Offenders, Deviants or Patients?

Offenders, Deviants or Patients? provides a practical approach to under-standing both the social context and treatment of mentally disordered offenders. Taking into account the current public concern, often heightened by media sensationalism, it addresses issues such as sex offending, homicide and other acts of serious bodily harm.

This fourth edition comes after extensive new research by academics and professionals in the field and reflects recent changes in law, policy and practice, including:

- New sex offending legislation
- Proposals to amend homicide legislation
- A new Mental Health Act

Using new case examples, Herschel Prins examines the relationship between mental disorders and crime and looks at the ways in which it should be dealt with by the mental health care and criminal justice systems.

Offenders, Deviants or Patients? is unique in its multidisciplinary approach and will be invaluable to all those who come into contact with serious offenders or those who study crime and criminal behaviour.

Herschel Prins has worked in the fields of criminal justice and forensic mental health for over fifty years. He has served on a number of public and voluntary bodies, authored numerous books and articles and continues to teach part-time at the Universities of Leicester and Loughborough.

Offenders, Deviants or Patients?

Explorations in clinical criminology

4th Edition

Herschel Prins

Routledge
Taylor & Francis Group

LONDON AND NEW YORK

First published 1980 by Tavistock

Second edition published 1995 by Routledge
11 New Fetter Lane, London EC4P 4EE
29 West 35th Street, New York, NY 10001

Third edition published 2005 by Routledge
27 Church Road, Hove, East Sussex BN3 2FA

Fourth edition published 2010 by Routledge
27 Church Road, Hove, East Sussex BN3 2FA

Simultaneously published in the USA and Canada
by Routledge
270 Madison Avenue, New York, NY 10016

Routledge is an imprint of the Taylor & Francis Group, an Informa business

© 2010 Herschel Prins

Typeset in Times by Garfield Morgan, Swansea, West Glamorgan
Printed and bound in Great Britain by TJ International Ltd, Padstow,
Cornwall
Paperback cover design by Andrew Ward

This publication has been produced with paper manufactured to strict
environmental standards and with pulp derived from sustainable forests.

British Library Cataloguing in Publication Data
A catalogue record for this book is available from the British Library

Library of Congress Cataloging in Publication Data
Prins, Herschel A.
    Offenders, deviants, or patients? : explorations in clinical criminology /
Herschel Prins. – 4th ed.
        p. cm.
    Includes bibliographical references.
    ISBN 978-0-415-46428-4 (hardback) – ISBN 978-0-415-46429-1 (pbk.)
1. Criminal psychology–Methods–Great Britain. 2. Prisoners–Psychology–
Great Britain. 3. Crime prevention–Great Britain. 4. Forensic psychiatry–
Great Britain. 5. Mental disorders–rehabilitation–Great Britain. 6. Mental
health services–Organization & administration–Great Britain. I. Title.
    HV8742.G72P74 2010
    364.3'8–dc22

                                                            2009038563

ISBN: 978-0-415-46428-4 (hbk)
ISBN: 978-0-415-46429-1 (pbk)

This book is dedicated to the memory of Dr Peter Duncan Scott, CBE, MD, FRCP – mentor and friend, and to all my colleagues past and present in forensic psychiatry (forensic mental health).

Tolle lege, tolle lege (Take up and read, take up and read)
 (St Augustine of Hippo, *Confessions* (AD 397–8), Book 8, Chapter 12)

Audi partem alteram (Hear the other side; sometimes rendered as 'Listen to both sides')
 (St Augustine of Hippo, *De duabus Animabus Contra Manicheos*,
Chapter 14)

Contents

Figures and tables

Figures

Tables

Note on case illustrations

No attempt has been made to conceal the identities of those persons whose cases have been in the public domain (for example, those who have been the subject of extensive media coverage). In all other instances, the cases derive from the author's personal knowledge. Every effort has been made to make the illustrations anonymous, and, to this end, composite accounts have been given. Despite these necessary ethical precautions, it is maintained that the illustrations provide sufficient authenticity concerning the issues presented.

The law – an advance apology

I have endeavoured to ensure that references to the law and its implementation are current at the time of going to press. However, such is the rapid pace of its evolution (some might say *re*volution!) it may be that in some places I have erred in my citation and/or interpretation. Should this be the case, I proffer my apologies and would request any reader who wishes to do to, to inform me of my 'fault'.

Preface: some explanations

I preface this book with a number of explanations. First, why a fourth edition in the light of the fact that considerably longer intervals have elapsed between the publication of the previous three? The answer is simple, and I hope acceptable. The pace of change in criminal justice and forensic mental health (or ill-health as I prefer to describe it) has been increasingly rapid – as is the accumulation of new research and other data. We have had new legislation on extended sentences, sexual offenders, changes in mental health law and proposals for the reform of the law of homicide, being just a few examples. In such times of rapid (and sometimes ill-thought-through) changes, a degree of explanation is required. I hope the foregoing comments have justified my decision. Second, why insert a subtitle? Although the first edition had one, the second and third editions did not have one, so why now? I decided that this fourth edition should be in the nature of my own personal explorations in the field of clinical criminology, this term now being an accepted description of the various issues to be discussed in the following pages. My emphasis is on the word *explorations*, since a degree of modesty dictates that I should not attempt to provide definitive answers to questions as emotive and complex as those addressed in the following pages. It may interest readers to know how I alighted upon the subtitle, *An Introduction to the Study of Socio-Forensic Problems*, in the first edition. On reflection, I consider that it was a fairly apposite (if perhaps slightly grandiose) description at the time of the book's inception. Forensic psychiatry, forensic psychology, forensic social work and forensic nursing have only really come of age in more recent times (see Chapter 1). There is another and slightly more personal take on that choice. Some years earlier, on the occasion of our marriage, my wife and I received a congratulatory telegram from my colleague Dr Peter Scott; it contained the words 'socio-forensic best wishes'. Such a term seemed to represent the nature of our task and thus it stayed in my memory until *Offenders, Deviants or Patients?* first came to be written.[1] Third, I have to explain one or two omissions in the present text. There are no chapters devoted specifically to female offenders or on the abuse of alcohol or other substances. However, both these areas are mentioned at various places in the text. Readers will see that, generally speaking, the book follows the sequence adopted in previous editions. However, there are one or two modifications. Chapter 1 is in the nature of a memoir of my fifty-plus years in the field. It is not included out of self-advertisement (at least I hope not), but I concluded that a personal statement concerning some of the general changes I have witnessed over such a lengthy period might provide a personal context for the rest of the book. I have to confess that the idea concerning its conclusion is not original. One of the assessors for the proposal for the third edition had suggested that I write something similar. At that time, I did not choose to pursue the matter, and now regret not having had the good sense to do so. Thus, I now make amends.[2] Finally, I have deleted the chapter on the uses of literature and drama. This is not because I have changed my mind concerning their usefulness, but because I have dealt with the topic in other places (see, for example, Prins 1991). This deletion has enabled me to include a specific chapter on homicide rather than subsume it under the general chapter on violence. And so, after this slightly self-indulgent Preface, I can now move to my second (and I hope final) piece of self-indulgence contained in Chapter 1.

Notes

1 At the time of the appearance of the first edition there were very few British texts on forensic-psychiatric matters. My work was never intended to be a substitute for these. However, it seems to have received general acclamation as an introductory text. And so later editions have been intended to be just that – an *introduction* to the field written by a comparative layman. The later works by forensic psychiatrists Robert Bluglass and Paul Bowden, John Gunn and Pamela Taylor, Malcolm Faulk, and Derek Chiswick and Rosemarie Cope provide more comprehensive accounts, as do the works of forensic psychologists such as Ronald Blackburn, Clive Hollin, Kevin Howells, Graham Towl and David Crighton, Mary McMurran and Dennis Howitt, and readers will find them referred to at various places in the following pages.
2 A fuller account of my personal context may be found in my memoirs – *Mad, Bad and Dangerous to Know: Reflections of a Forensic Practitioner*. Waterside Press, Hook, Hampshire. 2010.

Reference

Prins, H. (2001) 'Did Lady Macbeth Have a Mind Diseas'd? (A Medico-Legal Enigma)', *Medicine, Science and the Law* 41: 129–134.

Acknowledgements

The authors of books of reference owe considerable debts to those who have assisted in their gestation and birth. Mine is no exception. My thanks go to a number of kind folk. To Mr Nigel Shakleford who, over the years, has given me both information and advice from the Mental Health Unit at the one-time Home Office, now the Ministry of Justice. To Dr Sian Rees of the Department of Health for information concerning the state of the nation's mental health (or rather lack of it!), and for details of the revised procedures for instituting inquiries after mental health homicides. To Mr Paul McEvoy of the Fire and Rescue Service Directorate, Department of Communities and Local Government, for statistics relating to fires in the UK. To Mr Ben Manley of the Parole Board for supplying me with certain Parole Board publications. To Maya Bhudia of the British Crime Survey for printing me off a copy of a section of the latest British Crime Survey. Various academic colleagues and friends have come to my aid with great forbearance. Professor Ronnie Mackay of De Monfort University for assistance concerning matters relating to the insanity defence and disability in relation to the trial. To my former colleague Kate Brookes at Loughborough, and now reader in law at the University of Wolverhampton, for information concerning corporate manslaughter. To two of my former postgraduate students at Leicester University's Department of Criminology for help with a number of matters; Anna Hefford, Barrister, for help with matters relating to children who kill; to Carlene King Doctoral, researcher in the Department of Psychiatry, Manchester University, for downloading from the Internet a number of items – and for generally being very supportive of my endeavours.

Various publishers have kindly granted me permission to reproduce parts of previously published material as indicated in the text: to Professor A. Goode, Chairman of the Editorial Board, *Medicine, Science and the Law*, and to the British Academy of Forensic Sciences (which holds the copyright). To Wiley-Blackwells for permission to reproduce certain material contained in Chapter 1 – material which first appeared in my article 'Fifty Years' Hard Labour – a Personal Odyssey' (*Howard Journal of Criminal*

Justice, 2007, 46(2): 176–193). To the editorial staff at Routledge and Psychology Press for their continuing support. This book would never have seen the light of day without the expert word-processing skills of Mrs Janet Kirkwood, who has worked with me for over thirty years. Her forbearance and skill have been highly commendable in making such good copy out of my scrawled drafts. Finally, I have been singularly fortunate in having an exemplary copy-editor in Christine Firth. She has with charming good grace corrected errors and suggested improvements in both style and content.

Chapter 1

Some autobiographical reminiscences

> I HAVE been here before.
>
> (Dante Gabriel Rossetti, *Sudden Light*, 1853)

I should stress at the outset that what follows is somewhat partial; some readers may also find it idiosyncratic.[1] For example, I have not included anything but the barest details of my early life (for some of these, see Jones 2007; Prins 2007a, 2008, 2010). Suffice it to say that some of my family were heavily involved in work with adult offenders and with disadvantaged young people. Being orphaned as an adolescent no doubt played an important part in my subsequent career choices. Following a period of not entirely successful employment in industry and commerce, and a period of National Service in the Royal Air Force, I opted for teacher training. However, my applications to teacher training colleges were not successful; thus countless numbers of young minds were saved from my ministrations! A social science diploma was followed by probation training and subsequent employment in the probation service in 1952. Training for probation work in those early days was provided under the auspices and management of the Home Office. It was very much practice based and, by present-day standards, might possibly be regarded to some extent as not being very academic. In my view such criticism would be unwarranted, since the course equipped students for the very wide range of duties undertaken at that time. (For accounts of the development of probation work and training, see Prins 1964; Smith 2006; Burnett 2007; Prins 2007b; see also McKnight's (2009) critical article on the gradual demise of the probation service in its former role.) As stated above, what follows presents merely a bird's eye view of my experiences in criminal justice and forensic mental health. My reminiscences are not presented in discrete compartments. Instead, I have tried to provide a sequential account covering some fifty-five years, divided where helpful into year bands.

One phenomenon stands out very clearly. This was the small-scale nature of the work and its organization. For example, by present-day standards, the Probation Service was a comparatively small enterprise. It was not particularly hierarchical, as is the case nowadays. Some areas did not even have a Principal Probation Officer (as they were then called) in charge. Bedfordshire was one such example. It was headed by a Senior Probation Officer with a comparatively small number of main-grade staff. Contact with 'clients' in what was a predominantly rural area (apart from the Boroughs of Bedford, Luton and Dunstable) was facilitated by reporting centres. These were situated in a variety of locations, for example, church halls or local authority offices such as health centres. These were often in quite isolated locations. Nowadays, I have little doubt that these would be regarded as quite inappropriate (*pace* John Reid – 'not fit for purpose'). This would be largely on the grounds of breaching Health and Safety Regulations. I do not think any of us considered the possible hazards to which we were exposing ourselves. Whether this blithe indifference was a good or a bad thing is no doubt open to debate. In five years' service in the county I recall being physically intimidated on only one occasion (I found the chairman of our Quarter Sessions far more intimidating – see later!). Another more general aspect of the Probation Service in those early days was its country-wide small-scale membership. One could attend an annual general meeting of the National Association of Probation Officers (NAPO) and know personally more than a handful of those attending. Another notable feature was the almost total absence of female Principal Officers in the Service. I recall the one exception as being the redoubtable Kate Fowler, Principal Officer in Sheffield. As I shall demonstrate later, in more recent times things have changed significantly for the better.

Not only was the Probation Service small scale, but also other services were similarly constituted. The fairly recently established Children's Departments (through the Children Act 1948) were only just beginning to get into their stride. A notable exception to the predominantly male leadership in the Probation Service was the appointment of women as Children's Officers as heads of the new departments. Perhaps this was a reflection of the notion that women were more likely to have a better understanding of children's (particularly small children's) needs. Mental health services were also small scale, having their origins in Poor Law organization and practice. In those early days mental health duties were carried out by Relieving Officers, later by Duly Authorized Officers, then by Mental Welfare Officers, and of course much later by Approved Social Workers under the Mental Health Act 1983.[2]

The Prison Service was also comparatively small scale. Local prisons (for example Bedford) were run by a governor (sometimes a former senior military officer), a handful of warders (prison officers), a chaplain and a part-time medical officer (usually a visiting general practitioner (GP)). In the ensuing decades things have changed quite dramatically. The independent Prison Commission disappeared when the Home Office assumed total responsibility for prison affairs, and luminaries such as Sir Lionel Fox and Alexander Paterson disappeared from the scene. Prison administration now consists of a bewildering mixture of complicated organization and gross overcrowding, leading to hardship for inmates and staff alike.

To return to my early days in the Probation Service. My reason for this is that it was in these early days that I first developed my long-standing interest in the field of forensic psychiatry (now known as forensic mental health). This new title reflects the current multidisciplinary approach to mentally disordered offenders. My immediate predecessor had decided to emigrate with his family to Australia. However, his departure was in some jeopardy because one of his clients had killed his wife. The police were anxious that my former colleague should stay in the UK to give evidence at the Assizes. In the event, they were persuaded to rely upon a sworn statement as to his knowledge of his client. The latter was subsequently committed to Broadmoor (High Security) Hospital. I recall that there was no formal inquiry held into the circumstances leading up to the murder. The client had been known to the mental health authorities as well as being on probation. Nowadays an independent inquiry would have of course been mandatory (see later comments). Although I had no personal involvement in the case, its features intrigued me. My interest was heightened by the fact that the local asylum (as it was then called) was located within one of my court areas. Under the Criminal Justice Act 1948, the hospital could, if they agreed, receive offenders on probation with a requirement that they receive inpatient or outpatient treatment for their mental condition if this was of a fairly minor nature. Thus began my acquaintance with those offenders who became the subject of both criminal justice and mental health interventions. In those early days the probation officer's statutory functions were solely to be concerned with making arrangements (in consultation with the treating psychiatrist) for the amendment or discharge of the order. However, this limitation did not stop me from furthering my interest in matters forensic-psychiatric. This interest had been lying dormant since my student days on the Home Office training course. We were fortunate in having some excellent lecturers on the topic of psychiatric aspects of delinquency, examples being Professor Trevor Gibbens, seminars by the distinguished psychoanalytic psychiatrist-doctor Denis Carroll, and at a later stage by Dr Peter Scott, with whom I was subsequently to work as a psychiatric social worker at Stamford House Remand Home for Boys.[3] This is an appropriate point to refer to the ground-breaking Criminal Justice Act 1948; ground-breaking because some of its provisions tend to be forgotten in the welter of criminal justice legislation passed in the past few decades. In 2007 Lord Justice Judge, addressing an audience of law students and lawyers, noted that in the previous ten years Labour had created more than 3000 new criminal offences, produced 115,000 pages of legislation and passed numerous Bills including 24 criminal justice measures. He commented on the fact that between 1925 and 1985 we managed with only one each decade (as reported by Robert Verkaik, Law Editor, *The Independent*, 31 October 2007).[4]

The 1948 Act had appeared as a Bill in 1939, but was shelved on the outbreak of the Second World War, as were plans for the East Hubert psychiatric prison, later to become Grendon Underwood, now known as Grendon (see Home Office 1939). This milestone piece of legislation abolished flogging as a penalty (except for assaults on prison staff; this penalty was also subsequently abolished). The Act introduced the new sentences of Corrective Training (CT) and Preventive Detention (PD) for 'habitual criminals' (a provision first introduced in the Prevention of Crime Act 1908). Borstal was brought more into line with contemporary ideas, in the new guise of Borstal Training. And, as already noted, the Act introduced a new power for the courts to impose probation orders with a requirement for mental treatment. The statutory frameworks for this penalty have been modified over the years, for example, the offender's consent to the making of such an order is now no longer required, and the imposition of such an order counts as a conviction for sentencing purposes. The other point to note is that the former term 'probation order' is now subsumed as an option under a community treatment order. The term 'probation' and all that goes with it is sadly fast disappearing. Many of the provisions of the 1948 Act were subsequently to be abolished or amended substantially, for example, the discrete sentences of Corrective Training and Borstal Training. Preventive Detention was also abolished but has, to a certain extent, made a number of fresh appearances as the 'extended sentence' in its various guises, for example, the current provision in the Criminal Justice Act 2003 for those convicted of certain violent and serious sexual crimes to be given indeterminate sentences. One consequence of this particular penalty has been to exacerbate current overcrowding in our prisons (of which more later in this book). Later enactments introduced the Parole System, the suspended sentence and an ever-increasing range of community sanctions. It is worthy of note that the Parole System (as amended from time to time) relies heavily on forensic-psychiatric input and, from its inception in 1967, has mandated the presence of a psychiatrist on those panels of the Board considering life-sentence and other serious cases. In recent times, other forensic professionals (such as forensic psychologists) have become involved in the Board's work.

The 1950s and 1960s – the wider field

The 1950s and 1960s saw a further number of far-reaching innovations in the delivery of criminal justice and mental health care. My justification for a high degree of selectivity is that my observations arise out of personal acquaintance with some of them. The year 1957 witnessed a significant change in the law concerning the relationship between mental disorders and homicide. As I shall show subsequently, the Homicide Act 1957 was introduced following the *Report of the Royal Commission on Capital Punishment* of 1953 (Gowers 1953). In general terms, the Gowers Commission had recommended a widening of the scope for seriously disordered mental states to be proffered as a defence to a charge of murder. If such a defence was accepted, the charge of murder would be reduced to that of manslaughter on the grounds of diminished responsibility. This provision derived in part from its long-standing use in Scotland. In practice, it sits alongside the more restrictive M'Naghten rules. As is so often the case with new legislation, high hopes were raised during the statute's early days. However, the wording of Section 2 of the Act, and to some extent Section 3 (which deals with the vexed issue of provocation), have led over the years to a number of somewhat fraught exchanges between the law and psychiatry. Such exchanges were, of course, not new. Dr Henry Yellowlees received something of a mauling when he gave evidence for the defence in the trial of John George Haigh – the so-called 'acid bath murderer'. It is a sad fact that, because of such encounters, some general psychiatrists of my acquaintance have become reluctant to enter the criminal court arena. For discussion of a number of these issues, see Blom-Cooper and Morris (2004) and Law Commission (2006). Following closely on the heels of the Homicide Act 1957 came the Mental Health Act 1959. The Act modernized existing mental health legislation which had its roots in outmoded nineteenth-century emphasis on legalism. The Act was of considerable forensic-psychiatric importance. Under the new legislation, it became possible, on the basis of medical evidence, for the courts to commit seriously mentally disordered offenders to hospital in lieu of other penalties. Written medical evidence from two authorized medical practitioners (almost always psychiatrists) was required for the implementation of an unrestricted order. However, for the implementation of an order restricting the discharge of the patient (in order to protect the public from serious harm) one of the medical practitioners was required to give oral evidence. Prior to the 1959 Act, the procedures for admitting seriously mentally disordered offenders to hospital had proved to be somewhat cumbersome and not frequently used. Another important feature of the 1959 Act was the introduction of the controversial category of psychopathic disorder. This is a category that continues to bedevil law, psychiatry and psychology, and is dealt with in detail later in the book. The Act also introduced Mental Health Review Tribunals enabling patients, both under the Act's civil and criminal powers, to appeal against their detention. As with the Parole Board, psychiatric inputs (in respect of both reports to Tribunals and membership of Tribunal panels) were of considerable significance. During the 1960s I witnessed a number of other changes of 'socio-forensic' interest. The Suicide Act 1961 removed the offence of attempted suicide from the statute book. This liberalizing piece of legislation thus removed the albeit comparatively rare, but nonetheless distressing, criminal prosecutions for such behaviour – distressing not only for the defendant, but also for any relatives and professionals who might be involved (as in my case, as a probation officer). Another highly significant change occurred during the period. As a result of the Sexual Offences Act 1967, acts of adult consenting male homosexuality in private were decriminalized. In my early days as a probation officer, I remember having to attend court and to provide reports on adult males who were likely to receive a prison sentence for this behaviour. In addition, they were sometimes subjected to quite inappropriate homilies by sentencers (usually recorders or chairmen of Quarter Sessions). The manner in which the change in the law came about is of interest. It reveals the complex chains of events that are often involved in changes in policy and practice. As long ago as 1957, the Wolfenden Committee on Homosexual Offences and Prostitution (Home Office 1957) had recommended a change in the law on what they had come to regard as essentially private acts. They acknowledged that although many people considered these to be immoral and/or irreligious they should not be the concern of the criminal law. Some considerable time later a cause célèbre seems to have added weight to the Wolfenden Committee's proposals. A group of older men had been sentenced to varying terms of imprisonment for acts of indecency with a group of young airmen. An assumption seems to have been made that the older men had corrupted the younger. It subsequently transpired that this might not have been entirely the case. The imprisonment of the perpetrators caused some disquiet. As a result, those at the highest levels of law enforcement advised police forces to exercise restraint in bringing prosecutions unless public decency had been infringed or where consent was in doubt. Subsequently, the existing law appeared to fall into disuse and the time became right for the 1967 Act to be passed, with the decriminalization that followed.

Two further developments during this period are worthy of note. First, the ultimate success of the long-fought battle to abolish the death penalty for murder (by the Murder, Abolition of Death Penalty Act 1965). The cause had been championed by the efforts of protagonists such as the former Member of Parliament Sydney Silverman in the House of Commons, and by Frank Dawtry, who had been the secretary of the National Council for the Abolition of the Death Penalty (later to become the highly effective secretary of the National Association of Probation Officers) and others. Various attempts to reintroduce the death penalty since the 1965 Act have always failed, in my view mercifully. Not only had a number of people been hanged in error before abolition, but also a number of others would have suffered this fate as a result of wrong convictions since the Act. A further humane outcome for members of the psychiatric profession is that they do not have to attest to an offender's mental fitness to be hanged, as is the case with some of their American counterparts, in my view an odious and unethical practice. Another enactment that demonstrated a more sympathetic approach to human frailty was the introduction of a woman's lawful right to an abortion by the Abortion Act 1967. The movement for reform had been spearheaded by the likes of Madeleine Simms, and in the House of Commons by David (now Lord) Steel. Recent events indicate that abortion is still a somewhat contentious issue. Even its early supporters (such as Lord Steel) have expressed their concern in recent times about some untoward consequences of the legislation, such as the steady increase in the number of terminations in recent years. Overall, the period I have just outlined appears to reveal a trend towards a less legalistic and punitive approach to various forms of behaviour.

The 1970s onwards

The 1970s witnessed a number of further important changes. The Courts Act 1971 removed the ancient and somewhat arbitrary distinction between Courts of Quarter Sessions and Assizes. The latter courts were presided over by some colourful personalities. The formal opening of the County Assizes was looked forward to by many local onlookers – the 'red judge' carrying his nosegay of sweet-smelling herbs, a reminder of the days when the smell of bodily secretions and the threat of the plague were very evident. The judge would be followed by his retinue, including the bestockinged High Sheriff and other dignatories. Judges' reputations went before them. Some had reputations for severity, others demonstrated a more humane approach. Some were keen to expedite 'gaol delivery', one of the functions of the Assize being to empty the gaols of those awaiting trial. This latter function was one espoused with great enthusiasm and despatch by the former Lord Chief Justice Goddard when he occasionally vacated London to go on circuit. Occasionally those who presided over the then Quarter Sessions (chairmen in the counties and recorders in the boroughs) would demonstrate somewhat unprofessional behaviour. One such chairman of Quarter Sessions, before whom I used to appear occasionally, seemed to take a perverse delight in belittling the professionals who appeared before him, be they fellow members of the Bar, the police, psychiatrists, or the Probation Service. His behaviour became so unpleasant that complaints were made about his conduct, with the result that the County Sessions Committee did not renew his appointment when it expired. (However, sad to relate, he continued to sit as recorder in the borough.) For my part, I regarded him as one of the most unpleasant members of the legal profession I have ever met. My impression is that, with the introduction of Crown Courts under the 1971 Act and the subsequent rationalization of the courts of higher jurisdiction, such unwelcome 'eccentricities' have become far less common. With one or two exceptions, the judiciary now exercise their functions in a highly professional manner. Moreover, those holding high judicial office have been quick to champion the rule of law against over-heavy political reactions to antisocial behaviour (see my earlier comments concerning the proliferation of criminal justice legislation in recent years). Nowadays, such a stance is becoming increasingly important when we live in a risk-obsessed and over-safety-conscious society – a risk consciousness fuelled by some less than responsible elements of the media, who appear more intent on boosting sales than responsible journalism. The late 1960s and early 1970s witnessed significant changes in what we now describe as youth justice. In my early days as a probation officer, we often dealt with children who had committed offences or who were 'beyond parental control'. With the introduction of the new social services departments (SSDs) following the reports of the committees chaired by Dame Eileen Younghusband (Department of Health and Social Security (DHSS) 1959) and Sir Frederic Seebohm (Home Office et al. 1968) this aspect of our work passed to these new departments. For a variety of reasons, I did not think this was a particularly helpful development. First, probation officers had, over many years, built up a good deal of expertise in dealing with the needs and problems of antisocial children and young persons. Such experience was not very common among those who staffed the newly created SSDs. In addition, these children's needs had to be dealt with in competition with the needs of elderly people, those who were mentally ill and people with disabilities. (Prior to these post-Seebohm developments, the needs of children had been the specific focus of attention in the local authority children's departments established under the 1948 Act.) Second, the new service was based on the false assumption that the newly created generic social worker could be 'all things to all people'. Such an assumption seemed to be based on a mistaken interpretation of the Seebohm recommendations. What the Seebohm Report recommended was the introduction of *generic training* – a different matter entirely. Third, with the removal of involvement of probation officers' contact with this younger age group, a useful opportunity had been lost for the former to see at first hand the development of patterns of later antisocial behaviour – in other words, the loss of hands-on experience and awareness of an important aspect of human growth and development. Alongside these changes was a decision to decriminalize some forms of juvenile misbehaviour. Formal and informal police cautions (now known as warnings and reprimands) were to replace court appearances, provided the offence was of a fairly minor nature and was admitted by the young person involved. The changes referred to above in providing a less legalistic approach to juvenile offenders seem to have stemmed in part from the practice introduced in Scotland, namely those of 'Children's Hearings'. These followed the report by Lord Kilbrandon (Scottish Home and Health Department 1964). (A more recent helpful development has been the reintroduction of an awareness of the special needs of children in the combining of local authority children's and education services. For a brief account of other developments in the care and control of young delinquents in the 1970s to date, see Prins 2007a: 184–185.)

The 1980s onwards

The 1980s saw a number of other important developments in the fields of criminal justice and forensic mental health (or, as I prefer to describe it, forensic mental *ill*-health). The Mental Health Act 1983, in its reform of the 1959 legislation (see above), gave greater powers to Mental Health Review Tribunals (MHRTs). Under the 1983 Act, Tribunals could now authorize the absolute or conditional discharge of offender-patients detained under Hospital Orders with restrictions (Section 37/41). Under the 1959 Act they could only *recommend* discharge to the Home Secretary. As a result of this new power the presidents of Tribunals hearing such cases had to be of QC, recorder or circuit judge status. The Mental Health Act 2007 (implemented October 2008) does not change this practice, but abolishes the power to make restriction orders with limits of time (for further details of changes of forensic interest, see Prins 2007c). The 1983 Act also introduced the Mental Health Act Commission – a body charged *inter alia* with the inspection of psychiatric and mental handicap hospitals and units. As a former member of the commission, I thought the body was becoming somewhat unwieldy. I also considered that more oversight should have been provided in order to counteract the slightly over-zealous views and activities of one or two commission members. My past experience as a former member of a central government inspectorate – the Home Office Probation Inspectorate – had taught me that inspection not only was an onerous responsibility, but also was one that always needed a light, but nonetheless firm, touch. It was not a position to be held by the reformingly zealous. An important non-statutory body merits mention here. Following the lethal activities and subsequent conviction of the poisoner Graham Young, a non-statutory board was established (known initially as the 'Aarvold Board' after the chair of the inquiry into Young's activities). It subsequently became known as the Home Secretary's Advisory Board on Restricted Cases. Its purpose was to provide an additional screening device for cases such as Young's that were considered to require special care in assessment. Over the years, referrals to the Board by the Home Office became much less frequent (no doubt due to increasing confidence in MHRT decision-making) and the board was eventually wound up in September 2003. Forensic psychiatric representation on the board always played a very significant part in its activities.[5]

Since the late 1990s various proposals have been put forward for reform of mental health legislation. In essence, the *forensic* debate has hinged upon the resolution of the conflicting needs of the individual on the one hand and the protection of society on the other. Many trees must have been felled to provide the reams of paper for the various Green and White Papers and the three Bills that came before both Houses of Parliament. Some possible effect of the legislation eventually enacted will be considered in later chapters.

It now remains for me to consider one or two more general developments in criminal justice and mental health. My consideration of these is, again, highly selective. Women are now playing an increasing role in criminal justice and mental health, whether as perpetrators of crime or as professionals engaged in its prevention, detection and management. For highly complicated reasons that are not entirely clear, women appear to have become involved increasingly in the commission of sexual and violent criminality. One explanation may be that the distinction between the socially acceptable and conventionally dictated roles between the sexes have become increasingly blurred. Our attitudes towards, and expectations of, women still tend to be ambivalent. Women who offend tend to veer between being 'psychiatrized' on the one hand and 'demonized' on the other. As an example, consider the widely differing views that have been expressed about Lady Macbeth's mental state (see, for example, Prins 2001). There are some recent interesting examples of the increasing degree of gender parity in law and sentencing. Section 66 of the Sexual Offences Act 2003 makes the offence of indecent exposure no longer an exclusively male prerogative. Potential Lady Godivas be warned! (See Chapter 8 on sex offending.) It is gratifying to see that women now play a much more prominent part in advocacy in criminal justice and mental health. Some of them, for example Gareth Peirce, Shami Chakrabarti and Cherie Booth, have played significant parts in championing human rights. A growing number of women have been appointed as chief constables, as chief probation officers and as prison governors. Since 2001 the UK has had a woman as Chief Inspector of Prisons and, between 2007 and 2009, a female Home Secretary. In other spheres women have been playing increasingly important roles – as chairs and chief executives of hospital trusts (including mental health trusts) and a number of university vice-chancellors. No longer can the male chauvinists among us say 'Frailty thy name is woman' (*Hamlet*, Act 1, Sc. 2).

Recent times have witnessed what has been rightly described by two of my colleagues as *The Age of the Inquiry* (Stanley and Manthorpe 2004). In 1994, the Department of Health (NHS Executive) issued a directive making it mandatory to institute an independent inquiry into homicides committed by individuals known to the mental health services. (This directive has since been amended: for further details, see Prins 2007a.) It is fair to say that there are strongly differing views as to the purpose, practice and usefulness of homicide inquiries (see, for example, my chapter in Stanley and Manthorpe: Prins 2004). There had, of course, been a number of inquiries into mental health and other matters before the former became mandatory in 1994, for example, into the abuse and lack of care of children and into the care of psychiatric and mental handicap patients. More specifically, inquiries of the type envisaged in the 1994 directive had also been taking place, for example, into the circumstances in which Sharon Campbell killed her social worker, Isabel Schwarz; as already noted, into the case of Graham Young, convicted of poisoning his workmates while on discharge from Broadmoor High Security Hospital following previous convictions for similar offences by poisoning; into the case of Daniel Mudd – also a former Broadmoor patient – who killed a fellow hostel resident while on conditional discharge. In more general terms, we should be mindful of the cases of the nurse Beverley Allitt, Thomas Hamilton at Dunblane and the GP Harold Shipman – best regarded as a 'carer' killer rather than, as some have described, a serial killer. My personal experience of mental health inquiries involved the chairmanship of three somewhat different incidents. The first was into the death of Orville Blackwood – an African Caribbean offender-patient at Broadmoor; the second concerned the abscondion, while on escorted day parole, of an offender-patient from a medium secure unit in Hertfordshire. The man concerned had an established history of paedophilic-type conduct. The venue he was allowed to visit (with only a single escort) was a theme park and zoo – popular with children! The third was into the killing of a vagrant in the centre of Leicester by a 19-year-old man known to the mental health, education, social and probation services. My reflections on these three somewhat different inquiries and the very many others that I have read can be summarized very briefly. First, it is always easy to be wise after the event (described, as I recall, by my friend Dr Adrian Grounds at Cambridge as 'hindsight bias'). Second, the strain on all those involved in such inquiries is very considerable. This applies equally to families of the victims, perpetrators and their families (often forgotten) and not only those under scrutiny, but also the members of the inquiry team. Third, it seems right to question the extent to which these very costly activities produce 'the goods'. This is a very difficult question to answer. We do not really know the extent to which lessons are learned. It is satisfying to note that the recent guidance on the conduct of inquiries (already referred to) has focused more precisely on their remit and conduct. Offers of follow-up visits by inquiry teams are not always met with enthusiasm – indeed they may be refused, as our offer was in the Blackwood inquiry. This particular inquiry revealed a worrying failure to understand ethnic issues. Sadly I note that, despite much endeavour in this area, our understanding of what Sir William Macpherson and his colleagues described as 'institutional racism' is far from being as advanced as it could be (Home Office 1999). Recent instances of numerous racist attacks involving serious injury or homicide attest to this. Despite a vast literature on the topic, I cannot discover any fundamentally satisfying answers as to why black and other ethnic minority citizens continue to be represented disproportionately in the criminal justice and mental health populations. Perhaps the answers are too complex to produce clear resolution, or is the fear of 'dark strangers' still predominant? Fourth, the all too frequent claim that a killing by a mentally ill individual could have been prevented by more effective community care is misconceived. It is a worrying oversimplification to suggest that our community care problems commenced largely as a result of the rundown of the mental hospitals in the middle and late 1960s. The decarceration of mentally ill individuals had started in a small way long before that time. No doubt the problem was exacerbated by the somewhat unrealistic expectations that new pharmacological treatments would offer patients a speedy and non-relapsing return to the community. The recent claims that community care has failed, as so readily espoused by politicians and the media alike, are quite erroneous. Many patients and offender-patients are well and safely managed in the community, quietly, competently and without publicity. The other myth that needs dispelling is that deluded and hallucinated men and women are waiting to kill or seriously harm others at every opportunity. The truth is that such fellow citizens are more likely to kill or harm themselves. The seminal research by Taylor and Gunn (1999) belies this assumption. However, it is a sad truth that improved resourcing is still needed – both within general and forensic psychiatry. They appear to continue to be the 'Cinderella' services within health service provision.

Certain other developments are worthy of note by way of conclusion. A number of them are concerned with improvements in crime detection. The first has been accomplished by developments in information technology, particularly in the use of sophisticated computer techniques. Had such techniques been developed in the late 1970s and early 1980s the likes of Peter Sutcliffe might have been detected and apprehended sooner; he managed to evade arrest for some five years. Subsequent inquiries into the manner in which the investigation was carried out revealed that there had been an enormous overload of unlinked information contained on hundreds of index cards. This resulted in missed opportunities for what were, at the time, regarded as isolated incidents (see Bilton 2003). Nowadays there is rapid access to computerized national and international databases enabling systematized information retrieval. However, advances have their downsides. Witness the advent of cyber-stalking, Internet pornography and sexual grooming and, more recently, examples of missing sensitive personal data. Maybe we should be mindful of the advice of the chambermaid Prudence in Ben Jonson's play *The New Inn*: 'Beware you do not conjure up a spirit you cannot lay' (Act 3, Sc. 2). It seems to me that information technology can also facilitate over-hasty reactions to various events in our lives, for example, the use of the ubiquitous email. This seems to produce a veritable surfeit of often quite ill-thought-through and insubstantial over-reactive responses. Time expended in penning a well-considered response may prove to be more productive in the long run. The second aspect of crime detection that I have witnessed has been the ground-breaking introduction of DNA profiling by Dr, now Professor, Sir Alec Jeffreys, of the University of Leicester's Genetics Department. His pioneering work led to the first major criminal prosecution of a local man using such techniques. He was eventually convicted of the sexual assault and murder of two teenage girls. Perhaps we should note here that downsides also exist in this area of work. One or two recent cases have shown on appeal that some forms of DNA profiling do not possess the universal exactness once supposed, thus leaving areas of doubt concerning conviction in the courts. Other advances in forensic science should be noted. Forensic scientists have made a number of advances in the field of arson investigation (see Chapter 9 in this book) and in forensic entomology. This enables the time of death of a decomposing body to be established with a considerable degree of accuracy. Offender profiling (much popularized in the media, but in reality a much more modest enterprise) is now fairly commonplace. In a number of instances it has led to arrests and subsequent convictions that might have been difficult to obtain without it. However, in many cases it merely (but nonetheless importantly) serves to confirm for the police investigating officers that they are on the right track. (This was certainly my own experience when asked to help in a puzzling case of arson in the South-East of England.) Media involvement in criminal justice and forensic mental health has been referred to on one or two occasions in this chapter. Such comments now merit brief expansion. In my time in the field, both the written, oral and visual media have come into prominence. The likes of Arthur Conan Doyle, Dorothy Sayers and Agatha Christie have now become somewhat eclipsed by writers such as Ruth Rendell (Barbara Vine), P.D. (Phyllis) James, Val McDermid, Ian Rankin, Minette Walters, Mo Hayder and Simon Beckett in the UK, Patricia Cornwell, Kathy Reichs, Thomas Harris and Tess Gerritsen in the United States, Michael Dibdin in Canada, Italy and elsewhere, Donna Leon in Italy and Henning Mankell in Sweden, to name just a few. Television and the cinema have also played an important part in dramatizing the work of forensic professionals. Some readers may recall one of the first depictions of the work of a forensic scientist in the late 1960s, with Marius Goring as the pathology expert Dr Hardy and, at a somewhat later date, the ebullient *Quincy*. In recent times, UK television screens have produced some colourful if not very accurate portrayals, examples being *Cracker*, *Prime Suspect*, *Trial and Retribution*, *Silent Witness*, *Waking the Dead*, *Wire in the Blood*, *Messiah*, and in the United States *Crime Scene Investigation* and *Law and Order: Special Victims Unit*. To what extent these, for the most part, entertaining fictional representations have actually led to an enhanced understanding of these matters on the part of the general public is far from clear. Documentary programmes such as *Crime Watch UK* seem much more likely to aid the public's understanding, and in a number of cases they have assisted in the apprehension of offenders, such as Michael Stone (see Prins 2007d). I have always been interested in the manner in which our descriptions of aspects of sexual behaviour reflect shifts in cultural and moral beliefs. In my youth, sexual activities were always referred to euphemistically. For example, buggery was always described in the newspapers as a 'serious' or 'unnatural' offence. Nowadays, we speak or write quite freely about oral or anal sex, 'blow jobs', 'giving head' and 'going all the way' does not refer to reaching the bus terminus! Sexual behaviour as currently depicted in much written and visual media seems to have been stripped of much of its 'mystery'. Children are much more knowledgeable about sex at an earlier age. Maybe some of this mystery has been lost. Admittedly, there are gains in this, but are there not losses too?

Finally, I think it can be said with some confidence that forensic psychiatry (or forensic mental health), forensic psychology and forensic nursing have come of age.[6] Sadly, one of the most important agencies in the fields I have been describing seems to have been losing its influence, namely the Probation Service. I regard this as a tragic development since the Probation Service represents a powerful means of combining care and control. The remainder of this book is devoted to a fairly detailed consideration of a number of matters briefly discussed in these reminiscences.

Notes

1 Some of the material in this chapter appeared in Prins (2007a).
2 Under the Mental Health Act 2007 (implementated in October 2008) the role of the Approved Social Worker has been expanded to include non-social work professionals, such as clinical psychologists, occupational therapists and nurses. The explanatory notes to the Act do not dilate upon how such personnel are to be trained. This will be left to the relevant professional bodies (for a very thorough discussion of the Act and many issues arising from it, see Fennell 2007).
3 For those readers interested in examining the contribution, past and present, of psychoanalytic and associated approaches to probation work, see Prins (2007b, especially notes 1–6).
4 Lord Justice Judge's points were reinforced some three weeks later by the Lord Chief Justice (Lord Phillips of Worth Matravers) when he suggested that prison overcrowding was not only due to the fact that 'ministers had failed to recognize the impact of legislation enabling judges to hand down longer sentences'. He added that 'unless Parliament is prepared to provide whatever resources are necessary to give effect to the sentences judges choose to impose, *Parliament must re-examine the legislative framework for sentencing*' (emphasis added); reported in *The Independent* 17 November 2007).
5 The board's membership consisted of two forensic psychiatric members, two senior members from the Probation and Social Services and two 'independent members' with knowledge of the Criminal Justice System. It was chaired by a senior lawyer, usually a circuit judge. In addition to the setting up of the Aarvold Committee, the Home Secretary of the day established a wide-ranging committee of inquiry into the more general problems arising from the activities and management of mentally abnormal offenders. The report of the committee – under the chairmanship of Lord Butler of Saffron Walden (a former liberal-minded Home Secretary) – is essential reading for those who wish to understand present provision (Home Office and DHSS 1975).
6 For an account of the development of forensic psychiatry in Europe, see Gordon and Lindqvist (2007); for the current situation concerning the relationship between forensic psychiatry and general psychiatry, see Turner and Salter (2008).

Acts

Abortion Act 1967
Children Act 1948
Courts Act 1971
Criminal Justice Act 1948
Criminal Justice Act 1967
Criminal Justice Act 2003
Homicide Act 1957
Mental Health Act 1959
Mental Health Act 1983
Mental Health Act 2007
Murder, Abolition of the Death Penalty Act 1965
Sexual Offences Act 1967
Sexual Offences Act 2003
Suicide Act 1961

References

Bilton, M. (2003) *Wicked Beyond Belief: The Hunt for the Yorkshire Ripper*, London: HarperCollins.

Blom-Cooper, L., QC and Morris, T. (2004) *With Malice Aforethought: A Study of the Crime and Punishment for Homicide*, Oxford: Hart.

Burnett, R. (2007) 'Entry on "probation"', in R. Canton and D. Hancock (eds) *Dictionary of Probation and Offender Management*, Cullompton: Willan.

Department of Health (NHS Executive) (1994) *Guidance on the Discharge of Mentally Disordered People and their Continuing Care in the Community*, HSG 94/27, London: Department of Health.

Department of Health and Social Security (DHSS) (1959) *Report of the Working Party on Social Workers in Local Authority Health and Welfare Services* (Younghusband Report), London: HMSO.

Fennell, P. (2007) *Mental Health: The New Law*, Bristol: Jordan.

Gordon, H. and Lindqvist, P. (2007) 'Forensic Psychiatry in Europe', *Psychiatric Bulletin* 31: 421–424.

Gowers, E. (chair) (1953) *Report of the Royal Commission on Capital Punishment 1949–1953* (Gowers Report), Cmd 8932, London: HMSO.

Home Office (1939) *Report on the Psychological Treatment of Crime*, London: HMSO.

—— (1957) *Report of the Committee on Homosexual Offences and Prostitution* (Wolfenden Report), Cmnd 247, London: HMSO.

—— (1999) *The Stephen Lawrence Inquiry: Report of the Inquiry by Sir William Macpherson of Cluny* (Macpherson Report), Cm 4262-I. London: HMSO.

Home Office and Department of Health and Social Security (1975) *Report of the Committee on Mentally Abnormal Offenders* (Butler Report), Cmnd 6244, London: HMSO.

Home Office, Department of Education and Science, Ministry of Local Government and Ministry of Health (1968) *Report of the Committee on Local Authority and Allied Social Personal Services* (Seebohm Report), Cmnd 3703, London: HMSO.

Jones, C. (2007) 'Biography: Interview with Herschel Prins', *Journal of Forensic Psychiatry and Psychology* 18: 127–133.

Law Commission (2006) *Murder, Manslaughter and Infanticide*, Law Commission no. 304, HC 30, London: TSO.

McKnight, J. (2009) 'Speaking Up for Probation' (Bill McWilliams Memorial Lecture), *Howard Journal of Criminal Justice* 48(4): 327–343.

Prins, H. (1964) 'Training for Probation Work in England and Wales', *Federal Probation Quarterly USA* December: 1–7.

—— (2001) 'Did Lady Macbeth Have a Mind Diseas'd? (A Medico-Legal Enigma)', *Medicine, Science and the Law* 41: 129–134.

—— (2004) 'Mental Health Inquiries: "Cui Bono?"', in N. Stanley and J. Manthorpe (eds) *The Age of the Inquiry: Learning and Blaming in Health and Social Care*, London: Routledge.

—— (2007a) 'Fifty Years' Hard Labour (A Personal Odyssey)', *Howard Journal of Criminal Justice* 46: 176–193.

—— (2007b) 'Psychoanalysis and Probation Practice: A Brief Additional Perspective on Smith', *Probation: The Journal of Community and Criminal Justice* 54: 171–178.

—— (2007c) 'The Mental Health Act, 2007: A Hard Act to Follow', *Howard Journal of Criminal Justice* 47(1): 81–85.

—— (2007d) 'The Michael Stone Inquiry: A Somewhat Different Homicide Report', *Journal of Forensic Psychiatry and Psychology* 18: 411–431.

—— (2008) 'Half a Century of Madness and Badness: Some Diverse Recollections', *Journal of Forensic Psychiatry and Psychology* 19: 431–440.

—— (2010) *Mad, Bad and Dangerous to Know: Reflections of a Forensic Practitioner*, Hook, Hampshire: Waterside Press.

Scottish Home and Health Department (1964) *Children and Young Persons, Scotland* (Kilbrandon Report), Cmnd 2306, Edinburgh: HMSO.

Smith, D. (2006) 'Making Sense of Psychoanalysis in Criminological Theory and Probation Practice', *Probation: The Journal of Community and Criminal Justice* 53: 361–376.

Stanley, N. and Manthorpe, J. (eds) (2004) *The Age of the Inquiry: Learning and Blaming in Health and Social Care*, London: Routledge.

Taylor, P. and Gunn, J. (1999) 'Homicides by People with Mental Illness: Myth and Reality', *British Journal of Psychiatry* 174: 9–14.

Turner, T. and Salter, M. (2008) 'Forensic Psychiatry and General Psychiatry: Re-examining the Relationship', *Psychiatric Bulletin* 32: 2–6.

Further reading

On the growth and development of forensic psychology, see in particular:

McMurran, M., Khalifa, N. and Gibbon, S. (2009) *Forensic Mental Health*, Cullompton: Willan.

Oyebode, F. (ed.) (2009) *Mindreadings: Literature and Psychiatry*, London: Royal College of Psychiatrists.

Soothill, K., Rogers, P. and Dolan, M. (eds) (2008) *Handbook of Forensic Mental Health*, Cullompton: Willan.

Towl, G.J., Farrington, D.P., Crighton, D.A. and Hughes, G. (eds) (2008) *Dictionary of Forensic Psychology*, Cullompton: Willan.

Chapter 2

Non-responsibility, responsibility and partial responsibility

I am ashamed the law is such an ass.
(George Chapman, *Revenge for Honour*, Act 3, Sc. 2, 1654)

The law is the true embodiment of everything that's
excellent. It has no kind of fault or flaw.
(W.S. Gilbert, *Iolanthe*, Act 1, 1882)

To some extent the two quotations that preface this chapter epitomize the conflicting attitudes that exist towards the law. However, they are broad-brush statements and do not delineate the finer points of argument between, for example, lawyers on the one hand and forensic mental health experts on the other. The complexities of the issues to be outlined in this chapter are compounded by the manner in which certain terms are used, often synonymously, by many of the protagonists in the legal arena. This problem is, as we shall see shortly, exemplified by the meaning given to words such as 'responsibility', 'capacity', 'culpability' and 'liability'. I summarize here a statement I made in previous editions of this book. The story now to be unfolded is intended merely to provide a map, similar to those provided by motoring organizations, namely those giving an outline of the main terrain, but deliberately devoid of any fine detail. For the finer detail, the traveller must return to the more detailed directions provided by the Ordnance Survey or similar modern aids (I refer here to that somewhat unreliable device – sat nav)!

It is my hope that the references to various authorities cited in this chapter and my suggestions for Further Reading will serve to fill these gaps. To continue with my geographical analogy. The terrain surveyed in this outline map is divided, somewhat arbitrarily, into the following sections. First, a brief consideration of some of the terms used in discussion of responsibility for crime. Second, a comparatively brief historical account of the notion of responsibility and associated matters. Third, a description of the manner in which the law in England and Wales makes special provision for what in my view can best be regarded as 'erosions' of responsibility, summarized in Table 2.1 (p. 46). Fourth, a brief discussion of some aspects of the relationship between mental disturbances and crime which are discussed in detail in Chapter 4.

Some semantic issues

A layperson is likely to use terms such as responsibility or guilt in less precise fashion than would a lawyer or student of jurisprudence. Thus the former, if asked to define the word 'responsible', would probably come near to the dictionary definition: (1) 'liable to be called to account (to a person or for a thing)', (2) 'being *morally* accountable for one's actions; capable of rational conduct' (*Concise Oxford Dictionary*). The important point to be noted here is the emphasis I have added, because the law is not necessarily concerned with morally reprehensible conduct. In their discussion of the law relating to homosexuality and prostitution, the Wolfenden Committee made a very important distinction between private and public morality. They considered that:

> Unless a deliberate attempt is made by Society, acting through the agency of the law, to equate the sphere of crime with that of sin, there must remain a realm of private morality and immorality which is, in brief and crude terms not the law's business.
> (Home Office and Scottish Home Department 1957: 24)

The layperson may also use the word 'irresponsible' to denote something more than legal lack of responsibility. For our purposes, 'irresponsible' means simply lack of legal responsibility and is not used in any lay or pejorative sense.

The word 'culpable' is found, not infrequently, in the literature on responsibility and related matters. For the present purposes it means blameworthiness in the criminal sense. However, if we choose to use it in this way we must acknowledge that a moral quality may creep into its usage. The word 'capacity' is also sometimes used as a synonym for legal competency (as, for example, the capacity to give consent for various medical or surgical interventions). Thus, in legal terms, it would seem to denote a quality existing within an individual – for example, to form an intent to act in a certain way. The word 'liability' is sometimes used as being synonymous with responsibility. The *Concise Oxford Dictionary* defines 'liable' as being 'legally bound, or under an obligation'. For present purposes, the term responsibility merely means liability to be dealt with by the criminal law and the criminal justice system.

In 1984, my friend and former colleague, the late Professor Edward Griew, drew attention to these definitional problems; he stated that responsibility is a word 'so often bandied about; like an historical back-ground it gives an air of learning to a discussion . . . it is a muddying word . . . liability is the better word as being less ambiguous' (Griew 1984: 60).

One final, but very important, point needs to be made about the term 'liability'. As far as the law is concerned, liability can certainly go beyond responsibility in the sense of moral culpability. For example, there are a number of offences, those of so-called 'strict liability' (sometimes called 'absolute liability') for which individuals may be prosecuted and punished, even though they are unaware of the existence of facts which make their conduct a criminal offence. An example of this would be the case of a shopkeeper found to have purveyed contaminated meat or other foodstuffs even though he or she did not know they were contaminated. In recent years, the House of Lords (then as supreme judicial review body) indicated that there should be some restriction in the interpretation of offences of strict liability. A seminal case was that of *Sweet v. Parsley* (1969). This concerned a young woman who was originally convicted of being concerned in the management of premises (she being the tenant of a farmhouse in Oxfordshire which she sublet to various other tenants) in which the prosecution alleged cannabis had been smoked. Her conviction, after appeal, was eventually overturned as a result of a ruling in the House of Lords. (For some discussion of the pros and cons of this area of concern, see Buchanan 2000: 20, 21 and 97.)

Components of legal blameworthiness

There are one or two additional terms that require clarification. An act does not make a person *legally* guilty unless his or her mind is also legally blameworthy (see also earlier comments on the difference between legal blameworthiness and moral turpitude). Lawyers denote this concept of guilt through their use of the Latin term *mens rea*. Simply put, this means having legally guilty intent or, more precisely, having the intention to commit an act that is wrong in the sense that it is *legally forbidden*. (For a discussion, see Hart (1968) and, more recently, by a former Lord Chancellor, Lord Mackay (2008).) It should also be noted that there must be an act or omission, known in legal terms as the *actus reus*. An omission is a failure to do something; a simple example would be the failure to give precedence to persons on a pedestrian crossing. There are, of course, more complex and emotive situations in which a person may be charged with a failure to do something; such an act might amount in certain circumstances to serious negligence. Since the late 1980s there have been a number of instances where this has been an issue as, for example, in a number of multiple fatal injuries arising from disasters at sea and on land. Such negligent acts, if they caused the death of others, *could* lead to charges of manslaughter; charges can be brought against companies and persons in managerial positions having control over the activities of their more junior staff. Prosecutions of this nature are difficult to bring and are not often successful. This is because it is very difficult to discover what is known as 'a controlling mind' in the complex web of corporate organizational responsibility (for comment, see Chapter 7 on homicide).

Brief historical background

With certain exceptions (notably extreme youth or mental disturbance),[1] individuals are to be held responsible (liable) for their acts and adjudged capable of exercising control over them. History reveals that the issue has not always been clear cut. In earlier times, it was customary for punishment to be imposed for the commission of a criminal act regardless of the mental condition of the person concerned; indeed, in England and Wales, the common law gave considerable overriding priority to the need to preserve law and order. Further back in historical time, in the Old Testament, we find examples of severe forms of punishment without mitigating features being much in evidence. However, in a restricted number of cases, if the crime appeared to be unintentional, *some* mitigation of penalty was available through the use of the 'cities of refuge' for those who killed unintentionally. In addition, minors, the feeble minded and deaf mutes were often afforded special treatment under the terms of Shoteh (as described in the Jewish Talmud). In the Roman era, one can discern the beginnings of an attempt to introduce a primitive notion of diminished responsibility; and in thirteenth-century England, it seems to have been generally held that neither the child nor the madman should be held liable for crime. Henry de Bracton, author of one of the first major treatises on English law, stated that 'Furiosus non intelligit quod agit et anima et ratione caret, et non multimumdistas a brutis' – 'an insane person is one who does not know what he is doing, is lacking in mind and reason and is not far from the brutes' (quoted in Walker 1968: 33). Though obviously benign in intent, the statement seems to have a somewhat primitive element to it, associating mental illness with the behaviour of animals. Walker (1968) and Jacobs (1971) have drawn attention to what appears to be an interesting error in another of Bracton's statements. It is worth alluding to briefly because it exemplifies some of the problems involved in tracing the evolution of legal and allied concepts. Bracton is said to have stated:

> Then there is what can be said about the child and the madman (furiosus), for the one is protected by the innocence of design and the other is excused by the misfortune of his *deed*.
>
> (quoted in Jacobs 1971: 25, emphasis added)

It is not altogether clear from his text why the madman is not to be held responsible. Apparently, Bracton took his text from a translation of the work of Modestinus. In its original form, this referred not to the misfortune of his deed ('infelicitas *facti*') but to the misfortune of his fate ('infelicitas *fati*'). This would make more sense, for it would appear that in Roman law there seems to have been an assumption that an insane offender was punished sufficiently by his madness ('satis furore ipso punitur'). Complicated statements and concepts sometimes become lost or confused during translation. For example, it is highly likely that much of the controversy over some of Freud's views and findings has arisen because of difficulties in finding suitable English interpretations of terms originally conceived and described in the German language. Such difficulties have been usefully illustrated by the psychiatrist and philanthropist Bruno Bettelheim, as follows:

> conversations with friends have disclosed that many, who, like myself, are native German speakers, and emigrated to the States in the middle of their lives, are quite dissatisfied with the way Freud's works have been rendered in English. The number of inadequacies and downright errors in the translations is enormous.
>
> (Bettelheim 1983: vii)

In the seventeenth century, the lawyer Sir Edward Coke appeared to share the view of earlier authorities that the mad were punished sufficiently by their fate. In the same century, Sir Matthew Hale (in a treatise published in 1736, some sixty years after his death) tried to distinguish between the totally and the partially insane. In his view, the latter would not be exempt from criminal responsibility (see Clarke 1975; Jacobs 1971). It seems fairly safe to assume that only very serious mental disorder ('raving lunacy') would have been recognized as giving exemption from serious crime and, in particular, homicide. However, contrary to general belief, issues relating to madness (insanity) were gradually being raised more frequently in respect of crimes less serious than homicide. Eigen (1983: 426) states that: 'the jurisprudence of insanity appears to have arisen not out of sensationalistic murders or grotesque personal assaults, but from what were rather more "garden variety" crimes.'

In addition, broader interpretations of what might constitute mental disorder were being admitted. For example, in the case of Edward Arnold in 1724, the judge suggested that 'if a man be deprived of reason, and, consequently of his intention, he cannot be guilty' (cited in Jacobs 1971: 27). Similar views were expressed in a famous Leicestershire case, namely that of Laurence Shirley, fourth Earl Ferrers. He was tried in 1760 by his fellow peers in the House of Lords for the murder of his steward John Johnson. His history, trial and the climate of the times in which it took place have been described in lively yet scholarly fashion by a local Leicester author and solicitor, Arthur Crane (1990). A subsequent and more influential case was that of James Hadfield, who was tried for capital treason in 1800 for shooting at King George III in the Theatre Royal, Drury Lane in London. Thomas Erskine, Hadfield's counsel, obtained an acquittal on the basis of the defendant having sustained serious head injuries (through sword wounds) during war service. These injuries had led Hadfield to develop delusional ideas that impelled him to believe that he had to sacrifice his life for the salvation of the world. Not wishing to be guilty of suicide and the condemnation and obloquy this would call down upon his memory, he chose to commit his crime for the sole purpose of being executed for it. Hadfield's case is of interest for three reasons. First, it was probably the first time that brain damage (caused by a head injury) had been advanced as a relevant exculpatory factor. Second, Erskine, who was a brilliant advocate (a George Carman of his day and later to become a distinguished judge), was probably more easily able to secure Hadfield's acquittal at a time when public interest in, and sympathy towards, the 'mad' had been fostered by the long-standing and intermittent illness suffered by the King (a malady for which the diagnosis has always been subject to professional controversy – was it a manic-depressive disorder or symptomatic of porphyria?). The third area of interest is the consequence that flowed from Hadfield's acquittal. The question that arose was where to 'house' him? Despite the facilities afforded by the vagrancy laws, the common law permitted the detention of a person such as Hadfield only until he had regained his sanity. As Reznek (1997: 18) points out, 'this led to dangerous lunatics being released during "lucid intervals"'. Reznek goes on to point out that 'an act of parliament hastily established . . . the existence of the special verdict NGRI [not guilty by reason of insanity] – allowing Hadfield to be committed indefinitely to Bethlem [Hospital]'. (Reznek 1997: 18). As we shall see shortly, the 'special verdict' still exists, but is implemented comparatively rarely. Not all cases were brought to such a successful conclusion as was Hadfield's. For example, a similar plea to Hadfield's entered in the case of John Bellingham (who in 1812 shot the prime minister, Spencer Perceval) was unsuccessful and Bellingham was condemned to death. Walker (1968) reports how a similar fate befell a contemporary of Bellingham's – an epileptic farmer named Bowler, who had killed a neighbour. However, it is the case of Daniel M'Naghten in 1843 that is of particular interest, for it was the outcome of his case and the consideration of that outcome by the senior judiciary that resulted in the formulation of a legal test of insanity.[2] M'Naghten was a Glaswegian wood-carver (carpenter) who seems to have suffered from what would be described today as paranoid delusions (see Chapter 4). For example, among other delusions, he believed that the Tories were conspiring against him. Following his arrest M'Naghten gave the following statement to the police: 'The Tories in my native city have compelled me to do this. They follow and persecute me wherever I go, and have entirely destroyed my peace of mind' (Walker 1968: 91; also quoted by Reznek 1997: 19).

As a result of this particular delusion M'Naghten purchased a pair of pistols and, on 20 January 1843, mistaking Sir Robert Peel's secretary, Robert Drummond, for the prime minister himself, shot him in the back. Drummond died some days later. In March the same year, M'Naghten went on trial. He too was represented by a very able counsel – Alexander Cockburn. Cockburn produced mental state evidence in court which suggested that M'Naghten was insane because he lacked control over his actions. He endeavoured to make out a case for a defence of partial insanity 'that could lead him to commit crimes for which morally he cannot be held responsible' (Walker 1968: 94). However, the trial judge did not favour such a view and put it to the jury that if M'Naghten had been able to distinguish right from wrong, they should return a guilty verdict. The jury disagreed and returned a verdict of Not Guilty by Reason of Insanity (NGRI). This verdict caused much concern and the House of Lords decided to put to a group of senior judges certain questions that arose from it. Two of the five questions put to the judges have, in combined form, come to be known as the M'Naghten 'rules'; in my humble opinion this is a somewhat erroneous term as they are merely a legal 'test' of insanity. The 'test' states, in effect, that:

> [The] jurors ought to be told in all cases that every man is to be presumed sane and to possess a sufficient degree of reason to be responsible for his crimes until the contrary is proved to their satisfaction; and that to establish a defence of insanity, it must be clearly proved that, at the time of committing the act, the party accused was labouring under such a defect of reason from disease of the mind, as not to know the nature and quality of his act he was doing; or, if he did know it, that he did not know what he was doing was wrong.
>
> (quoted in Walker 1968: 100)

In essence, there are two significant parts to the above statement. An accused has a defence, first, if they did not know the nature and quality of their act or, second, if they did, they did not know that it was wrong (in law). From the time they were first posited, the so-called 'rules' have, understandably, been the subject of criticism. In the first place, they were framed at a time when the disciplines of psychology and psychiatry were in an embryonic state of development; a disproportionate degree of emphasis was placed upon the faculties of knowing, reasoning and understanding (cognitive processes) to the exclusion of emotional and volitional factors (connative processes). (For very helpful discussions of these issues in the Victorian era, see Smith 1991; Ward 2002.) Second, the 'rules' make use of such expressions as 'defect of reason', 'disease of the mind', 'nature and quality of his act'. These terms have involved numerous debates concerning their precise legal definition and interpretation. Third, and perhaps more importantly, the criteria for 'M'Naghten madness' were so tightly drawn that its use as a defence in serious cases such as homicide has always been fraught with difficulty. Since the introduction of the Homicide Act 1957, the Mental Health Acts 1959, 1983 and 2007 and the total abolition of the death penalty in 1965, the number of insanity defences resulting in the 'special verdict' in homicide cases has been very small. It should be remembered that the insanity defence is open for use in cases other than homicide and, as we shall see when we consider the second form of the 'special verdict' (unfitness to plead), it is sometimes pleaded in such cases. However, until the Criminal Procedure (Insanity and Unfitness to Plead) Act 1991, a finding of insanity or unfitness to plead involved a fixed disposal of detention, often in a secure hospital, usually without limit of time. (For an excellent survey of these provisions, see Mackay 1995.) Lack of satisfaction with the M'Naghten 'rules' led the Committee on Mentally Abnormal Offenders to suggest a number of amendments to the M'Naghten provisions and to call for the introduction of a new formulation of the special verdict, namely, not guilty on evidence of severe mental disorder (illness or impairment) (Home Office and DHSS 1975).

The Committee on Mentally Abnormal Offenders proposed a definition of severe mental illness which would contain one or more of the following characteristics:

(a) Lasting impairment of intellectual functions shown by failure of memory, orientation, comprehension and learning capacity.
(b) Lasting alteration of mood of such degree as to give rise to delusional appraisal of the patient's situation, his past or his future, or that of others, or to lack of any appraisal.
(c) Delusional beliefs, persecutory, jealous or grandiose.
(d) Abnormal perceptions associated with delusional misinterpretation of events.
(e) Thinking so disordered as to prevent reasonable appraisal of the patient's situation or reasonable communication with others.
(Home Office and DHSS 1975: para 18.35 and Appendix 10)

To date, there has not been a great deal of impetus from central government or other sources to change the basic components of the insanity defence (see Buchanan 2000; see also Chapter 7 on homicide).

Unfitness to plead (under disability in relation to the trial)

So far I have considered only the first form of the special verdict. In order to complete the picture in this section of the chapter we must consider the situation when an individual claims that he or she is unfit to be tried (known as 'unfitness to plead' or being 'under disability in relation to the trial'). By tradition, and in accordance with the principles of English justice, a court has to be satisfied that an accused person can, first, understand the charges against them, second, exercise their age-old right to challenge a juror, third, follow the evidence against them, and fourth, instruct counsel for their defence. If the accused is considered to be unable to put the foregoing into effect, he or she has customarily been held to be 'unfit to plead' or, to use the term now favoured, to be 'under disability in relation to the trial' ('under disability' for short). As De Souza (2007: 7) points out in a very useful article 'only one of the above criteria needs to be [answered in the negative] for an individual to be found unfit to plead'. Cases of deaf-mutism may also occur rarely or may be found to be 'mute of malice'. In earlier times when a prisoner was thought to be 'mute of malice' they would be subjected to the *peine forte et dure*, 'in which the mute prisoner was both starved and gradually crushed under increasing weights . . . until he was either dead or had agreed to enter a plea' (Grubin 1996: 10). (For further discussion of the history of such pleas, see Grubin 1996; Rogers et al. 2008 and 2009. For the implications of the abolition of the right to silence as it might affect such cases, see Gray et al. 2001. For a discussion of assessing fitness to plead in relation to people with a learning disability, see Brewster et al. 2008.)

A finding of unfitness to plead occurs fairly infrequently, mainly because a person has to be very seriously disabled psychiatrically in order to satisfy the relevant criteria. Three cases known to me professionally exemplify this aspect. The first concerned a man who was suffering from such serious psychotic delusions that in the course of them he killed his wife. He was still severely deluded at the time of his trial and subsequently. The second case was of a young man who was found to be so impaired in intelligence and understanding that he, too, was found unfit to plead. A third case concerned a man who, while in the grip of severe psychotic delusions, attacked a near relative.[3] Before the Criminal Procedure (Insanity and Unfitness to Plead) Act 1991, the only disposal available on a finding of 'disability' was committal to a psychiatric hospital. This might be for a considerable period of time and the *facts* of the case might never be determined. It is possible (and in some cases even probable) that someone found to be under disability might well have had a defence to the charge if it had been put to the test in court. Momentum for change from various sources led to the 1991 Act and its more flexible provisions. These were as follows:

1   Where a person is found not guilty by reason of insanity or found to be under disability (unfit to plead), a Crown or Appeal Court will no longer be bound to order detention in hospital under a restriction order within the terms, currently, of the Mental Health Act 1983 (Sections 37/ 41), *except in cases of murder*. (But for the legality of this, see Kerrigan 2002.)

2   The following disposals were then available:

(a) An order for admission to hospital (an 'admission order') with the option of an added restriction order.

(b) A Guardianship Order under Section 37 of the Mental Health Act 1983.

(c) An Order for Supervision and Treatment placing the person under the supervision of either a probation officer or local authority social worker for a period of two years. In addition, the person would also be required to be under the care of a qualified medical practitioner. That order was similar to a community rehabilitation (formerly probation) order with a requirement for mental treatment, except that, in the event of non-compliance, there were no provisions, as in a community rehabilitation order, for a return to court or revocation of the order.

(d) An order for absolute discharge.

(e) There was a requirement for the medical evidence to the court to be given by two registered medical practitioners, one of whom had to be approved under Section 12 of the Mental Health Act 1983.

(f) Provision for a speedy trial of the facts of the case (see above discussion) so that the question of guilt could be determined. Such determination would be carried out by a jury separate from that empanelled to determine the defendant's state of mind. Should the jury decide that the defendant was not guilty of the alleged act or omission the court had to acquit, irrespective of his or her mental state. (In such a case, it is likely that other powers of the mental health legislation would be invoked if the individual satisfied the criteria for compulsory admission to hospital.)

Further changes in practice have now been made by Section 23 of the Domestic Violence, Crime and Victims Act 2004. These may be summarized as follows:

The number of options available to the courts are now fewer and less complicated. The court can make a hospital order and, if appropriate, add a restriction order under the mental health legislation; make a supervision order; discharge the defendant absolutely. The question of unfitness will now be determined by the judge and not a jury.

Comments

The courts must now be satisfied that the criteria for admission under the mental health legislation are met.[4] A supervision order may now include treatment for a *physical* as well as a mental disorder. An order for absolute discharge would most likely be imposed in cases where the charge might be regarded as trivial 'and the accused does not require treatment in the community' (de Souza 2007: 10).

These recent more flexible provisions of the 1991 Act seem to have promoted a modest increase in both disposals (for detailed information, see Mackay et al. 2006, 2007).

Diminished responsibility

As stated earlier in this chapter, the criteria for establishing a defence of insanity are narrowly drawn and difficult to implement. Until the introduction of the Homicide Act 1957 the defence was used almost exclusively in cases of murder as a means of avoiding the imposition of the death penalty. The Homicide Act was introduced following the report of the Royal Commission on Capital Punishment (Gowers 1953). The purpose of the Act was to introduce a wider range of mental defences to a charge of what was then capital murder. Such a defence had been used in Scotland since the 1870s (see Buchanan 2000: 54; see also Blom-Cooper and Morris 2004, notably Chapters 3 and 4). It was introduced in Scotland following the case of *HM Advocate v. Dingwall* (1867), in which the presiding judge referred to 'murder with extenuating circumstances' (Collins and White 2003; see also Patrick 2003). In their article, Collins and White (2003) examine the history of its development and demonstrate similar problems of interpretation in both law and psychiatry in Scotland to those in England and Wales. Section 2 of the Act states that:

> Where a person kills or is party to the killing of another, he shall not be convicted of murder if he was suffering from such abnormality of mind (whether arising from a condition of arrested or retarded development of mind or any inherent causes or induced by disease or injury) as substantially impaired his mental responsibility for his acts or omissions in doing or being party to the killing.

The defence is available only in cases of murder, and a finding of diminished responsibility reduces a charge of murder to that of manslaughter. This permits the judge a wide degree of discretion in sentencing. Conviction on a charge of murder permits, at present, only one disposal – a mandatory sentence of life imprisonment with, if the judge so disposes, a recommendation as to the minimum length of time the convicted person should serve. Examination of Section 2 indicates the recognition of a degree of *partial* responsibility; this differs from a successful insanity defence where a finding of insanity (or for that matter unfitness to plead) acknowledges total exculpation from responsibility. The plea of diminished responsibility may be raised by the accused and, as we shall see shortly, if contested, will be decided by a jury 'on the balance of probabilities'. Such a test is somewhat less strict than the 'beyond all reasonable doubt' burden of proof required in most criminal trials. The number of instances in which diminished responsibility has been pleaded and the number of hospital disposals in these would seem to have been fluctuating in recent years. In an early study Dell (1984) suggested that this might have been due to reluctance on the part of some psychiatrists to treat those diagnosed as suffering from psychopathic disorder, either in secure conditions or in ordinary psychiatric hospitals. In addition to problems of disposal, the wording of Section 2 itself has presented serious problems in court. The notion of diminishment of responsibility is a difficult one to grasp. Many psychiatrists have occasionally been willing to go somewhat beyond their remit of diagnosing mental disorder and opine as to the extent to which this may have diminished responsibility. On the other hand, some psychiatrists question whether this latter function is properly within psychiatry's remit. Should it not be solely for the jury to decide? Case law has indicated that even if there is unanimous psychiatric opinion that responsibility is substantially diminished, the jury is not bound to accept that view (*R. v. Vernege* 1982). We shall see shortly that this was certainly the case in *R. v. Sutcliffe* 1981.

Returning to the issue of semantics, we may well ask ourselves what interpretation should be placed upon the words 'abnormality of mind'? At least two aspects of this question may be discerned. First, whether or not an abnormality of mind existed and second, whether it affected the defendant's 'mental responsibility' for his or her acts. Dr John Hamilton, one-time Medical Director of Broadmoor Hospital, once asked: 'What on earth does [mental responsibility] mean?' (Hamilton 1981: 434). And, as has already been suggested, are psychiatrists necessarily the most appropriate persons to give such opinions? Dr Jack Kahn, a very experienced general psychiatrist with a deep interest in mental health and philosophical issues, once posed the dilemma for psychiatrists having to testify in court very trenchantly:

> In deviation from the normal, particularly where behaviour is concerned, there may not necessarily be a medical contribution at all. The treatment may be purely legal or social action. The aim is to bring the behaviour into conformity . . . the psychiatrist comes into the study of some human problems only by invitation, and this invitation may not be wholehearted. It is as if the psychiatrist is expected to claim authority in every problem of living, only to have that claim challenged even while his help is being sought.
>
> (Kahn 1971: 230)

It is also worth noting here that Professor Thomas Szasz (1987, 1993) has for long championed the view that psychiatry should not be used over-enthusiastically in matters of morality and deviance. There would appear, then, to be a fundamental ambivalence to be overcome, even before matters of motivation and its interpretation are raised and challenged under our adversarial system of justice. Aspects of such ambivalence were well attested to in a seminal article by Kenny (1984). He began his contribution with an incisive discussion of the case of John Hinckley, who attempted to assassinate President Ronald Reagan. He too makes some trenchant observations about the role of expert witnesses, particularly psychiatrists:

> The law should be reformed by changing statutes which force expert witnesses to testify beyond their science, by taking the provision of expert evidence out of the adversarial context, and by removing from the courts the decision whether a nascent discipline is, or is not a science.
>
> (Kenny 1984: 291)

Brief reference has already been made to the notion of 'abnormality of mind'. In the case of Byrne – a sexual psychopath – Lord Parker, then Lord Chief Justice, described abnormality of mind and its legal implications in the following terms:

> Inability to exercise will-power to control physical acts, provided it is due to abnormality of mind from one of the causes specified [i.e. in the Homicide Act] is sufficient to entitle the accused to the benefit of the [defence]; difficulty in controlling his physical acts depending on the degree of difficulty may be. *It is for the jury to decide on the whole of the evidence* whether such inability or difficulty has, *not as a matter of scientific certainty but on the balance of probabilities* been established, and in the case of difficulty, is so great as to amount in their view to *substantial* impairment of the accused's mental responsibility for his acts.
>
> (*R. v. Byrne* 1960, emphases added)

Four further points arise from this statement. First, such a definition reinforces the much wider interpretation of mental disorder than that within the more narrow confines of the M'Naghten 'rules' referred to earlier. Second, it seems to acknowledge that will-power can be impaired, introducing to some extent the American concept of 'irresistible impulse' – a concept not popular hitherto with English jurists (see also Reznek 1997: 24 et seq.). Third, we can infer that the judiciary could permit the view that the mind can be answerable for behaviour. Fourth, the question of *substantial* impairment was also a matter for the jury to decide, but *how* it arose and its *causes* were questions for the doctors. As to the meaning of substantial, it has been held that '"substantial" does not mean total . . . the mental responsibility need not be totally impaired, destroyed altogether. At the other end of the scale, substantial does not mean trivial or minimal' (*R. v. Lloyd* 1967). (Not, you may consider, a very helpful ruling!) Some of these and associated problems have been usefully analysed by Mitchell (1997a, 1997b).

Case illustrations

In order to illustrate further some of the problems referred to above, I now present four cases.

Case illustration 2.1

The case of Peter Sutcliffe attracted such notoriety and media interest that some of the key issues concerning the diminishment, or otherwise, of his 'mental responsibility for his acts' have tended to be overshadowed by the horrendous nature of his crimes and the furore surrounding the circumstances of his detection or, to be more precise, his non-detection over a five-year period. The history of the latter has been described in detail by Michael Bilton (2003) and was referred to briefly in Chapter 1.[5] Sutcliffe's case, and the others to be described shortly, highlight in compelling fashion many of the issues I have sought to address in the previous few pages of this chapter. A court will frequently accept a plea of diminished responsibility on the basis of agreed and uncontested psychiatric evidence: that is, the psychiatrists for the prosecution and the defence are all agreed on the diagnosis. Acceptance by the courts of pleas of diminished responsibility on *agreed* psychiatric evidence has occurred only since 1962. Between 1957 and 1962, following a High Court decision in *R. v. Matheson* (1958), the issue had to be put to a jury in all cases (Bartholomew 1983). It will be recalled that the issue of diminished responsibility is raised by the defence and its proof rests on a *balance of probabilities*. If such a plea is accepted by the judge (in a non-contested case), or by a jury (after a trial of the issue), a person who would otherwise have been liable to conviction for murder will be convicted of manslaughter, allowing the judge a wide discretion in sentencing. As is now well known, the trial judge in Sutcliffe's case Mr Justice Boreham refused (as was his right) to accept the agreed views of both prosecution and defence and decided to put the issue of Sutcliffe's mental responsibility for his acts to a jury. It is important to ask why this very experienced judge embarked upon this particular course of action when four highly experienced senior forensic-psychiatrists were all agreed on Sutcliffe's disordered mental state. There are a number of possibilities. First, although a plea of Section 2 diminished responsibility is available only in a murder case, the judge may have been very conscious of the fact that the *public* might have considered it to be a somewhat contradictory and idiosyncratic state of affairs that allowed Sutcliffe to plead *guilty* to the *attempted murder* of seven women and *not guilty* to the murder of thirteen (when the fact that he had actually *committed* the murders was not being disputed – merely his criminal responsibility for so doing). To the general public (but of course not to the legally informed) it might have seemed somewhat disturbing that such pleas were acceptable when, presumably, only good fortune saved the lives of seven of his victims. Hence, the judge might well have considered that 'public interest' demanded that the issues involved be made absolutely clear. Second, the judge would no doubt have been very conscious of the public's more general concern about the case and its notoriety. It might well have seemed to him to have been doing both the case and the public less than full justice to have disposed of it without a full and public hearing about the defendant's alleged motivation and mental state. Third, the judge, having read the papers in the case before the actual hearing, might well have wondered at the apparent discrepancies between what Sutcliffe was alleged to have told the police in the course of their prolonged interviews with him, what he was alleged to have confided to the prison officers and what he told the psychiatrists who examined him. (For a full discussion of some of these aspects, see Spencer 1984: 106–113.) Fourth, no doubt the judge would have considered the possibility of putting the case to a jury in the knowledge that, following a conviction of murder, not only would he have to pass a life sentence, but also he could, by virtue of Section 1(2) of the Murder (Abolition of Death Penalty) Act 1965, add *a recommendation as to what the minimum sentence should be*. Such a possibility would not be available to him in a finding of Section 2 manslaughter. It is of interest to note here that the House of Lords decided in 2003 that a life sentence imposed on a mentally ill offender is not incompatible with Article 3 of the European Convention on Human Rights (*R. v. Drew* (2003) UKHL 25 in *The Independent, Law Report*, 15 May 2003, p. 18). The judge would doubtless also be mindful that a sentence of imprisonment would keep control over Sutcliffe's eventual release within the penal system even, as it eventually turned out, he was subsequently transferred to hospital. For all these reasons, the judge's decision to put the whole issue to the jury seems very understandable, though the final outcome of indefinite detention in prison or hospital could have been predicted. According to some of the media accounts of the trial we witnessed the somewhat unusual (some would say undignified) spectacle of all the psychiatric witnesses being cross-examined by the prosecution counsel – including their own, when only a few hours before all the parties in the case had been agreed on the course of action that should be taken.[6] The manner in which the psychiatric evidence was received and commented upon in the press during the trial revealed very clearly the ambivalence of society towards the intervention of psychiatry in matters of criminal behaviour referred to earlier in this chapter. This ambivalence is, of course, compounded by the fact that the UK adversarial system of justice does not lend itself readily to the discussion or deliberation of complex and finely drawn issues of intent and motivation. Psychiatrists, in their day-to-day practice, are accustomed to dealing with grey areas of motivation and far less with the black and white issues of fact demanded by the constraints of our justice system. Some people have suggested that the psychiatrists were wrong-footed in court; they were certainly subjected to a good deal of criticism, if not ridicule. On going over the various press accounts of the case, this appears to have been quite ill founded, given the constraints already referred to and the fact that journalistic accounts are inevitably highly selective.[7]

Although I shall be considering the relationship between mental disorders and criminality in some detail in Chapter 4, it is appropriate at this point to make brief comment about the relationship between some forms of schizophrenic illness and crime, since a form of schizophrenic illness was the diagnosis the psychiatrists gave to Sutcliffe's condition. We can say that the relationship between schizophrenic illnesses and crime in general is a modest one. However, the *particular* diagnosis given for Sutcliffe's disorder was a form of *paranoid* schizophrenia. This form of schizophrenia is characterized to a large extent (but not exclusively) by delusions. There are a number of well-documented cases concerning persons who have committed homicide and other serious offences while under the influence of these, the most historic of these probably being the case of Daniel M'Naghten already referred to. One of the most important points to remember about the paranoid disorders (and their variants) is that sufferers are likely to appear quite sane and rational in most aspects of their lives. It is only when the subject matter of their delusional beliefs is touched upon that their symptoms may emerge with unexpected and frightening impact. It is not altogether surprising, therefore, that Sutcliffe was able to cover his tracks, because one can be highly paranoid, yet also be evasive and cunning. It is also true to say that the problems encountered by the police in linking vital pieces of information, and the sending of the false tapes, served only to facilitate Sutcliffe's opportunities for evasion. As already indicated, the individual's delusional system may be so well encapsulated (highly contained) that it may not emerge until and unless the matters upon which the system has fastened are explored in a detailed and systematic manner by a skilled psychiatric assessor. It is understandable, therefore, that the police and prison officers obtained one impression of Sutcliffe and the psychiatrists another; much depends upon the questions one asks and the manner and skill with which one asks them. This of course presents its own difficulties, for one's questioning *may* be determined by a particular set of preconceptions. At the time of his trial, other diagnoses of Sutcliffe's disorder appear to have been ruled out. We know that he is alleged to have once suffered a head injury as a result of a motor cycle accident. In some instances, if head injuries are serious enough to result in brain damage, they can produce delusional symptoms (as in Hadfield's case referred to earlier). Neither does a diagnosis of psychopathic disorder appear to have been entertained. Given his past history, background and apparent long-standing paranoid ideation, such a diagnosis would seem unlikely. However, an unequivocal diagnosis of paranoid schizophrenia does not seem to be altogether without its difficulties, given Sutcliffe's conflicting statements and his apparent capacity for acting with insight in order to avoid detection. Spencer suggests that:

In his *apparent* simulation of insanity, his alleged and God-inspired delusions and the sadistic undertones of his killings, Sutcliffe falls exactly halfway between the murderers John George Haigh and Neville Heath.
(Spencer 1984: 112–113, emphasis added)

Spencer also suggests, in highly insightful fashion, that a more precise defence for Sutcliffe might have been that he suffered:

> from a clear-cut abnormality of mind of a strangely paranoid type. Starting in 1969, with an unexplained attack on a prostitute and enhanced in 1979 by trivial humiliation, it developed into a bizarre, homicidal hatred of women, particularly prostitutes or alleged prostitutes. It continues with a strongly sadistic overtone and possibly – perhaps probably – as the result of a low-grade schizophrenic process. Whether or not the basis was schizophrenic, there was surely substantially more than minimal or trivial diminishment of responsibility?
>
> (Spencer 1984: 113; see also Burn 1984; Jones 1992)

The rest of the story is well known and can be recounted briefly. The jury returned a majority (10–2) verdict finding Sutcliffe guilty of murder. It is worth emphasizing here, that in doing so they did not *necessarily* reject the proposition that Sutcliffe was suffering from a form of paranoid schizophrenia, only that it did *not constitute an abnormality of mind of sufficient degree to substantially impair his mental responsibility for his acts*. He was sentenced to life imprisonment, Mr Justice Boreham making a recommendation that he serve a minimum of thirty years. A year later he was refused leave to appeal. Subsequent events seem to have vindicated the views of all the psychiatrists who examined him before his trial. His mental state deteriorated in prison and he was the victim of an assault by a fellow prisoner. His severity of symptoms and his vulnerability to attack presented very real problems for the prison medical authorities; eventually, following further assessment, the Home Secretary gave authority for his transfer to a high security hospital (Broadmoor) – where he is currently detained. It is of interest to note that, even in a secure hospital setting, he has been the subject of a further serious assault by a fellow patient. The Sutcliffe case illustrates some of the problems involved in the diminished responsibility defence, not the least of these being the area of tension that inevitably exists between psychiatry and the law. Most of these problems would be avoided if we abandoned the mandatory life sentence for murder and allowed the judiciary the same sentencing discretion as in manslaughter cases. Such a proposal has had the backing of the judiciary and those who work in the criminal justice and forensic mental health systems for many years. Sadly, the political will to agree to such a change has not been forthcoming (see Chapter 7 on homicide). Sadly, I continue to conclude that this is due to the establishment's over-cautious approach and the apparent sacrifice of more effective and more humane disposals upon the altar of political expediency.

Case illustration 2.2

In 1983, very similar problems were to emerge in the almost equally notorious case of Dennis Nilsen. Nilsen admitted having sex with and killing fifteen young men and subsequently dissecting, boiling and burning their bodies in order to dispose of them. He was sentenced to life imprisonment, the judge adding a minimum recommendation that he serve twenty-five years. The jury had convicted him of murder by a majority verdict of 10–2 on all but one of the counts against him. In the latter case they reached a unanimous verdict. In arguing for a manslaughter verdict Nilsen's counsel had tried to convince the jury that 'anybody guilty of such horrific acts must be out of his mind' (*The Times*, 5 November 1983). In Nilsen's case, unlike Sutcliffe's, there had been no unanimity of opinion as to Nilsen's abnormality of mind among the psychiatrists who examined him. (Two opined for diminished responsibility, one was against.) Nor was Nilsen's alleged mental disorder as floridly psychotic or akin to a lay person's notion of 'madness' as was Sutcliffe's. Nilsen was said to be suffering from a severe personality (psychopathic) disorder, manifested in part by abnormal sexual behaviour. The psychiatrists disagreed not only as to the nature of the diagnosis in his case, but also as to whether it constituted an abnormality of mind within the meaning of the Homicide Act. However, no one reading the press accounts of Nilsen's life history, the nature of his crimes and his attitudes towards his victims, could fail to agree that his behaviour was decidedly abnormal by any standards (*The Times*, 5 November 1983; *Guardian*, 5 November 1983). (For a detailed account of Nilsen's developmental history, life and behaviour, see Masters 1985.) One of the key issues that emerges in Nilsen's case is similar to that in Sutcliffe's – namely the difficulty involved in fitting the inherently imprecise concepts used in psychiatry into the confining straitjacket of the law. There is an important difference between the two cases. Sutcliffe's disorder was one that might be improved (if not cured) by treatment. The more intrusive features of his delusions could be treated, and abated to some extent, by medication. In Nilsen's case, his personality disorder, even if it had constituted an abnormality of mind, was considered to be largely untreatable so that a penal as opposed to a mental health disposal may seem only marginally less helpful. However, as I shall show later in this book, some severe personality disorders are capable of some improvement given the right approach and environment.

Case illustration 2.3

In June 1984 M.T. was jailed for life for the manslaughter of his second wife. Following a nine-day trial, he was found guilty of manslaughter, but not murder, by a unanimous jury – a jury who took only two and a half hours to reach their verdict. It was alleged in court that M.T. had had a highly disturbed and somewhat tragic childhood. He lacked maturity and showed a marked inability to control his impulses and emotions. He was probably not helped by his wealthy background, which encouraged a degree of self-indulgent behaviour. Such a description resonates with that in the case of *R. v. Byrne* quoted earlier in this chapter. The facts in M.T.'s case are, to some extent, only minimally less bizarre than those in Sutcliffe's and Nilsen's. Admittedly he had committed only one crime, but the circumstances of that single killing and the aftermath are not only gruesome but also highly pathological.

According to a press report (*Guardian*, 30 June 1984), M.T. shot his wife after she had allegedly taunted him beyond endurance concerning her sexual relations with members of both sexes. After killing her, he moved her body around the house for a week or so, occasionally talking to and kissing her corpse. Allegedly he subsequently placed her body in a half-built sauna in the house. Five months later he decided to take the body to the West Country with a view to burying it. This proved unsuccessful (because of drought). He eventually left the body in some bracken overlooking a river, having cut off her head and taking it with him; it was subsequently found in the boot of his car. In M.T.'s case two psychiatrists testified that his responsibility was diminished and one testified against that view. It is difficult to tell whether the jury was more influenced by the opinions of the two psychiatrists who viewed him as suffering from a disorder that would substantially diminish his responsibility, or whether it was his bizarre activities following the killing which led them to the view that he 'must have been mad' to have behaved in such a fashion.[8] But was his behaviour more bizarre than Nilsen's? Nilsen had sex with his victims before and after death and then lived with the results of what he had done until he could no longer dispose of their corpses safely. Samuels (1975) has some very apt words on this latter aspect:

> If a defendant just kills his victim for what appears to be a very ordinary motive such as greed or jealousy, diminished responsibility stands little chance of being established, but if the defendant has a history of mental trouble, goes in for perverted sexual practices with the victim before and after death, mutilates the body, cuts it up [or] sends it through the post . . . then the more horrible the killing the more likely diminished responsibility will be established, because *the further removed from normal behaviour the behaviour of the defendant, the more he appears to be mentally ill*, or so the submission runs.
>
> (Samuels 1975: 199–200, emphases added)

M.T. was represented by the late George Carman, QC, who emphasized M.T.'s highly fraught background.

Case illustration 2.4

For my last example I turn to the United States. Although Jeffrey Dahmer committed his numerous murders in the United States and was dealt with by the US criminal justice system, his case has certain points in common with that of Dennis Nilsen. One of these was the attempt by his defence counsel to satisfy the court that his responsibility for his crimes was diminished by an abnormality of mind. In Dahmer's case, a defence of insanity had to be entered, because there is no exact US equivalent of the UK's Homicide Act. The relevant state statute contains reference to a lack of 'substantial capacity to appreciate the wrongfulness of his conduct or conform his conduct to the requirements of the law' (Masters 1993: 227). Dahmer's long career of killing ended, as had Sutcliffe's, by chance. He had been apprehended on another matter by two Milwaukee police patrolmen. On going to his apartment they were confronted by a gruesome collection of Polaroid pictures of dead males, severed heads and partially dismembered torsos. Later, the police were to discover even more tangible evidence – a refrigerator containing a severed head, a freezer containing two more heads and a human torso. Two skulls and a complete skeleton were found in a filing cabinet, as was a large plastic drum containing three further torsos in various stages of decomposition. Following his arrest, and for the ensuing two weeks, Dahmer confessed 'that he had killed sixteen men in Milwaukee over a period of four years' (Masters 1993: 4). To the outside world, Dahmer was a quiet, inoffensive factory worker. It is of interest to note that he had been the subject of investigation at one stage for non-consensual acts of indecency with other males in a 'bath house'. However, the proprietors are said not to have wished for the matter to be taken further on account of the adverse publicity it might have occasioned. It is also of some concern to note that on another occasion he had been convicted of a sexual assault, and that while waiting sentence for that offence he had committed his fifth murder. With hindsight, it would seem that he had already given indications of his sinister preoccupation with deviant sexuality and with death. From his history it emerges that he had an overpowering need to possess and control his victims – to the point of collecting and storing their remains after death. In my view this could well be regarded as a variant of necrophilia. (See Chapter 8 on sex offending for further discussion.)

As in Nilsen's case, Dahmer's advocate sought to convince the court that a person who indulged in such compulsive behaviour must be mad rather than merely bad, but that he could in fact 'retain a perfectly clear idea of what is right and good and still be compelled to do what is wrong and bad' (Masters 1993: 98). Much play was made of his long-standing sexual problems, prolonged alcohol abuse and difficulties in making social relationships with both males and females. Despite the expert evidence given on his behalf, his plea failed. The jury retired on Friday 14 February 1992 and returned earlier than anticipated with their verdicts – majority verdicts of 10–2 on five of the counts – on Saturday 15 February. He was sentenced to life imprisonment with no eligibility for parole before seventy years. He was subsequently murdered in prison.

Other 'erosions' of responsibility

My comments on infanticide and provocation should be read in conjunction with those I make on these matters in Chapter 7 on homicide.

Infanticide

In addition to the Homicide Act 1957, the law makes *specific* provision for the erosion of responsibility in cases of killing in one other way. This is through the Infanticide Act 1938. This enactment (which amended the earlier Infanticide Act 1922, which in turn had revised much earlier legislation) was introduced in order to relieve from the death sentence a woman who, under certain specific circumstances, had caused the death of her children. In such cases the judges had always felt a great deal of reluctance in having to impose the death penalty (Bluglass 1990). In the context of this chapter, its creation is of interest in that it gave statutory recognition to a *specific state of mind* in a *woman* who caused by any wilful act or omission, the death of her child *under the age of twelve months* when the balance of her mind was disturbed by reason of her not having fully recovered from the *effect of giving birth to a child or by reason of the effect of lactation (breast feeding) consequent upon that birth* (emphases added). The Act was passed at a time when more emphasis was placed upon what was considered to be the adverse effects of childbirth upon a woman's *mental state* than would perhaps be considered as relevant nowadays (see also Buchanan 2000: 102; and see Chapter 7 in this book). When one examines the figures for infanticide convictions they are very small; since the late 1990s, the average number of convictions per year has been about four. Almost all cases are dealt with by a community penalty such as a probation order (community rehabilitation order). There are almost always adverse social conditions or a highly complex personal situation that would more likely than not enable the case to be dealt with as a case of diminished responsibility under the provisions of the current Homicide Act 1957. The complexities and anomalies are exemplified strikingly in the following case – reported in the *Guardian* newspaper:

> A woman killed her four-year-old daughter shortly after the latter witnessed her mother killing her seventeen-month-old baby brother by strangulation. In this case, the prosecution accepted pleas of diminished responsibility and the woman was discharged on condition she receive hospital treatment. Defending counsel said the woman had experienced a slow build-up of pressure and had suffered a depressive disorder from the birth of her son. In theory, had she killed the child within the first twelve months of his life instead of at seventeen months, she could have been charged with infanticide as well as perhaps being charged with the murder of the four-year-old.
>
> (*Guardian*, 27 November 1984)

This case example illustrates the somewhat outmoded and arbitrary nature of the infanticide defence. The Butler Committee put forward the view that the offence could be subsumed under the umbrella of diminished responsibility, but retaining infanticide was favoured by the Criminal Law Revision Committee (1980: paras 100–104: 114:1). For a discussion of some of the implications of any change and their historical context, see Lambie (2001) and Law Commission (2006: Part 8).

Provocation

Buchanan (2000: 50) notes that 'the defence of provocation emerged in English law in the seventeenth century'. The Homicide Act 1957 made 'statutory provision for provocation to reduce what would otherwise be murder to manslaughter' (Buchanan 2000: 50) thus avoiding a conviction for the former. The defence hinges on the presence or otherwise of a *sudden* loss of control and whether or not a *reasonable* person would have acted as the defendant did. Numerous difficulties have arisen in the courts' interpretations of these requirements and have led to some contradictory decisions from the Court of Appeal (see later). It is not difficult to see that a claim of an abnormality of mind might be put forward as a reason for the defendant's response to provocation. Lord Justice Lawton held that psychiatric evidence was not necessarily admissible and in the case of *R. v. Turner* (1975) stated that:

> trial by psychiatrists would be likely to take the place of trial by jury and magistrates . . . psychiatry has not yet become a satisfactory substitute for the common sense of juries and magistrates on matters within their experience of life.
>
> (quoted in Hall Williams 1980: 279)

However, in many cases the dividing line between those behaviours that can be regarded as 'normal' and those that can be regarded as 'abnormal' may not be quite as clear cut as Lord Justice Lawton was implying. Some support for my contention is afforded by Dell (1984), who found in her study that 'in a few cases, the jury had found the defendant guilty on grounds both of diminished responsibility and provocation' (Dell 1984: 4).

More recently, further complicated legal issues have arisen; it has been held for many years that the events leading to an act carried out under circumstances of alleged provocation must be recent. In the case of *R. v. Ahluwalia* (1990) it was held by the Court of Appeal that a judge's direction to a jury:

> on a murder trial defining 'provocation' as conduct causing a 'sudden loss of self control' was in accordance with well established law and could not be faulted. If the law was wrong it was for Parliament to change it not the courts.

(However, it should be noted here that the defendant Kiranjit Ahluwalia won her appeal against a murder conviction on other grounds.) A great deal of concern has also been expressed as to the apparent arbitrary fashion in which acts of provocation have been defined. For example, those who have been worried about the rights of 'battered women' have been concerned that years of assaultive behaviour by husbands or partners that

is patiently borne by their victims may not constitute a situation of provocation that culminates in legal retaliation or defence. The fact that it has
to be a result of a *sudden* and *recent* incident of violent behaviour seems to
be quite arbitrary. One has much sympathy for this view and, as stated
earlier, the courts seem to reach conflicting decisions. For example, at
Belfast Crown Court a woman succeeded in her plea of provocation
in respect of a charge of murdering her husband. She had stabbed him
to death after she had 'snapped' during a drunken row. The judge is said to
have told her: 'I am satisfied that what caused you to snap was not just one
evening's ill treatment but the accumulation of six years' abuse'. He placed
her on probation (*The Independent*, 2 February 1993). Another case concerned a 'devoted father who battered and strangled his unfaithful wife'. He
was said to have 'snapped after years of humiliation at the hands of his
wife'. The judge is said to have told him: 'I have never before encountered a
more extreme case of *persistent* provocation or degrading behaviour by a
woman towards a man . . . you were goaded beyond anyone's breaking
point' (*The Independent*, 6 April 1993, emphasis added). The somewhat
contradictory state of the law has been usefully stated and supported by a
number of further case examples by Rix (2001; see also Hall 1998) and
more recently by the Law Commission (2006: Part 5). Clearly the present
state of affairs can be regarded only as unsatisfactory.

The special case of children

The position regarding children has already been referred to briefly. I
consider them in more detail in Chapter 7 on homicide. As with other parts
of this book, my decision is, perforce, somewhat arbitrary.

Some other mental defences

I now consider briefly some aspects of what can best be described as
involuntary conduct and the nature of the state known as automatism.

Involuntary conduct

An act or omission is considered to be *involuntary* where it can clearly be
shown to be beyond the control of the person. A frequently quoted case is
that of *Hill v. Baxter* (1958) in which it was alleged that the defendant had
contravened the Road Traffic Act 1930 by driving dangerously. The
defendant pleaded that he had become unconscious and that he remembered nothing of the alleged incident. His plea was accepted by the magistrates on the grounds that severe loss of memory must have been caused by
the sudden onset of illness which had overcome him. However, the High
Court did not accept this finding, suggesting that he might just have fallen

asleep. In expressing their view in this particular case, they did qualify it by stating that there might be some states of unconsciousness, or even clouded (interrupted) consciousness, such as those in a stroke or epileptic seizure, which might exclude liability in similar cases. One of the judges hearing the appeal suggested that similar exculpation from liability might have arisen if, for example, a man had been attacked by a swarm of bees and, because of their action, had lost directional control of the vehicle. In his classic work, Hart (1968) made a useful twofold distinction between those situations where the subject is conscious and where he or she is unconscious. I paraphrase it as follows:

1   **Conscious**
   (a) Physical compulsion by another person.
   (b) Muscular control impaired by disease; as in cases of chorea (for example Huntington's Chorea, now known as Huntington's Disorder).
   (c) Reflex muscular contraction (as in the hypothetical case of the swarm of bees mentioned earlier).
2   **Unconscious**
   (a) Natural sleep at normal time (see later discussion).
   (b) Drunken stupor. Hart (1968) cited the example of a woman in a drunken state 'overlaying' her child and thus killing it (it could, of course, have equally been a man).
   (c) Sleep brought on by fatigue (as, for example, in the case of the motorist cited above).
   (d) Loss of consciousness involving collapse, in certain medical conditions such as epilepsy or hypoglycaemic states.

It is likely that many of the above states could lead to a successful plea for negation or serious reduction of criminal liability. Courts will always have to interpret such pleas according to individual circumstances, so that no general ruling can be found in quoted law reports or legal texts that would be appropriate in all cases. For example, if I fall asleep at the wheel of my car and cause an accident, am I to be considered to be entirely exempted from liability, or will the court suggest, as it did in the well-known case of *Kay v. Butterworth* (1945), that I must have known that drowsiness was overcoming me and that, because of this, I should have stopped driving and averted an accident? (For an erudite but highly readable discussion of this topic, see Mackay 1995: Chapter 1.)

Automatism

Automatism is a phenomenon which may occur in situations where loss of consciousness is the cause of an *involuntary* (i.e. unintentional) act. Such an act may, in certain circumstances, be held to constitute a crime. For legal purposes then, automatism means being in a state capable of action but not being conscious of that action. A well-known definition was that given in the case of *R. v. Bratty*:

> the state of a person who, though capable of action, is not conscious of what he is doing. It means unconscious, involuntary action and is a defence because the mind does not know what is being done.
>
> (quoted in Buchanan 2000: 97)

Two types of automatism have been (rather arbitrarily) distinguished by the courts on various occasions – sane automatism and insane automatism. To oversimplify somewhat, it is the case currently that an insane automatism is one that is caused by some internal factor 'and which has on one occasion at least manifested itself in violence' (Buchanan 2000: 98). The dividing line between sane and insane automatism is not clear cut and courts have interpreted the differences in various ways. For a finding of sane automatism there usually has to be some *external* cause, such as a blow to the head, whereas an *internal* cause would consist of some form of abnormality of mind (as, for example, in a plea of diminished responsibility). A finding of insane automatism will lead to a disposal under the Criminal Procedure (Insanity and Unfitness to Plead) Act 1991. A finding of sane automatism will lead to an acquittal. Courts tend to favour restricting the automatism defence, holding that a state of automatism is not a defence if the accused is in some way to blame or is at fault for getting into that condition: for example, through getting into a state of acute intoxication (see later discussion also). A review of some of the recent case law reveals that it has usually been held that a person is responsible for the consequences of his decision either to do something (such as to ingest drink or other drugs) or not to stop some activity (for example, continuing to drive while beginning to feel overcome by the need for sleep).

One more obvious form of automatism is that of being in a somnambulistic state. Fenwick's (1990) monograph on the clinical aspects of automatism provides an excellent extended discussion of the relationship between somnambulism (sleep automatism) and criminal behaviour (Fenwick 1990: 12–18). In particular, he offers detailed guidance for those engaged in having to try to establish a defence to a criminal charge on these grounds. He cites a number of important diagnostic and prognostic factors, such as childhood and family history, disorientation on awakening, availability of evidence from witnesses to the event, amnesia for the event, trigger factors, lack of attempts to conceal the crime, the motiveless or out of character nature of the crime and, in cases of violent crime, the possibility of a previous history of violence during a period of sleep automatism. From time to time, successful pleas in these cases are reported in the press. For example, a teenager almost killed a friend during a nightmare, but was cleared of attempted murder by a Crown Court. It was alleged that, in the course of the nightmare, he stabbed the friend with a kitchen knife and beat him with a wooden club. A psychiatrist told the court that 'He committed this act during his sleep – during a night of terror.' The doctor told the court that he 'knew of eight or nine similar cases' (*The Independent*, 9 March 1990). In this case, the defendant secured an acquittal. However, as already noted, the law seems somewhat capricious in its interpretation and implementation. For example, in the case of *R. v. Burgess* (1991) the decision was somewhat different. Here, it was held that Barry Burgess who, while sleepwalking, acted violently without being consciously aware of what he was doing, was suffering from *a disease of the mind* and not from non-insane automatism and so could be found not guilty of the offence by reason of insanity. At his trial, Burgess had admitted attacking a sleeping female friend by hitting her on the head with a bottle and grasping her around the throat. He said that he, too, had fallen asleep and was sleepwalking. Such apparently contradictory cases are not uncommon and the law is in obvious need of clarification. (For a discussion of the ambiguities in the law, see, for example, Rix (2001) and Yeo (2002); although he cites Canadian cases, much of what Yeo (2002) says can be extended to other jurisdictions such as the UK.)

Intoxicating substances

It is not uncommon in criminal cases, particularly those involving serious violence against persons or property, for a plea to be made by the accused that their liability for their criminal acts should be diminished because of the effects of taking alcohol and/or other drugs. The law holds that being in a state of intoxication is no defence to a criminal charge; however, if the offence requires specific intent (such as that which would be required to fulfil the legal requirements for a finding of guilt on a charge of murder) the fact that the accused had been drinking might help to negate specific intent and thus might provide a defence. (For an extended discussion of this matter, see Mackay 1995.) Other crimes requiring specific intent are theft, fraud and burglary (see, for example, the cases of *R. v. Burns* 1973 and *R. v. Stephenson* 1979). However, various legal decisions and their interpretations appear to suggest some continuing conflict of opinion on this matter. For example, in the case of *Bratty* already referred to, it was held that, in crimes such as murder, where proof of a specific intent was required, the intent *might* be negated by drunkenness and the accused might thus be convicted of a lesser offence, for example manslaughter or even unlawful wounding. Other cases indicate just how complex the matter is. For example, in the case of *R. v. Gittens* (1984) the appellant had been tried on counts of murder of his wife and the rape and murder of his 15-year-old stepdaughter. An issue arose as to whether his admitted abnormality of mind which substantially impaired his 'mental responsibility' was caused by drink or the drugs he had taken, as the prosecution contended, or whether it was due to *inherent causes coupled with the ingestion of drugs and drink* as the defence sought to establish. The jury had been directed by the trial judge to decide whether it was, on the one hand, the *drink and drugs* or, on the other, the *inherent causes* which were the main factors which caused him to act as he did. He was convicted of murder but appealed on the grounds that the jury had been misdirected, the proper question for them being whether the abnormality arising from the inherent causes substantially impaired his responsibility for his actions. His appeal was upheld, and his conviction for murder substituted by a conviction for Section 2 manslaughter. Giving judgment, Lord Lane, a former Lord Chief Justice, said that it was improper *in any circumstances* to invite the jury to decide the question of diminished responsibility on the basis of 'what was the substantial cause of the defendant's behaviour?' The jury were to be directed, first, to disregard what they thought the effect on the defendant of the alcohol-and-drug-induced mental abnormality was, since discussion of such abnormality was *not* within Section 2(1). They were then to go on to consider whether the combined effect of *other matters* which *did* fall within Section 2(1) amounted to such abnormality of mind as substantially impaired his mental responsibility within the meaning of substantial as set out in *R. v. Lloyd* (1967). This being so in this case, the jury, said Lord Lane, had been misdirected. In the case of *R. v. Lipman* (1970), the accused claimed successfully that he was under the influence of LSD (lysergic acid diethylamide) when he killed the girl he was sleeping with. Part of Lipman's defence consisted of the claim that as a result of his being in a drug-induced state he thought he was being attacked by snakes; the immediate cause of his unlucky companion's death was asphyxia caused by having part of a sheet stuffed into her mouth. However, in the later well-known case of *R. v. Majewski* (1977) the House of Lords held that, in the case of an impulsive act such as an assault, intoxication of itself would not constitute a defence. It was alleged that Robert Majewski had been a drug addict and that he also had a personality disorder. He had been drinking heavily on the day in question and had mixed alcohol with quantities of sodium membutal and dexedrine. Having ingested what must have amounted to a highly lethal 'cocktail', Majewski became involved in a fracas in a pub, in the course of which he assaulted the landlord and another customer. Having been removed from the premises, he returned, brandishing a piece of broken glass (Hall Williams 1980). The case of Majewski tends to support the view that the law sees the ingestion of alcohol and other drugs as aggravating rather than mitigating factors and that voluntary intoxication is no defence. However, if an accused could show that he or she was in a state of *involuntary* intoxication, he or she may have a defence where, for example, the accused had been deliberately drugged or had had intoxicants poured into a non-intoxicating beverage without his or her knowledge. This, as we shall see in Chapter 8 on sex offenders, may play an important part in allegations of rape on females. A question of capacity to give 'consent' then arises. A form of defence in crimes requiring evidence of specific intent will not be likely to succeed if an accused takes alcohol against medical advice after using prescribed drugs or, for example, if he or she fails to take insulin for a diabetic condition. Mackay draws attention to the problems with the present law and suggests it is time for reforms (Mackay 1995: 176–178).

Finally, Rix (1989) has suggested that we should make an interesting distinction between *intoxication* and *drunkenness*. Such a clinical distinction would have interesting and potentially useful legal implications. He proposes that:

> (1) the term 'alcohol intoxication' should refer to a state in which alcohol is in the body; (2) its diagnosis should be based on toxicological evidence for the presence of alcohol in body fluids or tissues; and (3) the term 'drunkenness' should be used to describe behaviour displayed by people who have consumed, believe that they have consumed or want others to believe they have consumed, alcohol.
>
> (Rix 1989: 100)

Summary and conclusion

This chapter has, inevitably, been somewhat discursive; in order to achieve brevity, I have had to take some short cuts. The law in relation to responsibility and the various ways in which it may be 'eroded' has followed a complex and ever-changing route. For example, developments in our understanding of mental processes have affected the way in which personal responsibility for behaviour has to be viewed nowadays, compared with two hundred and fifty years ago. In addition, public attitudes to those who practise the art and science of medicine, particularly psychiatry, affect the climate of opinion in which such practitioners and judges, lawyers and others play out their roles within the arena of the courts. The ways in which responsibility may be 'eroded' may be summarized as follows: total erosion may be afforded by a finding of not guilty by reason of insanity and of being under disability (unfitness to plead) leading to the special verdict(s). Partial erosion may be afforded by a finding of diminished responsibility (but only in homicide cases) and in infanticide. Finally, other pleas may be based upon states of mind caused by, for example, provocation, automatism and intoxication. In Chapter 3 I provide an account of the disposals available to the courts for those adjudged to be mentally disturbed in a variety of ways and the methods through which these disposals are implemented. The options for disposal are summarized in Table 2.1. I must re-emphasize the need to view the information presented in this book *as a*

Table 2.1 Summary of options for disposal

A   *Special verdicts*
    (a)   Not guilty by reason of insanity (NGRI)
        ('M'Naghten madness')
    (b)   Under disability (formerly known as unfitness to plead)
B   *Diminished responsibility*[a]
    Homicide Act 1957, Sections 2, 3 and 4
C   *Plea in mitigation of penalty*[b]

Notes: (a) Diminished responsibility is available only as a defence to a charge of murder, whereas special verdicts can be applied in respect of all other offences. (b) Following a guilty plea or conviction, a defendant's mental state can be proffered in mitigation of penalty in respect of more minor offences or where the criteria for pleas under A and B above would not be satisfied. Such pleas are most likely to be made at the lower court level (for example, in the magistrates' courts).

whole. The material has been divided in somewhat arbitrary fashion in order to achieve a hoped-for clarity of presentation.[9]

Notes

1 In England and Wales, 'extreme youth' is exemplified by setting the age of criminal responsibility at 10 years and over. In Scotland, currently set at 8 years, it is proposed to raise this to 12. The government in England and Wales is not inclined to follow suit (see Chapter 7 on homicide).
2 Considerable controversy has raged over the correct spelling of McNaughten's name. For example, the variants include MacNaughton, M'Naghten, M'Naughton. His own signature reproduced in Diamond (1977: 89) does little to resolve the matter. I have adopted M'Naghten, the spelling used by Lord Mackay (2008: 9).
3 It is, of course, also open to the Crown Prosecution Service not to bring a prosecution on 'public interest' grounds.
4 The choice of the words 'mental health legislation' is deliberate since, at the time of writing, the Mental Health Act 2007 had not been implemented. This took place in October 2008.
5 Bilton (2003) makes a number of important points in connection with Peter Sutcliffe's ability to avoid detection for nearly five years. First, the antiquated system of data collection then in use. The data were stored on hundreds of index cards which defied any capacity to link them. Second, the investigating officers were misled by the infamous tape-recorded messages. (The culprit admitted his hoax activities many years later and was sentenced to a substantial term of imprisonment for attempting to pervert the course of justice.) Third, Sutcliffe had been arrested, questioned and then released on several occasions and had been found to be in possession of housebreaking implements, notably a hammer similar to that used to kill some of his victims. Finally, he was apprehended, almost by chance, by police officers who became suspicious when they saw Sutcliffe in a car with a prostitute. One of the officers went back to where Sutcliffe was being questioned and found, hidden under some leaves, a hammer and a knife which fitted the description of a set of knives in Sutcliffe's kitchen. The details of his arrest for questioning and subsequent events are set out in detail in Bilton (2003: Chapter 17).
6 See, for example. *Daily Telegraph*, 6.5.81; 23.5.81; *Guardian*, 7.5.81; 8.5.81; 9.5.81; 12.5.81; 13.5.81; 14.5.81; 15.5.81; 16.5.81; 19.5.81; 20.5.81; 21.5.81; 22.5.81; *Observer*, 25.5.81; *Sunday Telegraph*, 24.5.81.

7 For accounts by two of the forensic psychiatrists involved in the trial, see Kay (1993) and MacCulloch (1993).
8 Although M.T. obtained a finding of manslaughter, he did not receive a hospital disposal. The psychiatrists were of the opinion that his personality disorder would not be responsive to medical treatment. His case and the cases of Sutcliffe and Nilsen illustrate the serendipitous outcomes in such cases.
9 Since this chapter was written the implementation of the Coroners and Justice Act, 2009 (Section 52) replaces the wording of Section 2 of the 1957 Homicide Act and deals with some of the ambiguities of that Section. Sections 54 and 55 clarify the defence of provocation (loss of control) and Section 57 makes minor amendments to the law of infanticide.

Acts

Coroners and Justice Act 2009
Criminal Procedure (Insanity and Unfitness to Plead) Act 1991
Domestic Violence, Crime and Victims Act 2004
Homicide Act 1957
Infanticide Act 1922
Infanticide Act 1938
Mental Health Act 1969
Mental Health Act 1983
Mental Health Act 2007
Murder (Abolition of Death Penalty) Act 1965
Road Traffic Act 1930

Cases

HM Advocate v. Dingwall [1867] 5 Irv. 466.
Bratty v. Attorney General for Northern Ireland [1963] AC 386.
Hill v. Baxter [1958] 1 QB 277.
Kay v. Butterworth [1945] 173 LT 191.
R. v. Ahluwalia [1992] *Independent Law Report*, 4 August: 7.
R. v. Burgess [1991] *Independent Law Report*, 27 March: 9.
R. v. Burns [1973] 58 Cr.App.R. 364.
R. v. Byrne [1960] 2 QB 396–455.
R. v. Drew [2003] UKHL 25, *Independent Law Report*, 15 May: 18.
R. v. Gittens [1984] *Law Society Gazette*, 5 September.
R. v. Lipman [1970] 1 QB 152.
R. v. Lloyd [1967] 1 QB 175–181.
R. v. Majewski [1977] AC 443.
R. v. Matheson [1958] 42 Cr.App.R. 154 1 WLR 474.
R. v. Stephenson [1979] 3 WLR 143.
R. v. Sutcliffe (*The Times* and *Guardian*, May 1981).
R. v. Turner [1975] 2 WLR 56.

R. v. Vernege [1982] *Crim. Law Rev.* December, 598–600.
Sweet v. Parsley [1969] 1 All ER 347.

References

Bartholomew, A.A. (1983) *R. v. Sutcliffe*, 'Letter', *Medicine, Science and the Law* 23: 222–223.

Bettelheim, B. (1983) *Freud and Man's Soul*, London: Chatto & Windus.

Bilton, M. (2003) *Wicked Beyond Belief: The Hunt for the Yorkshire Ripper*, London: HarperCollins.

Blom-Cooper, L., QC and Morris, T. (2004) *With Malice Aforethought: A Study of the Crime and Punishment for Homicide*, Oxford: Hart.

Bluglass, R. (1990) 'Infanticide and Filicide', in R. Bluglass and P. Bowden (eds) *Principles and Practice of Forensic Psychiatry*, London: Churchill Livingstone.

Brewster, W., Willox, E.G. and Haut, F. (2008) 'Assessing Fitness to Plead in Scotland's Learning Disabled', *Journal of Forensic Psychiatry and Psychology* 19: 597–602.

Buchanan, A. (2000) *Psychiatric Aspects of Justification, Excuse and Mitigation: The Jurisprudence of Mental Abnormality in Anglo-American Criminal Law*, London: Jessica Kingsley.

Burn, G. (1984) *Somebody's Husband, Somebody's Son: The Story of Peter Sutcliffe*, London: Heinemann.

Clarke, M.J. (1975) 'The Impact of Social Science on Conceptions of Responsibility', *British Journal of Law and Society* 2: 32–44.

Collins, P. and White, T. (2003) 'Depression, Homicide and Diminished Responsibility: New Scottish Directions', *Medicine, Science and the Law* 43: 195–202.

Crane, A. (1990) *The Kirkland Papers: 1753–1869. The Ferrers Murder and the Lives and Times of a Medical Family in Ashby-de-la-Zouch*, Ashby-de-la-Zouch: Crane Press.

Criminal Law Revision Committee (1980) *Offences Against the Person*, Cmnd 7844, London: HMSO.

Dell, S. (1984) *Murder into Manslaughter: The Diminished Responsibility Defence in Practice*, Maudsley Monograph no. 27, Oxford: Oxford University Press.

De Souza, D.S.M. (2007) 'The Concept of Unfitness to Plead', *British Journal of Forensic Practice* 9: 7–14.

Diamond, B.L. (1977) 'On the Spelling of Daniel M'Naghten's Name', in D.J. West and A. Walk (eds) *Daniel McNaughton: His Trial and the Aftermath*, London: Gaskell.

Eigen, P.J. (1983) 'Historical Developments in Psychiatric Forensic Evidence: The British Experience', *International Journal of Law and Psychiatry* 6: 423–429.

Fenwick, P. (1990) *Automatism, Medicine and the Law*, Psychological Medicine Monograph, Supplement 17, Cambridge: Cambridge University Press.

Gowers, E. (chair) (1953) *Report of the Royal Commission on Capital Punishment 1949–1953* (Gowers Report), Cmd 8932, London: HMSO.

Gray, N.S., O'Connor, C., Williams, T., Short, J. and MacCulloch, M. (2000) 'Fitness to Plead: Implications from Case-law Arising from the Criminal Justice and Public Order Act 1994', *Journal of Forensic Psychiatry* 12: 52–62.

Griew, E. (1984) 'Let's Implement Butler on Mental Disorder and Crime', in R. Rideout and B. Jowell (eds) *Current Legal Problems*, London: Sweet & Maxwell for University College London.

Grubin, D. (1996) *Fitness to Plead in England and Wales*, Maudsley Monograph no. 38, Hove: Psychology Press.

Hall, J. (1998) 'Recent Legal Issues in the Defence of Provocation', *Medicine, Science and the Law* 38: 206–210.

Hall Williams, J.E. (1980) 'Legal Views of Psychiatric Evidence', *Medicine, Science and the Law* 20: 276–282.

Hamilton, J. (1981) 'Diminished Responsibility', *British Journal of Psychiatry* 138: 434–436.

Hart, H.L.A. (1968) *Punishment and Responsibility: Essays in the Philosophy of Law*, Oxford: Clarendon Press.

Home Office and Department of Health and Social Security (1975) *Report of the Committee on Mentally Abnormal Offenders* (Butler Report), Cmnd 6244, London: HMSO.

Home Office and Scottish Home Department (1957) *Report of the Committee on Homosexual Offences and Prostitution* (Wolfenden Report), Cmnd 247, London: HMSO.

Jacobs, F.G. (1971) *Criminal Responsibility*, London: Weidenfeld & Nicolson.

Jones, B. (1992) *Voices from an Evil God*, London: Blake.

Kahn, J. (1971) 'Uses and Abuses of Child Psychiatry: Problems of Diagnosis and Treatment of Psychiatric Disorder', *British Journal of Medical Psychology* 44: 291–302.

Kay, T. (1993) 'Review of Jones, B. (1992) *Voices from an Evil God*. London: Blake', *Journal of Forensic Psychiatry* 4: 380–383.

Kenny, A. (1984) 'The Psychiatric Expert in Court', *Psychological Medicine* 14: 291–302.

Kerrigan, K. (2002) 'Psychiatric Evidence and Mandatory Disposal: Article 5 Compliance', *Journal of Mental Health Law* 7: 130–138.

Lambie, I. (2001) 'Mothers Who Kill: The Crime of Infanticide', *International Journal of Law and Psychiatry* 24: 70–80.

Law Commission (2006) *Murder, Manslaughter and Infanticide*, Law Commission no. 304, HC 30, London: TSO.

MacCulloch, M. (1993) 'Letter: The Trial of Peter Sutcliffe', *Journal of Forensic Psychiatry* 4: 583–589.

Mackay, J.P. (Lord) (2008) 'The Lund Lecture: What Makes a Legal System Effective?', *Medicine, Science and the Law* 48: 2–14.

Mackay, R. (1995) *Mental Condition Defences in the Criminal Law*, Oxford: Clarendon Press.

Mackay, R.D., Mitchell, B. and Howe, L. (2006) 'Yet More Facts about the Insanity Defence', *Criminal Law Review* 399–411.

—— (2007) 'A Continued Upturn in Unfitness to Plead – More Disability in Relation to the Trial under the 1991 Act', *Criminal Law Review* 530–544.

Masters, B. (1985) *Killing for Company*, London: Jonathan Cape.

—— (1993) *The Shrine of Jeffrey Dahmer*, London: Hodder & Stoughton.

Mitchell, B. (1997a) 'Diminished Responsibility Manslaughter', *Journal of Forensic Psychiatry* 8: 101–117.

—— (1997b) 'Putting Diminished Responsibility into Practice: A Forensic Psychiatric Perspective', *Journal of Forensic Psychiatry* 8: 620–634.

Patrick, H. (2003) 'Scottish Parliament Acts on Mental Health Law Reform', *Journal of Mental Health Law* 9: 71–76.

Reznek, L. (1997) *Evil or Ill: Justifying the Insanity Defence*, London: Routledge.

Rix, K.J.B. (1989) '"Alcohol Intoxication" or "Drunkenness": Is There a Difference?', *Medicine, Science and the Law* 29: 100–106.

—— (2001) '"Battered Woman Syndrome" and the Defence of Provocation! Two Women with Something More in Common', *Journal of Forensic Psychiatry* 12: 131–149.

Rogers, T.P., Blackwood, N.J., Farnham, F., Pickup, G.J. and Watts, M.J. (2008) 'Fitness to Plead and Competence to Stand Trial: A Systematic Review of the Constructs and their Application', *Journal of Forensic Psychiatry and Psychology* 19: 579–596.

—— (2009) 'Reforming Fitness to Plead: A Quantitative Study', *Journal of Forensic Psychiatry and Psychology* 20: 815–834.

Samuels, A. (1975) 'Mental Illness and Criminal Liability', *Medicine, Science and the Law* 15: 198–204.

Smith, R. (1991) 'Legal Frameworks for Psychiatry', in G.E. Berrios and H. Freemen (eds) *150 Years of British Psychiatry, 1841–1991*, London: Gaskell.

Spencer, S. (1984) 'Homicide, Mental Abnormality and Offence', in M. Craft and A. Craft (eds) *Mentally Abnormal Offenders*, London: Baillière Tindall.

Szasz, T. (1987) *Insanity: The Idea and its Consequences*, New York: Wiley.

—— (1993) 'Curing, Coercing, and Claims-making: A Reply to Critics', *British Journal of Psychiatry* 162: 797–800.

Walker, N. (1968) *Crime and Insanity in England*, Volume 1, Edinburgh: Edinburgh University Press.

Ward, T. (2002) 'A Terrible Responsibility: Murder and the Insanity Defence in England, 1908–1939', *International Journal of Law and Psychiatry* 25: 361–377.

Yeo, S. (2002) 'Classifying Automatism', *International Journal of Law and Psychiatry* 25: 445–458.

Further reading

The following three books are recommended:

Buchanan, A. (2000) *Psychiatric Aspects of Justification, Excuse and Mitigation: The Jurisprudence of Mental Abnormality in Anglo-American Criminal Law*, London: Jessica Kingsley.

Mackay, R. (1995) *Mental Condition Defences in the Criminal Law*, Oxford: Clarendon Press.

Reznek, L. (1997) *Evil or Ill: Justifying the Insanity Defence*, London: Routledge.

In addition, for an excellent account of the new mental health legislation see:

Fennell, P. (2007) *Mental Health: The New Law*. Bristol: Jordan.

The *Criminal Law Review* and the *Journal of Mental Health Law* will also be found very helpful.

Chapter 3

By divers routes

At sundry times and in divers manners.

(A Letter to the Hebrews, 1: 1)

Brief reference has been made in previous chapters to some of the means of dealing with offenders adjudged to be mentally disordered. I emphasize the word *brief* because the manner in which they can be dealt with is a complex one, and it is not just a question of 'prison or hospital'. The extent to which offenders and offender-patients can fail to be dealt with through either the forensic mental health or the criminal justice systems is, to some extent, serendipitous. The four cases cited in Chapter 2 attest to this. This is a useful point at which to suggest the form of such possible serendipitous outcomes. Consider the following scenarios. (a) A mentally disordered offender may not be proceeded against at all, a decision having been reached by the Crown Prosecution Service (CPS) that such prosecution would not be in the 'public interest'. (b) He or she may be found not guilty by reason of insanity (NGRI) or under disability in relation to the trial. Both findings resulting in the 'special verdict'. (c) He or she may be afforded diversion from the criminal justice system through many of the diversion schemes that exist, either before, during or after court appearance and sentence. (d) Legal representatives may advise against offering any mental health defence. Even a clear-cut notion of prison versus hospital is misleading. In England and Wales there are now two 'psychiatric' prisons and three hospitals affording maximum security; for some of the residents this may well feel like a prison environment.

In the following pages I attempt to outline some of these facilities and their governance in enough detail to provide a starting point for those readers who wish to explore these matters further. What follows is divided into three sections. The first is devoted to a brief historical background against which current management practices may be viewed. The second consists of an account of the methods by which the mentally disordered may be diverted from the criminal justice system. The third outlines the main mental health care and penal disposals available to the courts, including brief descriptions of the facilities available. For a summary of current methods of disposal, see Figure 3.1 (p. 78).

Historical context and population

Historical context

The history of the treatment of mentally disturbed individuals who offend is closely bound up with the history of more general provision for the care of mentally disordered people. Such care and control appear to show a cyclical pattern – a kind of 'flavour of the month' quality, often demonstrated more by passionate (and often irrational) conviction than by objective appraisal of need. Those of cynical disposition might well consider that such patterns have much in common with our tendency to 'reinvent the wheel'. The phenomenon has been ably described in contributions by Allderidge (1979, 1985) and by Parker (1980, 1985). The latter has suggested that 'From early times the mentally disordered in England seem to have been afforded some protection, in principle at least, from the customary consequences of wrongdoing' (Parker 1980: 461). In a subsequent contribution she stated:

> The practice of confining the insane stretches back more than 600 years in England. The type of detained patient has varied, always including those considered to be dangerous . . . The forms of security employed have changed little over the period, perimeter security, internal locks and bars and individual restraint by both physical and chemical means have been in continuous use to a great or lesser degree in various guises up to the present day.
>
> (Parker 1985: 15)

I would add that these days physical and chemical restraints are more likely to be measures of last resort and, if used, tightly controlled.

A similar haphazard and sometimes irrational approach can be seen in the deployment of 'community care' services bedevilled as they have been (and to a great extent still are) by underfunding and lack of coordination (see, for example, Jewesbury and McCulloch 2002; Laurance 2003; Judge et al. 2004). History teaches us that to be both 'mad' and 'bad' places those so designated at the bottom of the social priority pecking order; these are truly 'the people nobody owns' (Prins 1993). There is another unfortunate consequence of this attitude – namely, that those who work with such 'ownerless' persons may themselves sometimes feel alienated and contaminated and, as such, may be exposed to as much adverse public opinion and action as are their patients or clients. Space precludes a detailed history of the relevant legislation, but a few observations will hopefully provide a context for what is to follow. From as early as the eighteenth century, some provision existed for those who were considered to be mad and dangerous as I showed in Chapter 2. This had to be extended eventually for those found unfit to plead or not guilty by reason of insanity. However, it was not until the nineteenth century that special measures were introduced for the *public* as well as the *private* care and treatment of mentally disordered individuals. Such provisions were almost entirely custodial in nature and services for 'criminal lunatics', as they were then called, developed separately and in piecemeal fashion as, for example, in cases such as Hadfield's described in Chapter 2. In the early twentieth century the trend to provide more specific legislation continued; for example, the Mental Deficiency Act 1913 enabled courts to deal more effectively with 'mentally defective' people who committed crimes, by removing them from the penal system and placing them in hospital care. Such provision, which at the time may have seemed humane, led in some circumstances to unfortunate consequences; for example, it linked promiscuity with mental deficiency. This led to numbers of women who had given birth to illegitimate children being labelled as 'moral defectives' and subjected them to long-term incarceration in a secure hospital. Minor refinements were made to the 1913 Act in the 1920s and, as outlined in Chapter 1, the Criminal Justice Act 1948 empowered courts, for the first time, to formalize the practice of placing offenders on probation with a requirement for psychiatric inpatient or outpatient treatment. The Homicide Act 1957 (see Chapter 2) and the Mental Health Acts 1959 and 1983 made a wider range of options available for the management of mentally disturbed offenders, and these have been further developed in the 2007 Act (see Prins 2008). Recent criminal justice legislation tends to place issues of public protection to the forefront, with consequential implications for human rights issues. A succinct but very fully referenced account of the history of provisions for mentally disordered offenders and, in particular, community provision may be found in Laing (1999: Chapter 2) (see also Prins 1999: Chapter 2). I conclude these brief contextual remarks by a short summary of certain trends since the late 1960s that have been influential in the treatment (and, sadly, sometimes non-treatment) of mentally disturbed individuals in general and mentally disturbed offenders in particular.

1   The rundown and closure of the older mental hospitals, with re-provision by smaller acute units, resulted in much reduced overall bed capacity. With the wisdom of hindsight, one can see that such policies were perhaps premature and based upon predictions about the size of future psychiatric populations and needs that were not altogether to be fulfilled. The move for rundown and closure was also fuelled by a degree of over-optimism concerning the long-term benefits of new forms of drug treatment.

2   A lack of emotional, professional and financial investment in community provision for a seriously disadvantaged and often unattractive group of people, the 'hard to like' or 'not nice, degenerate' patients so well described by Scott (1975). This reluctance to work with such individuals is exemplified with particular strength in the case of the severely antisocial personality disordered (see Chapter 5).

3   Challenges were being made to some powerfully held assumptions about the nature and causes of mental disorders. For discussion of these earlier views, see Laing and Esterson (1970) and Szasz (1974). An excellent more recent perspective may be found in Leff (2001). (See also Chapter 4 of this volume.)

4   Anxiety was being expressed about the rights of mentally ill individuals and an increasing concentration on civil rights issues; this concern received recent prominence because of the debates concerning the new mental health legislation. Such concern has many laudable aspects, but perhaps brings in its wake certain iatrogenic (literally – physician caused) consequences, not the least of these being a tendency towards the practice of 'defensive' psychiatry. This is likely to result in a consequential denial of patients' right to treatment. This trend is in part responsible for the worrying number of mentally disordered individuals in penal establishments (see later).

5   Growing concern about the degree to which black and other ethnic minority groups were being discriminated against and seriously over-represented in penal and psychiatric institutions; concern has also been expressed about their untimely deaths in such establishments and in the community (see Prins et al. 1993; Jasper 1998; Liebling 1998; Home Office 1999; Dixon and Ray 2007; Fitzgibbon 2007; McGhee 2007). Sir William Macpherson and his advisers bravely pinpointed the essence of racism, emphasizing its often 'hidden' nature – as follows:

> The collective failure of an organization to provide an appropriate professional service to people because of their colour, culture or ethnic origin. It can be seen or detected in processes, attitudes and behaviour which amount to discrimination through *unwitting* prejudice, ignorance, thoughtlessness and racist stereotyping which disadvantage minority ethnic people.
>
> (Home Office 1999: 28, 6.34, emphasis added)

See also Fitzgibbon (2007) and Ali et al. (2007).

6   There has been what perhaps can best be described as a reduction in the primacy of the purely medical discipline in the management of mentally disturbed individuals. This has been evidenced by the medical profession's own developing acknowledgment of the importance of a team approach to such management. It has now been given more formal

recognition in the Mental Health Act 2007. The Responsible Medical Officer (RMO) will not in future necessarily have primary and sole responsibility for the patient's care. The primacy of social workers as Approved Social Workers (ASWs) has also been replaced by the intro-duction of a range of professionals to act as what are now described as Approved Mental Health Professionals (AMHPs). These can now include nurses, occupational therapists and chartered psychologists 'as long as they have the right skills and training'. The form and content of training are not spelled out in the Act or the Explanatory Notes to it, but will be left to the relevant professional bodies. Presumably such training will build upon the useful programmes run for the former ASWs by local authorities. This widening of professional interventive possibilities is to be welcomed, but it would be wise to recognize that 'boundary disputes' may still occur and, certainly in the early days of implementation, will need sensitive handling.

The problems of multidisciplinary working will be discussed in the chapter on risk. I now comment upon the numbers of mentally disturbed offenders in penal establishments.

Mentally disturbed offenders in the prison population

In 1998 a report published by the Office for National Statistics indicated that there were currently a disturbing number of persons in prison suffering from mental illness (Singleton et al. 1998). This of course was not an altogether new development, for as long ago as 1991 the Home Office and Department of Health stated that in the UK:

> Although the actual number of prisoners requiring psychiatric services is not known, research has shown that the prison population has a high psychiatric morbidity . . . It is estimated that 2–3 percent of *sentenced* prisoners at any one time are likely to be suffering from a psychotic illness, and it is likely that the proportion is even higher in the remand population. Histories of alcohol and drug misuse are very common, as is neurotic illness.
>
> (Home Office and Department of Health 1991: Annex C, emphasis in the original)

In general, prisoners with personality disorders were more likely than other prisoners to be young, unmarried, from a white ethnic group and charged with acquisitive offences. There was a high prevalence of co-occurring mental disorders – a large proportion of prisoners having several mental disorders (co-morbidity) (Singleton et al. 1998: 22–23). Although the above extract provides an *overall* picture, some more detailed later studies of penal populations may be helpful. It would appear that about one-third of the prison population requires some kind of psychiatric intervention, and that in *remand* populations this number is likely to be higher. Numerous studies have been made of both remand and sentenced prisoners. For example, Gunn et al. (1991) examined a series of sentenced prisoners in England and Wales. They contended, by extrapolation from their sample, that 'The sentenced population included over 700 men with psychosis and [that] around 1,100 would warrant transfer to hospital for psychiatric treatment' (Gunn et al. 1991: 338; see also Gunn 2000). Studies of *remand* prisoners tend to give even higher rates of psychiatric morbidity. More worrying is the evidence that suggests that psychiatric morbidity may be missed due to poor prison screening devices. Gavin et al. (2003) suggest that some 75 per cent of major mental illnesses in men and 66 per cent in women may be missed in this way. These authors reviewed screening processes in a local North of England prison taking male sentenced and remand prisoners. They concluded that:

> The findings in terms of numbers of new receptions screening positive for mental illness, and those in fact suffering from serious mental illnesses, were both in the range predicted from our earlier research, and in line with prevalence rates described in large scale remand prison surveys ([see for example] Singleton et al. 1998).
>
> (Gavin et al. 2003: 251)

Based on an admittedly small sample (616 new receptions over a 15-week period) the authors suggested that 'it does not appear that large demands will be placed upon psychiatric resources if the proposed new reception health screening processes were in place, although a reorganization of the way in which services are delivered will almost certainly be required' (Gavin et al. 2003: 253; see also Duffy et al. 2003). This question of reorganization is of vital importance. As things stand, prisoners still cannot be afforded the application of compulsory powers for treatment under current mental health legislation because prison hospitals are not deemed to be hospitals within the terms of the Health Acts 1983 and 2007, the only exceptions being the need for urgent treatment without consent under the common law. There are those who considered that designating prison health-care facilities as hospitals within the meaning of the Act would solve a number of problems, particularly in relation to suicidal behaviour (see, for example, Home Office 1990a, 1991, 1999; also Towl et al. 2000). This may seem an attractive solution, but perhaps some caution should be espoused. If prison hospitals were to be designated as hospitals within the meaning of the Mental Health Acts it *might* mean that, unless rigorous safeguards were introduced, they could become the 'dumping grounds' of the 'not nice' patients the National Health Service (NHS) seems reluctant to take. The most satisfactory answer then seemed to reside in the 'policy shift towards formal partnership between the NHS and the Prison Service for the provision of health care as a whole'. Such a partnership has taken place (see Department of Health 2002d). Additionally, the ongoing provision of 'in-reach teams' in prisons has helped to alleviate some of the problems caused by inappropriate detention.

Some final words of caution are necessary in concluding this section. This concerns the tendency to accept too readily that those mentally disturbed offenders detained in prison are there because if they were not, they would be in hospital. For many years the view put forward by the distinguished geneticist Sir Lionel Penrose (1939) that there was an inverse relationship between prison and mental hospital populations had held considerable sway. In 1939 he published his well-known study which became known in criminological circles as 'Penrose's law', namely that as the prison population rose mental hospital populations declined and vice versa. Bowden (1993), in a critical study of this so-called 'law', stated that:

> The suggestion appears to have been that there was a relatively stable mass of individuals who were in one form of environment, asylums, rather than another, prison. The two were used interchangeably. The benefit of the asylum was its effect on reducing crime.
>
> (Bowden 1993: 81)

Careful examination of remand and sentenced penal populations reveals that such a state of affairs is not as clear cut as Penrose (1939) and some later writers had suggested. Further support for Bowden's (1993) criticisms comes from Fowles (1993), who made a meticulous study of prison and mental hospital populations over a twenty-five-year period. He suggested that:

> The mental hospitals have been run down but the full-blooded closure programme is still in its relatively early stages and its effects will not be felt for some time to come. Those remaining in the mental hospitals are unlikely to be of the age and sex normally associated with crime. [Moreover,] it is not possible to obtain comparable age distributions for prison populations and hospital residents.
>
> (Fowles 1993: 71)

Fowles goes on to suggest another complicating factor, namely:

> The former patients who are discharged from long-stay mental hospitals may be defined officially as living in the community but that may only mean that they are in the wards of a privately owned nursing home. The 'community' means any hospital/home not owned by the NHS.
>
> (Fowles 1993: 71)

Similar criticisms of hypotheses that may have been all too readily accepted in the past indicate that the relationship between criminality and mental disturbance is much more complicated than would appear at first sight; this is examined in Chapter 4. The somewhat simplistic thinking of the kind briefly alluded to above has very important implications for the provision of both prison and health care services and the best use of resources for their maintenance and governance.

Diversion: keeping the mentally disturbed individual out of the criminal justice and penal systems

Even if we adopt a somewhat cautious approach to the estimates of the numbers of mentally disturbed persons held in penal establishments at various stages of their careers, and accept the caveats entered by Fowles (1993), Bowden (1993) and others, we are still compelled to acknowledge that a sizeable proportion of them should not be there. Moreover, we are also forced to conclude that not only should they not be *in prison*, but also perhaps they *should not have entered the criminal justice system in the first place*. In Chapter 2, I demonstrated how one form of diversion from the criminal justice system operates through a finding of 'unfitness to plead' (being under disability). As long ago as 1975, the Butler Committee recommended that mentally disturbed offenders might be dealt with other than through the courts:

> Where any apparent offender is clearly in need of psychiatric treatment and there is no risk to members of the public the question should always be asked whether any useful purpose would be served by prosecution . . . these remarks apply in cases of homicide or attempted homicide or grave bodily harm as in less serious cases.
>
> (Home Office and DHSS 1975: 266)

Some fifteen years later the Home Office, in its now well-known Circular 66/90 (Home Office 1990b), reiterated this view as follows:

> It is government policy that, wherever possible, mentally disordered persons should receive care and treatment from the health and social services. Where there is sufficient evidence, in accordance with the principles of the *Code for Crown Prosecutors*, to show that a mentally disordered person has committed an offence, careful consideration should be given to whether prosecution is required by the public interest.
>
> (Home Office 1990b: Paragraph 2)

The circular went on to provide very detailed advice to all those agencies likely to be involved in dealing with mentally disturbed offenders (for example, the police, crown prosecution service, probation, social services, courts, health authorities, the then titled prison medical service). The stress on inter-agency cooperation has continued to be a central theme in mental health policy, as illustrated in various government documents. Concern about the most appropriate action to be taken in respect of mentally disturbed offenders is, of course, not new. Two examples from history will suffice to make my point.

Case illustration 3.1

This concerns a young man named Hwaetred, as recounted by St Guthlac (AD 674–714), who lived in so-called Dark Ages rural England.

> A young man named Hwaetred became afflicted with an evil spirit. So terrible was [his] madness that he tore his own limbs and attacked others with his teeth. When men tried to restrain him, he snatched up a double-bladed axe and killed three men. After four years of madness and with emaciated body, he was taken by his parents to several sacred shrines, but he received no help. One day, when his parents were wishing more for his death than his life, they heard of a hermit (Guthlac) on the Isle of Crowland. They took their possessed son, with limbs bound, to the hermit.
>
> (Felix, *Life of St. Guthlac*, quoted in Roth and Kroll 1986: 100)

The modern recounters of this ancient story make some interesting and very relevant comments. First, they indicate that the young man's condition was seen as an illness; second, his deviance was *not* minor, for he killed three men. Third, there is no talk of revenge or attribution of criminality or of guilt; it would have been quite simple to have hunted him down and killed him, but instead attempts were made to restrain and control him within his own community. Fourth, his parents, desperate as many of the parents of the seriously mentally ill are today, seek yet further remedy in the guise of a 'wise man' – a latter day psychiatrist perhaps? – in the hope that a cure might be effected. One would not wish to make too much of this vignette, but it does encapsulate some of the issues raised in Roth and Kroll's (1986) account and, one wonders, how a multidisciplinary case-conference today would answer the question: 'What would you have done with this young man?'

Case illustration 3.2

Some twelve hundred years later, an incident showing the other side of the coin is recorded in *The Lancet* (14 April 1883: 648–649).

Malice or madness?
What is justly described as a 'shocking scene in a prison' has just occurred in Dartmoor. An exceptionally 'bad' young man, who was sentenced to seven

years penal servitude in August, 1879, he having been no less than nine times previously convicted and flogged, was being examined in prison on Tuesday last on a charge of a violent assault on a warder, whom it seems, he nearly killed with a spade when his violence was such that with great difficulty several warders put him in irons. The story is sickening in its brutality. What, however, must most powerfully strike the medical reader is that the narrative very closely resembles one of the old stories of a struggle with a madman in the days before the humane system of non-restraint was introduced into the asylums in this country. The question we are actuated to ask – and it is one which ought to be pressed strongly on the consideration of the Home Office – is whether this young man is not mad? He was convicted nine times before he reached the age of eighteen. Moreover, his rage is manifestly that of mania, rather than a sane being . . . Looking at the treatment – wholly unworthy of a civilized country – which Thomas Jones is undergoing in a dark cell at Dartmoor, it would be well if the enquiry necessary to reassure the public mind that a madmen is not being punished when he ought to be placed under treatment could be instituted at once . . . it cannot be permitted that prison authorities should reproduce the horrors of the Spanish inquisition in one of Queen Victoria's gaols, and withal mistake a lunatic for a felon.

(quoted by Rollin 1993: 475)

Diversion as an aspect of discretion

The practice of diversion involves the exercise of discretion at various stages of the criminal justice process; it has a long, if somewhat obscure, history. Hetherington (1989) traces its origins to the reign of Henry VIII. However, it was not until the latter part of the nineteenth century that the office of Director of Public Prosecutions was introduced. Currently, the decision to prosecute rests with the Crown Prosecution Service, which is guided by a Code for Crown Prosecutors within which the prosecutor has to have regard for the need for prosecution in 'the public interest'. A number of factors govern this latter consideration, such as likely penalty, staleness (that is, the offence was committed so long ago that its prosecution would be of questionable merit), youth, old age and infirmity, complainant's attitude, and *mental illness or stress*. On this last aspect the Code states:

Whenever the crown prosecutor is provided with a medical report to the effect that an accused or a person under investigation is suffering from some form of psychiatric illness . . . and the strain of criminal proceedings may lead to a considerable worsening of his condition, such a report should receive anxious consideration. This is a difficult field because, in some instances, the accused may have become mentally disturbed or depressed by the mere fact that his misconduct has been discovered and the crown prosecutor may be dubious about a prognosis that criminal proceedings will adversely affect his condition to a significant extent. Where, however, the crown prosecutor is satisfied that the probable effect upon the defendant's mental health outweighs the interests of justice in that particular case, he should not hesitate to discontinue proceedings. An independent medical examination may be sought, but should generally be reserved for cases of such gravity as plainly require prosecution but for clear evidence that such a course would be likely to result in a permanent worsening of the accused's condition.

(Crown Prosecution Service n.d.: 4)

A number of questions arise from this statement. First, what variations are there in practice in making decisions whether not to prosecute, or to discontinue prosecution once it is underway within the terms of the general power to withdraw or to offer no evidence through Section 23 of the Prosecution of Offences Act 1985? Grounds (1991) indicated that 'There is a large gap in research knowledge in this area. Little is known about what happens to mentally disordered offenders *who do not enter criminal proceedings* and these gaps need to be filled if a complete picture is to be obtained' (emphasis added). He continued: 'Such research might also indicate whether more mentally disordered offenders could, or should, be diverted away from criminal proceedings' (Grounds 1991: 40). Since the time Grounds (1991) called for such research, some headway has been made. For example, Rowlands et al. (1996) indicated in a follow-up study that a number of individuals subjected to the diversionary process and, in particular, those with substance abuse problems were lost to the psychiatric services; on a follow-up after one year, 17 per cent had reoffended. They called for further long-term research. Shaw et al. (2001) reported that on a two-year follow-up period, one-third of those diverted to inpatient services had lost contact at twelve months; for those diverted to outpatient and community services, about one-third had also lost contact. They recommend better 'out-reach' assertive services (see also Green et al. 2005; Dyer 2006; Orr et al. 2007).

Geelan et al. (2001) report more positive results. They suggest that 'if *appropriately* assessed in court, and *appropriate* hospital placements are arranged, successful outcome can be achieved for the majority of people diverted from custody to hospital in terms of improved mental states and a planned discharge' (Geelan et al. 2001: 127, emphasis added). Examination of this and other studies (for example James and Hamilton 1991; Joseph 1992; Joseph and Potter 1993) would appear to indicate that success is heavily dependent upon detailed professional assessment and good communication within the system, that is, between the various professionals involved, magistrates, police, psychiatric, social and probation services (see also Exworthy and Parrott 1993, 1997). Most studies have concentrated on male offenders and reports on diversion for females are somewhat sparse. However, Parsons et al. (2001) carried out a major survey of the prevalence of mental disorder in female remand prisons and found, unsurprisingly, high rates of psychiatric morbidity, and that existing screening on reception (in prison) did not identify the majority of cases of mental disorder. In addition, the plight of women sentenced to imprisonment, who are then perforce separated from their children, has been highlighted by the Children's Commissioner for England, Sir Al Aynsley-Green (as reported by Sarah Cassidy, *The Independent*, 30 January 2008).

A formal diversionary measure was originally contained in Section 136 of the Mental Health Act 1959 and re-enacted with the same section number in the Mental Health Acts 1983 and 2007. This provides a police officer with a power to remove to a place of safety a person found in a place to which the public have access, who appears to be suffering from mental disorder within the meaning of the Act and appears to be in immediate need of care, protection or control. (It should be noted that the Act specifies 'to which the public have access'. The provision is frequently misquoted, describing it as 'a public place'; the correct interpretation of the definition allows a much wider interpretation of the location.) The person may be detained for a maximum of 72 hours for the purposes of being examined by authorized mental health professionals. Such examination may or may not lead to admission to hospital, either informally, or under the compulsory powers of the Act.[1] The section has merits, but it also has some accompanying disadvantages. Often, a police station is used as a place of safety and police stations are clearly not the best places for detaining mentally distressed individuals. Although the police are not always certain of their powers, research seems to indicate that they are reasonably competent at recognizing a florid psychosis when they see one. There are often delays in the arrival of the relevant professionals (for example approved doctor and approved mental health professional) and communications between the parties have not always been as good as one might wish.

Past research has indicated that the implementation of the provision afforded by Section 136 is not uniform country-wide (Bean et al. 1991; NACRO (formerly National Association for the Care and Resettlement of Offenders) 1993; later research is summarized in some detail by Laing 1999, notably Chapter 3). Diversion may also take place at the point of arrest. Riordan et al. (2000) showed that intervention at the point of arrest had been successful in preventing some mentally disordered individuals being 'inappropriately taken into custody *and had fostered lasting and productive links between psychiatric services, the police and other agencies*' (Riordan et al. 2000: 683, emphasis added; see also Riordan et al. 2003; Hean et al. 2009).

Second, how much notice should be taken of an accused's view of his or her right to prosecution? Would some mentally disordered offenders *prefer* to be prosecuted in the normal way? This is of vital importance since the iatrogenic consequences of psychiatric disposal may be considerable. As we have seen, until the introduction of the Criminal Procedure (Insanity and Unfitness to Plead) Act 1991 – as subsequently amended (see Chapter 2) – a successful defence of insanity or unfitness to plead would involve immediate hospitalization – sometimes with a restriction order and a comparatively rare chance of the *facts* of the case being explored and determined. Hospitalization under the mental health legislation for offences may well result in a much longer spell of incarceration than if the defendant had been dealt with by way of imprisonment.

Third, given the current state of psychiatric services (and in particular *general* psychiatric services) is it certain that a psychiatric disposal will necessarily offer the best solution? This applies with considerable force to the severely personality disordered. As already noted, hospitals and psychiatrists have often seemed reluctant to accept such persons. Current government arrangements for dealing with those showing severe personality disorder, and who are considered to be highly dangerous to others, are considered in some detail in Chapter 5.

Fourth, we have already seen how prisoners, particularly those on remand, may have varying degrees of mental disturbance which are not spotted by prison staff. For example, the depressed prisoner may be difficult to pick out in an already overcrowded remand prison; moreover, depression is an illness often unrecognized by the unwary and often contributes to suicides and suicidal gestures (see Towl et al. 2000; see also Chapter 4 of this volume). Some prisoners may conceal the fact that they have a serious mental health problem as, for example, in the case of the highly encapsulated delusional system of the morbidly jealous or psychotically deluded individual. Coid (1991) found a small number of inmates whose psychotic delusions appeared to be quite unknown to the prison staff. Recent changes in prison health care already referred to should, one hopes, help to remedy this problem.

Fifth, an important jurisprudential question needs consideration. To what extent should offenders, even though mentally disturbed, be held responsible for their actions? We might exclude the floridly psychotic at the time of the offence and perhaps some of the seriously mentally impaired offenders. How far down the line of what some have termed the 'psychiatrization' of delinquency should we go? Such a practice tends to make the prison system the dumping ground for 'badness'; it also enables professionals to use prisons for the projection of their own 'badness', and it continues to negate rehabilitative measures within them. The *disadvantages* of non-prosecution have been alluded to by some forensic psychiatrists. For example, Smith and Donovan (1990) have suggested that:

> Excusing offending may not always be in the patient's interests. The formal legal process can be a valuable exercise in reality testing. The

patient [in this instance they are writing about offences committed by psychiatric in-patients] . . . can measure his or her own perceptions of his or her own behaviour against those of society. This can be a useful preparation for life outside hospital. The knowledge that prosecution is routine rather than exceptional, may deter further assaults and help aggressive patients to accept responsibility for their behaviour. Sometimes encouraging such patients to accept responsibility can be clinically beneficial and help to instil a sense of justice in other patients on a ward.

(Smith and Donovan 1990: 380)

They also state that non-prosecution

can reinforce the patient's belief that he or she need not control his or her behaviour. It may also leave staff feeling unsupported and there may be similar consequences if the court imposes a minimal penalty.

(Smith and Donovan 1990: 381)

For example, it is possible that had Christopher Clunis's serious offence behaviour been dealt with by a hospital order with restrictions, it could have been possible to exert more adequate control over his whereabouts and to have avoided the situation where he was able to disappear from view with, as we now know, lethal results (Ritchie et al. 1994). Similar concerns have been echoed elsewhere. In an article on the issue of determining criminal responsibility in France, Lloyd and Bénézech (1991) state:

The main problem . . . was how to determine the exact amount of free will each individual had at the time of the criminal offence. It was relatively easy to assess the absence of criminal responsibility in cases of severe mental disorder or handicap; intermediate mental states, however, present considerable difficulties in assessment, as did the measuring of constraints on the free will of normal men and women.

(Lloyd and Bénézech 1991: 282)

Sixth, in deciding upon diversion or discontinuance, how much consideration should be given to the views of victims? This is a delicate and difficult matter with considerable ethical implications. It needs to be seen against the climate of increasing attempts to allow victims more 'say' in what should happen to offenders and the establishment of opportunities for some offenders and victims to enter into 'dialogue'. It is an aspect of 'restorative' justice in which offenders witness at first hand the damage they have caused. In the past, such schemes have been limited to younger offenders, but they have now been extended to adults. Such participation has much to commend it, but the role of victims and the extent to which they actually participate in criminal justice and forensic-psychiatric decision-making processes requires very careful consideration. There is a fine dividing line between what may be quite appropriate involvement and undue influence being exerted by those who have been the victims, or who are a victim's family members. It should be remembered that our long-established system of law making and the delivery of justice have their roots in the avoidance of personal vengeance.

Finally, can we identify more clearly those aspects of law and practice that tend to militate against the effective use of diversion? There is anecdotal evidence to suggest that agencies tend to disclaim responsibility (notably financial) for the individual. For example the sad history of patchy development of medium and low secure accommodation attests to the importance of trying to ensure that funds are 'ring-fenced' (Department of Health and Home Office 1992). At the individual (case) level, would not the notion of funds travelling with the patient-offender offset a great deal of buck-passing? At a more personal level, professionals are often reluctant to see a problem from a colleague's point of view. This is not necessarily deliberate obfuscation or intransigence on their part, but is a product of differences in role perceptions among professionals trained in different ways. Far more needs to be done to address relationship problems of this kind and forensic-psychiatric or criminology centres could play a significant role in this (see, for example, Riordan et al. 2003). In the midst of inter-professional squabbles the offender-patient suffers and, as previously stated, the more inadequate of them continue to play their 'stage army' parts in the criminal justice and health care arenas; parts so well described by Rollin as long ago as the late 1960s (Rollin 1969). Homeless people, ethnic minority groups, particularly African Caribbean populations, fare particularly badly in this respect. Mentally handicapped people are another sad illustration – a truly vulnerable group whom nobody really wishes to own. They may find themselves with increasing frequency back within the criminal justice system – a phenomenon that the Mental Deficiency Act 1913 was designed specifically to prevent.

In an excellent review of ten years' published and unpublished contributions on diversion, James (1999) concluded that:

> Court diversion can be highly effective in the identification and acceleration into a hospital of mentally disordered offenders . . . However, most court diversion services are currently inadequately planned, organized or resourced and are therefore of limited effect . . . a central strategy is required, and properly designed and adequately supported court services should be incorporated into, and understood to be a core part of mainstream psychiatric provision . . . without such action, the future of court diversion lies in doubt.
>
> (James 1999: 507)

Two further specific problems can be identified: a reluctance on the part of courts to grant bail in some suitable cases (see Hucklesby 1997) and a problem in obtaining reports from increasingly busy general psychiatrists. Vaughan et al. (2003) suggest that more use could be made of a wider range of mental health professionals in the penal and community systems for obtaining information that would assist the courts in making mental health disposals. They state:

> By using existing court diversion schemes, prison mental health teams [and other professionals] . . . it is hoped that this will result in more timely and reliable flow of psychiatric information . . . the mentally disordered defendant should benefit from a better informed bench when they are considering his/her disposal.
>
> (Vaughan et al. 2003: 255)

In summary, diversionary practice may be set out in somewhat over-simplified fashion in five stages – as follows:

Stage 1   Informal diversion by the police.
Stage 2   Formal implementation of Section 136 of the Mental Health Act 2007.
Stage 3   Referral for psychiatric examination before court hearing and discontinuance of prosecution at any stage thereafter.
Stage 4   Disposal through mental health services at court or after sentence (see later discussion under 'Other health care disposals', p. 67).
Stage 5   Disposal through these services at a later stage in sentence – for example, transfer under the Mental Health Act 2007 from prison to hospital.
Note: The above stages may, of course, overlap.

For a critical and comprehensive review of diversion in its various aspects see *The Bradley Report* (2009).

The *effectiveness* of diversion will be limited if we do not take into account the following factors:

* Placing interest and activity concerning diversionary activities within an historical context.
* Recognizing that collaboration, cooperation and effective team-work are much harder to achieve than might appear to be the case on first inspection.
* Recognizing that these fundamental difficulties may make their appearance in disguised form, for example, through the guise of financial constraints and limitations.
* Recognizing the *possibility* that for some offenders, diversion to the health care system in its under-funded and under-resourced state may be a less satisfactory option than entry into the criminal justice system.

- Recognizing that, despite some useful research, we still lack detailed information about the effectiveness of diversionary activity and about what happens *long term* to those diverted.
- Recognizing that it is all too easy to assume that offenders wish to be diverted and that, for some, diversion may reduce their sense of personal responsibility to adverse effect.
- Recognizing that diversion may deflect attention from the lack of medical and psychiatric facilities within penal establishments.

I made brief reference to imprisonment in Chapter 1. It seems very important to emphasize at this point that our over-enthusiasm for imprisoning people has been the cause of the current gross overcrowding. We now lock up a wide range of ill-assorted offenders and alleged offenders (including terrorists), and those detained in immigration detention centres. It should come as no great surprise that the mental health needs of such a wide range of incarcerated individuals receive but scant or no attention. The Chief Inspector of Prisons, Dame Anne Owers, like many of her predecessors, has constantly drawn attention to this problem (see Nigel Morris, *The Independent*, 25 October 2007). Suicides and attempts by inmates is a profound worry. It is no doubt compounded by this gross overcrowding (*The Independent*, 22 September 2007). More recently we are informed that there are 'soaring levels of inmate violence'. It is reported by the Ministry of Justice that 'the number of assaults on prisoners by cell-mates have rocketed from 1,790 in 1996 to 11,826 [in 2007]' (*The Independent*, 3 March 2008). This worrying increase will come as no surprise to those with even a basic knowledge of (non-human) animal ethology. Overcrowding in unsatisfactory conditions is likely to produce extreme stress which, in turn, is likely to produce violent behaviour.

Other health care disposals

In order to keep the material in this section within reasonable limits, I provide merely an outline account of facilities. Readers wishing to obtain more detailed information will find it in the works cited and in the works listed for Further Reading at the end of the chapter. As already noted, the *legal basis and structure* of mental health services in the United Kingdom have undergone considerable changes in recent years, and are described in considerable detail by Eldergill (2002). Those readers wishing to examine international comparative provisions will find the *International Journal of Offender Therapy and Comparative Criminology*, *International Journal of Law and Psychiatry* and *International Journal of Forensic Mental Health* useful sources of information.

I have confined my description, almost exclusively, to provisions for adult offenders and offender-patients. However, there is continuing concern about the circumstances of young people (children and young persons under 16) who have committed homicide and other grave crimes and who are held in a variety of institutions. Such young people will often have to cross the boundaries between psychiatric, social and penal care. *Public* concern is not difficult to register; witness the fact that it is alleged that some 200,000 people signed a petition to ensure that the then Home Secretary 'imprisoned for life' the two young killers of the toddler James Bulger. Happily, good sense and humanity prevailed and the two young men concerned were released under conditions of anonymity, but not without further public outcry. A person convicted of murder, who was less than 18 at the time of the offence was committed, will be ordered to be detained 'during Her Majesty's Pleasure' (Section 53(1) Children and Young Person's Act 1933, as amended by the powers of the Criminal Courts (Sentencing) Act 2000). To all intents and purposes, this is similar to a life sentence, except that the offender may be detained 'in such place and under such conditions as the Secretary of State may direct'. The places chosen for such detention will vary according to the age and the mental condition of the offender and his or her circumstances, all of which may change over time. Thus, a youthful offender so detained may commence his or her sentence in a local authority residential establishment, a health care establishment, or in a secure hospital or unit, Young Offenders' Institution or, if detained for long enough, may be transferred to an adult prison. Such would have been the outcome for the killers of James Bulger had they not been released before this became a distinct probability. Persons who are under 17 and convicted of crimes other than murder, for which a sentence of life imprisonment may be passed on an adult, may be sentenced to detention for life under Section 53 of the 1933 Act (as amended by the Criminal Justice Act 1961, the Criminal Justice Act 1991 and the Criminal Justice and Public Order Act 1994). The effect of the 1994 Act was to extend the age range to those aged 10 or over, for the same range of offences as applied before to those aged 14 and under 18 (NACRO 1996: 1). Such a sentence has virtually the same effect as one of detention during Her Majesty's Pleasure. The oversight of the care and control of children and young persons subject to the sentences just outlined rests with the Youth Justice Board under the supervision of the Ministry of Justice.

The backgrounds and conditions under which the above offenders are detained have been examined very fully by Boswell (1996). Her study revealed a number of serious problems concerning their care and containment. These included: lack of adequate help in assisting these young people to understand the reasons for their behaviour (though it has to be said in fairness that in the case of the killers of James Bulger this issue seems to have been addressed); disruption to their education caused by their being moved from child care to penal provision as they grew older (see above); and a lack of adequate training in social skills. Boswell (1996) also found a very high degree of child physical and sexual abuse in their backgrounds. Sadly, the care of such disturbed children and young people has been found wanting in other institutions in recent times as, for example, in certain child care homes in Leicestershire (Kirkwood Report: see Leicestershire County Council 1993) and Sir Stephen Tumim's inquiries into prison suicides by young people (Home Office 1990a). The problem seems to be a perennial one (Prins 1991). As I write this there is an ongoing investigation into allegations of serious child abuse in a former children's home in Jersey.

The material that now follows is divided into three subsections. The first is concerned with 'enquiries into mental state and allied matters', the second deals with 'hospital provision' and the third covers 'penal provision'. In order to enhance clarity of presentation the subsections have been further divided into subdivisions.

Inquiries into mental state and allied matters

In Chapter 2, reference was made to the state of mind of those accused of offences such as homicide and other grave crimes. I now consider, briefly, the procedures available for causing inquiry to be made into the mental state of these and other defendants. In the case of those charged with murder, reports are usually prepared automatically by the Prison Health Care Service. The practice seems to have arisen mainly because of the importance attached in the past to the need to secure psychiatric evidence in cases where the death penalty could still be imposed and because of the seriousness with which all accusations of murder were (and still are) treated. The statutory requirements for the provision of mental condition reports are laid down in the Powers of Criminal Courts (Sentencing) Act 2000 and the Criminal Justice Act 2003. In essence they are as follows:

Before passing a custodial sentence other than one fixed by law [i.e. murder] on an offender who is, or appears to be mentally disordered, a court should consider:
(a) any information before it which relates to his mental condition [whether given in a medical report, or a pre-sentence report* or otherwise]; and
(b) the likely effect of such a sentence on that condition and on any treatment which may be available for it.

Note: *Pre-sentence reports are normally provided by the National Probation Service; they were previously known as probation or social inquiry reports. Reports into an accused's mental and physical state may also be prepared at the instigation of the Director of Public Prosecutions (DPP), or by the accused's legal advisers. In almost all cases of alleged murder, the reports will be prepared in custody but, in certain exceptional cases, an accused may be granted bail on condition that they remain in a psychiatric hospital for reports to be prepared. In cases of grave crimes, where the accused's mental condition may give rise to doubts as to diagnosis or the case is problematic in other ways, the investigations should also include thorough physical, neurological and biochemical investigations.

As indicated earlier, psychiatric reports will be prepared in cases of alleged murder and in other cases where the motivation for the offence may seem unclear. Certain sexual offences and cases of arson would fall into this category (see Chapters 8 and 9), as would cases involving less serious crimes which seem to have occurred out of the blue, or in repetitive fashion and in front of witnesses. It is difficult to obtain precise figures for the number of psychiatric reports prepared in any one year, but a reasonable estimate is that they are provided in about 2–4 per cent of all cases coming before the courts.

Remands to hospital

Currently, Section 35(1) of the Mental Health Act 1983 (as amended)[2] empowers magistrates' and Crown Courts to order the remand of an accused person to *hospital* for the preparation of a report into his or her mental condition. This provides an alternative to remanding an accused in custody in situations where it would not be practicable to obtain the report on bail (for example, if the accused decided to breach a *bail* requirement that he or she should reside in hospital for examination, the hospital would be unable to prevent that person from leaving; the *remand to hospital* under Section 35 gives the hospital the power to *detain* the accused). This power to remand to hospital applies also to any person *awaiting trial* by the Crown Court for any offence punishable by imprisonment, or any person who has been convicted but not yet sentenced (but excludes persons charged with murder). The power may be exercised only if an appropriately authorized medical practitioner (see below) reports orally or in writing that there is reason to believe that the accused is suffering from mental disorder. In the first instance, a remand may be for up to 28 days; after this initial period, the accused may be remanded for periods of up to 28 days for a maximum of 12 weeks. It should be noted that the criteria for *remands to hospital* are more limited than those which obtain for *remands on bail*. In the case of remands to hospital the court has to be satisfied that the accused is suffering from mental disorder as defined in the Act. In a review of Section 35, Bartlett and Sandland (2000) outline a number of problems that beset the provision 'both in terms of resources and frameworks and in terms of the legislative detail' (Bartlett and Sandland 2000: 169). Readers should consult their work for a detailed account of their criticisms.

Remands for treatment

Section 36 of the Mental Health Act 1983 (as amended) empowers the Crown Court to remand an accused person to hospital for treatment (other than a person charged with murder). The court must be satisfied on the written or oral evidence of *two* medical practitioners authorized under Section 12 of the Act that the accused is suffering from mental disorder of a nature or degree which makes it appropriate for him or her to be detained in hospital for medical treatment, and appropriate medical treatment is available to him. In the first instance, the remands may be for up to 28 days. The remand may be renewed at 28-day intervals for a period of up to 12 weeks. The court is also empowered to terminate the remand for treatment at any time, for example, in the event of the accused recovering, or in the event of the court hearing that no effective treatment is possible. This section appears to be used quite rarely (see Bartlett and Sandland 2000: 167).

Interim hospital orders

In addition to their powers under Sections 37 and 41 of the Act (as amended) (see below) courts are empowered under Section 38 to make an interim hospital order. As with the preceding provisions, the court has to be satisfied on duly approved medical evidence that this is the most appropriate course of action and that an accused person is suffering from mental disorder. The provision is likely to be of use in those cases where the court wishes to make some evaluation of an accused's likely response to treatment without irrevocable commitment on either side. Such an order may be made in the first instance for a period of up to 12 weeks; it may be renewed for periods of up to 28 days to a maximum total period of 12 months. The court may also terminate an interim hospital order after considering written or oral evidence or, if it makes a full hospital order (see below), or decides to deal with the offender in some alternative fashion.

Hospital orders

Section 37 of the Act (as amended) enables courts to make hospital or guardianship orders. (The latter are not considered here, as their use is currently infrequent in both civil and criminal cases: see Fennell 2007: 206–208.) In order to make a hospital order the court must be satisfied as to the following:

(a) That having regard to all the circumstances, including the nature of the offence, antecedents of the offender, and the unsuitability of other methods of disposal, a hospital order is the most suitable method of dealing with the case.

(b) The accused has been *convicted of an offence* punishable with imprisonment (other than murder). In the magistrates' court an order may be made without proceeding to conviction provided the court is satisfied that the defendant committed the act or made the omission charged, and that the person is suffering from mental disorder.

(c) The mental disorder from which the offender is suffering is of a nature or degree which makes it appropriate for him to be detained in a hospital and appropriate medical treatment is available to him, and that the court is of the opinion, having regard to all the circumstances, including the nature of the offences and the character and antecedents of the offender, and to the other available methods of dealing with him, that the most suitable method of disposing of the case is by means of an order under this section. It should be stressed that the condition *must* be one that merits compulsory detention in hospital and is *not* one that could be treated by other means, for example by a requirement for mental treatment under a community order (formerly known as a probation order).

A hospital order lasts initially for six months, is renewable for a further six months and is then renewable at annual intervals. A patient so detained may be discharged by the Responsible Clinician (formerly known as Responsible Medical Officer). At any time the patient or, within certain limitations, his or her nearest relative may also make application to a Mental Health Review Tribunal (MHRT) at regular intervals. Under Section 117(2) of the amended Act, after-care must be provided for those who cease to be detained under Section 37 and who leave hospital. The implementation of such after-care is now to be the responsibility of the Primary Care Trust or Local Health Board, and of the local social services authority in cooperation with relevant voluntary agencies.

Restriction orders

Section 41 of the Act (as amended) enables a Crown Court or an Appeal Court (but *not* a magistrates' court) to make a restriction order. The criteria for making such an order are as follows: first, that, following conviction, it appears to the court, having regard to

(a) the nature of the offence
(b) the offender's antecedents
(c) the risk of his or her committing further offences if discharged, that a restriction order is necessary *for the protection of the public from serious harm.*

Second, that at least one of the doctors authorized under Section 12(2) of the Act whose written evidence is before the court has also given that evidence orally. The criterion I have italicized did not appear in the Mental Health Act 1959 and was inserted in the 1983 Act to ensure that only those offender-patients who were considered likely to constitute a serious risk to the public would be subjected to the serious restrictions on liberty that follow the making of such an order (see below). Serious harm to the public is not defined in the Act. However, the Court of Appeal has, through a number of its decisions, provided guidance as to the nature and quality of serious harm. In particular, in the case of Birch in 1989, it was decided that

> the court is required to assess not the seriousness of the *risk* that the defendant will re-offend, but the risk that if he does so the public will suffer serious harm . . . the potential harm must be *serious*, and a high possibility of a recurrence of minor offences will no longer be sufficient.
>
> (quoted in Jones 2001: 222, emphasis in the original)

Up until now very little was known about judges' views and considerations when making a restriction order. However, a study by Quarshi and Shaw (2008) has thrown interesting light on this matter. Of an admittedly small sample of twelve judges interviewed, there was a unanimous view expressed that

> where a hospital order was being considered involving a serious offence a psychiatrist should take a firm view on whether a restriction order was also required. Furthermore, the interviewees stated that they would also anticipate a positive recommendation from psychiatrists in cases involving homicide, arson and serious sexual and violent offences.
>
> (Quarshi and Shaw 2008: 57)

In recent years there has been a modest increase in the number of restriction orders made (Quarshi and Shaw 2008; see also Ministry of Justice 2007).

Until 2007, a restriction could be made for a specific period *or* without limit of time. The 2007 Act removes the option or orders with specific time limit on the sensible assumption that the assessment of risk should not be impeded by a constraint imposed by a finite period of detention.

A restriction order places serious curbs on the liberty of the subject.

1   The offender-patient cannot be given leave of absence from the hospital (as he or she can be under non-restricted orders), be transferred elsewhere, or be discharged by the responsible clinician without the consent of the Secretary of State.

2   The Secretary of State may remove the restrictions if he or she con-
     siders they are no longer needed to protect the public from serious
     harm. Should the order continue in force without the restriction clause,
     it has the same effect as an order made under Section 37 of the Act.
3   The Secretary of State may, at any time, discharge the offender-patient
     absolutely or subject to conditions. In considering those restricted cases
     (a) which were considered to be particularly problematic, (b) which
     were considered to be in need of special care in assessment, and (c)
     where there might have been a fear of possible future risk to the public,
     the Secretary of State would in the past have sought the advice of the
     Advisory Board on Restricted Patients (formerly known as the Aarvold
     Board). The Board was stood down in 2003. See later for details of the
     Board's one-time constitution and functions.

Under Section 73 of the Act (as amended) a Mental Health Review Tribunal may exercise its own powers concerning restricted patients in the
following manner: first, the Tribunal *shall* order the patient's *absolute*
discharge if it is satisfied that:

(a) an offender-patient is not now suffering from mental disorder as
     specified in the Act which makes it appropriate for him or her to be
     detained in hospital for medical treatment; *or*
(b) it is not necessary for the health and safety of the offender-patient or
     for the protection of other persons that he or she should receive such
     treatment; *and*
(c) it is not appropriate for the offender-patient to remain liable to be
     recalled to hospital for further treatment. (For detailed discussion of
     the medical evidence required in cases requiring recall, see Azvonye
     (2007). For the Secretary of State's powers, see Pezanni (2007).)

In the important case of *R. v. K* (1990) it was held that a tribunal which was
satisfied that the restricted patient was not suffering from a mental or
psychopathic disorder was nevertheless entitled to order the conditional
discharge of the patient and was not, as had hitherto held to be the case,
obliged to order his or her absolute discharge. The court appeared to have
in mind the possibility of a need for a residual power to recall the patient in
the event of a relapse at some future date.

Second, a conditionally discharged offender-patient may be recalled to
hospital by the Secretary of State at any time during the duration of the
restriction order, but the patient has to be referred to a Mental Health
Review Tribunal for a prompt hearing into the recall, the reasons for it
and any representations the offender-patient may wish to make. It has also
been held by the Court of Appeal (*R. v. Secretary of State for the Home*

Department ex parte K 1990) that the Home Secretary did not have to rely on medical evidence in order to recall a restricted patient to hospital, even if medical opinion was of the view that the patient was not suffering from mental disorder (see also Azvonye 2007). This wide discretion was held to lie entirely in the hands of the Secretary of State, and the public interest would, if necessary, take precedence. However, this view was subsequently challenged by the offender-patient who took his case to the European Court of Human Rights. The court held that 'in the absence of an emergency, there had been a breach of Article 5(1) in recalling "K" without up-do-date medical evidence to demonstrate that he was suffering from a true mental disorder' (*Kay v. United Kingdom* 1998). In citing this case Jones (2001: 234) indicates that 'the recall of conditionally discharged patients should conform with this judgement'. An order for conditional discharge may contain a range of requirements held to be conducive to the welfare of the offender-patient and, more importantly, for the protection of the public. (For a helpful analysis of the management of restricted offender-patients in the community, see Street 1998.)

Under the 1959 Act tribunals could only *advise* the then Home Secretary on the discharge of restricted patients. As can be seen, they now have the power themselves to order the patient's discharge. In order to exercise these wider powers, tribunals must be chaired by a senior legal practitioner approved by the Lord Chancellor, such as a circuit judge or person of equivalent status (see later discussion of functions of MHRTs). For a discussion of the role of the Home Secretary (now Minister for Justice) in dealing with restricted cases, see Snow and Moody (2005).

Hospital and limitation directions

Section 46 of the Crime (Sentences) Act 1997 introduced a new disposal (a hospital direction) which is to be found in Sections 45A and 45B of the Mental Health Act 1983 (as amended); it is known in the vernacular as a 'hybrid order'. A hospital direction is defined in the 1983 Act as 'a direction that, instead of being removed to and detained in a prison, the offender may be removed to and detained in such hospital as may be specified in the direction'. The court may also add a 'limitation direction' which is similar to the effect of a restriction order made under Section 41 of the Act. The disposal is available only to a Crown Court. Its purpose is to ensure that should a mentally disordered offender not respond to hospital treatment, he or she may be transferred to prison (for further descriptions, see Bartlett and Sandland 2000: 189–194; Jones 2001: 240–245; Fennell 2007: 402–403). Detailed criticisms of the use of such orders have come from the legal, criminological and forensic-psychiatric quarters. For examples of the former, see Walker (1996) and Laing (1997), and for the latter, see Eastman (1996) and Darjee et al. (2000, 2002).

Transfer of prisoners found to be mentally disordered

Sections 47–52 of the Mental Health Act 1983 (as amended) enable the Secretary of State to order the transfer of sentenced or unconvicted prisoners from prison to hospital if they are found to be suffering from mental disorder as defined in the Act (see, for example, the case of Peter Sutcliffe described in Chapter 2). Under the provisions of Section 47 an order in respect of a sentenced prisoner *may* be made without restrictions, but it will be much more likely to be made with restrictions under the provisions of Section 49. Bartlett and Sandland (2000: 196) report that in the period 1997–98 'of 247 orders made under Section 47 only 31 were unrestricted'. If the Secretary of State is notified by the RMO (now Responsible Consultant) or a Mental Health Review Tribunal that such a person no longer needs treatment for mental disorder, there are two possibilities open to the Secretary of State:

1   If the offender-patient has become eligible for parole or has earned statutory remission, the Secretary of State can order his or her discharge.
2   Alternatively, the Secretary of State can order that the patient be remitted to prison to serve the remainder of his or her sentence (for examples of the effects of such transfer upon sentenced prisoners, see Grounds 1990a, 1990b, 1991). Despite attempts on the part of government to obviate delays in transferring mentally disordered offenders from prison to hospital, the problem has continued. One difficulty is that acutely mentally ill prisoners do not always conform to advice to take anti-psychotic medication. Such medication cannot, of course, be enforced in prison as prison hospitals are not designated as such within the meaning of the mental health legislation. However, McKenzie and Sales (2008), in a useful study, discovered that under the new transfer procedures there was 'a trend towards shorter delay times for transfer to hospital – from 11 weeks to 7 weeks'. Despite this encouraging trend, they concluded that 'unacceptable delays in transfer to hospital of mentally ill prisoners are likely to remain, even after the introduction of new procedures by the Department of Health and the Prison Service' (McKenzie and Sales 2008: 22).[3]

'Psychiatric probation orders'

The heading has been placed in quotation marks because although they are commonly known as 'psychiatric probation orders', their correct title under recent legislation should be a mental health treatment requirement under a community order. The provision has been available under statute since the Criminal Justice Act 1948 and is now provided under the Criminal Justice Act 2003 (Sections 207 and 208). This permits such treatment, provided:

1   A hospital, or other establishment, will receive him or her and is willing to provide treatment by a registered medical practitioner or chartered psychologist.

2   The court has before it the oral or written evidence of one doctor (approved under Section 12(2) of the Mental Health Act 1983, as amended) indicating that the offender's condition requires, and may be susceptible to, treatment (but is not such as to warrant his or her detention in pursuance of a hospital or guardianship order). Such an order may be on an inpatient or outpatient basis.

As far as a hospital or other institution is concerned, the offender-patient has informal status and there is no power to detain him or her compulsorily (as there is under the provisions of the Mental Health Act). Should the offender-patient leave, the probation officer may, of course, take action for breach of requirement of the order. However, it is not open to the court to sanction proceedings for a breach of the order if, for example, the offender-patient refuses a physical form of treatment such as electroconvulsive therapy (ECT). Such orders are of use in cases of milder forms of mental illness and where it is considered there is no indication of potential serious harm to the offender and/or the public. The limited research that has been carried out into this form of treatment indicates that it is useful in circumstances where there is good cooperation between the psychiatric and probation services. However, the use of such orders is not frequent, and has been declining somewhat (Home Office 1997; see also Clark et al. 2002; Richardson et al. 2003; Stone 2003).[4]

An outline of the arrangements for the disposal of mentally disturbed offenders is set out in Figure 3.1.

Hospital provision: high security, semi-secure and low secure accommodation

A number of mentally disordered and disturbed offenders will be detained in ordinary psychiatric hospitals. Those who have committed grave crimes, and who are considered to be an immediate danger to the public if at large may, as we shall see shortly, be detained in a high security (formerly known as a 'special') hospital. In the latter stages of their rehabilitation towards the community, such offender-patients may be transferred to an ordinary psychiatric hospital or, more likely, to a medium and subsequently perhaps to a low security unit. Until fairly recently, due to the absence of these less secure units and a reluctance on the part of ordinary psychiatric hospitals to take offender-patients, some of them might remain in conditions of high security for far longer than their condition or the safety of the public warranted. The situation is not so serious nowadays, but sadly there are still some instances of lengthy delays in transfer. The Glancy (Department of

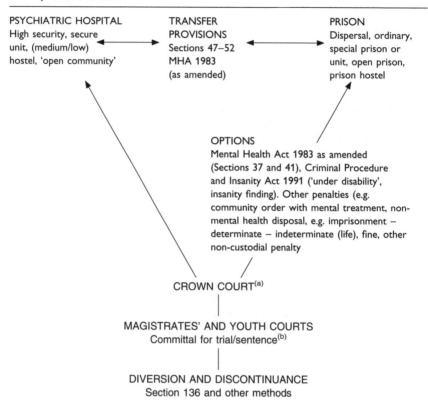

PSYCHIATRIC HOSPITAL
High security, secure
unit, (medium/low)
hostel, 'open community'

TRANSFER
PROVISIONS
Sections 47–52
MHA 1983
(as amended)

PRISON
Dispersal, ordinary,
special prison or
unit, open prison,
prison hostel

OPTIONS
Mental Health Act 1983 as amended
(Sections 37 and 41), Criminal Procedure
and Insanity Act 1991 ('under disability',
insanity finding). Other penalties (e.g.
community order with mental treatment, non-
mental health disposal, e.g. imprisonment –
determinate – indeterminate (life), fine, other
non-custodial penalty

CROWN COURT[a]

MAGISTRATES' AND YOUTH COURTS
Committal for trial/sentence[b]

DIVERSION AND DISCONTINUANCE
Section 136 and other methods

Notes: (a) The powers available to the Crown Court are also exercisable on appeal by the Court of Appeal. (b) Magistrates may also commit to the Crown Court with a view to a hospital order being made *with restrictions*.

Figure 3.1   Disposal of mentally disordered and disturbed offenders through the criminal justice, forensic mental health and penal systems

Health and Social Security 1974) and Butler Committees (Home Office and Department of Health and Social Security 1974, 1975) both stressed the need for the setting up of medium secure units and the need for earmarked funds to be made available for the purpose. In the event, such funds were used by some health authorities for other purposes and it took a considerable time to free up the necessary funding.

Over the years there have been a number of problems in developing the *range* of units required to meet the varied problems presented by offender-patients. First, in the past, the secure units tended to be seen as an answer to the problem of the management of the difficult or disruptive patient detained in *ordinary* psychiatric hospitals. (It is important to note here that about one-third of offender-patients detained in one or other of the three high security hospitals – to be described shortly – are not offenders, but have been transferred to high security accommodation because of their severely disruptive or violent behaviour.) To some extent the situation has been eased by the establishment of special units catering for such patients who demonstrate what is known as 'challenging behaviour'. Second, in the past, secure units have tended to be seen as 'mini high security' hospitals. Third, most of the medium secure units were designed to take offender-patients for a maximum of two years. A number of such patients have longer term needs for some form of secure accommodation. To meet this need, a small number of low security units have been set up. They are seen largely as a final staging post before return to rehabilitation in the open community. Fourth, medium secure units are likely to cater on their admission wards for some quite acutely mentally ill patients. For some patients who are considered suitable for transfer from a high security hospital, the presence of such ill patients is likely to have an unfortunate impact on them on arrival at a unit. This is because, over the years, they are likely to have reached a degree of emotional and mental stability and achieved freedom from acute psychotic symptoms. To suddenly find themselves placed in such a setting can be a very traumatic experience. Sometimes, such a placement has led to a breakdown in a secure hospital patient's phased rehabilitation. Since the late 1980s, there have been a number of studies describing the characteristics of treatment regimes for offender-patients located in conditions of medium security. The short selection of references that follows may help readers who wish to research this aspect further; many of the articles provide details of other relevant literature (see, for example, James et al. 1997). Murray (1996) surveyed the use of beds in NHS medium secure units in England. Trends in admissions to one Regional Secure Unit over a fifteen-year period have been described by Brown et al. (2001). Demographic and other characteristics of first admission patients in a similar unit have been described by Ricketts et al. (2001). The needs of rural areas have been described by Jones et al. (2002). Watson (1998) has described the factors that influenced the design of regional secure units (see also Greenhalgh et al. 1996). Moss (1998) has provided a book-length account of the development and practice of medium secure provision by the private sector. Castro et al. (2002) have published a small-scale follow-up study of such patients. Follow-up studies of patients in the public sector have been made by Quinn and Ward (2000). For further studies, see also Davies et al. (2007), Neille et al. (2007) and Riordan and Humphreys (2007).

High security (formerly) special hospitals

Under the provisions of Section 4 of the National Health Service and Community Care Act 1990, the Secretary of State for Social Services is required to provide and maintain such institutions as are necessary for persons subject to detention under the mental health legislation who, in his opinion, require treatment in conditions of special security because of their 'dangerous, violent or criminal propensities'. However, as already noted above, about one-third of all such detained patients are *not* offenders, but are detained because of their difficult, disruptive or violent behaviour in ordinary psychiatric or mental handicap hospitals. There are three (formerly four) high security hospitals in England (Broadmoor, Rampton and Ashworth (formerly Moss Side and Park Lane)) but none in Wales or Northern Ireland. The State Hospital at Carstairs in Scotland is the approximate equivalent of an English high security hospital and the Central Mental Hospital at Dundrum in Dublin performs some of the functions of its UK counterparts. Because Northern Ireland has no high security hospital, it sends a few of its more dangerous offender-patients to Carstairs or, more frequently, to Ashworth. The former 'special hospitals' have had a long and, from time to time, somewhat chequered history. Formerly administered directly by the Department of Health, then by a specially created health authority – the Special Hospitals Service Authority (SHSA) – they have now been merged with general NHS provision. The aim is to bring these establishments along-side more general psychiatric practice and to reduce the isolation that seems to have plagued them over the years. A short account now follows of the three hospitals in question. They have about 1000 patients, divided pretty much in equal numbers between them (Fennell and Yeates 2002). (The *overall* number of restricted patients in various forms of psychiatric hospital care at the end of 2006 was 3601: Ministry of Justice 2007.)

BROADMOOR

Broadmoor in Berkshire is the oldest of the hospitals, having been estab-lished in 1863. Once beset by severe overcrowding, some relief was afforded by the building of Park Lane (now Ashworth) Hospital. However, the provision for female patients has been the subject of continued criticism in recent years and, at one time, its handling of ethnic minority (particularly African Caribbean) patients left something to be desired (see Prins et al. 1993). However, it appears that ethnic and other minority issues have now begun to be addressed in a more sympathetic and constructive manner.

RAMPTON

Rampton Hospital in North Nottinghamshire was established in 1914 and in its earlier days tended to specialize in the management of mentally impaired offender-patients. It now has a more mixed population and there has been recent concentration on work with individuals with a severe personality disorder, notably those considered to be dangerous. This is evidenced by the establishment of a pilot special unit for the treatment of such patients. Overcrowding was once a serious problem, and the hospital was the subject of an intensive inquiry into allegations of ill-treatment of patients. However, since the late 1980s, the hospital has moved out of its backwater status (DHSS 1980: iii) and been revitalized by the introduction of more proactive review processes and of more forward-looking staff at all levels.

ASHWORTH

Ashworth Complex is located at Maghull, Liverpool. The complex consists of the former Moss Side (established 1933) and Park Lane (established 1974) hospitals. At one time, Moss Side took mainly mentally impaired patients, but following integration with Park Lane, it now takes all three categories – people who are learning disabled, mentally ill and severely antisocial personality disordered (see later).

THE FUTURE OF HIGH SECURITY

As already indicated, the high security hospitals have come in for a good deal of criticism in the past, and a lot of it was justified. However, even their severest critics acknowledge that such institutions have to undertake a tremendously difficult task in attempting to combine containment, clinical treatment and rehabilitation in a climate of opinion that does not give high priority to the care of the 'mad and the bad'. There have been abuses, as witnessed in the damning report of Sir Louis Blom-Cooper's inquiry into conditions at Ashworth (Department of Health 1992) and an inquiry into managerial and other deficiencies at the personality disorder unit at the same hospital (Fallon et al. 1999). The authors of that report described the establishment as 'A Scandalous and Corrupt Hospital'. One result of the Fallon inquiry was increased concern over security. Sir Richard Tilt, former director of the English Prison Service, was commissioned to carry out an inquiry (Tilt et al. 2000). He and his team made numerous recommendations which included increasing physical perimeter security, increasing security measures within the hospital and increasing staff levels in the security service departments. The report was criticized by two senior forensic psychiatrists, Dr Tim Exworthy and Professor John Gunn (Exworthy and Gunn 2003). In brief, they regretted the report's overemphasis on physical means of security and the extent to which these could be damaging to 'relational' aspects of the hospital's environment. Tilt (2003), in a reply to these criticisms, took a different view, stating: 'I believe firmly, as did all the members of my team, that the key to running successful treatment-orientated high security hospitals lies in ensuring that the public, patients and staff feel safe about their operation' (Tilt 2003: 548).

In the past there have been calls for the high security hospitals to be closed down and replaced by smaller units. Wisdom suggests that the expertise that *does* reside in the secure hospitals needs to be maintained and not dissipated. Dr David Tidmarsh (1998), a very experienced former senior consultant at Broadmoor, indicated that patients at the hospital would prefer its current good facilities over and above proximity to relatives and friends. He put the position very clearly:

> To decant these patients into worse facilities would be inhumane. To provide the equivalent safety in half a dozen mini Special Hospitals would be extremely expensive. If they were built on green field sites they would suffer from all the problems of isolation that have beset the existing Special Hospitals . . . It would seem therefore both humane and politically expedient to give up this idea, to lift the planning blight from the existing Special Hospitals and to provide them with the strong leadership they need to escape from the more unfortunate aspects of their recent history.
>
> (Tidmarsh 1998: 508)

Without being over-optimistic about their future, it is reasonable to suggest that the high security hospitals are likely to embrace better times. Being part of NHS general psychiatric provision should go some way to offset their former 'splendid isolation' – an isolation that served to foster complacency in the past. Better trained and motivated staff are coming forward and the past sometimes less than helpful attitudes of the Prison Officers' Association have been dissipated to a major extent. The fact that the two pilot centres for the management of dangerous personality disordered patients are located in Rampton and Broadmoor also augurs well for the future. Major research projects have been undertaken; some of these are described briefly but helpfully by Kaye and Franey (1998), and more fully by Thomas et al. (2004a, 2004b) and by Harty et al. (2004).

Maximum secure accommodation in Scotland and Ireland

The clientele of the State Hospital at Carstairs (established in 1944) are, for all intents and purposes, the same as those in the high security hospitals in England. It normally houses some 200 or so offender-patients, the majority suffering from psychotic illness. As already indicated, it very occasionally receives patients from Northern Ireland.

Ireland

The Central Mental Hospital at Dundrum, Dublin, has a predominantly male population of some 100 or so offender-patients, about half of whom are said to suffer from schizophrenic illness. A large percentage of these patients are the subjects of transfer from prison.

Penal provisions

Prison psychiatric services

Brief reference has already been made to prison mental health care. This section merely provides some further detail. Acts of 1774 and 1779 required prisons to appoint a physician, and an organized full-time medical service began with the establishment of the Prison Commission in 1887. Such appointments can be seen as the forerunners of a range of other professional appointments which were subsequently to swell the ranks of prison staffs, for example chaplains, psychologists, specialist nursing officers, probation officers (formerly prison welfare officers), education personnel and works and occupations staff. The history of mental health services in prisons reveals that there were a number of early attempts to describe and classify mentally disordered offenders received in prison. Perhaps one of the most significant was the report authored by East and de Hubert (1939) which, as referred to in Chapter 1, paved the way to some extent for the foundation of Grendon Underwood psychiatric prison in 1962 (see below). It is possibly not widely known that, over the years, prison medical staff have had general oversight of the total care of *both prisoners and prison staff and also a concern with environmental health matters*. As indicated earlier in this chapter, such work has now become an NHS responsibility and the specific post of prison medical officer is being phased out. Sadly, as stated earlier, there are still a number of mentally disordered offenders who should be in hospital (though the numbers of 'transfer directions' under the Mental Health Act have increased modestly in recent years), and an even greater number who, while not fulfilling the strict criteria for transfer under the mental health legislation, would benefit from better psychiatric oversight and management. Dr John Reed, former Chief Medical Inspector, HM Inspectorate of Prisons, has also expressed his concern over the continuing delays in transferring mentally disturbed prisoners to NHS hospitals. However, he is cautious about extending treatment for non-consenting patients in prison beyond emergencies, as advocated by some (see, for example, Wilson and Forrester 2002; Earthrowl et al. 2003), on the grounds that prisons currently do not have adequate medical resources to carry out such treatments safely.

A substantial analysis of the work of Grendon Psychiatric Prison is that by Genders and Player (1995). The views of what prisoners think of Grendon have been thoughtfully described by Wilson and McCabe (2002), and a more anecdotal account has been provided by Smartt (2001). There are a number of other therapeutically orientated units within the prison system (examples being at HM Prisons Wakefield and Wormwood Scrubs and the Young Offenders' Institution at Feltham). A 'second Grendon' was opened at HM Prison Dovegate, Staffordshire in 1991. An interesting feature of this establishment is that it was procured under private contract (see Genders 2003). Three further developments should be noted by way of concluding this section. First, the report entitled *The Future Organisation of Prison Health Care* published in 1999 set out the policy of prison health care being provided by a partnership with the NHS based upon the principle of equivalence (Department of Health 1999c). Second, the development of prison 'mental health in-reach services' has seen a process of rapid development. Third, in 2001 the Department of Health, HM Prison Service and the National Assembly for Wales published an important document setting out a strategy for the development and modernizing of mental health services in prisons (Department of Health et al. 2001).

Supervision in the community

At some point in their careers, attempts will be made to relocate offenders and offender-patients into the community. Those dealt with through the penal system, even though they may have mental health problems, will be dealt with through release on parole, or life licence. Those who have been dealt with under the terms of a hospital order with restrictions will be released on what is known as a 'conditional discharge'. Supervision of those dealt with through the penal system will be undertaken by a probation officer and, if there are mental health problems, supervision may also include psychiatric intervention. Those released through the mental health system will be supervised by either a probation officer or a local authority social worker. At one time, the supervision of restricted patients was almost always undertaken by the probation service; nowadays, supervision is more likely to be undertaken by a local authority social worker. Individual circumstances will govern the choice. If the offender-patient has been previously well known to the probation service, then it will most likely be the probation service who will be asked to supervise. If additional community resources are required, such as a hostel or day-care facility, then social services will be most likely to be chosen. In addition to social supervision, almost without exception, the offender-patient will also be under the care and supervision of a named psychiatrist and perhaps a community psychiatric nurse. In both penal and health care orders for release there will be specific requirements, such as place of residence, notification of change of address etc. and any other requirements that are deemed to be in the interests of the offender or offender-patient and, importantly, the safety of the public.

Issues relating to public safety and the assessment and management of risk are extremely important and are dealt with in detail in Chapter 10. In restricted cases, it is essential that there is open and constructive liaison between the social supervisor and the psychiatrist. Clear procedures for this should be established between the parties involved: offender-patient, social supervisor, psychiatrist and community nurse. The Home Office (now Ministry of Justice) issues guidelines on best practice and these are updated from time to time. Not infrequently, decisions have to be made at a time of crisis. For example, an offender-patient's behaviour may have deteriorated to the extent that recall to hospital may need to be considered or, in the case of a parolee or life licensee, recall to prison. The worker carrying responsibility for the case (and by definition they will almost always be complex and difficult) should have easy access to their line management for support and advice. Access for further advice from the relevant department of the Ministry of Justice (Mental Health Unit or Parole Unit) is essential. Cases in which advice would need to be sought would include those where there appears to be an actual or potential risk to the public, where contact with the offender or offender-patient has been lost, where there has been a substantial breach of the discharge conditions, or where the individual's behaviour suggests a need for recall for further inpatient treatment, or where the offender or offender-patient has been charged with, or convicted of, a further offence. An offender-patient who is recalled to hospital by order of the Secretary of State has to have his or her case referred to a Mental Health Review Tribunal within one month of his or her recall (see earlier discussion of the evidence required for such recall). In deciding whether or not to issue a warrant for recall, the Secretary of State will treat each case on its merits. If an offender-patient has been hospitalized in the past for very serious violence or homicide, comparatively minor irregularities of conduct or failure to cooperate within the terms of the conditional discharge *might* well be sufficient to merit the consideration of recall. Similar considerations apply in relation to offenders released on parole or life licence. If all goes well, the conditions of a life licence, such as the requirement to live in a specific place, to report to a probation officer, to receive visits or not to take specific employments, may be cancelled – but customarily not before at least four or five years have elapsed; the life licence itself remains in force for life. In the case of conditionally discharged restricted patients, the requirements for supervision, or the order for conditional discharge itself, may be lifted by the Secretary of State or by a Mental Health Review Tribunal. At the time of writing, there are several hundred life-sentence prisoners being supervised by the probation service and in excess of a thousand conditionally discharged restricted patients by local authority social workers, probation officers and psychiatrists (and in some cases community mental health staff) (Ministry of Justice 2007). (For a survey of community forensic psychiatric services in England and Wales, see Judge et al. 2004.)

National decision-making and advisory bodies

Brief reference has been made to the mechanism of parole, to the Mental Health Review Tribunal and to the Home Secretary's one-time Advisory

Board on Restricted Patients. Each of these is now considered in a little more detail.

Parole Board

The arrangements for release on parole and life licence were initiated in the Criminal Justice Act 1967 and have been amended from time to time. The 1967 Act established the Parole Board as an independent body, appointed by the then Home Secretary, to offer him or her advice and to take decisions on his or her behalf on the early release of determinate or life-sentence prisoners. More recent enactments and rulings have increased the categories of prisoners who are made subject to parole supervision. Over the years its independence has been further marked as, for example, by the board's establishment as an executive non-departmental public body in 1996. Its current statement of purposes is as follows: 'The Parole Board is an independent body that works with its criminal justice partners to protect the public by risk assessing prisoners to decide whether they can be safely released into the community' (Parole Board 2007). Concern has been expressed in recent times as to the *real* extent of the Parole Board's independent status. This independence has been the subject of recent review in the High Court (Administrative Division). The court found that though 'there is no question about the independence of mind and impartiality of members of the Board' and 'no sign of any attempt by the executive to influence individual cases', there is a valid basis for concern regarding the board's independence. The court in its judgment went on to declare 'that the present arrangements for the Parole Board do not sufficiently demonstrate its objective independence of the Secretary of State as required by English common law and ECHR [European Convention on Human Rights] Article 5(4)', as reported by Stone (2008) concerning the case of R. (on the application of Brooke and others) v. The Parole Board and the Secretary of State for Justice (September 2007). At the time of writing this chapter, the case has not yet been formally reported by the *Law Reports* (Stone 2008: 115–116).

The work of the Parole Board has been accompanied by a considerable increase in the size of its membership. Under the terms of the 1967 Act the board was required to include among its members the following categories of persons:

- a person who holds, or has held, judicial office
- a psychiatrist
- a person who has experience of the supervision or after-care of discharged prisoners (usually a chief or assistant chief probation officer)
- a person who has made a study of the causes of crime and the treatment of offenders (usually an academic criminologist).

The Parole Board currently includes a number of members of each of these categories; in addition, it now includes psychologists and its 'independent' members are qualified by a range of varied experiences to make significant contributions to the board's work. Membership of the board for the year 2006–07 consisted of a full-time chairman, two full-time members, and over a hundred other members.

The detailed functions of the Parole Board are set out in its annual report for 2006–07 (Parole Board 2007). A former member of the board, John Harding, has provided a stimulating discussion of the problems facing the board, particularly those relating to risk and the need to recall a licensee (Harding 2006; see also Fitzgibbon 2008). For a discussion on some of the problems involved in releasing on parole those prisoners who continue to maintain their innocence, see Naughton (2009).

Mental Health Review Tribunal (MHRT)

Mental Health Review Tribunals were introduced by the Mental Health Act 1959. They were intended to serve as a replacement for the role of the lay magistracy under previous lunacy legislation in safeguarding the rights of patients subject to detention; they also replaced some of the functions of the Board of Control to which a patient could make representations against detention in hospital. The role and scope of the Tribunals were extended under the Mental Health Act 1983; the Act gave greater opportunities for appeal against detention and for the automatic review of patients' cases at regular intervals if they had not applied themselves. The MHRT is a *judicial* body and has considerable statutory powers which are independent of any government agency such as the Ministry of Justice and the Department of Health. Currently, the main purpose of the MHRT is to review the cases of compulsorily detained patients and, if the relevant criteria are satisfied, to direct their discharge. This task involves examination of complex and often conflicting elements giving rise to concern for the liberty of the patient (or offender-patient) on the one hand and, as with the Parole Board, the protection of the public on the other. With the advent of the Mental Health Act 2007 certain changes have been introduced into the tribunal's organization. The previous multiple tribunals for various regions in England are replaced by one tribunal under the direction of a president (Wales already had a presidential arrangement). Those who hitherto had been designated as presidents of *individual* tribunal hearings will henceforth be known as chairmen. And, in future, tribunals will now come under the management of the Ministry of Justice and not the Department of Health (see also Fennell 2007: 29–30). Concerning appeals, procedures, etc., tribunals are now overseen under the terms of the Tribunals, Courts and Enforcement Act 2007. (For a discussion of these matters, see Gledhill 2009.)

MHRT panels normally consist of three members; a legal member who chairs the panel, a medical member (almost always a psychiatrist of considerable experience) and a so-called lay member, who is neither a lawyer nor a doctor. As indicated earlier, panels hearing restricted cases must be chaired by a circuit judge or lawyer of equivalent standing. All three tribunal members have equal status, and an equal role in the decision-making process and in drafting the reasons for the final decision. Hearings are almost always in private but, in certain circumstances, a patient may request a public hearing. Nowadays patients are almost always legally represented. In particularly difficult or possibly contentious cases, other interested parties, such as the Ministry of Justice, may be legally represented, usually by counsel. Tribunals have not been without their critics. Peay (1989) made an extensive critical study of tribunal decision-making. Two inquiries into homicides committed by former offender-patients made serious criticisms of the system. In the first of these, the case of Andrew Robinson, details of his original offence were so inadequate that the tribunal had to make decisions on imperfect evidence. At one of his tribunals, the patient had refused to be examined by the medical member (a requirement under the Tribunal Rules). Despite this, the tribunal went ahead, determined the case and gave the patient an absolute discharge. The inquiry team acknowledged that at the various tribunal hearings the members were often having to act upon the information before them, and that this information was often seriously inadequate (Blom-Cooper et al. 1995). In the second case, that of Jason Mitchell, the inquiry team made further criticisms of tribunal practice. The first of these concerned the making of a deferred conditional discharge that contained requirements beyond the tribunal's legal remit. Blom-Cooper et al. (1996) made a number of recommendations: first, clinical psychologists should be added to the list of lay members who can be appointed to MHRTs. Second, MHRTs should have available more detailed information about an offender-patient's index offence (this has subsequently been remedied by the Ministry of Justice). Third, in restricted cases (as was Mitchell's), the medical member of the tribunal should preferably be a forensic psychiatrist. Fourth, MHRT members should be afforded follow-up; in those cases where an offender-patient had reoffended in serious fashion after discharge, a confidential retrospective review should be held (see Brunning 1996). For those readers wishing to learn more about tribunals, their functions and the issues arising from them, Eldergill's magisterial work offers a wealth of information (Eldergill 1997).

The MHRT is not to be confused with the Mental Health Act Commission. The latter was established by the Mental Health Act 1983 to oversee the welfare and interests of detained patients. Some of its functions are to deal with complaints and to appoint 'second opinion' doctors who are required to intervene in certain circumstances when compulsory treatment is being proposed. It is required to present a report on its work to

Parliament every two years. The commission has no power to order the release of detained patients. Under the new legislation the commission's work is now part of the Care Quality Commission (established in April 2009) (see Fennell 2007: 31–32; see also Lelliott 2009).

Home Secretary's Advisory Board on Restricted Patients

Following the conviction and sentence of Francis Graham Young for murder by poisoning, the then Home Secretary, acting on the recommendation of an inquiry into Young's case (Home Office and DHSS 1973), established a non-statutory advisory committee (known then as the Aarvold Board) to advise him in those restricted cases: (a) which were considered to be particularly problematic; (b) which were considered to need special care in assessment; and (c) where there was thought to be a fear of possible future risk to the public. This committee, subsequently known as the Home Secretary's Advisory Board on Restricted Patients, merely proffered advice to the Home Secretary. In more recent times, it had dealt with very few cases and its workload decreased considerably to the extent that, as already noted, the Board was stood down in September 2003. This currently leaves the MHRT as the sole body in cases where the Secretary of State has not approved the offender-patient's conditional discharge himself or herself. Membership of the Committee was small; it included a legal chairperson, two psychiatrists, a director of social services, a chief probation officer and two other members who were considered to have wide experience of the criminal justice system.

Brief background to changes enshrined in the 2007 Act

It seems appropriate to comment briefly on the path that led to the new Mental Health Act. The Mental Health Act 1983 was hailed as a much needed reform of previous mental health legislation, notably the Mental Health Act 1959. However, over the ensuing years, various deficiencies in the 1983 Act were apparent. Some of these concerned problems of interpretation of the Act and, in particular, the legal requirements in respect of offender-patients. Under the 1959 Act, very few cases went to judicial review on points of law and practice; under the 1983 Act, a very large number of cases were reviewed by this means. One thing that emerged from these various deliberations and decisions was the highly complex nature of the 1983 Act. These facts, coupled with excessive anxiety about the behaviour of a number of mentally disturbed individuals in the community, for example, the activities of people like Michael Fagan, who gained entry to the Queen's bedroom, and Ben Silcock's intrusion into the lion's enclosure at the London Zoo, all helped to provoke a need for change; a change that was further promoted by a small number of homicides committed by patients or former patients of the mental health services. Such events led ministers to the view that 'community care' was failing; this gave further impetus to an already acknowledged need for reform. There is also little doubt that media hype added to these concerns. The proposals for reform followed a lengthy and complicated route; it is possible to refer to them only in outline here. Those wishing to pursue them should consult the works quoted below. In November 1999, the government published a Consultation Document (Department of Health 1999a) based in part upon the advice of an expert committee chaired by Professor Genevra Richardson. Professor Richardson's committee (Department of Health 1999b) were given a narrow and highly prescribed remit by the Department of Health; in the event, a number of their very sensible proposals did not appear in the Consultation Document. For summaries of the main proposals see Prins (2001a, 2001b). The second of my two articles aimed to reflect the ambiguity and uncertainty which surrounded 'high risk' patients and offender-patients as evidenced in the White Paper. The governmental reviews were then followed by further government publications, entitled *Reforming the Mental Health Act* (Department of Health 2000). There were three parts to this documentation: Part I set out the New Legal Framework, Part II dealt with the 'high risk' patients and the third element consisted of a Summary of the Consultation Responses to the earlier government proposals. Following these publications, the government published in 2002 its Draft Mental Health Bill (Department of Health 2002a) which was accompanied by Explanatory Notes and a Consultation Document (Department of Health 2002b, 2002c). With the publication of what would seem to most observers to be a deluge of consultation material, one can only conjecture that the government had in mind that many of the far-reaching changes it had proposed would not be favourably received. This proved to be the case, and criticisms of the proposals came from numerous quarters in the mental health field. Most of the criticisms centred around the proposed all-embracing definition of mental disorder and the possibilities of abrogation of individual human rights for those adjudged to be severely personality disordered and dangerous. The draft Bill did not, as anticipated, appear in the Queen's Speech in November 2002. However, in June 2004 the Secretary of State for Health indicated that a draft Bill *would* be introduced in time for the Queen's Speech in November that year (*The Independent*, 16 June 2004). In the event, the 2007 Act followed on a third draft Bill. Seldom can an Act of Parliament have had such an elephantine gestation period. Expressions of the almost unanimous criticisms and opposition to the original proposals may be found in Peay (2000), Grounds (2001), Moncrieff (2002), Sugarman (2002), and Bindman et al. (2003). For a review of recent Scottish proposals, see also Darjee (2003). For an excellent account of the detail of the current legislation, see Fennell (2007).

Concluding comment

This chapter has covered a wide range of topics concerning the legal and administrative arrangements for dealing with mentally disturbed and disordered offenders. It is important to re-emphasize that most of the reforms introduced by the Mental Health Act 2007 are being introduced in stages. The chapters that follow attempt to delineate the more clinical aspects of management.

Notes

1 Readers may also wish to note that under Section 135 of the Mental Health Act 1983 (as amended by the 2007 Act) a police officer, approved mental health professional or other authorized person may (on application to a magistrate for a warrant) enter premises where there is reason to believe that a person suffering from mental disorder is being, or has been, ill-treated or neglected or is not being kept under proper care and control. Such a person may then be removed to a place of safety as defined in Section 136 of the Act (for further details, see Fennell 2007: 482–483).
2 I have used the words 'as amended' to save repetition, and to indicate that only minor changes are envisaged with the Act's implementation. Any major change will, of course, be identified specifically.
3 Readers should be aware that the procedures outlined in this chapter provide only the barest outline. The references in the text, and guidance for further reading, should be consulted for elaboration.
4 What started life as a probation order with a requirement for mental treatment (as an inpatient or outpatient) became, in 2005, part of a Community Sentence (Community Order) (Criminal Justice Act 2003); it is now known as a Mental Health Treatment Requirement (MHTR). The criteria for making such orders remain much the same as in previous legislation. Currently their use by the courts appear to be somewhat limited. (For a helpful discussion of such orders, see Seymour et al. 2008.)

Acts

Children and Young Persons Act 1933
Crime (Sentences) Act 1997
Criminal Justice Act 1948
Criminal Justice Act 1961
Criminal Justice Act 1967
Criminal Justice Act 1991
Criminal Justice Act 2003
Criminal Justice and Public Order Act 1994
Criminal Procedure (Insanity and Unfitness to Plead) Act 1991
Homicide Act 1957
Mental Deficiency Act 1913
Mental Health Act 1959
Mental Health Act 1983

Mental Health Act 2007
Powers of Criminal Courts (Sentencing) Act 2000
Prosecution of Offences Act 1985
Tribunals, Courts and Enforcement Act 2007

Cases

K. v. United Kingdom [1998] 40 B.M.L.T. 20
R. v. Birch [1989] 11 Cr.App.R.(S) 202. CA
R. v. Merseyside Mental Health Review Tribunal – ex parte K. [1990]
1 ALL ER 694 CA
R. v. Secretary of State for the Home Department – ex parte K. [1990]
3 ALL ER 3. 562 CA

References

Ali, S., Dearman, S.P. and McWilliams, C. (2007) 'Are Asians at Greater Risk of
Compulsory Psychiatric Admission than Caucasians in the Acute General Adult
Setting?', *Medicine, Science and the Law* 47: 311–314.
Allderidge, P. (1979) 'Hospitals, Madhouses and Asylums: Cycles in the Care of the
Insane', *British Journal of Psychiatry* 134: 321–324.
—— (1985) 'Bedlam: Fact or Phantasy', in W.F. Bynum, R. Porter and M.
Shepherd (eds) *The Anatomy of Madness: Essays in the History of Psychiatry*,
Volume 2: *Institutions and Society*, London: Tavistock.
Azvonye, I.O. (2007) 'Medical Evidence for the Purpose of Recall under Section
42(3) of the Mental Health Act, 1983', *Journal of Forensic Psychiatry and
Psychology* 18: 443–451.
Bartlett, P. and Sandland, R. (2000) *Mental Health Law: Policy and Practice*,
London: Blackstone.
Bean, P., Bingley, W., Bynoe, I., Rassaby, E. and Rogers, A. (1991) *Out of Harm's
Way*, London: MIND.
Bindman, J., Maingay, S. and Szmukler, G. (2003) 'The Human Rights Act and
Mental Health Legislation', *British Journal of Psychiatry* 182: 91–94.
Blom-Cooper, L., QC, Hally, H. and Murphy, E. (1995) *The Falling Shadow: One
Patient's Mental Health Care, 1978–1993*, London: Duckworth.
Blom-Cooper, L., QC, Grounds, A., Parker, A. and Taylor, M. (1996) *The Case of
Jason Mitchell: Report of the Independent Panel of Inquiry*, London: Duckworth.
Boswell, G. (1996) *Young and Dangerous: The Backgrounds and Careers of Section
53 Offenders*, Aldershot: Avebury.
Bowden, P. (1993) 'New Directions for Service Provision', in W. Watson and A.
Grounds (eds) *The Mentally Disordered Offender in an Era of Community Care*,
Cambridge: Cambridge University Press.
Bradley, The Rt. Hon. Lord (2009) *The Bradley Report*, London: Department of
Health.
Brown, C.S.H., Lloyd, K.R. and Donovan, M. (2001) 'Trends in Admissions to a
Regional Secure Unit (1983–1997)', *Medicine, Science and the Law* 41: 35–40.

Brunning, J. (1996) 'The Case of Jason Mitchell: Report of the Independent Panel of Inquiry', *Mental Health Review Tribunal's Members' News Sheet* 17: 5–7.

Castro, M., Cockerton, T. and Birke, S. (2002) 'From Discharge to Follow-up: A Small Scale Study of Medium Secure Provision in the Private Sector', *British Journal of Forensic Practice* 4: 31–39.

Clark, T., Kenney-Herbert, J., Baker, J. and Humphreys, M. (2002) 'Psychiatric Probation Orders: Failed Provision or Future Panacea', *Medicine, Science and the Law* 42: 58–63.

Coid, J. (1991) 'Psychiatric Profiles of Difficult Disruptive Prisoners', in K. Bottomley and W. Hay (eds) *Special Units for Difficult Prisoners*, Hull: Centre for Criminology and Criminal Justice, University of Hull.

Crown Prosecution Service (n.d.) *Code for Crown Prosecutors*, London: Crown Prosecution Service.

Darjee, R. (2003) 'The Reports of the Millan and Maclean Committees: New Proposals for Mental Health Legislation for High Risk Offenders in Scotland', *Journal of Forensic Psychiatry* 14: 7–25.

Darjee, R., Crichton, J. and Thomson, L. (2000) 'Crime and Punishment (Scotland) Act, 1997: A Survey of Psychiatrists' Views Concerning the Scottish "Hybrid Order"', *Journal of Forensic Psychiatry* 11: 608–620.

—— (2002) 'Crime and Punishment (Scotland) Act, 1997: A Survey of Sentencers' Views Concerning the Scottish "Hybrid Order"', *Medicine, Science and the Law* 42: 76–86.

Davies, S., Clark, M., Hollin, C. and Duggan, C. (2007) 'Long-Term Outcomes after Discharge from Medium Secure Care: A Cause for Concern', *British Journal of Psychiatry* 191: 70–74.

Department of Health (1992) *Report of the Committee of Inquiry into Complaints about Ashworth Hospital*, Volumes 1 and 2 (Chairman, Sir Louis Blom-Cooper, QC), Cm 2028-I and Cm 2028-II, London: HMSO.

—— (1999a) *Reform of the Mental Health Act, 1983: Proposals for Consultation*, Cm 4480, London: TSO.

—— (1999b) *Report of the Expert Committee: Review of the Mental Health Act, 1983* (Richardson Report), London: TSO.

—— (1999c) *The Future Organisation of Prison Health Care*, London: Department of Health.

—— (2000) *Reforming the Mental Health Act: Part I – The New Legal Framework, Part II – High Risk Patients, Part III – Summary of Consultation Responses*, Cm 5016-I and Cm 5016-II, London: TSO.

—— (2002a) *Draft Mental Health Bill*, Cm 5538-I, London: TSO.

—— (2002b) *Draft Mental Health Bill – Explanatory Notes*, Cm 5538-II, London: TSO.

—— (2002c) *Consultation Document*, Cm 5538-III, London: TSO.

—— (2002d) 'Prison Health Transferred to Department of Health', *Department of Health Press Release* 64N/02, 24 September.

Department of Health and Home Office (1992) *Review of Health and Social Services for Mentally Disordered Offenders and Others Requiring Similar Services* (Chairman, Dr John Reed, CB), Final Summary Report, Cm 2088, London: HMSO.

Department of Health, HM Prison Service and National Assembly for Wales (2001)

Changing the Outlook: A Strategy for the Development and Modernising of Mental Health Services in Prisons, London: Department of Health.

Department of Health and Social Security (DHSS) (1974) *Revised Report of the Working Party on Security in NHS Psychiatric Hospitals* (Glancy Report), London: DHSS.

—— (1980) *Report of the Review of Rampton Hospital* (Boynton Report), Cmnd 8073, London: HMSO.

Dixon, L. and Ray, C. (2007) 'Current Issues and Developments in Race Hate Crime', *Probation Journal: The Journal of Community and Criminal Justice* 54: 109–124.

Duffy, D., Lenihan, S. and Kennedy, H. (2003) 'Screening Prisoners for Mental Disorders', *Psychiatric Bulletin* 27: 241–242.

Dyer, W. (2006) 'The Psychiatric and Criminal Careers of Mentally Disordered Offenders Referred to a Custody Diversion Scheme in the U.K.', *International Journal of Forensic Mental Health* 5: 15–27.

Earthrowl, M., O'Grady, J. and Birmingham, L. (2003) 'Providing Treatment to Prisoners with Mental Disorders', *British Journal of Psychiatry* 182: 299–302.

East, W.N. and de Hubert, W.H.B. (1939) *Psychological Treatment of Crime*, London: HMSO.

Eastman, N. (1996) 'Hybrid Orders: An Analysis of their Likely Effects on Sentencing Practice and on Forensic Psychiatric Practice and Services', *Journal of Forensic Psychiatry* 7: 481–494.

Eldergill, A. (1997) *Mental Health Review Tribunals: Law and Practice*, London: Sweet & Maxwell.

—— (2002) 'The Legal Structure of Mental Health Services', *Journal of Mental Health Law* 7: 139–168.

Exworthy, T. and Parrott, J. (1993) 'Evaluation of a Diversion Scheme from Custody at Magistrates' Courts', *Journal of Forensic Psychiatry* 4: 497–505.

—— (1997) 'Comparative Evaluation of a Diversion from Custody Scheme', *Journal of Forensic Psychiatry* 8: 406–416.

Exworthy, T. and Gunn, J. (2003) 'Taking Another Tilt at High-Secure Hospitals', *British Journal of Psychiatry* 182: 469–471.

Fallon, P., QC, Bluglass, R., Edwards, B. and Daniels, G. (1999) *Report of the Committee of Inquiry into the Personality Disorder Unit, Ashworth Special Hospital*, 2 Volumes and Executive Summary, Cm 4194-I, Cm 4194-II and Cm 4195, London: TSO.

Fennell, P. (2007) *Mental Health: The New Law*, Bristol: Jordan.

Fennell, P. and Yeates, V. (2002) 'To Serve Which Master? – Criminal Justice Policy, Community Care and the Mentally Disordered Offender', in A. Buchanan (ed.) *Care of the Mentally Disordered Offender in the Community*, Oxford: Oxford University Press.

Fitzgibbon, D.W. (2007) 'Institutional Racism, Pre-emptive Criminalisation and Risk Analysis', *Howard Journal of Criminal Justice* 46: 99–114.

—— (2008) 'Fit for Purpose? OASys Assessments and Parole Decisions', *Probation Journal: The Journal of Community and Criminal Justice* 55: 55–69.

Fowles, A.J. (1993) 'The Mentally Disordered Offender in an Era of Community Care', in W. Watson and A. Grounds (eds) *The Mentally Disordered Offender in an Era of Community Care*, Cambridge: Cambridge University Press.

Gavin, N., Parsons, S. and Grubin, D. (2003) 'Reception Screening and Mental Health Needs Assessment in a Male Remand Prison', *Psychiatric Bulletin* 27: 251–253.

Geelan, S.D., Campbell, M.J. and Bartlett, A. (2001) 'What Happens Afterwards? A Follow-Up Study of Those Diverted from Custody to Hospital in the First 2.5 Years of a Metropolitan Diversion Scheme', *Medicine, Science and the Law* 41: 122–128.

Genders, E. (2003) 'Privatisation and Innovation – Rhetoric and Reality: The Development of a Therapeutic Community Prison', *Howard Journal of Criminal Justice* 42: 137–157.

Genders, E. and Player, E. (1995) *Grendon: A Study of a Therapeutic Prison*, Oxford: Clarendon Press.

Gledhill, K. (2009) 'The First Flight of the Fledgling: The Upper Tribunal's Substantive Debut', *Journal of Mental Health Law* 18: 81–93.

Green, G., Smith, R. and South, N. (2005) 'Court Based Psychiatric Assessment: Case for an Integrated and Public Health Role', *Journal of Forensic Psychiatry and Psychology* 16: 577–591.

Greenhalgh, N.M., Wylie, K., Rix, K.J.B. and Tamlyn, D. (1996) 'Pilot Mental Health Assessment and Diversion Scheme in an English Metropolitan Petty Sessional Division', *Medicine, Science and the Law* 36: 52–58.

Grounds, A.T. (1990a) 'Transfers of Sentenced Prisoners to Hospital', *Criminal Law Review* June: 544–551.

—— (1990b) 'The Transfer of Sentenced Prisoners to Hospital 1960–1963: A Study of One Special Hospital', *British Journal of Criminology* 31: 54–71.

—— (1991) 'The Mentally Disordered Offender in the Criminal Process: Some Research and Policy Questions', in K. Herbst and J. Gunn (eds) *The Mentally Disordered Offender*, London: Butterworth-Heinemann in association with the Mental Health Foundation.

—— (2001) 'Reforming the Mental Health Act', *British Journal of Psychiatry* 179: 387–389.

Gunn, J. (2000) 'A Millennium Monster is Born', *Criminal Behaviour and Mental Health* 10: 73–76.

Gunn, J., Maden, A. and Swinton, M. (1991) *Mentally Disordered Prisoners*, London: Home Office.

Harding, J. (2006) 'Some Reflections on Risk Assessment, Parole and Recall', *Probation Journal: The Journal of Community and Criminal Justice* 53: 389–396.

Harty, M.A., Shaw, J., Thomas, S., Dolan, M., Davies, L., Thornicroft, G., Carlisle, J., Moreno, M., Leese, M., Appleby, L. and Jones, P. (2004) 'The Security, Clinical and Social Needs of Patients in High Security Psychiatric Hospitals in England', *Journal of Forensic Psychiatry and Psychology* 15: 208–221.

Hean, S., Warr, J. and Staddon, S. (2009) 'Challenges at the Interface of Working between Mental Health Services and the Criminal Justice System', *Medicine, Science and the Law* 49(3): 170–178.

Hetherington, T. (1989) *Prosecution in the Public Interest*, London: Waterlow.

Home Office (1990a) *Report of a Review into Suicides and Self-Harm in Prison Service Establishments in England and Wales (Report by Judge Tumim to the Home Secretary)*, Cm 1383, London: HMSO.

—— (1990b) *Provision for Mentally Disordered Offenders*, Circular 66/90, MNP/90/1/55/8, London: Home Office.

—— (1991) *Prison Disturbances, 1990, Report of an Inquiry by The Rt. Hon. Lord Justice Woolf* (Parts 1 and 2) *and His Honour Judge Stephen Tumim* (Part 1), London: HMSO.

—— (1997) *Probation Statistics, England and Wales*, London: Government Statistical Service.

—— (1999a) *Suicide is Everyone's Concern: Thematic Review by H.M. Chief Inspector of Prisons for England and Wales*, London: Home Office.

—— (1999b) *The Stephen Lawrence Inquiry: Report of the Inquiry by Sir William Macpherson of Cluny* (Macpherson Report), Cm 4262-I and Cm 4262-II, London: HMSO.

Home Office and Department of Health (1991) *Review of Health and Social Services for Mentally Disordered Offenders and Others Requiring Similar Services: Steering Committee* (Chairman Dr John Reed, CB), *Report of the Services Advisory Groups with Glossary*, London: HMSO.

Home Office and Department of Health and Social Security (1973) *Report of the Review of Procedures for the Discharge and Supervision of Psychiatric Patients Subject to Special Restrictions* (Aarvold Report), Cmnd 5191, London: HMSO.

—— (1974) *Interim Report on the Committee on Mentally Abnormal Offenders* (Butler Report), Cmnd 5698, London: HMSO.

—— (1975) *Report of the Committee on Mentally Abnormal Offenders* (Butler Report), Cmnd 6244, London: HMSO.

Hucklesby, A. (1997) 'Court Culture: An Explanation of Varieties in the Use of Bail by Magistrates' Courts', *Howard Journal of Criminal Justice* 36: 129–145.

James, D. (1999) 'Court Diversion at 10 Years: Can It Work, Does It Work and Has It a Future?', *Journal of Forensic Psychiatry* 10: 507–524.

James, D.V. and Hamilton, L.W. (1991) 'The Clerkenwell Scheme – Assessing Efficacy and Cost of a Psychiatric Liaison Service to a Magistrates' Court', *British Medical Journal* 303: 282–285.

James, D., Cripps, J., Gilluley, P. and Harlow, P. (1997) 'A Court-focused Model of Forensic Psychiatry Provision to Central London: Abolishing Remands to Prison', *Journal of Forensic Psychiatry* 8: 390–405.

Jasper, L. (1998) 'Black Deaths in Custody: A Human Rights Perspective', in A. Liebling (ed.) *Deaths of Offenders: The Hidden Side of Justice*, Winchester: Waterside Press.

Jewesbury, I. and McCulloch, A. (2002) 'Public Policy and Mentally Disordered Offenders in the UK', in A. Buchanan (ed.) *Care of the Mentally Disordered Offender in the Community*, Oxford: Oxford University Press.

Jones, C., Jones, B. and Ward, S. (2002) 'Mentally Disordered Offenders: The Need for a Diversion Service in a Rural Area', *British Journal of Forensic Practice* 4: 19–23.

Jones, R. (2001) *Mental Health Act Manual*, 7th edn, London: Sweet & Maxwell.

Joseph, P. (1992) *Psychiatric Assessment at the Magistrates' Courts*, London: Home Office and Department of Health.

Joseph, P. and Potter, M. (1993) 'Diversion from Custody': 'I – Psychiatric Assessment at the Magistrates' Court' and 'II – Effect on Hospital and Prison Resources', *British Journal of Psychiatry* 162: 325–330 and 330–334.

Judge, J., Harty, M.A. and Fahy, T. (2004) 'Survey of Community Forensic Psychiatric Services in England and Wales', *Journal of Forensic Psychiatry and Psychology* 15: 244–253.

Kaye, C. and Franey, A. (1998) 'Research and Development', in C. Kaye and A. Franey (eds) *Managing High Security Psychiatric Care*, Forensic Focus 9, London: Jessica Kingsley.

Laing, J. (1997) 'The Likely Impact of Mandatory and Minimum Sentences on the Disposal of Mentally Disordered Offenders', *Journal of Forensic Psychiatry* 8: 504–508.

—— (1999) *Care or Custody? Mentally Disordered Offenders in the Criminal Justice System*, Oxford: Oxford University Press.

Laing, R.D. and Esterson, A. (1970) *Sanity, Madness and the Family: Families of Schizophrenics*, Harmondsworth: Penguin.

Laurance, J. (2003) *Pure Madness: How Fear Drives the Mental Health System*, London: Routledge.

Leff, J. (2001) *The Unbalanced Mind*, London: Weidenfeld & Nicolson.

Leicestershire County Council (1993) *The Leicestershire Inquiry, 1992: Report of an Inquiry into Aspects of the Management of Children's Homes in Leicestershire between 1973 and 1986* (Chairman Andrew Kirkwood, QC), Leicester: Leicestershire County Council.

Lelliott, P. (2009) 'Role of the Clinical Professions in the Regulation of Health Care in England: Walking the Tightrope', *Psychiatric Bulletin* 33: 321–324.

Liebling, A. (1998) *Deaths of Offenders: The Hidden Side of Justice*, Winchester: Waterside Press on behalf of the Institute for the Study and Treatment of Delinquency.

Lloyd, M.G. and Bénézech, M. (1991) 'Criminal Responsibility in the French Judicial System', *Journal of Forensic Psychiatry* 2: 281–294.

McGhee, D. (2007) 'The Challenge of Working with Racially Motivated Offenders: An Exercise in Ambivalence', *Probation Journal: The Journal of Community and Criminal Justice* 54: 213–226.

McKenzie, N. and Sales, B. (2008) 'New Procedures to Cut Delays in Transfer of Mentally Ill Prisoners to Hospital', *Psychiatric Bulletin* 32: 20–22.

Ministry of Justice (2007) *Statistics of Mentally Disordered Offenders, 2006*, London: Ministry of Justice.

Moncrieff, J. (2003) 'The Politics of a New Mental Health Act', *British Journal of Psychiatry* 183: 8–9.

Moss, K.R. (1998) *Medium Secure Psychiatric Provision in the Private Sector*, Aldershot: Ashgate.

Murray, K. (1996) 'The Use of Beds in NHS Medium Secure Units in England', *Journal of Forensic Psychiatry* 7: 504–524.

NACRO (National Association for the Care and Resettlement of Offenders) (1993) *Community Care and Mentally Disordered Offenders*, Policy Paper no. 1, Mental Health Advisory Committee (Chairman H. Prins), London: NACRO.

—— (1996) *Youth Crime Section: Briefing Paper, September*, London: NACRO.

Naughton, M. (2009) 'Does the NOMS Risk Assessment Bubble Need to Burst for Prisoners Who May Be Innocent to Make Progress?', *Howard Journal of Criminal Justice* 48(4): 357–372.

Neille, D., Saini, M.S. and Humphreys, M. (2007) 'Characteristics of Mentally Disordered Offenders for Low Secure Forensic Rehabilitation', *Medicine, Science and the Law* 47: 213–219.

Orr, E.M., Baker, M. and Ramsay, L. (2007) 'Referrals from the Glasgow Sheriff Court Liaison Scheme since the Introduction of Referral Criteria', *Medicine, Science and the Law* 47: 325–329.

Parker, E. (1980) 'Mentally Disordered Offenders and their Protection From Punitive Sanction', *International Journal of Law and Psychiatry* 3: 461–469.

—— (1985) 'The Development of Secure Provision', in L. Gostin (ed.) *Secure Provision: A Review of Special Services for the Mentally Ill and Mentally Handicapped in England and Wales*, London: Tavistock.

Parole Board (2007) *Annual Report and Accounts, 2006–2007 and Business Plan, 2003–2004*, HC 1022. London: TSO.

Parsons, S., Walker, L. and Grubin, D. (2001) 'Prevalence of Mental Disorder in Female Remand Prisons', *Journal of Forensic Psychiatry* 12: 194–202.

Peay, J. (1989) *Tribunals on Trial: A Study in Decision Making under the Mental Health Act, 1983*, Oxford: Clarendon Press.

—— (2000) 'Reform of the Mental Health Act, 1983: Squandering a Lost Opportunity', *Journal of Mental Health Law* 3: 5–15.

Penrose, L. (1939) 'Mental Disease and Crime: Outline for a Study of European Statistics', *British Journal of Medical Psychology* 18: 1–15.

Pezanni, R. (2007) 'The Recall of Conditionally Discharged Patients: The Breadth of the Secretary of State's Discretion', *Journal of Mental Health Law* 16: 219–223.

Prins, H. (1991) 'The Avoidance of Scandal: A Perennial Problem', *Medicine, Science and the Law* 31: 277–279.

—— (1993) 'The People Nobody Owns', in W. Watson and A. Grounds (eds) *The Mentally Disordered Offender in an Era of Community Care*, Cambridge: Cambridge University Press.

—— (1999) *Will They Do It Again? Risk Assessment and Management in Criminal Justice and Psychiatry*, London: Routledge.

—— (2001a) 'Whither Mental Health Legislation [Locking Up the Disturbed and the Deviant]', *Medicine, Science and the Law* 41: 241–249.

—— (2001b) 'Offenders, Deviants or Patients – Comments on Part Two of the White Paper', *Journal of Mental Health Law* 5: 21–26.

—— (2008) 'The Mental Health Act 2007: A Hard Act to Follow', *Howard Journal of Criminal Justice* 47: 81–85.

Prins, H., Backer-Holst, T., Francis, E. and Keitch, I. (1993) *Report of the Committee of Inquiry into the Death in Broadmoor Hospital of Orville Blackwood and a Review of the Deaths of Two Other Afro-Caribbean Patients: 'Big, Black and Dangerous?'*, London: Special Hospitals Service Authority (SHSA).

Quarshi, I. and Shaw, J. (2008) 'Sections 37/41 Mental Health Act, 1983: A Study of Judge's Practice and Assessment of Risk to the Public', *Medicine, Science and the Law* 48: 57–63.

Quinn, P. and Ward, M. (2000) 'What Happens to Special Patients Admitted to Maximum Security?', *Medicine, Science and the Law* 40: 345–349.

Reed, J. (2003) 'Mental Health Care in Prisons', *British Journal of Psychiatry* 182: 287–288.

Richardson, T., Kenney-Herbert, J., Baker, J. and Humphreys, M. (2002) 'Probation Orders with a Condition of Psychiatric Treatment: A Descriptive Study', *Medicine, Science and the Law* 43: 80–84.

Ricketts, D., Carnell, H., Davies, S., Kaul, A. and Duggan, C. (2001) 'First Admissions to a Regional Secure Unit Over a 16 Year Period: Changes in Demographic and Service Characteristics', *Journal of Forensic Psychiatry* 12: 78–89.

Riordan, S. and Humphreys, M. (2007) 'Patient Perceptions of Medium Secure Care', *Medicine, Science and the Law* 47: 20–26.

Riordan, S., Wix, S., Kenney-Herbert, J. and Humphreys, M. (2000) 'Diversion at the Point of Arrest: Mentally Disordered People and Contact with the Police', *Journal of Forensic Psychiatry* 11: 683–690.

Riordan, S., Wix, S., Haque, M.S. and Humphreys, M. (2003) 'Multiple Contacts with Diversion at the Point of Arrest', *Medicine, Science and the Law* 43: 105–110.

Ritchie, J., Dick, D. and Lingham, R. (1994) *Report of the Committee of Inquiry into the Care and Treatment of Christopher Clunis*, London: HMSO.

Rollin, H. (1969) *The Mentally Abnormal Offender and the Law*, Oxford: Pergamon.

—— (1993) 'A Hundred Years Ago: Malice or Madness?', *British Journal of Psychiatry* 162: 475.

Roth, M. and Kroll, J. (1986) *The Reality of Mental Illness*, Cambridge: Cambridge University Press.

Rowlands, R., Inch, H., Rodger, W. and Soliman, A. (1996) 'Diverted to Where? What Happens to Diverted Mentally Disordered Offenders?', *Journal of Forensic Psychiatry* 7: 284–296.

Scott, P.D. (1975) *Has Psychiatry Failed in the Treatment of the Offender?*, London: Institute for the Study and Treatment of Delinquency.

Seymour, L., Rutherford, M., Khanon, H. and Samele, C. (2008) 'The Community Order and the Mental Health Treatment Requirement', *Journal of Mental Health Law* 17 (May): 53–65.

Shaw, J., Tomenson, B., Creed, F. and Perry, A. (2001) 'Loss of Contact with Psychiatric Services in People Diverted from the Criminal Justice System', *Journal of Forensic Psychiatry* 12: 203–210.

Singleton, N., Meltzer, H., Gatward, R., Coid, J. and Deasy, D. (1998) *Psychiatric Morbidity among Prisoners in England and Wales*, London: Office for National Statistics.

Smartt, U. (2001) *Grendon Tales: Stories from a Therapeutic Community*, Winchester: Waterside Press.

Smith, J. and Donovan, M. (1990) 'The Prosecution of Psychiatric In-patients', *Journal of Forensic Psychiatry* 1: 379–383.

Snow, P. and Moody, E. (2005) 'Mental Health Unit', *British Journal of Forensic Practice* 7: 21–26.

Stone, N. (2003) *A Companion Guide to Mentally Disordered Offenders*, 2nd edn, Crayford, Kent: Shaw and Sons.

—— (2008) 'Independence of the Parole Board: In Court', *Probation Journal: The Journal of Community and Criminal Justice* 55: 115–116.

Street, R. (1998) *The Restricted Hospital Order: From Court to the Community*,

Home Office Research Study 186, London: Home Office Research and Statistics Directorate.

Sugarman, P. (2002) 'Detaining Dangerous People with Mental Disorders', *British Medical Journal* 325: 659.

Szasz, T. (1974) *The Myth of Mental Illness*, New York: Harper & Row.

Thomas, S., Dolan, M. and Thornicroft, G. (2004a) 'Revisiting the Role of the High Security Hospitals in England', *Journal of Forensic Psychiatry and Psychology* 15: 197–207.

Thomas, S., Leese, M., Dolan, M., Harty, M.A., Shaw, J., Middleton, H., Carlisle, J., Davies, L., Thornicroft, G. and Appleby, L. (2004b) 'The Individual Needs of Patients in High Secure Psychiatric Hospitals in England', *Journal of Forensic Psychiatry and Psychology* 15: 222–243.

Tidmarsh, D. (1998) 'Asylums or Crude Cauldrons of Containment? The Future of the Special Hospitals', *Journal of Forensic Psychiatry* 9: 505–508.

Tilt, R. (2003) Letter, *British Journal of Psychiatry* 182: 548.

Tilt, R., Perry, N. and Martin, C. (2000) *Report of the Review of Security at the High Security Hospitals*, London: Department of Health.

Towl, G., Snow, L. and McHugh, M. (eds) (2000) *Suicides in Prisons*, Leicester: British Psychological Society Books.

Vaughan, P., Austen, C., le Feuvre, M., O'Grady, J. and Swyer, B. (2003) 'Psychiatric Support to Magistrates' Courts', *Medicine, Science and the Law* 43: 255–259.

Walker, N. (1996) 'Hybrid Orders', *Journal of Forensic Psychiatry* 7: 469–472.

Watson, W. (1998) 'Designed to Care: The Clinician-Led Development of England's Regional Secure Units', *Journal of Forensic Psychiatry* 9: 519–531.

Wilson, D. and McCabe, S. (2002) 'How HMP Grendon Works in the Words of Those Undergoing Therapy', *Howard Journal of Criminal Justice* 41: 279–291.

Wilson, S. and Forrester, A. (2002) 'Too Little, Too Late? The Treatment of Mentally Incapacitated Prisoners', *Journal of Forensic Psychiatry* 13: 1–8.

Further reading

Mental health law etc.

Department of Health and Welsh Office (2008) *Mental Health Act 1983: Code of Practice*, London: TSO (guide to best practice in the mental health care and management of detained patients and certain others).

Fennell, P. (2007) *Mental Health: The New Law*, Bristol: Jordan.

Forrester, A., Ozdural, S., Muthukumaraswamy, A. and Carroll, A. (2008) 'The Evolution of Mental Disorder as a Legal Category in England and Wales', *Journal of Forensic Psychiatry and Psychology* 19: 543–560.

Peay, J. (2003) *Decisions and Dilemmas: Working with Mental Health Law*, Oxford: Hart.

Stone, N. (2003) *A Companion Guide to Mentally Disordered Offenders*, 2nd edn, Crayford, Kent: Shaw and Sons.

Female offender-patients

Allen, H. (1987) *Justice Unbalanced: Gender, Psychiatry and Judicial Decisions*, Milton Keynes: Open University Press.

Kesteven, S. (2002) *Women Who Challenge: Women Offenders and Mental Health Issues*, London: NACRO.

Walklate, S. (2004) *Gender, Crime and Criminal Justice* 2nd edn, Cullompton: Willan.

High and medium security

Black, D.A. (2003) *Broadmoor Interacts: Criminal Insanity Revisited*, Chichester: Barry Rose (clinical aspects of the work of Broadmoor Hospital for the years between 1959 and 1983, written by its one-time head psychologist).

Winchester, S. (1999) *The Surgeon of Crowthorne*, Harmondsworth: Penguin (fascinating biographical account of a Broadmoor patient who made a significant contribution to the work on the first version of the Oxford English Dictionary).

For critical accounts of medium security, see selection of articles in *Journal of Forensic Psychiatry and Psychology*, special issue 20(1), April 2009. See also 20(2).

Parole

A full account of the Board's remit, organization and work may be found in *The Parole Board for England and Wales: Annual Report and Accounts: 2006–07 (2007)*, London: TSO, *The Parole Board for England and Wales: Business Plan 2007–08*, London, *The Parole Board for England and Wales: Corporate Plan 2007–2010*, London.

Statistics – Restricted Mentally Disordered Offenders, Ministry of Justice Statistical Bulletin (2007), London (provides detailed information on numbers of restricted patients detained in, and discharged from, hospitals and units).

Chapter 4

'Thick coming fancies'

As she is troubled with thick coming fancies
That keep her from her rest.
> (The doctor to Macbeth concerning his wife's mental state,
> in *Macbeth*, Act 5, Sc. 3)

This chapter considers some of the 'thick coming fancies' – namely disturbed mental states – that have been alluded to briefly in earlier chapters. Three other quotations may help readers to focus upon the content of this chapter. Othello says, 'It is the very error of the moon; She comes more nearer earth than she was wont, and makes men mad' (*Othello*, Act 5, Sc. 2). King Lear says, 'Oh, let me not be mad, not mad, sweet heaven! Keep me in temper: I would not be mad!' (*King Lear*, Act 1, Sc. 5) and Macbeth asks of his wife's physician: 'Canst thou not minister to a mind diseas'd?' (*Macbeth*, Act 5, Sc. 3). The first quotation serves as a reminder of the many myths that surround 'madness'; the second suggests most powerfully the fear of 'madness'; and the third is indicative of our attempts to replace madness with sanity in offenders and offender-patients. The myths and fear surrounding madness (particularly if 'madness' is linked to 'badness') account for many of the problems involved in establishing various forms of community provision for those who have this dual label. In a study carried out by Claire Holden, one of my former students, and her colleagues into the use of public consultation exercises in relation to establishing secure mental health facilities, the authors found that health trusts 'tended to underestimate the depth of public feeling and this fostered . . . [local] residents' suspicions and hostility'. To offset these problems, the authors suggest that their findings 'highlight the need for trusts to be open with all interested parties as early as possible. The maintenance of an on-going dialogue with local residents, politicians, media, service-user groups, community health councils and statutory bodies is essential' (Holden et al. 2001: 513). In a thought-provoking article which is highly relevant to this problem, Pilgrim and Rogers (2003) critically examine the extent to which politicians (in particular) 'remain concerned about the special threat which psychiatric patients allegedly pose to public safety'. They note 'three contextualising factors: public prejudice; the widening remit of deviance control by psychiatry during the twentieth century; and inconsistent societal sanctions about dangerousness' (Pilgrim and Rogers 2003: 7). In providing a degree of support for this view, Walsh et al. (2003) found that in a study of some 700 patients with established psychotic disorders, those with psychosis were found to be 'at considerable risk of violent victimisation in the community' (Walsh et al. 2003: 233). This is a helpful countervailing view to the political and public notion of the dangers posed *by* those who are mentally ill. In preceding chapters I made reference to certain forms of mental disturbance and their possible relationship to criminal behaviour. Such reference was in very general terms; in this chapter, I consider aspects of mental disturbance and its relationship to criminality in more detail. The term 'mental disturbance' is used here, as in preceding chapters, to include mental disorder as now defined in the Mental Health Act 2007 in England and Wales. The 1983 Act definition included mental illness (not further defined in that Act), mental impairment, severe mental impairment, psychopathic disorder, and any other disability of the mind. The new Act simply defines it as 'any disorder or disability of mind'. As Fennell (2007) states in his excellent comprehensive discussion of the 2007 Act, 'Once the Act is in force, a person will be able to be detained if suffering from "any disorder or disability of the mind", regardless of whether the detention is for a short or long period' (Fennell 2007: 45). Personally, I prefer, for the purpose of this chapter, to use the term 'mental disturbance', since it allows us to consider states of mind that would not necessarily satisfy the strict criteria for compulsory admission to hospital or a community treatment order under the 2007 Act. The term is used in this chapter merely to encompass a range of disordered mental states, but its imperfections are recognized. (For a more detailed definition, see NACRO 1993: 4.) As I hope to demonstrate, it is reasonably easy to define mental illnesses, especially those with clear-cut aetiology (cause); it is harder to define, with a degree of acceptable precision, such conditions as mental handicap (learning disability), particularly in its milder presentations and, to a marked degree, such conditions such as severe personality (psychopathic) disorder. However, what we do know with some degree of certainty, is that mental disturbance is likely to be present in all cultures (though it may present in a variety of ways) and at all levels of society, including political and other leaders. This latter possibility can have frightening possibilities, as Freeman has demonstrated (see, for example, Freeman 1991).

'Changing the goalposts'

At the outset we are faced with the difficult task of trying to establish any clear causal connections, or even associations, between mental disturbance and criminality. This is because we are trying to make connections between very complex and different phenomena; and these phenomena are the subject of much continuing debate concerning both definition and substance. It is as though the goalposts for the game are constantly being shifted. Let me take the case of mental illness as an example of this phenomenon. There are those who seek to suggest that some forms of mental illness do not even exist. A well-known proponent of this view is Professor Szasz who, in many of his books and papers, has suggested that persons are often diagnosed as mentally ill on the grounds that they have problems in living and that these problems may affront society. Society then turns to psychiatrists to remove them from public view and conscience (see, for example, Szasz 1987). The foregoing is a somewhat bald and simplistic view of Szasz's work and, to be fair, he has written substantial rebuttals of his critics (see, for example, Szasz 1993). However, his arguments do have a kernel of truth in that he alerts us to the manner in which psychiatry may be abused. They also have a certain attractive seductiveness, but they also contain a quality of rhetoric which has been criticized by both psychiatrists and non-psychiatrists (see, for example, Sedgewick 1982; Roth and Kroll 1986). In the 1960s, there existed a popular view that much mental illness had its origins in 'conspiracies' and 'mixed messages' within families. This view is exemplified in the work of Ronald Laing and his colleagues (see, for example, Laing and Esterson 1964). (For a challenging perspective on this problem, see Bean 2008: Part Four.) At the other end of the 'spectrum' we have the more biologically orientated view that found expression in some of the earlier textbooks of psychiatry. Professor John Gunn put the position into perspective very ably when he stated that:

> somewhere in the confusion there is a biological reality of mental disorder . . . this reality is a complex mixture of diverse conditions, some organic, some functional, some inherited, some learned, some acquired, some curable, others unremitting.
>
> (Gunn 1977a: 317)

This complex picture is also compounded by the fact that the prevalence and presentation of mental disturbances appear to change over time. Some investigators such as Hare (1983) and Scull (1984) have concluded, albeit very tentatively, that the schizophrenic illnesses as we now know them possibly did not exist on any large scale in earlier times. However, anecdotal and clinical evidence would suggest that such assertions need to be viewed with a degree of caution (see Bark 1985; Eastman 1993; Gunn 1993). It is worth mentioning here that, in earlier times, there may well have been individuals presenting with psychiatric signs and symptoms in whom, these days, we would recognize a physical or organic origin. In the Middle Ages, for example, malnourishment produced a pellagric (nutritional deficiency) state with its psychological and psychiatric consequences. The use of bad or adulterated flour could produce ergot poisoning which, in turn, could produce signs and symptoms of mental illness. It has even been suggested that episodes of the so-called 'dancing mania' seen in post-medieval Italy and surrounding countries were probably due to such a cause (Camporesi 1989). Lead was commonly used in making cooking utensils, in water pipes and in wine production. This could have had harmful results, which might have produced confused and disturbed behaviour. Some people afflicted by states of so-called 'possession' probably may have suffered from similar organic causes. (For discussion of such states, see Prins 1990: Chapter 3; Enoch and Ball 2001: Chapter 11.) Occupations have also been shown to have their hazards. We may infer from Lewis Carroll's depiction of the 'Hatter', at the famous tea party in *Alice's Adventures in Wonderland*, that he was 'mad', although the author does not say so specifically; people who worked in the hat-making industry were exposed to mercury, and mercurial poisoning can produce signs and symptoms of mental disturbance. It has been suggested that Isaac Newton's well-known episodes of apparent depression, leading to withdrawal from public life and activity, may have been due to the effect of the mercuric substances with which he experimented (see Klawans 1990; Gleick 2003). Since the 1990s, much concern has been expressed about the effects of lead emissions on children's behaviour; there is also a school of thought that maintains that poor quality diet (particularly if it contains amounts of 'junk' foods and excess additives) may produce not only hyperactivity, but also antisocial behaviour in some children. However, unequivocal evidence of this, both in the United States and in Britain, does not yet appear to be available. It is difficult to provide precise figures for the numbers of people suffering from mental disorders. In a government publication *Modernising Mental Health Services* (Department of Health 1998), it was suggested that depression in one form or another 'will affect nearly half of all women and a quarter of all men in the UK before the age of 70'. They quote from a major survey published in 1995 which showed that

> one in six adults aged 16–64 had suffered from some type of mental health problem in the week prior to being interviewed, the most common being 'neurotic' conditions like anxiety and depression; and a very small proportion of the population – less than 1 per cent – had a more severe and complex psychotic mental illness, such as schizophrenia.
>
> (1.2–1.4)

The rates found in 2000 were much in line with those reported in 1995, but the proportion of people actually receiving treatment had increased considerably. Such statistics can provide only a very rough indicator of the mental health of a nation. This is because there are likely to be not inconsiderable numbers of individuals suffering from a degree of mental disturbance or distress who do not present for treatment at either their general practitioner (the most likely first port of call) or at a hospital (unless acutely mentally unwell, suicidal etc.). What we do know is that the cost of mental disorders, in terms of distress to the sufferers and their families and others close to them, is very considerable. These predicaments are well described by Jeremy Laurance, Health Editor of *The Independent*, in his book on the mental health system (Laurance 2003). Much of it is hidden from view and the figures we have represent only the tip of the iceberg. It is worth noting here that the same is true for the hidden nature of much criminal activity; the iceberg phenomenon is equally important in this respect.

When we come to consider criminal behaviour we are faced with problems similar to those outlined above. At its simplest, crime is merely that form of behaviour defined by society as illegal and punishable by the criminal law. At various times in our history, acts once judged as criminal have been redefined, or even removed from the statute books – as, for example, in the case of attempted suicide and adult (or now near adult) male consenting homosexual acts committed in private. *New* offences are also created, particularly in times of war or civil commotion. Moreover, our increasingly complex technological society has required the introduction of a wide range of laws and regulations governing many aspects of our conduct. Since much criminal behaviour is somewhat arbitrarily defined, and there are arguments about the existence and definitions of mental disturbances, it is hardly surprising that we find difficulty in trying to establish the connections between these two somewhat ill-defined and complex behaviours. Be this as it may, there are occasions when some mental disturbances do seem to be closely associated with criminal conduct, and aspects of this connection are now considered in some detail.

Mental disturbances (disorders) have been classified in a variety of ways. The two most widely acknowledged classification systems – particularly for purposes of cross-cultural research – are the *Diagnostic and Statistical Manual of Mental Disorders*, published by the American Psychiatric Association (APA 2005: 4th edn (text revision) DSM-IV-TR) and the *International Classification of Mental and Behavioural Disorders*, published by the World Health Organization (WHO 1992: ICD-10). These substantial texts cover every aspect of diagnosis and classification. Readers should also consult one of the standard textbooks of psychiatry, a good example being the very detailed two-volume work *The New Oxford Textbook of Psychiatry* (Gelder et al. 2009). Table 4.1 provides a much simplified classification of mental disorders followed by some explanatory comment.

Table 4.1 Simplified classification of mental disorders (disturbances)

Main categories[a]	Subcategories
The functional psychoses	Affective disorders Schizophrenic illnesses
The neuroses: psychoneuroses, neurotic reactions, post-traumatic stress disorder (PTSD)[b]	Mild depression, anxiety states, hysteria (hysterical reactions), obsessive-compulsive disorder
Mental disturbance as a result of infection, disease, metabolic and similar disturbance, physical trauma	Including the epilepsies[c]
Mental disturbance due to the ageing process	For example, the various dementias, certain unusual psychiatric syndromes ('eponymous' conditions)[d]
Personality abnormalities: including severe personality (psychopathic) disorder; some sexual deviations)	
Substance abuse (alcohol, other drugs, solvents)	
Mental impairment: including learning disability, mental handicap, mental retardation[e]	

Notes: (a) The following general classification could be slightly misleading, implying that the disorders are discrete entities. This is not the case. Disorders may coexist and such states are usually described as co-morbid, leading to the need for a dual diagnosis. The importance of this should never be overlooked. Childhood disorders are not included in this table (for example, childhood depression, autistic spectrum disorders such as Asperger Syndrome); I have confined myself largely to adult disorders. However, where developmental issues are relevant, they are discussed in various parts of the text (for example, in the possible genesis of severe personality disorder). (b) In recent times there has been a marked development of interest in the relationship between post-traumatic stress disorders and criminality. See, for example, Crisford et al. (2008), Friel et al. (2008) and Morel (2008). (c) The epilepsies (note the use of the plural) are essentially neurological disorders, but are included here because of their psychiatric and psychological consequences (sequelae). (d) 'Eponymous' conditions, are named after those who first identified them. This is common in both psychiatry and general medicine. See Table 4.2 (p. 123) for some psychiatric examples (see also Prins 1990: Chapter 2). (e) Mental impairment has been the subject of various titles over historical time. Some of the older terminology was highly pejorative (for example 'Mongolism', later called Down's Syndrome after the doctor who first recognized and described it clinically, feeble-mindedness, idiocy and moral defectiveness).

Some common misnomers

It is not uncommon for some of the specialist terms used in psychiatry to fall into common use or be used in a pejorative fashion. My sometime colleague on the Mental Health Review Tribunal, Dr John Grimshaw, used to make this clear in our induction courses for new MHRT members (John Grimshaw, unpublished course lecture notes, 1997). For example, demented does not mean agitated, hysterical does not mean excited and noisy, manic does not mean rushing around (although, as we shall see, people in a manic state may act somewhat frenetically). Schizophrenia does not mean split personality as in Robert Louis Stevenson's story of Dr Jekyll and Mr Hyde in 1886; rather, it refers to a gradual 'splintering' or disintegration of the personality. Neurotic does not mean over-fussy or over-anxious, and depression in the clinical sense, means being decidedly unwell and not just 'pissed off' or 'miserable'. Barbara Vine, in her novel *Gallowglass*, provides a wonderful short distinction between the two phenomena (Vine 1990: 14–15).

The functional psychoses

This term is used to describe a group of severe mental disorders for which, as yet, no evidence of underlying organic brain disorder has been demonstrated conclusively. However, there is some evidence to suggest that in time a biochemical basis for these disorders may be found. The two illnesses subsumed under this heading are the *affective disorders (bipolar or manic-depressive illness)* and the *schizophrenic illnesses*. I consider first the affective disorders. In doing so I must emphasize again that only the barest outline is provided of this and the following disorders. Specialist texts should be consulted for detailed accounts of their aetiology and management.

Affective disorders

The underlying characteristic of an affective disorder is a basic disturbance of mood (hence the term affective, meaning relating to affect or mood). In cases of *mild* depressive disorder (see later), the disturbance of mood may be sufficiently slight for it to be almost unnoticeable to those quite close to the person – to such an extent that its onset may be unnoticed. As noted in Chapter 3, this may account for the occasional failure of prison staffs to 'spot' depression in a newly remanded prisoner. In *severe* depressive disorder, the mood disturbance is much more pronounced; a useful aide-memoire is that the main characteristics are those of 'loss' (of energy, of libido (sexual drive), weight, appetite, interest in oneself and one's environment). Such features may be so pronounced that the person concerned may be quite unable to perform normal daily routines and functions. Accompanying characteristics may include varying degrees of tension, severe feelings of guilt, lack of concentration, disturbances in sleep patterns and preoccupation with what the sufferer believes to be disturbed bodily functions (such as bowel or bladder functions). For example, loss of appetite may lead to constipation, which in turn may lead to acute abdominal discomfort; the depressed person may then come to believe that some kind of cancerous tumour is eating away at their bowels – maybe as a punishment for some imagined 'sin'. Some forms of depressive disorder are also characterized by agitation, restlessness and irritability; such presentations, being somewhat atypical of depression, can lead to possible misdiagnoses. In very severe states of depression, the degree of retardation of function may be such that suicidal action will be precluded. However, as recovery takes place, such thoughts may become prominent and the person may have enough psychic and physical energy to put them into action. It is therefore of the utmost importance that such patients and their families are counselled as to the risks involved in premature discharge from hospital. This is demonstrated in the following case illustration.

Case illustration 4.1

A male patient, aged 45, had developed many of the signs of serious depression over the preceding few months (abnormally high level of anxiety, disturbed sleep pattern, loss of appetite resulting in weight loss and consequent preoccupation with bowel functions, believing he might have a tumour). He took an overdose of sleeping tablets (prescribed by his GP for his insomnia), was admitted to a local hospital and subsequently transferred to a psychiatric unit. Having received some treatment for his depression he felt better; his brother persuaded him to take his discharge (against medical advice). Two days later, he went out alone for a walk, threw himself under an express train and was decapitated.

At the other end of the spectrum is the condition known as mania or hypomania (the latter condition being the more common and is just below 'full-flight' mania). The condition is the very opposite of depressive illness. Here, activities are speeded up in gross and frenetic fashion, grandiose ideas are developed and the person becomes uncontrollably excitable, overactive, socially (and sometimes highly sexually) disinhibited, and is totally lacking in insight. Attempts by family, friends and professionals to interfere with what the sufferer believes to be his or her lawful activities may result in serious injury to themselves. This total lack of insight normally demands admission to hospital under compulsory powers. Given treatment (usually drugs like lithium) the condition can be remedied, the mood quietens down and some degree of insight regained.

There is no universal consensus as to the classification and aetiology of affective disorders. Some authorities take the view that two types may be discerned – *endogenous* (that is, where no clear precipitating factors can be seen) and *exogenous* (or *reactive*); in the latter, some stressful life event is thought to have precipitated the illness. When states of depression alternate with episodes of manic illness, the term *manic-depressive psychosis* is sometimes used. Some authorities refer to the depressive phase of this particular illness as bipolar depression, using the term unipolar depression for those cases in which manic illness is not present. Bipolar depressive states need careful monitoring, since someone may suffer a severe depressive state following a manic episode; in such cases, *suicide is always a risk*.

Classification, even if somewhat crude, is of importance from the point of view of treatment. Generally speaking, endogenous depression, if it is proving intractable, responds best to moderate applications of ECT (electroconvulsive therapy) and exogenous depression seems to respond best to medication supplemented by psychotherapy of some kind. However, I should stress that the modes of treatment I have outlined briefly, *and the indicators for them, are not necessarily as clear cut as I have suggested*.

Severe depressive disorder and crime

From time to time, we find cases in which a person charged with a grave offence such as homicide is found to be suffering from severe depressive disorder at the time of the crime. West (1965), in an early and informative study of cases of *Murder Followed by Suicide*, suggested that sufferers from psychotic depression may

> become so convinced of the helplessness of their misery that death becomes a happy escape. Sometimes, before committing suicide, they first kill their children and other members of the family . . . Under the delusion of a future without hope and the inevitability of catastrophe overtaking their nearest and dearest as well as themselves, they decide to kill in order to spare their loved ones suffering.
>
> (West 1965: 6)

Schipkowensky (1969) also stressed the extent to which the 'patient feels his personality is without value (delusion of inferiority). His life is without sense, it is only [one of] everlasting suffering, and he feels he "deserves" to be punished for his imaginary crimes' (Schipkowensky 1969: 64–65).

Case illustration 4.2

The Independent (16 February 2002) reported the case of a young mother who was found dead at the foot of a cliff in Scotland. It was said that she was suffering from postnatal depression. She was believed to have thrown her two children over the cliff and then killed herself. The police reported that the mother and her children had 'plunged about 100 feet to a ledge on the side of [a] hill. It was reported that she had a history of mental health problems.

Case illustration 4.3

This is the case of a young man under my supervision many years ago during my work as a probation officer. He had become severely depressed and became so convinced that the world was a terrible place in which to live that he attempted to kill his mother, his sister and then himself. Only swift medical intervention saved all their lives. Following a court appearance, he was made the subject of hospital care; he responded well to treatment and made a good recovery.

Trying to estimate the extent and duration of a depressive illness and its relevance to serious offences such as homicide is very difficult. Gunn et al. (1978) put the position very clearly:

> It is very difficult to establish *unless several helpful informants are available* whether a depressed murderer is depressed because he has been imprisoned for life, depressed because of the conditions in which he has been imprisoned, depressed by the enormity of his crime, or whether he committed murder because he was depressed in the first place.
>
> (Gunn et al. 1978: 35, emphasis added)

The comment by Gunn et al. emphasizes the importance of the availability of a full social history of the offender and the detailed circumstances in which the crime was committed.

Finally, in this brief discussion of depression and crime, a significant comment is made by Higgins (1990; see also White 2005):

> Depression may result in serious violence, tension and pre-occupation building up over a protracted period and an assault committed in a state of grave psychological turmoil. The act itself might then act as a catharsis, the individual not afterwards appearing depressed nor complaining of depression *and the diagnosis then being missed.*
>
> (Higgins 1990: 348, emphasis added)

Hypomanic disorder and crime

I have already alluded to some of the main features of this disorder. From time to time, persons suffering from manic disorder of varying degrees of severity may come to the attention of the courts because of their outrageous, insightless and potentially dangerous behaviour. The following two case examples illustrate the nature of the condition; in the second example, the outcome was such that a court appearance was avoided.

Case illustration 4.4

This is the case of a car salesman in his twenties. He initially impressed his employer as a bright, energetic and very enthusiastic worker. However, it was not long before his ideas and activities took a grandiose and highly unrealistic turn. For example, he sent dramatic and exaggerated letters daily to a wide range of motor manufacturers. His behaviour began to deteriorate rapidly, he lost weight through not eating (he 'never had time') and he rarely slept. One night, in a fit of rage directed towards his 'unsympathetic' employer, he returned to the car showrooms, smashed the windows and did extensive damage to several very expensive cars. He appeared in court, was remanded for psychiatric reports, and was eventually hospitalized under the Mental Health Act.

Case illustration 4.5

A young woman became increasingly convinced that certain members of the Cabinet were her close friends and would assist her in her grandiose schemes for the development of a quite unrealistic business enterprise. When her calls to Downing Street were not reciprocated, she became increasingly angry and threatened with physical violence those she saw as obstructing her. She was quite without insight, did not believe she was ill, and because of her threats to others she was hospitalized, but not before some consideration was given to prosecuting her for threatening behaviour. Following treatment by medication, her mood became slightly less high, though she remained very irritable, somewhat disinhibited and showed little insight. It was envisaged that she would need to remain in hospital for some time until her mood stabilized and her potentially dangerous preoccupations diminished.

The characteristics of this type of patient are worth re-emphasizing, since they justify the 'mental illness' label very clearly. They consider themselves to be omnipotent and become convinced that their wildest ideas are, in fact, entirely practical. Because there is no impairment of memory, they are capable of giving persuasive rationalized arguments and explanations for support of their actions. It is important to stress that such persons are very difficult to treat without the use of compulsory powers, since they fiercely resist the idea that anything is wrong with them. However, though lacking insight, they can appear deceptively lucid and rational; it is this that makes their behaviour a very real risk to others. As already noted, they can be not only verbally hostile, but also physically aggressive to those they consider are obstructing them in their plans and activities. Persons in full-flight hypomanic states can be some of the most *potentially* dangerous people suffering from a definable mental illness (see also Higgins 1990).

Schizophrenic illnesses

At one time, it was customary to speak of schizophrenia in the singular; to some extent, this is still the case, but increasingly, the recognition that there are a variety of 'illnesses' within this term has led some to prefer the use of the word in the plural, using the descriptive term, the *schizophrenias*.

Debate exists concerning both the causes and classification of these disorders. Currently, it seems safe to suggest that environmental and social factors play a significant part in the onset and duration of the illnesses, but there are certainly likely to be neuro-biochemical factors which may determine the onset and course of the illness in the first instance. In other words, a person may have an 'in-built' predisposition to develop the disorder which may be enhanced or precipitated by environmental stresses (see Murray et al. 2002; Gelder et al. 2009).

The most important single characteristic feature of schizophrenic illness is the disintegration and, in some cases, apparent destruction of the personality. In the schizophrenic illnesses, we are dealing with what can best be regarded as a 'splintering' of the mind – the personality shatters and disintegrates into a mass of poorly operating components rather than a near division into two parts – as lay interpretations of the word would imply (see earlier discussion). In particular, there is likely to be a degree of incongruity between thoughts and emotions. The main signs and symptoms of the illnesses fall under the following broad simplified headings, though they will not necessarily be present in every case. As we shall see, some of them are of considerable forensic importance.

- *Disorders of thinking:* delusions are common; for example, a person may believe that his or her thoughts are being stolen by others.
- *Disorders of emotion:* these may range from excessive anxiety and perplexity, and a flattening of mood (sometimes interrupted by severe outbursts of rage) on the one hand, to complete incongruity of affect (emotion) on the other: for example, giggling at something non-sufferers would consider sad.
- *Disorders of volition:* the key characteristic here is likely to be apathy and a consequent withdrawal from social intercourse. The individual may behave in a very negative fashion – a presentation sometimes described technically as *negativism.*
- *Psychomotor symptoms:* periods of complete lack of emotion or a stuporose state may be interspersed with outbursts of sudden and unpredictable violence.
- *Hallucinations:* in the schizophrenias these are mostly (but not exclusively) of an auditory nature. They may consist of voices which tell the sufferer to do certain things or, alternatively, the person may state that his or her thoughts can be heard and controlled by others. Occasionally, the individual may believe that people are interfering with them: for example, if this supposed interference is sexual, it may result in an unprovoked assault on an innocent stranger.

Over the years, psychiatrists and others (with varying degrees of agreement) have classified the schizophrenic illnesses. For example, one of the two major textbooks on psychiatric classification and presentation, the DSM-IV-TR (APA 2005: 19), gives a fivefold classification as follows: Paranoid Type, Disorganized Type, Catatonic Type, Undifferentiated Type and Residual Type. I have simplified this classification but not, I hope, to the point of oversimplification. In practical terms, the divisions I list below are usually more complicated and not so clear cut; readers should be aware of this. For example, I have not made reference above to those illnesses on the borderland of schizophrenia such as the so-called schizo-affective disorders where, as the term implies, the sufferer may demonstrate signs and symptoms of both a schizophrenic and an affective (depressive) disorder. It is also very important to recognize that some of the signs and symptoms of schizophrenic illness can be present in other disorders, including certain organic conditions and alcohol or drug induced psychoses. Such co-morbidity has important implications when we come to consider forensic-psychiatric aspects of the schizophrenias.

- *Simple schizophrenia:* in these cases, the onset appears to be fairly gradual, occurs in early adult life and is so insidious that the initial signs and symptoms may not be recognized by those near to the sufferer. Social behaviour is impoverished and the emotions appear to be blunted or shallow. The course of the illness and its lengthy duration may gradually wear away the personality, involving a schizophrenic process of steady deterioration.
- *Hebephrenic schizophrenia* (from the Greek 'youthful'): the onset, which occurs most frequently in late teenage or early adult life, is often quite florid and dramatic and accompanied by delusions and hallucinations. The individual may deteriorate fairly rapidly and require urgent treatment.
- *Catatonic schizophrenia:* this condition is seen much more rarely today than in the past; this is due, in part, to the early use of certain drugs that seem helpful in this condition. The key characteristics are withdrawal from social intercourse accompanied by muteness; the latter sometimes interspersed with occasional episodes of unprovoked violence. In some cases, the limbs may be rigid and board-like. In others, they take on a curious characteristic known as *flexibilitas cerea* (waxy flexibility) in which the limbs are placed and then left in the most contorted positions almost indefinitely. Attempts to return them to normal merely result in the patient returning them to their original position. The violent outbursts shown by such patients are fortunately rare; these, and the violence exhibited in cases of acute hypomania, may account for the small number of incidents of *serious* violence committed by some psychiatric inpatients.
- *Paranoid schizophrenia and paranoid states:* in these cases, the keynotes are irrational over-suspiciousness and ideas of self-reference. Such

persons may be convinced that people are continually talking about them, for example accusing them of sexual indiscretions or persecuting them in other ways. As I shall demonstrate shortly, such ideas are quite irrational and are highly impervious to reasoned explanation and discussion.

Schizophrenic illnesses, violence and dangerous obsessions

This is an emotive topic and rational discussion is not helped by the manner in which the media tend to hype up individual cases and, in the process, lead the public to extrapolate from these singular and rare events to those suffering from schizophrenic illnesses more generally. However, it has to be acknowledged that research since the late 1960s has indicated that, given certain conditions, there does seem to be an association between some forms of schizophrenia (notably the paranoid varieties) and violence. Indications of such evidence may be found in contributions by McNeil et al. (1988), Linquist and Allebeck (1990), Swanson et al. (1990), Hodgins (1992), Link et al. (1992), Monahan (1992), Gunn (1993), Link and Steuve (1994), Wesseley et al. (1994), Taylor (1995), Hodgins and Muller-Isberner (2001), Monahan et al. (2001), Hodgins and Gunnar-Janson (2002), and Monahan (2002). Two more recent contributions add to the evidence, Walsh et al. (2002) and Moran et al. (2003). Notorious cases tend to 'hit the headlines', with Peter Sutcliffe, referred to in Chapter 2, being a case in point. Many years earlier, a man called John Ley – a former Australian senior law officer – was convicted of conspiring to murder a man he deludedly believed to have seduced his wife. Ley was sentenced to death but, after sentence, was found to be suffering from a paranoid illness; he was sent to Broadmoor where he subsequently died. In more recent times, Ian Ball was ordered to be detained in a (special) high security hospital as a result of an elaborate and skilful (yet highly delusional) plan to kidnap Princess Anne in the Mall in London. And, of course, there have been cases in the United States of murderous attacks on political figures by individuals allegedly suffering from some form of schizophrenic illness. It is important to stress that people suffering from this type of disorder may begin to demonstrate 'oddnesses' of behaviour *for some time before the disorder emerges in an acute or very obvious form.* Intervention at this stage may, in some cases, help to prevent a tragedy. Some of the research studies quoted above suggest that certain factors may help to contribute to violence in some schizophrenic patients. It is very important to consider these factors in order to give the lie to the popular media conception that all schizophrenic patients are potentially violent. In point of fact, they are more likely to harm or suffer harm to themselves than others (Walsh et al. 2003). The delusional ideas would appear to be as follows.

First, active delusions seem to be powerful factors where the patient perceives some threat, where there is a lessening of mechanisms of self control and dominance of the patient's mind by perceived forces that seem to be beyond his or her control. These phenomena are sometimes described in the literature as

> perceived threat and control override (TCO) . . . TCO involves the belief that (1) others are controlling one's thoughts by either stealing thoughts or inserting them directly into one's mind; and (2) others are plotting against one, following one and wanting to hurt one physically.
>
> (Bjorkly and Havik 2003)

Professor Tony Maden describes them very succinctly. 'The typical scenario is the persecutory delusion in which the sense of threat is used to justify pre-emptive action and overrides a person's normal inhibitions against violence' (Maden 2007: 27). However, Monahan (2002) suggests the espousal of a degree of caution in respect of delusions. In the very large-scale MacArthur study of the relationship between psychotic illness (notably schizophrenia) and violence, he and his colleagues found that

> the presence of delusions [did] not predict higher rates of violence among recently discharged psychiatric patients . . . In particular, the much discussed findings of a relationship between threat/control over-ride delusions and violence were not confirmed . . . on the other hand, non-delusional suspiciousness – perhaps involving a tendency towards misperception of others' behaviour as indicating hostile intent – does appear to be linked with subsequent violence, and may account for the findings of previous studies.
>
> (Monahan 2002: 68–69)

Second, when the disorder is associated with the ingestion of drugs or other forms of substance abuse. For example, Wheatley (1998) studied a sample of schizophrenic patients detained under the Mental Health Act in a medium secure unit. His results confirmed a high degree of co-morbidity of alcohol and substance abuse and schizophrenia in detained and forensic patients (see also Marshall 1998). Similarly, in a large-scale American survey involving patients in the community, Steadman et al. (1998) found the incidence of violence was substantially elevated by the abuse of drugs and alcohol.

Third, the impact of co-morbid personality disorder on violent behaviour in psychosis has been emphasized by Moran et al. (2003). They examined a sample of 670 patients with established psychotic illness. When screened for the presence of co-morbid personality disorder, they found 28 per cent exhibited the disorder and these patients 'were significantly more likely to behave violently over the two-year trial period [involved in the study]' (Moran et al. 2003: 129). The importance of co-morbidity and dual diagnosis is also emphasized in a comprehensive review by Crichton (1999). He concluded that

> the more *specific* that studies have been in comparing particular diagnosis and symptom cluster with *specific* criminal behaviour, the more useful they have been in establishing causality. An emerging theme is the importance of dual diagnosis, particularly substance misuse and psychosis and violent crime.
>
> (Crichton 1999: 659, emphases added)

Finally, concurrent social problems such as loss of family ties and homelessness may tend to contribute to the likelihood of violence.

Paranoid disorder and 'dangerous obsessions'

I am aware that this heading does not bear much relationship to conventional classificatory practice, but I have provided it in order to try to simplify somewhat complex forms of behaviour. I trust any of my psychiatrist colleagues who chance upon this book will afford me a degree of latitude!

As already noted, one of the key characteristics of those suffering from one or other of the forms of paranoid illness is their systematized delusional beliefs (and sometimes hallucinatory experiences). These may take the form of irrational and unshakeable beliefs that they are being persecuted by others, or that they have a need to be the persecutor (as we saw in Sutcliffe's case). It is important to emphasize here that such systems of belief are not necessarily peculiar to those suffering from a schizophrenic disorder; they may be part of an affective illness or be associated with chronic alcohol abuse or, in some cases, organic disorder. Two points of cardinal importance need emphasizing here. First, such sufferers may begin to develop certain oddnesses of behaviour for some time *before the disorder emerges in an acute or very obvious form*; sensitive observation and possible intervention *may*, in some cases, help to prevent a tragedy. However, it has to be acknowledged that this may be very difficult on both clinical and ethical grounds. Second, persons developing paranoid beliefs may do so in an encapsulated (contained) form; thus, a seriously paranoid person may appear perfectly sane and in command of him or herself in all other respects. The illness may be so well encapsulated that an unwary or unskilled observer may be very easily misled. It is only when the matters which the delusional system has fastened on are broached, that the severity of the disorder may be revealed.

The sinister and potentially highly dangerous nature of these forms of disorder are clearly delineated in a condition known variously as 'morbid jealousy', 'sexual jealousy', 'delusions of infidelity', the 'Othello Syndrome' etc. This disorder will now be used as an example of these particular distortions of thinking and behaviour. Dealing with the phenomena in this way can be used to illustrate by way of extrapolation similar kinds of behaviours in which obsessional preoccupations can become highly dangerous. For this reason, I shall also include a brief discussion of the fairly recently described preoccupation with the phenomenon of 'stalking', though of course not all stalkers suffer from mental disorder in a strict medical sense. As indicated above, some of these conditions are given a variety of titles. It might be more helpful to abandon these discrete categories and consider the totality of these phenomena within a framework of 'dangerous obsessions', irrespective of the focus of the unwanted attentions. In suggesting this, I am conscious that I am dealing here with a highly selected range of dangerous obsessions; others are, of course, equally dangerous, particularly when they are motivated by overwhelming desires for control and subjugation, as in some forms of serious personality (psychopathic) disorder. In the 1940s, Lagach (1947) made the important observation that love involved two elements: a desire to dedicate and give oneself to the beloved – 'amour oblatif' – and the desire to possess and subjugate, which he called 'amour captatif'. He considered that those who fell into the second category were especially prone to jealousy. Jealousy is, of course, a universal phenomenon which varies in intensity from the so-called 'normal' to the intensely pathological. A very useful discussion of the 'generality' of jealousy may be found in Pines (1998) and clinical management of the condition is discussed in a comprehensive account by White and Mullen (1989). Jealousy has been described in a variety of ways in the world's great literature. There are examples in Giovanni Boccaccio's *The Decameron* and in the work of Leo Tolstoy; and, of course, one of the best descriptions of its potential lethality and intractability is graphically described by Shakespeare in *Othello*. Emilia, wife to Iago and maid to Desdemona, puts it in these terms:

> But jealous souls will not be answer'd so;
> They are not ever jealous for the cause;
> But jealous for they are jealous; 'tis a monster
> Begot upon itself, born on itself.
> $\qquad$ (*Othello*, Act 3, Sc. 4)

And the condition is further depicted graphically by Shakespeare in *The Winter's Tale*, where the irrationally jealous Leontes says:

> Were my wife's liver
> Infected as her life, she would not live
> The running of one glass.
> (*The Winter's Tale*, Act 1, Sc. 2)

In my view, the characterization of Leontes gives a more powerful exemplification of delusional jealousy than the description of Othello – to the extent that I have suggested elsewhere that we might better describe the condition as the *Leontes* rather than the *Othello* Syndrome (Prins 1996). In more modern times, the crime novelist Patricia Cornwell has an apt observation on the nature of dangerous obsessive love:

> Attraction turns to obsession, love becomes pathological. When he loves, he has to possess because he feels so insecure and unworthy, is so easily threatened. When his secret love is not returned, he becomes increasingly obsessed. He becomes so fixated his ability to react and function becomes limited.
>
> (Cornwell 1995: 221)

She also makes a further compelling and disturbing observation: 'Murder never emerges full blown from a vacuum. Nothing evil ever does' (Cornwell 1995: 312). Such an observation has great importance when we attempt to discover and assess risk triggers.

The boundary between 'normal' and 'abnormal' in this field is difficult to delineate with precision. Mullen (1981), who has made highly significant contributions to the study of pathological love, states:

> In our culture, jealousy is now regarded not just as problematic or undesirable, but increasingly as unhealthy, as a symptom of immaturity, possessiveness, neurosis and insecurity.
>
> (Mullen 1981: 593)

In similar fashion, Higgins (1995; see also Maden 2007) believes that 'the boundary between normal and morbid jealousy is indistinct':

> Jealousy, or a tendency to be jealous, can be a normal relative transient response in an otherwise well adjusted individual to frank infidelity; one feature in an individual with a paranoid personality disorder . . . or a frankly delusional idea arising suddenly and unexpectedly either as a single delusional idea or one of a number of related ideas in a typical psychosis.
>
> (Higgins 1995: 79)

There is no universal agreement as to the causes of 'encapsulated' delusional jealousy. However, a number of explanations have been offered. For example, the person suffering from the delusion may themselves have behaved promiscuously in the past and have harboured an expectation that the spouse or partner will behave in similar fashion. Other explanations have embraced the possibility of impotence in the sufferer with consequent projection of feeling a failure on to the spouse or partner. Freudian and neo-Freudian explanations stress the possibility of repressed homosexuality resulting in fantasies about the male consort of a spouse or partner. Pines (1998) suggests the importance of a 'triggering event'; she states that 'Although jealousy occurs in different forms and in varying degrees of intensity, it always results from an interaction between a certain predisposition and a particular triggering event' (Pines 1998: 27). She considers that predispositions to jealousy vary widely between individuals. For someone with a high predisposition, a triggering event can be as minor as a partner's glance at an attractive stranger passing by. For most people, however, the trigger for intense jealousy is a much more serious event, such as the discovery of an illicit affair. For others, the trigger can be imagined (as reported by R. Dobson in *The Independent*, 3 September 1998).

The following three case illustrations demonstrate the varied and irrational nature of such sufferers' beliefs.

Case illustration 4.6

This is the case of two men described by the nineteenth-century physician Clouston and presented in the first edition of Enoch and Trethowan's classic work *Uncommon Psychiatric Syndromes* (1979):

> I now have in an asylum, two quite rational-looking men, whose chief delusion is that their wives, both women of undoubted character, have been unfaithful to them. Keep them off the subject and they are rational. But on that subject they are utterly delusional and insane.
>
> (Enoch and Trethowan 1979: 47)

Case illustration 4.7

This case, drawn from my own experience, supports the irrationality of belief so graphically described by Clouston. This concerned a man in his sixties, detained in a high security hospital without limit of time (Mental Health Act 1983, Sections 37/41) with a diagnosis of mental illness. He had been convicted of the attempted murder of his wife and had a history of infidelity during the marriage. There was a family history of mental illness. The index (original) offence consisted of an attempt to stab his wife to death and a serious assault on his daughter, who tried to intervene to protect her. He gave a history of prolonged, but quite unfounded, suspicions of his wife's infidelity. He arranged to have her followed, interrogated her persistently as to her whereabouts (which were always quite innocent) and searched her personal belongings for proof of her alleged unfaithfulness. He even inspected her under-clothing for signs of seminal staining in order to confirm his delusional beliefs. He also believed that neighbours and others were colluding with his wife to aid her in her alleged unfaithfulness. As is so often the case, he was regarded as a model patient, well liked by staff and other patients and, to the unwary and uninformed observer, presented himself as completely rational and reasonable. It was only when asked about his wife at his Mental Health Review Tribunal hearing that his delusional ideas about her expressed themselves with ominous intensity. Although he had been detained in hospital for some years and his delusional ideas were not as intrusive as they were on admission, they were still easily evoked. The likelihood of his release was remote. His wife had been urged to sever her connections with him entirely and make a new life for herself. However, as is sometimes the case, she was reluctant to do so, hoping that her husband's attitude would change. The wife's attitude is of considerable importance. This is because, in such cases, the irrational beliefs held by the sufferer are not easily amenable to treatment; the wife is likely, therefore, to be at considerable risk whenever the offender or offender-patient is released. Some slightly cynical professionals, when asked 'What's the best treat-ment?', have been known to respond by saying 'Geographical', meaning that the woman would be strongly advised to move home and change her name; it seems that the woman in such an instance is doubly victimized. Supervision of these and similar cases requires the utmost vigilance and a capacity to spot subtle changes in both mood and circumstances. It is well known that sufferers from delusional jealousy and similar delusional states have what my friend, Dr Murray Cox, used to describe as 'unfinished business' to complete. Even if, sadly, the first victim dies as a result of the delusionally held beliefs, surrogate victims may be sought out and be similarly at risk. Careful questioning of the pathologically jealous individual is essential. Mullen (1996) describes it cogently as follows:

> The clinician attempting to treat a patient or client in whom jealousy features must keep constantly in mind the possibility of an escalation of conflict pro-ducing resort to violence. Careful and repeated questioning of the jealous individual and their partner is advisable, and, wherever possible, informants outside the relationship should be consulted.
>
> (Mullen 1996: 204)

Case illustration 4.8

The third example demonstrates the manifestation of the disorder in a less severe form and is somewhat unusual in that it was described by the sufferer. It demon-strates the possibility of improvement (in a less severe case) and was provided by

Christine Aziz (1987) in a national newspaper. Her jealousy, which developed in relation to her partner:

> came unannounced one warm autumn day; a tight pain in the stomach, sweating and nausea. Still cocooned in the intense early days of love, I discovered Simon [her partner] had slept with someone else and, even more hurtful, had denied it. Jealousy had come to stay. The occasional twinge was bearable, but this torment was the surgeon's knife without the anaesthetic. It came unannounced and for hours; the evil turned me into a stranger to those who knew and loved me.
>
> (Aziz 1987: 15)

Case illustration 4.9

A near-psychotic state of jealousy was depicted in the BBC's adaptation of Trollope's novel *He Knew He was Right* (April–May, 2004). In the television presentation, Louis develops an unshakeable delusional belief that his wife has been having an affair with a Member of Parliament – a man who, it must be said, has an alleged reputation as a 'womanizer'. He eventually dies in a severely weakened and highly distressed state.

In Christine Aziz's case, she was happily able to realize to some degree that her behaviour was irrational; she was eventually helped through behavioural psychotherapy to deal with it and find some peace of mind.

Erotomania

The notion of pathological (obsessive) possessiveness may assist us in linking pathological jealousy on the one hand, and erotomania on the other. It will also act as a useful springboard for a discussion of 'stalking'. Erotomania (*psychose passionelle*) is a condition in which the sufferer believes with passionate and irrational conviction that a person, who is usually older and socially quite unattainable (such as an important public figure), is in love with them. The condition is sometimes described eponymously as De Clérambault's Syndrome (see Table 4.2). Taylor et al. (1983) suggest five criteria for making the diagnosis in the female:

- Presence of the delusion that the woman is loved by a specific man.
- That the woman has previously had very little or no contact with this man.
- The man is unattainable in some way.
- That the man nevertheless watches over, protects or follows the woman.
- That the woman should remain chaste.

Table 4.2 Some less well-known psychiatric and eponymous conditions

Othello Syndrome[a]	The patient (most often male) harbours the delusional belief that their spouse or partner is unfaithful
Capgras Syndrome	A rare disorder, in which the sufferer believes that a closely related relative has been replaced by a double
Frégoli's Syndrome	A disorder in which a false identification of persons connected with the individual occurs in strangers
De Clérambault's Syndrome	The patient believes that someone not known to them personally (and usually of some fame) is in love with them
Cotard's Syndrome	Sufferer has delusions of nihilism and poverty
Ekbohm's Syndrome	Patient has delusions of infestation by insects, maggots, etc
Munchausen's Syndrome and Munchausen by Proxy	The individual seeks attention by repeated attempts to gain hospital admission for non-existent medical conditions. Munchausen by proxy is similar, but a child is the focus of the 'false illness' in order for the parent to gain attention; the harm to the child often being caused by the parent (usually the mother). The preferred, more recently introduced, term is Fabricated and Induced Illness (FII)
Gilles de La Tourette's Syndrome	Seen almost exclusively in childhood and adolescence; main features are uncontrollable tics, suggestive, and sometimes obscene, utterances by the patient
Folie à Deux, Folie à Trois, Folie à Plusieurs	A condition in which beliefs of delusional intensity are transmitted from the patient to significant others in their close environment
Couvade Syndrome[b]	A husband exhibits the features of pregnancy as being experienced by his wife or partner
Koro (Shook Yang) genital retraction syndrome[c]	The patient believes that his penis is shrinking

Notes: (a) Syndrome means, in general terms, the signs and symptoms of a disease or combination of behavioural characteristics. (b) Both 'Couvade' and 'Koro' are best described as 'culture bound syndromes'; other examples are 'amok' and 'possession' states. (c) For additional references to a number of these conditions, see Friedmann and Faguet (1982), Prins (1990), Franzini and Grossberg (1995), Bhugra and Munro (1997) and Enoch and Ball (2001).

Some of the above criteria could, of course, be applied if the sufferer was male. Taylor et al. (1983) found that medication helped their patients to feel more relaxed, but that this did not lead necessarily to an early resolution of their amorous beliefs. As with delusional jealousy, the condition can be a potentially dangerous one, since sufferers may seek to attack those who reject their 'advances' and those who they consider to be their rivals for the attentions of those they obsessively love. Some of these activities are characteristic of the behaviour of certain so-called 'stalkers'; I consider these next.

'Unwelcome attentions' – stalking

Each era seems to produce its own shibboleths, be they adult sexual behaviour (and abuse), child abuse, including child sexual abuse of various kinds (for example, ritual satanic abuse), so-called 'serial killing' and, more recently, errant medical practitioners, Internet pornography and violence in the workplace. To this last we must now add the behaviour known popularly as 'stalking'. As Meloy (1998) aptly states: 'Stalking is an old behaviour, but a new crime. Shakespeare captured certain aspects of it in the obsessive and murderous thoughts of Othello'. He goes on to remind his readers that 'Louisa May Alcott . . . author of *Little Women* . . . also wrote a novel about stalking in 1866. *A Long Fatal Love Chase* remained undiscovered and unpublished for over a century' (Meloy 1998: xix). There is a growing recent literature on the topic and in what follows I have been highly selective; readers will find the books and articles referred to helpful in filling in the gaps in my presentation. The UK has been somewhat slower than other countries to introduce legislation to deal with the problem; for example, the North Americas have had anti-stalking (harassment) legislation for some time. The Protection from Harassment Act 1997 came into being because of a growing concern about the phenomenon fostered by the publication of a number of cases of well-known people who had been the subject of what can perhaps best be described as 'unwelcome attentions'. Section 1(1) of the 1997 Act states that a person must not pursue a course of conduct which amounts to harassment of another, and which he knows, or ought to know, amounts to harassment of another. The Act does not provide a specific definition of harassment and the courts tend to rely on the subjective experiences of victims. The Act creates two 'levels' of the offending behaviour. The first is to be found in Section 2 of the Act and may be dealt with summarily (i.e. by a magistrates' court) and is currently punishable by a maximum sentence of six months' imprisonment. The second, and more serious form of the offence, is that of causing fear of violence (Section 4) and is punishable on indictment by a maximum penalty of five years' imprisonment imposable by a crown court. (For a detailed critical discussion of the Act, see Finch 2002.) Harris (2000) carried out a study into the effectiveness of the legislation. She found that

> the most common reason given for harassment was that the complainant had ended an intimate relationship with the suspect. Victims

were often unaware of the existence of the legislation and that [they] had often endured the unwanted behaviour for a significant time before reporting it.

(Harris 2000: 2)

Overall, the conviction rate in those cases ending in a court hearing was 84 per cent; a conditional discharge was the most frequent disposal. Over a half of the convictions were accompanied by a 'restraining order'; this is an option available to the courts under the Act as a means of endeavouring to prevent a repetition of the harassment. A study by Petch (2002) adds weight to Harris's (2000) findings into the effectiveness of the Act. He concluded that 'The Act would be more effective if it was used by police, prosecutors and the courts more consistently. A programme of widespread dissemination of the provisions within the Act is now called for' (Petch 2002: 19). Legal and psychological aspects have also been reviewed by McGuire and Wraith (2000). The extent to which the 'public' have a clear perception of what constitutes 'stalking' has been explored in an interesting article by Sheridan and Davies (2001).

Readers may be surprised to know how widespread the problem is. In a study conducted by Budd and Mattinson (2000), as part of the regular updating of the *British Crime Survey*, it was estimated that in defining stalking as 'an experience of persistent and unwanted attention' (Budd and Mattinson 200: 3), 2.9 per cent of adults aged between 16 and 59 had been stalked in the year of the survey. This, they state, equates to 900,000 victims. An estimated 770,000 victims had been distressed or upset by the experience and 550,000 victims had been subjected to violence, threatened with violence or had been fearful that violence would be used. Risks of these unwanted attentions were particularly high for young women between 16 and 19. About one-third of the incidents were carried out by someone who was in an intimate relationship with the victim, a further third involved an acquaintance of the victim and only one-third of incidents involved strangers. The victims' most common experiences were 'being forced to talk to the offender, silent phone calls, being physically intimidated and being followed' (Budd and Mattinson 2000: 3). A quarter of male victims and a fifth of the women said the perpetrator had used physical force. 'Seven in ten victims said they had changed their life-style as a result of the experience. Women were more likely to have done so than men' (Budd and Mattinson 2000: 3). Other research carried out into the perceptions of stalking on the part of both men and women tends to add weight to these findings (see Sheridan et al. 2000; Sheridan et al. 2001; Sheridan et al. 2002). There have been numerous attempts to classify stalkers by their motives and behaviour. Kamphuis and Emmelkamp (2000) conducted an extensive review of these aspects. In particular, they noted the work of Zona et al. (1993), Harmon et al. (1995), Wright et al. (1996) and Mullen et al. (1999,

2000). The authors of the review suggest that 'most authors agree on the importance of the relationship between stalking in the context of some sort of prior relationship and stalking where there has not been a real relationship at all' (Kamphuis and Emmelkamp 2000: 207). They quote the classification by Zona et al. (1993):

> (a) the 'classic' erotomanic stalker who is usually a woman with the delusional belief that an older man of higher social class or social esteem is in love with her [see entry under de Clérambault in Figure 4.2], (b) the love-obsessional stalker, who is typically a psychotic stalker targeting famous people or total strangers and, most common, (c) the simple obsessional stalker, who stalks after a 'real' relationship has gone sour leaving him with intense resentment following perceived abuse or rejection.
>
> (Kamphuis and Emmelkamp 2000: 207)

They also quote Mullen et al. (1999), who have made significant contributions to this topic. Kamphuis and Emmelkamp (2000) present a slightly different classification under five headings:

> (a) the rejected stalker, who has had a relationship with the victim and who is often characterised by a mixture of revenge and desire for reconciliation; (b) the stalker seeking intimacy, which includes individuals with erotomanic delusions; (c) the incompetent stalker – usually intellectually limited and socially incompetent individuals; (d) the resentful stalker, who seeks to frighten and distress the victim; and finally (e) the predatory stalker, who is preparing a sexual attack.
>
> (Kamphuis and Emmelkamp 2000: 207)

It is not difficult to see that the individuals illustrated in both these classifications can prove to be potentially highly dangerous. For this reason Kamphuis and Emmelkamp suggest that

> there is a clear need to derive a consensus on a typology of stalkers, with associated diagnostic criteria. At present there is no evidence that one proposed typology is superior to another. The typology eventually agreed upon should have clear implications for treatment.
>
> (Kamphuis and Emmelkamp 2000: 207)

For a contribution to the state of the art on this topic, see Meloy (2007); for a description of a group of patients in high security with a history of stalking behaviour, see Whyte et al. (2008) and for harassment of Members of Parliament in Canada, see Adams et al. (2009); for treatment by means of dialetical behaviour therapy, see Rosenfeld et al. (2007). Before leaving this subject, we should note that abuse of Internet facilities has added another dimension in the form of what has been described as 'cyberstalking'. Interesting examples of this phenomenon have been provided by Bocij and McFarlane (2003), Bocij et al. (2003) and Sheridan and Grant (2007).

Minor offences

Those suffering from schizophrenic illnesses sometimes commit minor offences. What forms do these take? In some cases, where the illness is of insidious onset, there is often an accompanying decline in social competence; in which case the sufferer may well succumb to temptations (sometimes prompted by others) that they might well have resisted had they been in good mental health. Those suffering from so-called 'simple schizophrenia' may demonstrate a steady diminution of social functioning accompanied by withdrawal from society. Such sufferers may come to the attention of the authorities through offences such as begging, breach of the peace (insulting words and behaviour) or acts of vandalism (criminal damage). They often form part of the sad 'stage army' described so aptly in the late 1960s by Rollin (1969), shunted as they are between hospital, prison and community.

Section summary

Although, as I have indicated, the contribution of schizophrenic and associated illnesses to criminality is very low, they may be of considerable importance in *particular cases*, notably when a degree of co-morbidity and substance abuse exists and any delusions experienced are of a persecutory nature. For those who may have professional involvement with the individual concerned (for example, probation officers and other social workers, penal institution and other residential staffs, the police, general practitioners etc.) it is as well to be aware of the significance of even slight changes in behaviour, but also, more importantly, to be aware of *atypical* behaviour. These may give clues (along with other evidence) to the possibility of an underlying schizophrenic illness (see, for example, Gunn and Taylor 1993: Chapter 8).

The neuroses, psycho-neuroses, neurotic reactions and crime

The terms 'neuroses' and 'psycho-neuroses' (which, for the most part, are used synonymously – psycho-neuroses being the older of the two terms) when used correctly (and not pejoratively – see earlier discussion) describe a wide range of conditions which are characterized by certain specific mental and physical signs and symptoms. It is erroneous to think that the neuroses are less disabling than psychotic conditions. Although the signs and symptoms in neurosis may not be so florid and intrusive, the effects of some neurotic conditions can be severely disabling, as in obsessive-compulsive states where sufferers are compelled to undertake ritualistic activities which gravely affect their lives. As with the classifications of mental disturbances more generally, there is no absolute consensus as to classification, but for our purposes I trust the following will suffice:

- mild depression
- anxiety states
- hysterical and associated states
- obsessive-compulsive states.

In this section I have concentrated upon mild depression, anxiety states and hysterical and associated states; even this concentration will inevitably be somewhat superficial. Those readers wishing to obtain comprehensive accounts of them should consult works like the two-volume *New Oxford Textbook of Psychiatry*, edited by Gelder et al. (2009). It is also as well to remember that any classification is not discrete; that is, the conditions and their signs and symptoms frequently overlap. We also need to remember an important distinction between (a) common neurotic traits (seen in most of us!); (b) more serious neurotic traits or reactions; and (c) fully developed neurotic illness. The notion of a continuum (as with more serious mental illnesses such as the psychoses) is a useful one.

Mild depression and crime

Instances of mild depression may not always be recognized immediately. This is because the behaviour of the sufferer may depart only slightly from the 'norm'. However, many of the signs and symptoms of serious (psychotic) depression referred to earlier may be present but in less severe form. The following is an example.

Case illustration 4.10

A married woman of 60, of impeccable previous character, for no apparent reason (she had plenty of money with her) stole a tin of beans from a supermarket. The offence seemed quite out of character and when she appeared in court she was remanded for a psychiatric examination. This subsequently showed that she had suffered for a considerable time from mild depression. One of the effects of her depression was to leave her confused. She was made the subject of a community rehabilitation order (probation order) with a requirement for outpatient treatment.

In a study carried out in the 1950s, but still relevant, Woddis (1964) cited several cases in which stealing occurred against a background of depressive illness. Most of his examples were of middle-aged or late-middle-aged women. However, he also cited the unusual case of a young man of 21 charged with the persistent theft of motor vehicles. He had a history of recurrent mild depressive attacks which seemed to be clearly associated timewise with his thefts. Drug-induced abreactive treatment helped him to reveal, while under its influence, that his offences had started at the time his father had been burned to death in a lorry accident. The young man had intense feelings of guilt that he had not reached his father in time to rescue him. When these matters were brought more clearly into consciousness and clarified, the stealing stopped. From time to time, I have come across cases of young men and women who have claimed that they have embarked on a series of crimes because they felt low or fed-up – as though the offending behaviour would supply a buzz or a lift for their low spirits. This element of needing a 'high' will be referred to again in relation to individuals who are seriously personality disordered in Chapter 5. Occasionally, the past and recent histories of these young men and women have revealed a number of depressive elements, but it would have been difficult to have applied the clinical label 'neurotically depressed' to many of them. Such examples illustrate the need for very careful history-taking so that the relevance of depressive factors may be assessed as accurately as possible.

Anxiety states and crime

True anxiety states are characterized by a morbid or pervasive fear or dread. They may occur as a single symptom or in conjunction with other psychiatric disturbances – such as depressive illness. Often, such anxiety can be said to be associated with some specific environmental situation or stress as in the phenomenon of post-traumatic stress syndrome (see Table 4.1). This latter disorder has been the subject of much argument and litigation following war service and natural or human-made disasters of one kind or another. In other cases, the anxiety state is said to be 'free-floating' – a nameless and non-specific dread. Symptoms can include palpitations, giddiness, nausea, irregular respiration, feelings of suffocation, excessive sweating, dry mouth and loss of appetite. Anxiety states in 'pure culture' rarely account for criminal acts, but morbidly anxious individuals may feel so driven by their anxieties that they may commit an impulsive offence. Such rare offences also seem to occur in individuals where the anxiety is accompanied by, or associated with, an obsessive and perfectionist personality. The following case is an example of such phenomena.

Case illustration 4.11

A young man in his early twenties made a serious and unprovoked attack upon an innocent passer-by in the street. As he put it, 'I just exploded. I don't know why; the tension I had been feeling lately become unbearable.' Subsequent psychotherapy over a long period revealed a very vulnerable personality accompanied by a lack of self-esteem and a compulsive need to work in order to keep unnamed anxieties at bay. Later, as psychotherapy continued, it became apparent that many of his problems were associated with his relationship with his father, which bordered upon hatred. The innocent passer-by just happened to look like his father and, therefore, the assault was in many respects no mere accident. I usually describe this type of offence to my students as the 'innocent stranger in the street syndrome'. This is dealt with later in Chapter 10 on risk.

Finally, I should emphasize that anxiety has been discussed here in a very specific and narrow sense. I am not referring to situations where an offender or alleged offender is apparently almost pathologically anxious in the context of his or her present predicament (for example, facing a court hearing or being detained in prison). The comments by Gunn et al. (1978) quoted earlier in relation to depression, are equally relevant in this connection.

Hysterical and associated states and crime

The clinical condition of hysteria has a long history and can be defined very loosely as the existence of mental or physical symptoms for the sake of some advantage (for example, compensation or attention of some kind), although the sufferer is not completely aware of the motive. As I have already suggested, the term is often used quite incorrectly by lay people. It is not to be taken to mean 'having hysterics' or acting histrionically (highly dramatically), though both these characteristics *may* be demonstrated by hysterics in certain situations. It needs also to be distinguished from hysterical personality. Hysterical symptoms can be classified in a somewhat oversimplified fashion as follows:

* Those associated with the senses, for example deafness or blindness.
* Those associated with motor symptoms, for example paralysis, spasms or tremors (somatization disorder or Briquet Syndrome).
* Those where mental symptoms present, such as memory loss (which may sometimes be associated with a fugue or wandering state), pseudo-dementia, Ganser Syndrome (see later), stupor, hysterical phobias. These may also present as anxiety and depressive states in which the person may react in difficult or unpleasant situations with symptoms of these latter disturbances of mind. The keynotes in all these disorders are symptoms of *conversion* or *dissociation* (sometimes known nowadays as dissociative states). Conversion symptoms may occur, for example, in hysterical states in the form of fits which may be superficially similar to those produced in epilepsy (see later). Dissociation arises when the

individual has a conflict which produces anxiety as described, for example, in Breuer and Freud's (1936) early work on hysteria, but the latter is overcome by some manifestation of physical or mental illness which submerges the real anxiety. Because of the processes at work, one may notice in hysterical individuals that the emotions which should accompany events, or memories of them, are often inappropriate; thus an account of an experience given by an hysteric, which one would expect to produce sadness, may be given with a bland smile on the face (*la belle indifférence*).

From a forensic-psychiatric point of view, it will be fairly obvious that a number of these conditions are of considerable importance – of these, hysterical amnesia, fugues and Ganser Syndrome are the most significant and are now considered in more detail. Amnesias due to *organic* disorders or disease are dealt with in the section concerned with these states but again, as with other mental conditions, there are degrees of overlap. In some instances, it is difficult, if not impossible, to distinguish a genuine hysterical illness from simulation or malingering. The following are pointers to possible differences:

- In malingering, the motivation is more or less at a conscious level. The symptoms are usually of sudden onset and have some connection with a situation the malingerer is keen to avoid; see Enoch (1990) and Heinze (2003) for the uses of psychological testing. See also Resnick (1994), Pollock (1996) and Kucharski et al. (2006).
- The malingerer's 'symptoms' are usually over-acted and exaggerated, as was the case with John Haigh, the so-called 'acid bath murderer', who feigned insanity to avoid conviction and sentence for murder (for details, see Prins 1990: Chapter 5). It is possible for even highly skilled professional workers to be misled occasionally; some chronic mental hospital patients or clinic attenders can become adept at picking up and simulating a range of psychiatric signs and symptoms.
- Symptoms may sometimes be made to order. For example, if the examiner of the suspected malingerer suggests a certain symptom of illness being feigned is absent in the individual's presentation, the malingerer will sometimes try to produce it.
- When feigning illness, many of the usual signs and symptoms associated with the illness may be missing.
- The signs may be present only when the malingerer is being observed. This is very important from a forensic-psychiatric point of view, as a true picture of the supposed malingerer may emerge only after fairly lengthy and close observation. Generally speaking, it is exceptional for skilled observers to be fooled but, very occasionally, it can happen as in the following case illustration.

Case illustration 4.12

A man was sentenced to be detained in hospital under the Mental Health Act, having been convicted of a series of serious sexual assaults on males. The doctors who examined him had always shared *some* doubts about the nature of his illness. Over time, it emerged that he had feigned illness. He was discharged from hospital, arrested immediately following discharge, prosecuted and sentenced for perverting the course of justice; the prison sentence passed was of a length commensurate with what he would have received had he been given a penal disposal in the first instance. (For an interesting account of malingered psychosis, see Broughton and Chesterman 2001.)

There are two other conditions allied to malingering that must be mentioned as they are also of forensic-psychiatric interest. The first is pseudo-dementia and the second is Ganser Syndrome. Pseudo-dementia, as the name implies, is closely akin to malingering or simulation of insanity. An individual of normal intelligence may say, for example, that 4+4=9, or will incorrectly give, or strangely twist, the most simple facts. In these cases, the examiner will usually have the impression that the person knows the right answers. However, differential diagnosis is sometimes very difficult, because pseudo-dementia may coexist alongside a genuine organic defect or illness. Ganser Syndrome is, in many ways, very like pseudo-dementia and takes its name from the physician S.J.M. Ganser, who first described the condition in a lecture given in 1897 – calling it 'A Peculiar Hysterical State'. Ganser stated that:

> The most obvious sign they present consists of their inability to answer correctly the simplest questions which are asked of them, even though by many of their answers they indicate they have grasped, in large part, the sense of the question, and in their answers they betray at once a baffling ignorance and a surprising lack of knowledge which they most assuredly once possessed, or still possess.
>
> (Ganser, translated in Schorer 1965: 123)

Another phenomenon that should be mentioned here is so-called 'hysterical amnesia'. From time to time, offenders may claim an amnesic episode for their crime or the events leading up to it. A classic example was that of Gunther Podola, tried and convicted in 1959 for killing a police officer (*R. v. Podola* [1959] 3 All ER 418). There appears to be a consensus that the difference between a genuine and feigned amnesia attack is more likely to be one of degree than of kind. Both conditions may exist in the same person and be serving a common purpose, namely loss of memory for an alleged crime. Power (1977), an experienced prison medical officer, has suggested that the following pointers may help to elicit whether an amnesia is genuine:

- An amnesic episode of sudden onset and ending may be suggestive of a feigned loss of memory.
- The crime itself may give clues. Motiveless crime may be committed in an impulsive fashion, without any premeditation or attempt to conceal it; it may be committed with unnecessary violence and in the presence of witnesses.
- Careful comparisons of the accounts given by police and by the defendant may provide helpful evidence of inconsistencies.
- Have there been past amnesic episodes? If so, the current episode may be more likely to be a genuine one. This is also true, of course, in determining the relevance of past episodes of somnambulism in cases where somnambulism is being used as a defence against responsibility for crime (Power 1977).

In an interesting and somewhat provocative article, Stone (1992) suggests that it is often unproductive to try to determine with any degree of exactness whether an amnesia is organic or psychogenic. He also notes that *victims*, especially of violent crime 'can suffer from memory loss similar to that seen in . . . perpetrators' (Stone 1992: 342). He goes on to state that:

> It is perhaps in this direction that the way forward lies in understanding the causes of psychogenic amnesia without the hindrance of having to decide whether the amnesia is genuine or not, a task that is fruitless.
>
> (Stone 1992: 342)

For discussion of amnesia more generally, see Whitty and Zangwill (1977), Lishman (1997) and Porter et al. (2001), and, more specifically, for forensic implications, see Pyszora et al. (2003), Birch et al. (2006) and Vattakatuchery and Chesterman (2006).

Before passing on to 'organic' factors, it is important to mention two 'hysterical-type' phenomenon that have assumed an increasing degree of interest in recent years. The first concerns the controversial phenomenon of so-called 'multiple personality disorder'. The currently accepted criteria are, first, the existence within the person of two or more distinct personalities, each with its own relatively enduring pattern of perceiving, relating to and thinking about the environment and self, and second, at least two of these personalities or personality states taking full control of the person's behaviour. The presentation is likely to be characterized by the coexistence of relatively consistent, but alternate separate, sometimes very numerous, identities with recurring episodes of distortion of memory and frank amnesia. Various studies have suggested that this strange disorder may not be as uncommon as was once thought to be the case. However, an alternative (and somewhat convincing) view is that the medical attention such persons receive merely serves to facilitate the expression of the symptomology and adds to its proliferation (see Merskey 1992; Wilson 1993; Keyes 1995; James 1998, James and Schramm 1998; Enoch and Ball 2001: Chapter 6).

The second concerns the phenomenon known as Munchausen's Syndrome and Munchausen's Syndrome by Proxy or, as it is now known, Fabricated and Induced Illness. As we noted earlier in this chapter, in the first form of the disorder the person complains of, and receives, extensive treatment for various somatic complaints, travelling from one hospital to the next (sometimes they are described as 'hospital hoboes' or 'hospital addicts'). The term Munchausen Syndrome is something of a misnomer. First, because the famous eighteenth-century nobleman, Baron Münchhausen, from whom the name of the condition is derived may have been a great fabricator and wanderer, but he was *not* addicted to hospitals. Second, the term is considered by some to be too narrow for what is believed to be a wide range of personality disorders. In an interesting article, Hardie and Reed (1998) suggest that conditions such as fantastic lying (pseudologia fantastica) and factitious disorder (Munchausen type syndrome) and what they call impostership, could usefully be subsumed under a new heading of 'Deception Syndrome'. Gibbon (1998) has described a case of Munchausen's Syndrome as presenting as an acute sexual assault. In a subsidiary condition, Munchausen's Syndrome by Proxy (Fabricated and Induced Illness), a mother or significant other may inflict a variety of injuries upon a child, requiring hospital treatment. In such cases, there appears to be a pattern of attention-seeking behaviour and the derivation of vicarious satisfaction from the attention given to the child. In recent times, the methods used by those professionals to detect this particular syndrome have been considered to be somewhat questionable and over-intrusive (see Tantam and Whittaker 1993; Adshead and Bluglass 2005).

Mental disorder (disturbance) as a result of 'organic' and allied conditions

For the sake of simplicity I propose to consider all of the above under the broad, but somewhat unscientific, rubric of 'organic' disorders. The reason for including them is that although some of them figure but rarely in criminal activity, *it is their very rarity that makes them important.* This is because professionals without a medical training or orientation are often, understandably, somewhat ill informed about physical (organic) conditions that may play an important part in a person's behaviour or misbehaviour. This applies with particular force to those in the probation, social work and counselling professions, where an understanding of human behaviour is frequently, and perhaps understandably, based on an emphasis on psychological, social and emotional influences. The importance of what might be described as 'brain behaviour' in determining responsibility for crime, in an age in which we now have sophisticated devices for measuring such activity (such as a variety of brain scanning techniques) have been described by Buchanan (1994) (see also Howard 2002; Blair et al. 2005). Further reference to this aspect is to be found in Chapter 5 of this volume.

Infections

These include meningitis, encephalitis and a number of other infections. It is not uncommon for marked changes in behaviour to occur after an infective illness such as encephalitis, particularly in children; these changes may sometimes be accompanied by the development of aggressive and antisocial tendencies. It is also worth noting here that in older or elderly persons infections of the urinary tract (UTIs) may produce confusion and disorientation, and unless a urine analysis is undertaken, the signs and symptoms may be mistaken for a stroke or other cerebral disorder.

Huntington's Disorder (formerly known as Huntington's Chorea)

This is a comparatively rare, directly transmitted, hereditary condition. The onset of the disorder (which is terminal) is most likely to occur in the middle years of life and is characterized by a progressive deterioration of physical, mental and emotional functioning, including the choreiform (jerky) movements characteristic of the disorder. Sufferers from the condition may sometimes behave unpredictably and antisocially, though such instances are uncommon. Because of the hereditary transmission of the disorder and its terminal nature, relatives need active counselling and support.

General paresis and crime

This is a form of neurosyphilis and has sometimes been described as dementia paralytica or General Paralysis of the Insane (GPI). The disorder develops as a result of a primary syphilitic infection and attacks the central nervous system (CNS). Symptoms may appear many years after the original infective incident. Individuals suffering from the disorder may begin to behave unpredictably and irritably. Such signs may be accompanied by euphoria and grandiosity; indeed the presenting signs and symptoms may be mistaken for a hypomanic attack (see earlier discussion). Any acts of 'outrageous' behaviour in a person of previous good character on the part of a person so afflicted should alert professionals to the possibility of the disorder being present. Nowadays neurosyphilis is not seen with any great degree of frequency (whereas in the nineteenth and early twentieth centuries it was fairly widespread). Its disappearance is due largely to early diagnosis and the use of antibiotics.

Alcoholic poisoning and crime

The prolonged and regular ingestion of alcohol may bring about serious brain damage with consequent behaviour changes. It may lead to disorders of consciousness, known as 'twilight states'. One such phenomenon has sometimes been described as *mania à potu* in which the afflicted individual may react in an extreme manner to even very small amounts of alcohol; such states may result in violent outbursts. Both chronic alcoholism and alcoholic psychosis are characterized by impairment of memory. Such impairment often results in the person trying to fill in gaps in their accounts of event by use of their imagination – a phenomenon known technically as 'confabulation'. It is seen in conditions such as Korsakoff's Syndrome. This particular condition also presents with nutritional deficiency and abnormalities in the peripheral nerve endings. Alcohol acts as a cerebral depressant. The Porter in *Macbeth* describes it well in relation to sexual matters – as follows. He is asked by Macduff: 'What three things does drink especially provoke?' In reply the Porter refers to lechery among other things, and says:

> Lechery, sir, it provokes, and unprovokes: it provokes the desire, but it takes away the performance. Therefore much drink may be said to be an equivocator with lechery: it makes him, and it mars him; it sets him on, and it takes him off; it persuades him and disheartens him, makes him stand to and not stand to.
>
> (*Macbeth*, Act 2, Sc. 3)

Here we have in the most graphic terms the role of strong drink in relation to erectile function and performance. Drink is sometimes consumed in the hope that it will enhance sexual performance; whereas, in fact, as alcohol is a cerebral depressant it has the reverse effect. Anecdotally, it has been said that publicans who abuse alcohol to a chronic extent may lose erectile function – hence the condition known rather crudely as 'brewer's droop'. This is defined in *The New Partridge Dictionary of Slang and Unconventional English* as 'a temporary inability to achieve an erect penis caused by drinking too much alcohol, especially beer' (Dalzell and Victor 2006: 263). The source appears to be Australian, circa 1970 (Dalzell and Victor 2006).

The effects of alcohol on individuals who may already have brain damage from other causes may be considerable and have catastrophic consequences, notably of a violent kind.

Other toxic substances

Earlier in this chapter, reference was made to the effects on behaviour of such substances as contaminated flour, mercury etc. In addition, chemicals used in industrial processes where there is inadequate fume extraction may affect behaviour and produce states of confusion; these may lead occasionally to aggressive outbursts. Such instances are, of course, rare, but again, because of their comparative rarity, their importance may be overlooked by the unwary.

Metabolic, other disturbances and crime

Low blood sugar (hypoglycaemia) may occur in certain predisposed individuals who have gone without food for a prolonged period. Judgement may become impaired, they may show extreme irritability coupled with a degree of confusion and in such a state they may come into conflict with the criminal justice system. Such states are important in cases such as diabetes or, more particularly, unrecognized diabetes. Prompt action may be necessary before coma or even death intervene(s). Those with untreated excess thyroid levels (thyrotoxicosis) may become irritable, aggressive and occasionally antisocial. In recent years, some interest has been focused on the relevance of the menstrual cycle to criminality, particularly violent criminality. Dr Katharina Dalton (1982) was involved in a small number of homicide cases where pleas had been put forward that pre-menstrual syndrome (PMS) constitutes an abnormality of mind within the meaning of the Homicide Act 1957. However, such pleas do not appear to have become widespread (D'Orban 1983).

Brain trauma, tumour, brain diseases and crime

It is important to emphasize that, from time to time, cases of brain trauma or tumour are missed – sometimes with tragic consequences. An injury to the brain (however caused) is quite likely to produce a degree of concussion which may sometimes be prolonged. Such injuries may give rise to mental retardation (learning disability) or to forms of epilepsy (see later discussion of both these phenomena). Such persons may be amnesic, but such amnesia will differ from the amnesia described earlier. Following recovery of consciousness, there may be noisy delirium – a condition *not* observed in hysterical or malingered amnesia. Organically, amnesic individuals may sometimes appear to be normal initially and only gradually, following careful examination, does it emerge that they have been behaving 'automatically' (see Fenwick 1990, 1993; Ebrahim and Fenwick 2008). In contrast, in cases of hysterical amnesia, memory may return spontaneously within twenty-four hours or so. Organically amnesic persons are likely to want to do their best to remember events and may appear to be annoyed by their defective memory. In contrast, hysterical amnesics may show a complete inability to recall any events before a specific time. In addition, hysterically amnesic individuals, unlike those showing organic amnesia, may have perfect command of their speech and be well in control of their other faculties (see Williams 1979). The following case illustrates some of the tragic forensic consequences of brain damage.

Case illustration 4.13

This concerned a former miner, aged 36, whose personality changed after suffering severe head injuries in a pit accident. Following essential brain surgery, he suffered hallucinations and became aggressive towards his family. During one of these episodes, he threw burning coals around the living room, setting fire to the house. He was charged with arson, convicted, and made the subject of a probation order with a requirement that he undertake medical treatment. (Leicester Mercury, 29 September 1984: 11) (see also discussion of Hadfield's case in Chapter 2).

Occasionally, the dementing processes of developing old age (of which Alzheimer's Disease is perhaps the best known example) may be associated with behaviour that not only is out of character, but also may be highly impulsive, disinhibited and aggressive. Any such behaviour occurring out of the blue in late mid-life that seems odd, out of character, and carried out (perhaps repeatedly) in the presence of witnesses, should alert police, prosecuting and probation authorities to the possibility of a dementing process, or to the presence of a malignancy of some kind. In respect of the latter, tests are now available which enable even quite small brain tumours to be diagnosed. In addition, clinical and forensic psychologists have developed a range of tests that can determine the presence and extent of a dementing process (see L. Miller 1992; E. Miller 1999). In a timely contribution, Yorston (1999) reminds us that research into elderly people is sparse and, as he states:

> With an ageing population and ever-dwindling continuing care resources, the elderly are going to come into conflict with the law more often. If justice and humanitarian principles are to be upheld, the need for specialist assessment and management of elderly offenders is likely to increase.
>
> (Yorston 1999: 193)

(See also Curtice et al. 2003; Nnatu et al. 2005; O'Sullivan and Chesterman 2007.) We should also note here that increasing attention is being paid to elderly people as *victims* of aggression and violence (see Brogden and Nijhar 2000; Brogden 2001).

Epilepsies and associated disorders and crime

The epilepsies in their various presentations are not, strictly speaking, psychiatric illnesses, but neurological disorders manifested primarily by an excessive or abnormal discharge of electrical activity in the brain. Many thousands of people will have an epileptic attack of one kind or another at some stage in their lives; even for those who have major attacks, it is usually possible to lead a perfectly normal life with the aid of medication. There are many forms of epilepsy and they have been reviewed extensively in the standard textbooks, such as that by Lishman (1997) in the various editions of his book *Organic Psychiatry*. Some forms of epilepsy may be caused by head injury or brain damage, others are of unknown origin (*idiopathic*). There are several types of epileptic phenomena: *grand mal* (major convulsions); *petit mal* (often so minor as to be non-discernible to the onlooker); *temporal lobe epilepsy* (sometimes characterized by sudden unexpected alterations of mood and behaviour – and of particular forensic-psychiatric interest); *Jacksonian epilepsy* (a form of the disorder named after Hughlings Jackson, himself a sufferer, who first identified it). This is a localized cerebral convulsion following traumatic brain damage; partial seizures and more generalized convulsive seizures. Fenwick, in a number of papers, has described in some detail the relationship between epileptic seizures and diminishment of responsibility for crime (see, for example, Fenwick 1993). Gunn (1977b) and Gunn et al. (1978) carried out a number of classic and important surveys into the relationship between epilepsy and crime more generally (particularly violent crime). It was found that more epileptic males were taken into custody than would have been expected by chance – a ratio of some seven or eight per thousand. This is considerably higher than the proportion of epileptics found in the general population. About one-third of Gunn et al.'s (1978) cases were found to be suffering from temporal lobe epilepsy and temporal lobe cases were found to have a higher previous conviction rate. But it was the group suffering from idiopathic epilepsy who had received disproportionately more convictions for violence than any other group.

However, Gunn cautions us not to place too much emphasis on the relationship between epilepsy and crime. In doing so, he makes three important points. First, the epilepsy itself may generate social and psychological problems, which in turn can lead to antisocial reactions. Second, harmful social factors, such as overcrowding, parental neglect and allied problems, may lead to a higher than average degree of both epilepsy and antisocial behaviour. Third, environmental factors such as those just described may lead to behavioural disturbances that not only lead to brushes with the law, but may also aggravate accident and illness proneness. Such disturbances in themselves may produce an excess prevalence of epileptic phenomena. In this respect, it is of interest to note a study by Fearnley and

Zaatar (2001) in which they explored the presence of a family history of epilepsy in prisoners detained in HM Prison Liverpool. The indications were 'that prisoners have a high prevalence of family history of epilepsy'. The study also showed that 'prisoners who report such a history have significantly more psychological problems than those prisoners without such a family history' (Fearnley and Zaatar 2001: 305). Although it has been stated that there is no very strong *proof* of a general relationship between epilepsy and crime (particularly violent crime), it may well be very important in the individual case (see Delgado-Escueta et al. 1981). For this reason, expert assessment is very important as is careful community monitoring. This is particularly the case if the person is on medication. Not only does this need to be taken regularly but also, as stated earlier, horrendous results may occur if such medication is taken with alcohol (even in small amounts) or with illicit drugs. It is also important to note that repetitive fits over prolonged periods may result in further brain damage.

There is a further collection of signs and symptoms akin to epileptic phenomena, described as the Episodic Dyscontrol Syndrome; sometimes also described as 'intermittent explosive disorder' or 'limbic' rage. Lucas (1994), in a comprehensive review of the literature on the condition, cites some fifteen or so alternative labels that have been used over the years. The features, found in a very small group of individuals who, in the absence of demonstrable epilepsy, brain damage or psychotic illness, may show explosively violent behaviour without any clearly discernible stimuli, so that the explosive reaction seems out of all proportion to minimal provocation. Lewis and Carpenter (1999), in an article discussing the legal implications of the condition, suggest that:

> Episodic dyscontrol is relatively easy to diagnose and responds very well to drug therapy, eliminating any unwanted (by the sufferer as well as society) existing violent behaviour and any possible future 'criminal' behaviour. Recognition of the condition may result in justice being meted out for genuine, remorseful sufferers, differentiated from people who *choose* violence (for whatever reason) or at least have the capacity to choose violence.
>
> (Lewis and Carpenter 1999: 21)

They go on to suggest that individuals engaging in this form of behaviour should be able to claim partial exculpation of criminal responsibility by an extension of the existing law as framed under the Homicide Act 1957. However, Lucas (1994), in his extensive review of the topic, is less sanguine about the diagnosis, suggesting that:

> Despite its 25 year survival, episodic dyscontrol may represent [an] impracticable or obsolete idea . . . and as such may be destined for the compost heap of history . . . The fate of psychiatric concepts, however,

is not determined by merit alone and episodic dyscontrol may yet prove another tenacious perennial, which to change metaphors, will long survive its obituaries.

(Lucas 1994: 401)

The debate continues.

Mental impairment (learning disability) and crime

As indicated earlier, various descriptive terms have been used for what we now term learning disability. It is important to emphasize at this point that lay people sometimes confuse mental *illness* with *mental impairment* (the term I shall use henceforth); the two conditions are entirely separate, but they can coexist in some individuals. In general and oversimplified terms, it can be said that the mentally *ill* person starts life with normal intelligence but, for a variety of reasons (as described earlier in this chapter), becomes ill and deviates from the so-called norm. The mentally impaired person never had the endowment of normal intelligence, or lost it in infancy or in early life. This point is demonstrated clearly in the use of the now obsolete descriptive terms for the condition, 'amentia' or 'oligophrenia', both of which mean lack or absence of mind. It must be stressed that mental impairment is a relative concept. It used to be assumed, quite incorrectly, that the degree of impairment could be assessed purely in terms of intellectual capacity as measured by IQ tests. Though these are still of some importance, it is imperative to have regard for the social functioning of the individual, in particular family and social supports or lack of them.

CAUSAL FACTORS

There are a very large number of known possible causes for mental impairment. Some of the most familiar are listed below:

- Infection in the mother, notably rubella (German measles) contracted in early pregnancy.
- Illness in infancy or early childhood, for example, meningitis or encephalitis (as already discussed).
- Brain damage to the infant before, during or after birth. This may occur as a result of prematurity, or as a result of anoxia (lack of oxygen) due to various causes. Brain damage (mild or severe) after birth may occur as a result of physical child abuse or neglect by parents or others.
- Chromosomal abnormalities, of which the best known is Down's Syndrome – named after Dr Langdon Down, who first described it as a specific condition.

- Other 'inborn' causes, for example, the disorder known as phenyl-ketonuria – a condition in which some children are unable to cope with the phenyaliline content of normal diets; failure to observe a correct dietary regime will result in severe mental impairment.
- Exacerbation of an existing mild impairment (from whatever cause) by lack of social and intellectual stimulation, poor nutrition and poor antenatal and postnatal care.
- Exposure to excess alcohol and certain illicit drugs in pregnancy, or occasionally exposure to certain therapeutic drugs and vaccines used in infancy.
- Exposure to radiation.

Mental impairment and crime

Cases of mild or moderate mental impairment are the most likely conditions to come to the attention of the criminal justice system. In any event, as my colleague Dr Ken Day pointed out, 'The contribution of the mentally handicapped to the criminal statistics is small'. He goes on to suggest that:

> Although the prevalence of offending in the mentally handicapped appears to have remained unchanged over the years, increase is to be anticipated in the coming years as implementation of Care in the Community policies expose more mentally handicapped people to greater temptations and opportunities for offending and the 'hidden offences' which occur regularly in institutions become more visible.
>
> (Day 1993: 116)

(See also Reid 1990; Day 1997; Crossland et al. 2005; Hogue et al. 2006; Smith et al. 2008.)

The following is a summary of the ways in which mentally impaired individuals are likely to come to the attention of the criminal justice system:

1 The degree of impairment may be severe enough to prevent the individual from understanding that his or her act was legally wrong. In such cases, issues of responsibility will arise and decisions will have to be made as to whether or not to prosecute the alleged offender (see earlier comments in this chapter and Chapter 2).
2 The moderately impaired individual may be more easily caught in a criminal act.
3 Such offenders may be used very easily by others (dupes) in delinquent escapades and find themselves acting as accomplices – sometimes unwittingly, sometimes not.

4   An individual's mental impairment may be associated with a disorder that may make him or her particularly unpredictable, aggressive and impulsive.
5   Some mentally impaired offenders have problems in making understood their often harmless intentions. Thus, a friendly overture by them may be misinterpreted by an uninformed or unsympathetic recipient as an attempted assault. The initial overture may be rebuffed therefore. This may lead to surprise and anger on the part of the mentally impaired individual and he or she may then retaliate with aggression.
6   A moderately mentally impaired individual may be provoked quite readily into an uncharacteristic act of violence.
7   The attitude to legitimate expressions of sexuality in some of the mentally impaired may be naïve, primitive, unrestrained and lacking in social skills. Such deficits may account for the number of sexual offences that appear to be found in the backgrounds of detained mentally impaired patients in the high security hospitals (see Day 1997; Green et al. 2003).
8   Mentally impaired persons may be especially vulnerable to changes in their social environments that would not have the same impact upon their more well-endowed peers. A moderately mentally impaired person may manage perfectly well as long as he or she has the support of parents, other relatives or friends. Should this be interrupted by death, or for any other reasons, such persons may then indulge in delinquent acts as a means of trying to relieve the stresses of their situation.

The following case examples will help to demonstrate the vulnerability of the mentally impaired to changes in circumstances and other pressures. (For epidemiological and related issues, see Kearns 2001; see also special issue of *British Journal of Forensic Practice* 2001, 3(1); special section of *Legal and Criminological Psychology* 2003, 8(2): 219–266; Scott et al. 2006; Koolhof et al. 2007.)

Case illustration 4.14

A man of 26 was charged with causing grievous bodily harm to a young woman by hitting her over the head with an iron bar. She was entirely unknown to him, and though he denied the offence vehemently, he was convicted by the Crown Court on the clearest possible evidence. As a child he had suffered brain damage, which had resulted in a mild degree of mental impairment, accompanied by the kind of impulsive, aggressive and unpredictable behaviour referred to in (4) above. He had been before the courts on a number of occasions and had eventually been sent to a hospital for mentally handicapped people. He was discharged some years later to the care of his mother. Subsequent to his discharge, he committed the offence described above and was placed on probation. His response was poor. He was impulsive and erratic, and regressed to very childish behaviour when under stress. The family background was problematic: the parents had divorced (acrimoniously) when the offender was quite small; a brother suffered from a disabling form of epilepsy; and other members of the family showed decidedly eccentric lifestyles. (Such a family would no doubt today be described as 'dysfunctional'.) Shortly after the probation period expired, he committed a particularly vicious and unprovoked assault on a small girl and was sentenced to a long term of imprisonment.

Case illustration 4.15

This case illustrates some of the problems identified under (6) above. For many years, a mildly mentally impaired man in his forties had worked well under friendly but firm supervision. His work situation changed, with the result that his new employers felt he was being lazy and did not have much sympathy for his disabilities. In addition, his new workmates teased and picked on him. One day, one of them taunted him about his lack of success with the opposite sex. Goaded beyond endurance, the defendant stabbed his tormentor with a pitchfork in his chest, causing quite serious internal injuries. When the case came to the Crown Court, evidence was given as to his mental condition, his social situation and the manner in which he had been provoked. The court made a Hospital Order under the Mental Health Act.

Suggestibility

From the foregoing comments it can be seen that the mentally impaired individual may be especially vulnerable to pressures from others. When this takes the form of alleged pressure to commit crimes they may not have committed, the situation can become very serious indeed. Unfortunately, there have been a number of cases in which impressionable and suggestible individuals (some of them formally assessed as mentally impaired) have been the victims of miscarriages of justice. For example, three young men were alleged to have been responsible for the murder of a man named Maxwell Confait. All three were deemed to be vulnerable because of varying degrees of handicap. The same applied to Stefan Kiszko, also accused, convicted of, and sentenced for murder. In upholding his appeal, the court ruled that 'special care needs to be taken where the defendant suffers from a "significant degree of mental handicap" if the only evidence against him is his confession' (Kellam 1993: 361). Kellam goes on to make the important point that 'There seems no reason to think that the court meant to limit (handicap) to lack of mental capacity alone' (Kellam 1993: 362). The Police and Criminal Evidence Act 1984, and subsequent codes of practice, introduced certain safeguards in respect of police interrogations, most notably the availability of an 'appropriate adult', when vulnerable persons are being interviewed (Pearse and Gudjonsson 1996; Nemitz and Bean 2001). In this context, vulnerability would be held to include both mentally ill and mentally impaired individuals, and those thought for other reasons to be especially suggestible (Pearse and Gudjonsson 1997; Norfolk 2001; Blair 2007; Hartwig et al. 2007). Better formal training for 'appropriate adults' and police interrogators is gradually being introduced and clinical and forensic psychologists have made impressive contributions to this work (see, for example, Gudjonsson 1992; Shepherd 1993; McBrien et al. 2003).

Chromosomal abnormalities and crime

In the early 1960s, a considerable degree of interest was aroused by the finding that a number of men detained in high security hospitals and prisons carried an extra Y chromosome (XYY).[1] Such men were often found to be taller than average, came from essentially *non-delinquent backgrounds* and occasionally had records of violence. Subsequent research has proved inconclusive concerning the prevalence of such abnormalities, not only in penal and similar populations, but also in the community at large. Although the leads offered have potential for further and interesting development, there appears to be no strong evidence to suggest a causal link between specific genetic defects or abnormalities and crime, particularly violent crime. In a review of a number of studies in this area, Day (1993) concluded that 'the personal variables of tallness, intelligence and educational grade and the social variables of parental and family background bore closer relations to the possibility of conviction than genotypic abnormalities'. For an excellent account of the complex relationship between genes and behaviour, see Rutter (2006).

A concluding cautionary note

This chapter has had to encompass in brief form a wide range of complex material. Because of this, it would be all too easy for the reader to conclude that we are on sure ground in describing and delineating mental disturbances and disorders. The truth is that there are still vast grey areas in this field, and much more work is needed before we can be at all certain about aetiology (causes) and the best methods of management. Despite this, much valuable work has been, and is being done, notably in the field of brain biochemistry and its allied disciplines. Trying to equate mental disturbances with criminal behaviour is therefore quite hazardous, especially when we remember that crime itself is not a 'static' phenomenon. It is also very important to recall that both gender and race play a very important part in any study of the relationship between mental disturbances and crime. Despite much research, we are still not sure why certain ethnic minority groups (and notably African Caribbeans) seem over-represented in penal and psychiatric populations (Prins et al. 1993). Women, when they offend, tend to receive proportionately more psychiatric disposals than men. Fewer women seem to be assessed as 'psychopathic'; they seem more likely to be described as having 'neurotic' characteristics. Is this because the latter labels are regarded as more clinically correct, or because a male dominated society and criminal justice system tend to label women in this way? Some researchers (for example, Allen 1987) have suggested that the apparent discrepancies in sentencing are less than obvious. Allen's central thesis is that such divergences cannot be explained entirely by differences in the mental make-up of male and female offenders and that such divergences may occur regardless of their psychiatric symptomatology. She makes the often forgotten point that 'the importance of the current imbalance lies not so much in the excess of psychiatry in relation to female offenders as its deficiency in relation to males' (Allen 1987: xii). Some of the behaviours only touched upon in this chapter are now given more detailed treatment in those that follow; I begin in Chapter 5 with the vexed topic of severe personality (psychopathic) disorder.

Note

1 A brief word of explanation concerning normal chromosome distribution may be helpful to those new to this field. Normal human cells contain forty-six chromosomes; these are arranged in twenty-three pairs of different shapes and sizes. They may be seen and classified under high power, for example electron-microscopy, once they have been suitably prepared for examination. Different chromosomes contain different genes. One pair of chromosomes called X and Y determine sex. In the female, these consist of a matched pair, XX, and in the male an unmatched pair, XY. This normal patterning may sometimes become altered (translocated) in a variety of ways, resulting in an extra X or extra Y chromosome or some other variant.

Acts

Homicide Act 1957
Mental Health Act 1983
Mental Health Act 2007

Cases

R. v. Podola [1959] 3 All ER 418

References

Adams, S.J., Hazelwood, T.E., Pitre, N.L., Bedard, T.E. and Landry, S.D. (2009) 'Harassment of Members of Parliament and the Legislative Assemblies in Canada by Individuals Believed to be Mentally Disordered', *Journal of Forensic Psychiatry and Psychology* 20: 801–814.

Adshead, G. and Bluglass, K. (2005) 'Attachment Representations in a Mother with Abnormal Illness Behaviour by Proxy', *British Journal of Psychiatry* 187: 328–333.

Allen, H. (1987) *Justice Unbalanced: Gender, Psychiatry and Judicial Decisions*, Milton Keynes: Open University Press.

American Psychiatric Association (APA) (2005) *Diagnostic and Statistical Manual of Mental Disorders*, 4th edn (text revision) (DSM-IV-TR), Washington, DC: APA.

Aziz, C. (1987) 'Prey to the Green-eyed Monster', *The Independent*, 10 November.

Bark, N.M. (1985) 'Did Shakespeare Know Schizophrenia? The Case of Poor Mad Tom in King Lear', *British Journal of Psychiatry* 146: 346–348.

Bean, P. (2008) *Madness and Crime*, Cullompton: Willan.

Bhugra, D. and Munro, A. (1997) *Troublesome Disguises: Undiagnosed Psychiatric Syndromes*, Oxford: Blackwell.

Birch, C.D., Kelln, B.R.C. and Aquino, E.P.B. (2006) 'A Review and Report of Pseudologia Fantastica', *Journal of Forensic Psychiatry and Psychology* 17: 299–320.

Bjorkly, S. and Havik, O.E. (2003) 'TCO Symptoms as Markers of Violence in a Sample of Seventy Violent Psychiatric In-patients', *International Journal of Forensic Mental Health* 2: 87–97.

Blair, J.P. (2007) 'The Roles of Interrogation, Perception and Individual Difference in Producing False Confessions', *Psychology, Crime and Law* 13: 173–186.

Blair, J., Mitchell, D. and Blair, K. (2005) *The Psychopath: Emotion and the Brain*, Oxford: Blackwell.

Bocij, P. and McFarlane, L. (2003) 'Seven Fallacies about Cyberstalking', *Prison Service Journal* 149: 37–42.

Bocij, P., Bocij, H. and McFarlane, L. (2003) 'Cyberstalking: A Case Study of Serial Harassment in the U.K.', *British Journal of Forensic Practice* 5: 25–32.

Breuer, J. and Freud, S. (1936) *Studies in Hysteria*, New York: Putnam.

Brogden, M. (2001) *Geronticide: Killing the Elderly*, London: Jessica Kingsley.

Brogden, M. and Nijhar, P. (2000) *Crime, Abuse and the Elderly*, Cullompton: Willan.

Broughton, N. and Chesterman, P. (2001) 'Malingered Psychosis', *Journal of Forensic Psychiatry* 12: 407–422.

Buchanan, A. (1994) 'Brain, Mind and Behaviour Revisited', *Journal of Forensic Psychiatry* 5: 232–236.

Budd, T. and Mattinson, J. (2000) *Stalking: Findings from the 1998 British Crime Survey*, Research Findings no. 129, London: Home Office Research, Development and Statistics Directorate.

Camporesi, P. (1989) *Bread of Dreams: Food and Fantasy in Early Modern Europe*, Cambridge: Polity Press.

Cornwell, P. (1995) *Body of Evidence*, London: Warner.

Crichton, J.M. (1999) 'Mental Disorder and Crime: Coincidence, Correlation and Cause', *Journal of Forensic Psychiatry* 10: 659–677.

Crisford, H., Dare, H. and Evangeli, M. (2008) 'Offence-related Post Traumatic Stress Disorder (PTSD) Symptomatology and Guilt in Mentally Disordered Violent and Sexual Offenders', *Journal of Forensic Psychiatry and Psychology* 19: 86–107.

Crossland, S., Burns, M., Leach, C. and Quinn, P. (2005) 'Needs Assessment in Forensic Learning Disability', *Medicine, Science and the Law* 45: 147–153.

Curtice, M., Parker, J., Wismayer, F.S. and Tomison, A. (2003) 'The Elderly Offender: An 11 Year Survey of Referrals to a Regional Forensic-Psychiatric Service', *Journal of Forensic Psychiatry* 14: 253–265.

Dalton, K. (1982) 'Legal Implication of PMS', *World Medicine* 17: 93–94.

Dalzell, T. and Victor, T. (eds) (2006) *The New Partridge Dictionary of Slang and Unconventional English*, London: Routledge.

Day, K. (1993) 'Crime and Mental Retardation', in K. Howells and C.R. Hollin (eds) *Clinical Approaches to the Mentally Disordered Offender*, Chichester: Wiley.

—— (1997) 'Sex Offenders with Learning Disabilities', in S.G. Read (ed.) *Psychiatry in Learning Disability*, London: Saunders.

Delgado-Escueta, A.V., Mattson, R.H. and King, L. (1981) 'The Nature of Aggression during Epileptic Seizures', *New England Journal of Medicine* 305: 711–716.

Department of Health (1998) *Modernising Mental Health Services, Section I*, December, London: Department of Health.

D'Orban, P.T. (1983) 'Medico-Legal Aspects of the Pre-Menstrual Syndrome', *British Journal of Hospital Medicine* 30: 404–409.

Eastman, N.L.G. (1993) 'Forensic Psychiatric Services in Britain: A Current Review', *International Journal of Law and Psychiatry* 16: 1–26.

Ebrahim, A. and Fenwick, P. (2008) 'Sleep Related Violence', *Medicine, Science and the Law* 48: 124–136.

Enoch, D. (1990) 'Hysteria, Malingering, Pseudologia Fantastica, Ganser Syndrome, Prison Psychosis, and Munchausen's Syndrome', in R. Bluglass and P. Bowden (eds) *Principles and Practice of Forensic Psychiatry*, London: Churchill Livingstone.

Enoch, D. and Ball, H. (2001) *Uncommon Psychiatric Syndromes*, 4th edn, London: Arnold.

Enoch, D. and Trethowan, W. (1979) *Uncommon Psychiatric Syndromes*, 2nd edn, London: Butterworth-Heinemann.

Fearnley, D. and Zaatar, A. (2001) 'A Cross-Sectional Study which Measures the Prevalence and Characteristics of Prisoners who Present with a Family History of Epilepsy', *Medicine, Science and the Law* 41: 305–308.

Fennell, P. (2007) *Mental Health: The New Law*, Bristol: Jordan.

Fenwick, P. (1990) *Automatism, Medicine and the Law*, Psychological Medicine Monograph, Supplement 17, Cambridge: Cambridge University Press.

—— (1993) 'Brain, Mind and Behaviour: Some Medico-Legal Aspects', *British Journal of Psychiatry* 163: 565–573.

Finch, E. (2002) 'Stalking: A Violent Crime or a Crime of Violence', *Howard Journal of Criminal Justice* 41: 422–433.

Franzini, L.R. and Grossberg, J.M. (1995) *Eccentric and Bizarre Behaviours*, Chichester: Wiley.

Freeman, H. (1991) 'The Human Brain and Political Behaviour', *British Journal of Psychiatry* 159: 19–32.

Friedmann, C.T.H. and Faguet, R.A. (eds) (1982) *Extraordinary Disorders of Human Behaviour*, New York: Plenum Press.

Friel, A., White, T. and Hull, A. (2008) 'Post-traumatic Stress Disorder and Criminal Responsibility', *Journal of Forensic Psychiatry and Psychology* 19: 64–85.

Gelder, M.G., Lopez-Ibor, J.J. and Andreasen, N.C. (eds) (2009) *New Oxford Textbook of Psychiatry*, 2nd edn, 2 Volumes, Oxford: Oxford University Press.

Gibbon, K. (1998) 'Munchausen's Syndrome Presenting as an Acute Sexual Assault', *Medicine, Science and the Law* 38: 202–205.

Gleick, J. (2003) *Isaac Newton*, London: Fourth Estate.

Green, G., Gray, N.S. and Willan, P. (2003) 'Management of Sexually Inappropriate Behaviours in Men with Learning Disabilities', *Journal of Forensic Psychiatry* 13: 85–110.

Gudjonsson, G. (1992) *The Psychology of Interrogations, Confessions and Testimony*, Chichester: Wiley.

Gunn, J. (1977a) 'Criminal Behaviour and Mental Disorders', *British Journal of Psychiatry* 130: 317–329.

—— (1977b) *Epileptics in Prison*, London: Academic Press.

—— (1992) 'Personality Disorders and Forensic Psychiatry', *Criminal Behaviour and Mental Health* 2: 202–211.

—— (1993) 'Epidemiology and Forensic Psychiatry', *Criminal Behaviour and Mental Health* 3: 180–193.

Gunn, J. and Taylor P.J. (eds) (1993) *Forensic Psychiatry: Clinical, Legal and Ethical Issues*, London: Butterworth-Heinemann.

Gunn, J., Robertson, G., Dell, S. and Way, C. (1978) *Psychiatric Aspects of Imprisonment*, London: Academic Press.

Hardie, T.J. and Reed, A. (1998) 'Pseudologia Fantastica, Factitious Disorder and Impostership: A Deception Syndrome', *Medicine, Science and the Law* 38: 198–201.

Hare, E. (1983) 'Was Insanity on the Increase?', *British Journal of Psychiatry* 142: 439–455.

Harmon, R., Rosner, R. and Owens, H. (1995) 'Obsessive Harassment and Erotomania in a Criminal Court Population', *Journal of Forensic Sciences* 40: 188–196.

Harris, J. (2000) *The Protection from Harassment Act, 1997: An Evaluation of its Effectiveness*, Research Findings no. 130, London: Home Office Research, Development and Statistics Directorate.

Hartwig, M., Granhag, P.A. and Strömwall, L.A. (2007) 'Guilty and Innocent Suspects' Strategies during Police Interrogations', *Psychology, Crime and Law* 13: 213–227.

Heinze, M.C. (2003) 'Developing Sensitivity to Distortion: Utility of Psychological Tests in Differentiating Malingering and Psychopathology in Criminal Defendants', *Journal of Forensic Psychiatry* 14: 151–177.

Higgins, J. (1990) 'Affective Disorders', in R. Bluglass and P. Bowden (eds) *Principles and Practice of Forensic Psychiatry*, London: Churchill Livingstone.

—— (1995) 'Crime and Mental Disorder II: Forensic Aspects of Psychiatric

Disorder', in D. Chiswick and R. Cope (eds) *Seminars in Practical Forensic Psychiatry*, London: Gaskell.

Hodgins, S. (1992) 'Mental Disorder, Intellectual Deficiency and Crime', *Archives of General Psychiatry* 49: 476–483.

Hodgins, S. and Gunnar-Janson, C. (2002) *Criminality and Violence among the Mentally Disordered: The Stockholm Metropolitan Project*, Cambridge: Cambridge University Press.

Hodgins, S. and Muller-Isberner, R. (2001) *Violence, Crime and Mentally Disordered Offenders: Concepts and Methods For Effective Treatment and Prevention*, Chichester: Wiley.

Hogue, T., Steptoe, L., Taylor, J.L., Lindsay, W.R., Mooney, P., Pinkey, L., Johnston, S., Smith, A.H.W. and O'Brien, G. (2006) 'A Comparison of Offenders with Intellectual Disability across Three Levels of Security', *Criminal Behaviour and Mental Health* 16: 13–28.

Holden, C., Lacey, A. and Monach, J. (2001) 'Establishing Secure Mental Health Facilities: The Outcome of Public Consultation Exercises', *Journal of Mental Health* 10: 513–524.

Howard, R.C. (2002) 'Brainwaves, Dangerousness and Deviant Desires', *Journal of Forensic Psychiatry* 13: 367–384.

James, D. (1998) 'Multiple Personality Disorder in the Courts: A Review of the North American Experience', *Journal of Forensic Psychiatry* 9: 339–361.

James, D. and Schramm, M. (1998) 'Multiple Personality Disorder Presenting to the English Courts: A Case Study', *Journal of Forensic Psychiatry* 9: 615–628.

Kamphuis, J.H. and Emmelkamp, P.M.G. (2000) 'Stalking: A Contemporary Challenge for Forensic and Clinical Psychiatry', *British Journal of Psychiatry* 176: 206–209.

Kearns, A. (2001) 'Forensic Services and People with Learning Disabilities in the Shadow of the Reed Report', *Journal of Forensic Psychiatry* 12: 8–12.

Kellam, A.M.P. (1993) 'False Confessions: A Note on the McKenzie Judgement', *Psychiatric Bulletin* 17: 361–362.

Keyes, D. (1995) *The Minds of Billy Milligan*, Harmondsworth: Penguin.

Klawans, H.L. (1990) *Newton's Madness and Further Tales of Clinical Neurology*, London: Bodley Head.

Koolhof, R., Loeber, R., Wei, E.H., Pardini, D. and D'Escury, A.C. (2007) 'Inhibition Deficits of Serious Delinquent Boys of Low Intelligence', *Criminal Behaviour and Mental Health* 17: 274–292.

Kucharski, L.T., Falkenbach, D.M., Egan, S.S. and Duncan, S. (2006) 'Anti-Social Personality Disorder and Malingering of Psychiatric Disorder: A Study of Criminal Defendants', *International Journal of Forensic Mental Health* 5: 195–204.

Lagach, E.D. (1947) *La Jalousie Amoureuse*, Paris: Presses Universitaires de France.

Laing, R.D. and Esterson, A. (1964) *Sanity, Madness and the Family*, London: Tavistock.

Laurance, J. (2003) *Pure Madness: How Fear Drives the Mental Health System*, London: Routledge.

Lewis, O. and Carpenter, S. (1999) 'Episodic Dyscontrol and the English Criminal Law', *Journal of Mental Health Law* 1: 13–22.

Lindquist, P. and Allebeck, P. (1990) 'Schizophrenia and Crime: A Longitudinal

Follow-up of 644 Schizophrenics in Stockholm', *British Journal of Psychiatry* 157: 345–350.

Link, B.J. and Steuve, A. (1994) 'Psychotic Symptoms and Violent/Illegal Behaviour of Mental Patients Compared to Community Controls', in J. Monahan and H.J. Steadman (eds) *Violence and Mental Disorder: Developments in Risk Assessment*, Chicago, IL: University of Chicago Press.

Link, B.J., Andrews, H. and Cullen, F.T. (1992) 'The Violent and Illegal Behaviour of Mental Patients Reconsidered', *American Sociological Review* 57: 275–292.

Lishman, A. (1997) *Organic Psychiatry*, 3rd edn, Oxford: Blackwell.

Lucas, P. (1994) 'Episodic Dyscontrol: A Look Back at Anger', *Journal of Forensic Psychiatry* 5: 371–407.

McBrien, J., Hodgetts, A. and Gregory, J. (2003) 'Offending and Risky Behaviour in Community Services for People with Intellectual Disabilities in One Local Authority', *Journal of Forensic Psychiatry* 14: 280–297.

McGuire, B. and Wraith, A. (2000) 'Legal and Psychological Aspects of Stalking: A Review', *Journal of Forensic Psychiatry* 11: 316–327.

McNeil, D.E., Binder, R. and Greenfield, T. (1988) 'Predictions of Violence in Civilly Committed Acute Psychiatric Patients', *American Journal of Psychiatry* 145: 965–970.

Maden, A. (2007) *Treating Violence: A Guide to Risk Management in Mental Health*, Oxford: Oxford University Press.

Marshall, J. (1998) 'Dual Diagnosis: Co-Morbidity of Severe Mental Illness and Substance Misuse', *Journal of Forensic Psychiatry* 9: 9–15.

Meloy, J.R. (ed.) (1998) *The Psychology of Stalking: Clinical and Forensic Perspectives*, San Diego, CA: Academic Press.

—— (2007) Editorial: 'Stalking: The State of the Science', *Criminal Behaviour and Mental Health* 17: 1–7.

Merskey, H. (1992) 'The Manufacture of Personalities: The Production of Multiple Personality Disorder', *British Journal of Psychiatry* 160: 327–340.

Miller, E. (1999) 'The Neuropsychology of Offending', *Psychology, Crime and Law* 5: 297–318.

Miller, L. (1992) 'Neuropsychology, Personality and Substance Abuse in a Head Injury Case: Clinical and Forensic Issues', *International Journal of Law and Psychiatry* 15: 303–316.

Monahan, J. (1992) 'Mental Disorder and Violent Behaviour: Perceptions and Evidence', *American Psychologist* 74: 511–521.

—— (2002) 'The MacArthur Studies of Violence Risk', *Criminal Behaviour and Mental Health, Supplement: Festschrift to John Gunn* 12: S67–S72.

Monahan, J., Steadman, H.J., Silver, E., Appelbaum, P.S., Robbins, P.C., Mulvey, E.P., Roth, L.H., Grisso, T. and Banks, S. (2001) *Rethinking Risk Assessment: The MacArthur Study of Mental Disorder and Violence*, Oxford: Oxford University Press.

Moran, P., Walsh, E., Tyrer, P., Burns, F., Creed, F. and Fahy, T. (2003) 'Impact of Combined Personality Disorder and Violence in Psychoses: Report from the UK 700 Trial', *British Journal of Psychiatry* 182: 129–134.

Morel, K.R. (2008) 'Development of a Validity Scale for Combat Related Post-traumatic Stress Disorder: Evidence from Simulated Malingerers and Actual Disability Claimants', *Journal of Forensic Psychiatry and Psychology* 19: 52–63.

Mullen, P. (1981) 'Jealousy: The Pathology of Passion', *British Journal of Psychiatry* 158: 593–601.

—— (1996) 'Jealousy and the Emergence of Violent and Indimidatory Behaviours', *Criminal Behaviour and Mental Health* 6: 194–205.

Mullen, P.E., Pathé, M. and Purcell, R. (1999) 'Study of Stalkers', *American Journal of Psychiatry* 156: 1244–1249.

—— (2000) *Stalkers and their Victims*, Cambridge: Cambridge University Press.

Murray, R., Walsh, E. and Arseneault, L. (2002) 'Some Possible Answers to Questions about Schizophrenia that have concerned John Gunn', *Criminal Behaviour and Mental Health, Supplement: Festschrift to John Gunn* 12: S4–S9.

NACRO (National Association for the Care and Resettlement of Offenders) (1993) *Community Care and Mentally Disordered Offenders*, Policy Paper no. 1, Mental Health Advisory Committee (Chairman H. Prins), London: NACRO.

Nemitz, T. and Bean, P. (2001) 'Protecting the Rights of the Mentally Disordered in Police Stations: The Use of the Appropriate Adult in England and Wales', *International Journal of Law and Psychiatry* 24: 595–605.

Nnatu, I.O., Mahomed, F. and Shama, A. (2005) 'Is There a Need for Elderly Forensic Psychiatric Services?', *Medicine, Science and the Law* 45: 154–160.

Norfolk, G. (2001) 'Fit to be Interviewed by the Police: An Aid to Assessment', *Medicine, Science and the Law* 41: 5–12.

O'Sullivan, P.C.J. and Chesterman, L.O. (2007) 'Older Adult Patients Subject to Restriction Orders in England and Wales: A Cross-Sectional Survey', *Journal of Forensic Psychiatry and Psychology* 18: 204–220.

Pearse, J. and Gudjonsson, G. (1996) 'How Appropriate are Appropriate Adults?', *Journal of Forensic Psychiatry* 7: 570–580.

—— (1997) 'Police Interviewing and Legal Representation: A Field Study', *Journal of Forensic Psychiatry* 8: 200–208.

Petch, E. (2002) 'Anti-Stalking Laws and the Protection from Harassment Act, 1997', *Journal of Forensic Psychiatry* 13: 19–34.

Pilgrim, D. and Rogers, A. (2003) 'Mental Disorder and Violence: An Empirical Picture in Context', *Journal of Mental Health* 12: 7–18.

Pines, A.M. (1998) *Romantic Jealousy: Causes, Symptoms, Cures*, London: Routledge.

Pollock, P.H. (1996) 'A Cautionary Note on the Determination of Malingering', *Psychology, Crime and Law* 3: 97–110.

Porter, S., Birt, A.R., Yuille, J.C. and Hervé, H.F. (2001) 'Memory for Murder: A Psychological Perspective on Dissociative Amnesia in Legal Contexts', *International Journal of Law and Psychiatry* 24: 23–42.

Power, D.J. (1977) 'Memory, Identification and Crime', *Medicine, Science and the Law* 17: 132–139.

Prins, H. (1990) *Bizarre Behaviours: Boundaries of Psychiatric Disorder*, London: Routledge.

—— (1996) 'Othello, Leontes or What You Will: A Comment on Crichton', *Journal of Forensic Psychiatry* 7: 630–633.

Prins, H., Backer-Holst, T., Francis, E. and Keitch, I. (1993) *Report of the Committee of Inquiry into the Death in Broadmoor Hospital of Orville Blackwood and a Review of the Deaths of Two Other Afro-Caribbean Patients: 'Big, Black and Dangerous?'*, London: Special Hospitals Service Authority (SHSA).

Pyszora, N.M., Barker, A.F. and Kopelman, M.D. (2003) 'Amnesia for Criminal Offences: A Study of Life-Sentence Prisoners', *Journal of Forensic Psychiatry and Psychology* 14: 475–490.

Reid, A. (1990) 'Mental Retardation and Crime', in R. Bluglass and P. Bowden (eds) *Principles and Practice of Forensic Psychiatry*, London: Churchill Livingstone.

Resnick, P. (1994) 'Malingering', *Journal of Forensic Psychiatry* 5: 1–4.

Rollin, H. (1969) *The Mentally Abnormal Offender and the Law*, Oxford: Pergamon.

Rosenfeld, B., Galietta, M., Ivanoff, A., Garcia-Mansilla, A., Martinez, R., Fava, J., Fineran, V. and Green, D. (2007) 'Dialetical Behaviour Therapy for the Treatment of Stalking Offenders', *International Journal of Forensic Mental Health* 6: 95–103.

Roth, M. and Kroll, J. (1986) *The Reality of Mental Illness*, Cambridge: Cambridge University Press.

Rutter, M. (2006) *Genes and Behaviour: Nature-Nurture Interplay Explained*, Oxford: Blackwell.

Schipkowensky, N. (1969) 'Cyclophrenia and Murder', in A.V.S. Ruck and R. Porter (eds) *The Mentally Abnormal Offender*, London: J. and A. Churchill.

Schorer, C.E. (1965) 'The Ganser Syndrome', *British Journal of Criminology* 5: 120–131.

Scott, D., McGilloway, S. and Donnelly, M. (2006) 'The Mental Health Needs of People with Learning Disability Detained in Police Custody', *Medicine, Science and the Law* 46: 111–114.

Scull, A. (1984) 'Was Insanity on the Increase? A Reply to Edward Hare', *British Journal of Psychiatry* 144: 432–436.

Sedgwick, P. (1982) *Psycho-politics*, London: Pluto Press.

Shepherd, E. (ed.) (1993) *Aspects of Police Interviewing*, Division of Legal and Criminological Psychology, Monograph no. 18, Leicester: British Psychological Society.

Sheridan, L. and Davies, G.M. (2001) 'What is Stalking? The Match between Legislation and Public Perceptions', *Legal and Criminological Psychology* 6: 3–17.

Sheridan, L. and Grant, T. (2007) 'Is Cyberstalking Different?', *Psychology, Crime and Law* 13: 627–640.

Sheridan, L., Gillett, R. and Davies, G. (2000) 'Stalking: Seeing the Victim's Perspective', *Psychology, Crime and Law* 6: 267–280.

Sheridan, L., Davies, G. and Boon, J. (2001) 'The Course and Nature of Stalking: A Victim Perspective', *Howard Journal of Criminal Justice* 40: 215–234.

Sheridan, L., Gillett, R. and Davies, G. (2002) 'Perceptions and Prevalence of Stalking in a Male Sample', *Psychology, Crime and Law* 8: 289–310.

Smith, H., White, T. and Walker, P. (2008) 'Offending in the Learning Disabled Population: A Retrospective Audit of Tayside Learning Disability Service Court Reports', *Medicine, Science and the Law* 48: 31–36.

Steadman, H., Mulvey, E.P., Monahan, J., Robbins, P.C., Appelbaum, P.S., Grisso, T., Roth, L.H. and Silver, E. (1998) 'Violence by People Discharged from Acute Psychiatric Inpatient Facilities and by Others in the Same Neighbourhoods', *Archives of General Psychiatry* 55: 393–401.

Stone, J.H. (1992) 'Memory Disorders in Offenders and Victims', *Criminal Behaviour and Mental Health* 2: 342–356.

Swanson, J.W., Holtzer, C.E., Ganju, V.K. and Juno, R.T. (1990) 'Violence and Psychiatric Disorder in the Community: Evidence from the Epidemiologic Catchment Area Surveys', *Hospital and Community Psychiatry* 41: 761–770.

Szasz, T. (1987) *Insanity: The Idea and its Consequences*, New York: Wiley.

—— (1993) 'Curing, Coercing and Claims-making: A Reply to Critics', *British Journal of Psychiatry* 162: 797–800.

Tantam, D. and Whittaker, J. (1993) 'Self Wounding and Personality Disorders', in P. Tyrer and G. Stein (eds) *Personality Disorder Reviewed*, London: Gaskell.

Taylor, P.J. (1995) 'Motives for Offending among Violent and Psychotic Men', *British Journal of Psychiatry* 147: 491–498.

Taylor, P.J., Mahendra, B. and Gunn, J. (1983) 'Erotomania in Males', *Psychological Medicine* 13: 645–650.

Vattakatuchery, J.J. and Chesterman, P. (2006) 'The Use of Abreaction to Recover Memories in Psychological Amnesia: A Case Report', *Journal of Forensic Psychiatry and Psychology* 17: 647–653.

Vine, B. (1990) *Gallowglass*, London: Viking.

Walsh, E., Buchanan, A., and Fahy, T. (2002) 'Violence and Schizophrenia: Examining the Evidence', *British Journal of Psychiatry* 180: 490–495.

Walsh, E., Moran, P., Scott, C., McKenzie, K., Burns, T., Creed, R., Tyrer, P., Murray, R.M. and Fahy, T. (2003) 'Prevalence of Violent Victimisation in Severe Mental Illness', *British Journal of Psychiatry* 183: 233–238.

Wesseley, S.C., Castle, D., Douglas, A.J. and Taylor, P.J. (1994) 'The Criminal Careers of Incident Cases of Schizophrenia', *Psychological Medicine* 24: 483–502.

West, D.J. (1965) *Murder Followed by Suicide*, London: Macmillan.

Wheatley, M. (1998) 'The Prevalence and Use of Substance Abuse in Detained Schizophrenic Patients', *Journal of Forensic Psychiatry* 9: 114–130.

White, G.L. and Mullen, P.E. (1989) *Jealousy: Theory, Research and Clinical Strategies*, New York: Guilford Press.

White, T. (2005) 'Patients with Affective Disorders Admitted to Maximum Secure Care (1990–2003)', *Medicine, Science and the Law* 45: 142–146.

Whitty, C.W.M. and Zangwill, O.L. (eds) (1977) *Amnesia: Clinical, Psychological and Legal Aspects*, London: Butterworth.

Whyte, S., Petch, E., Penny, C. and Reiss, D. (2008) 'Who Stalks? A Description of Patients at a High Security Hospital with a History of Stalking Behaviour', *Criminal Behaviour and Mental Health* 18: 27–38.

Williams, M. (1979) *Brain Damage, Behaviour and the Mind*, Chichester: Wiley.

Wilson, S. (1993) 'Multiple Personality Personality', in P. Tyrer and G. Stein (eds) *Personality Disorder Reviewed*, London: Gaskell.

Woddis, G.M. (1964) 'Clinical Psychiatry and Crime', *British Journal of Criminology* 4: 443–460.

World Health Organization (WHO) (1992) *The ICD-10 Classification of Mental and Behavioural Disorders: Clinical Descriptions and Diagnostic Guidelines*, Geneva: WHO.

Wright, J.A., Burgess, A.G., Burgess, A.W., Laszlo, A.T., McCrary, G.O. and Douglas, J.E. (1996) 'A Typology of Interpersonal Stalking', *Journal of Interpersonal Violence* 11: 487–502.

Yorston, G. (1999) 'Aged and Dangerous: Old Age Forensic Psychiatry', *British Journal of Psychiatry* 174: 193–195.

Zona, M.A., Sharma, K.K. and Lane, J.C. (1993) 'A Comparative Study of Erotomania and Obsessive Subjects in a Female Sample', *Journal of Forensic Sciences* 38: 894–903.

Further reading

Brain mechanisms

Pinker, S. (1999) *How the Mind Works*, London: Penguin (stimulating discussion of mind–body–society relationships).

Genetic aspects

Rutter, M. (2006) *Genes and Behaviour: Nature-Nurture Interplay Explained*, Oxford: Blackwell (probably the best and easiest-to-read account available).

Psychiatry – general and forensic

Gelder, M.G., Lopez-Ibor, J.J. Jr, Andreasen, N.C. and Geddes, J.R. (eds) (2009) *New Oxford Textbook of Psychiatry*, 2nd edn, Oxford: Oxford University Press (this two-volume Oxford textbook is extremely comprehensive on both general and forensic matters).

Historical

Anything by Professor Roy Porter is highly illuminating. For a splendid survey see Porter, R. (2006) *Madmen: A Social History of Mad – Doctors and Lunatics*, Stroud: Tempus.

Fiction

Novelists such as P.D. James and Ruth Rendell in the UK and Patricia Cornwell and Kathy Reichs in the United States (among many others) shed additional light on some of the issues described and discussed in this chapter. A compelling account of a young army officer's probable personality change (PTSD) as a result of a war-induced serious head injury may be found in Minette Walters' (2007) novel *The Chameleon's Shadow*, London: Macmillan.

Chapter 5

A failure to register

What's in a name? That which we call a rose
By any other name would smell as sweet.

(Juliet, in *Romeo and Juliet*, Act 2, Sc. 2)

I can't define an elephant, but I know one
when I see one.

(Curran and Mallinson 1944, quoted in East 1949: 130)

For there are mystically in our faces certain
characters which carry in them the motto of
our souls.

(Thomas Browne, *Religio Medici* 1643)

A word or two by way of explanation is needed for the title of this chapter and, by implication, the three quotations that head it. In all that I have read, and had first-hand knowledge of, those we describe as severely antisocial ('psychopathic'), their *central* characteristic seems to me to be that of a devastating and long-term failure to 'register' the needs of others (and often themselves). I am hoping that this chapter will justify my chapter title and the rationale for it. As I shall demonstrate, naming is also a highly problematic area, hence the three quotations above.[1] It is also important to note here that in what follows I am dealing with the criminally psychopathic, i.e. those who have come to the attention of the criminal justice and forensic mental health care systems. There are others who have not done so, as illustrated in a most interesting article by Board and Fritzon (2005).

Some of the material in this chapter appeared in an article written by myself and my former colleague Kate Brookes (Moss), 'Severe (Psychopathic) Personality Disorder: A Review', *Medicine, Science and the Law* 2006, 46(3): 190–207. It is reproduced here with the kind agreement of my co-author and with the permission of the publishers.

Since the late 1980s, there has been an increasing, largely politically and media driven, degree of concern with issues of public protection. Such concern has been given high priority in a veritable deluge of statutes supplemented by government circulars of prescription and guidance. Since the Criminal Justice Act 1991, rafts of statutes have made their appearance, culminating in the mammoth-sized Criminal Justice Act 2003. In the mental health field, the scope of the Mental Health Act 1983 was broadened with the passing of the Mental Health (Patients in the Community) Act 1995 and, as noted in previous chapters, now modified by the 2007 Act. The introduction of the label Dangerous Severe Personality Disorder (DSPD) is of considerable significance. This, it should be remembered, is a *political* and not a clinical term and is the product of the kind of moral panic as originally described by Cohen (2002). It is therefore appropriate to place some of these concerns in a short historical context.

Psychopathic disorder: a complex history

No attempt is made here to provide a detailed historical account of the development of the concept. A very comprehensive history may, however, be found in Millon et al. (2003) and Blackburn (2007). Although the nineteenth-century French alienists (equivalent to psychiatrists today) Philippe Pinel and Jean-Etienne Esquirol and the alienist and anthropologist James Prichard are usually quoted as forerunners in the descriptive field, there is evidence that mental and moral philosophers were taking an interest in the topic well before the nineteenth century. Of course, those showing what we would describe today as psychopathic characteristics appear throughout history. For example, the nobleman Gilles de Rais – a contemporary of Jean D'Arc – was a sadistic serial killer of children of both sexes. Vlad the Impaler would probably be given the label of psychopath today. Shakespeare's depictions of Richard III and Lady Macbeth might also be so described; the latter's condition providing a useful illustration of the presence of co-morbidity – that is, possible severe personality disorder accompanied by depression. Nowadays, no doubt, she would be given a dual diagnosis (see Prins 2001, 2005: 295–301). An American academic, Dr Eric Altschuler, of the University of California, describes the biblical Samson as having psychopathic characteristics. As a child he is said to have shown severe personality disorder, 'setting things on fire, torturing animals and bullying other children'. Altschuler also mentions Samson's mother as a possible pathogenic element in his development. Apparently, in the Book of Judges, 'she is warned not to drink when she is pregnant'. He concludes (perhaps somewhat tongue in cheek) that 'recklessness and a disregard for others may have run in the family'. It is perhaps fair to Altschuler to point out that the triad of enuresis (which is *not* indicated in Altschuler's account), cruelty to animals and fire setting have in the past been seen as precursors of later severe antisocial personality disorder (see *The Independent*, 15 February 2002, citing an unsourced paper in *The New Scientist*; for a further biblical example, see Stein 2009).

To continue with more recent history, reference has already been made to Pinel, whose descriptions included a number of cases that would probably not be considered as falling with the category of psychopathic disorder today. Somewhat nearer present-day formulations would be that advanced by Prichard with his description of moral insanity. Changes of *name* are often favoured, since it is hoped that they may facilitate changes of *attitude*. Gunn (2003: 32), for example, suggests that such changes may make a condition less 'horrid and worrying'. He adds that 'Perhaps the concept is a bit like that of "the privy", "the water closet", "the lavatory", "the toilet" or "the rest room"' (see later discussion of the hoped for results of further name changes). Prichard (1835) described his concept of moral insanity thus:

> a madness, consisting of morbid perversion of the natural feeling, affections, inclinations, tempers, habits, moral dispositions and natural impulses, without any remarkable disorder or defect of the intellect or knowing or reasoning faculties, and particularly *without any insane illusion or hallucination*.
>
> (Prichard 1835: 85, emphasis added)

In considering this quotation, we should note that 'moral' meant emotional and psychological and was not intended to denote the opposite of 'immoral' as used in modern parlance. This view of 'moral insanity' rested on the then, fairly widely held, controversial belief that there could be a separate moral sense that could, as it were, be diseased; however, these views need to be seen against the background of the very rudimentary state of psychiatric and psychological knowledge during his lifetime. This notion does find resonance in Cleckley's (1976) opinion that psychopathy could actually be a form of 'illness'. Koch (1891) formulated the concept of *constitutional psychopathy*, implying that there was a considerable innate predisposition; a line of thinking much in keeping with the [then] contemporary interest in hereditary factors in the causation of delinquency. As noted in Chapter 4, we have witnessed a relatively recent return to this in the study of neuro-physio-psychological processes in the causation of persistent deviancy (see, for example, Dolan 1994; Blair and Frith 2000; Spence et al. 2004; Blair et al. 2005). In the early 1900s the terms 'moral defective' and 'moral imbecile' found their way into the Mental Deficiency Act 1913 (subsequently replaced by less pejorative descriptions in an amending Act in 1927). Explorations in the 1930s were of importance. Findings from the disciplines of neurology and physiology were being applied to behaviour disorders – prompted no doubt by the behaviour disordered consequences of the widespread epidemics of illnesses such as encephalitis. Freudian perspectives were also being applied to deviant behaviour, as evidenced by the work of psycho-analytically orientated medical and non-medical professionals such as Melitta Schmideberg, Kate Friedlander, Anna Freud, August Aichorn, George Lyward and Otto Shaw, all of whom were interested in the possible childhood roots of serious antisocial behaviour. For an interesting compilation of work in the 1930s and 1940s in this field, see Eissler (1949). In 1939, Sir David Henderson – a distinguished British psychiatrist – published his famous work *Psychopathic States*, in which he divided psychopaths into the creative, inadequate and the aggressive. He considered that the psychopath's 'failure to adjust to ordinary social life is not a mere wilfulness or badness which can be threatened or thrashed out . . . but constitutes a true illness' (Henderson 1939: 19). The later work of Lee Robins (1966) is also seminal, as are works by Bowlby (1946, 1971, 1979), Ainsworth (1962) and Rutter (1999). Since the 1960s, attention has been focused on the management of adult psychopathically disordered individuals within institutional settings, notably those adopting a therapeutic community or 'social milieu' approach. Figures in this field include psychiatrists such as Jones (1963), Whiteley (1994) and Campling (1996).

In summarizing the foregoing, it is possible to trace three important themes in the development of the concept. The first, as Coid (1993) suggests, was the concept of abnormal personality as defined by social maladjustment – developed in France and later in the UK – which led to the one-time somewhat contentious legal definition of psychopathic disorder (of which more later). The second was the concept of mental degeneracy, also originating in France. The third was the German notion of defining abnormal psychopathic personality types, as illustrated in the seminal work of Schneider (1958). In addition, over the years, the concept has not been without attention from central government. It was considered by the Butler Committee as long ago as the early 1970s (Home Office and DHSS 1975), subsequently in a joint DHSS and Home Office Consultation Document (DHSS 1986), by the Reed Committee (Department of Health and Home Office 1994) and in the joint Home Office and Department of Health (1999) policy document concerning DSPD. Aspects of the problem were further considered in 1999 by the Fallon Committee in its inquiry into the Personality Disorder Unit at Ashworth Hospital, Volume II of which contains extensive expert evidence on the nature of personality disorder (Fallon et al. 1999) and in the report of the Richardson Committee (Department of Health 1999). A representation of the stages through which the concert has passed is provided in Figure 5.1.

Defining personality and personality disorder

There have always been problems in defining personality with any degree of consensus. It is a word used in common parlance to cover a wide range of

Manie sans délire (madness without delirium or delusion) ——▶ moral insanity ——▶ moral imbecility (defectiveness) Mental Deficiency Act 1913 ——▶ (constitutional) psychopathic inferiority ——▶ 'neurotic character' ——▶ psychopathy ——▶ sociopathy (USA) ——▶ anti social personality disorder (DSM-IV) ——▶ dissocial personality disorder (ICD-10) ——▶ dangerous severe personality disorder (Home Office and Department of Health).

Figure 5.1   From Pinel (1806) to the Home Office and Department of Health (1999)

attributes and behaviours. However, Trethowan and Sims (1983) offer the following useful statement:

> Personality may be either considered subjectively i.e. in terms of what the [person] believes and describes himself as an individual, or, objectively in terms of what an observer notices about his more consistent patterns of behaviour . . . Personality will include such things as mood state, attitudes and opinions and all these must be measured against how people comport themselves in their social environments. If we describe a person as having a 'normal' personality, we use the word in a statistical sense indicating that various personality traits are present in a broadly normal extent neither to gross excess nor extreme deficiency. Abnormal personality is, therefore, a variation upon an accepted yet broadly conceived, range of personality.
>
> (Trethowan and Sims 1983: 9)

The words of a non-psychiatric professional offer a slightly broader 'take' on their definition. Miri Rubin – a medieval historian – writes:

> Personal and group identity is best thought of as a cluster of attributes and associations including aspects of age, gender, region, occupation, experience and training. *Areas of identity are always heightened when they seem most different.*
>
> (Rubin 2005: 8, emphasis added)

When we consider what Trethowan and Sims (1983) describe as the *extremes* of personality, the two definitions of personality disorder as given in the DSM-IV (*Diagnostic and Statistical Manual of Mental Disorders*: APA 2005), and ICD-10 (*International Classification of Mental and Behavioural Disorders*: WHO 1992) amplify these. The DSM-IV defines them as:

> An enduring pattern of inner experience and behaviour that deviates markedly from the expectations of the individual's culture, is pervasive and inflexible, has an onset in adolescence or early childhood, is stable over time, and leads to distress or impairment.
>
> (quoted in National Institute for Mental Health in England (NIMHE) 2003: 9)

(See also Snowden and Kane 2003.)

The ICD-10 defines personality disorder in the following terms:

> A severe disturbance in the characterlogical and behavioural tendencies in the individual involving several areas of the personality, and nearly always associated with considerable personal and social disruption.
>
> (quoted in NIMHE 2003: 9)

(See also Tyrer 1990; Tyrer et al. 1990; Tyrer et al. 2003.)

Both these definitions indicate that personality disorders may present in a variety of forms. To my mind the ICD definition comes nearest to indicating the seriously deviant (and delinquent) end of the spectrum (for example, 'considerable personal and social disruption'). It was that aspect that was stressed in the Mental Health Act 1983 *legal* definition of psychopathic disorder.

> A persistent disorder or disability of mind (whether or not including significant impairment of intelligence) which results in abnormally aggressive or seriously irresponsible conduct on the part of the person concerned.
>
> (Mental Health Act 1983: Section 1(2))

The term psychopathic disorder (which many have considered to be pejorative and confusing) has now disappeared from current legislation and is subsumed under the broad definition of any disorder or disability of the mind (see Fennell 2007: Chapter 3).

In summary, we may consider that the modern concept of personality disorder seems to represent two interlocking notions. The first suggests that it is present when any abnormality of personality causes problems, either to the person themselves or to others. The second carries a more pejorative connotation; it implies unacceptable, antisocial behaviour incurring dislike for the person showing such behaviour and a rejection of them (see later). It is in embracing this latter interpretation that the term 'psychopath' is so often applied.

Causes and characteristics

There is a vast literature concerning the possible origins of psychopathic disorder and an equally vast literature on its characteristic features. No attempt is made here to review this literature at great length, merely to address certain aspects of it as a prelude to some discussion of the problems of management. Postulated origins have included genetic and hereditary factors and close familial environmental influences. There has always been much debate and speculation concerning the possible origins of serious antisocial conduct. The early work of John Bowlby was seminal in this field. In its early days, Bowlby's work had been the subject of considerable misunderstanding. In his study of forty-four juvenile thieves, Bowlby (1946) suggested that if children were deprived of maternal care they might become delinquent. But he added an important 'rider' that was sometimes forgotten, namely that this absence of maternal care might be offset by the presence of a mother substitute. Bowlby developed his early work into his more general study of attachment theory (see Bowlby 1971, 1979), and other workers have made significant contributions, such as Ainsworth (1962), Robins (1966) and Rutter (1999). One of the possible unfortunate byproducts of all this seminal work has been the notion that absent or inadequate parental care might be the predominating cause of a failure in bonding. Thus severe criticism and blame would be made of the parents for their poor parenting skills. But, consider the following possibility. What if, for various reasons (possibly neurologically based), from infancy the child had a defective 'mechanism' for responding to affection and showed a marked and lasting lack of empathic response? It takes a novelist to demonstrate this possibility in graphic terms. Lionel Shriver (2005), in her story of the development of one such child into 'psychopathic' adulthood, does just this.[2] Coid (1989) advocates caution in espousing the notion of psychopathic disorder as a *single* entity and suggests that:

> The sheer complexity and range of psychopathology in psychopathic disorder has previously led to the suggestion that these individuals could be considered to suffer from a series of conditions that would best be subsumed under a broad generic term 'psychopathic disorders' rather than a single entity.
>
> (Coid 1989: 756)

During the 1990s, interest has been revived concerning possible 'organic' causes, including both major and minor cerebral 'insults' in infancy and the consequences of obstetric complications. If such developments subsequently prove to have unequivocally firm foundations, one could envisage a situation where issues of responsibility (and notably diminished responsibility) may well have to be addressed by the courts. This is an arena already fraught with problems concerning the relationship between medicine (particularly psychiatry and neuro-psychiatry) and the law (see Spence et al. 2004). It has also been suggested that the environment plays a significant part in the aetiology of the disorder. It may well be that, as with other mentally disturbed states such as the schizophrenias, it is the interplay of social forces and pressures acting upon an already vulnerable personality (arising for whatever reason) that may tend to produce the conditions. As already indicated, some of the highly complicated and sophisticated neuro-physio-chemical research undertaken in recent years fosters speculation that *some* of the answers to the problem of aetiology may well be found in the area of brain structure and biochemistry. Similar possibilities are of equal interest. For example, one cannot ignore the evidence, admittedly laboratory based, of such factors as low anxiety thresholds, cortical immaturity (childlike patterns of brainwaves in adults), frontal lobe damage and, perhaps most relevant of all, the *true*, as distinct from the wrongly labelled, psychopath's need for excitement – the achievement of a 'high'. Such a need is described graphically in Wambaugh's (1989) account of the case of Colin Pitchfork.

Pitchfork was convicted of the rape and murder of two teenage girls in Leicestershire during the period 1983–86. In interviews with the police, it is alleged he stated that he obtained a 'high' when he exposed himself to women (he had previous convictions for indecent exposure prior to his two major offences). He also obtained a 'high' from the knowledge that his victims or likely victims were virgins. He is said to have described an additional aspect of his excitement, namely obtaining sex outside marriage. As with others assessed as psychopathic, he also demonstrated a great degree of charm; for example, he was able to get his wife to forgive him for a number of instances of admitted unfaithfulness. (Pitchfork's case is also of interest in that it involved the earliest attempt to use DNA profiling – a practice now fairly routine.)

Whether this disorder is inherited, acquired through some learning process, or due to other neurophysiologic factors, whether organic or trauma induced, is unknown at this time. It is suggested that the characteristics of severely personality disordered (SPD) individuals might be capable of modification by the environment so that while some can be found at the most severe end of the spectrum or personality disorder, possibly engaged in crime or certainly having come to the attention of the criminal justice system in some way, others manage to live in a relatively normal and certainly law-abiding way, though they still make the lives of those around them thoroughly stressful and miserable. A more extensive analysis of the current possibilities in relation to the genesis of SPD can be found in Millon et al. (2003). (See also Patrick 2007; also special issue of *Psychology, Crime and Law* 2007, 13(1), ed. K. Howells.) It is worth emphasizing that in terms of causation, since the late 1980s there has been an increase in the number of likely postulations regarding the causal factors in relation to SPD. This must, in part, be due to advances both in medical technology and in terms of a developing willingness on the part of society to accept that there may be a multiplicity of explanations for this complex condition. The reader is cautioned that what follows is neither an exhaustive nor a definitive list.

The biochemical-neurophysiologic approach and the limbic system

As already indicated, it is a relatively recent suggestion that SPD might be caused by alterations of, or abnormalities in, the normal chemical processes of the brain, which in turn may adversely affect the motivational processes that guide thoughts and perceptions. Such alterations of the normal chemical processes of the brain, or brain activity, can result from brain diseases such as cancer, nutritional deficiencies, brain injury, pollutants (such as lead) and even hypoglycaemia (see also Chapter 4).

In many instances such brain damage goes unnoticed, since the brain has an innate capacity to compensate itself for damaged areas. This appears not to be the case, however, where the limbic system is concerned. The limbic system is located in the upper brain stem and lower cerebrum portion of the brain. It is thought to be directly involved with brain processes relating to motivation and aggression. When the limbic system is damaged it can result in a person presenting with uncontrollable rage and violence. Such damage can be organic (such as the viral infection rabies, which specifically attacks the limbic system) or alternatively non-organic resulting from brain injury or trauma.

This approach is relatively new and unique, since it moots the possibility that a person's behaviour can be explained without necessarily having to refer to provocation by an external event.

The cerebral cortex

To date there has been relatively little systematic study of psychopathy from a *neurological* perspective. This is probably due to two reasons. First, since, as already mentioned, psychopathy as a term is controversial and difficult to define, it follows that empirical research regarding such a broad and ill-defined term is difficult to carry out. Second, studying the neurobiology of cohorts of psychopaths is difficult because a great many psychopaths will never find themselves in a clinical psychiatric setting. This said, the seminal work of Cleckley (1976), built upon by Hare et al. (1990) in their development of a research scale (the Psychopathy Checklist, now known as the PCL-R), has shown that valid and reliable research can indeed be carried out to predict recidivism in criminal populations. This is done using a two-factor structure, consisting first of personality traits such as glibness, lack of remorse and failure to accept responsibility, and second, antisocial traits and aggression. In this context the possibility of developing a neurobiological approach to psychopathy becomes feasible.

Neurobiological underpinnings to this condition have been furthered in the findings of studies of the cerebral cortex using the electroencephalogram (EEG). These have tended to show that the 'slow wave' activity of the brain of some aggressive psychopaths bears some degree of resemblance to the EEG tracings found in children. Such findings have led to the formulation of a hypothesis of cortical immaturity, which may explain why the aggressive behaviour of some psychopaths seems to become less violent with advancing years because, as in the case with children, the brain matures.

Heredity

It is by now fairly well established that some types of behaviour run in families. Notwithstanding this, the nature versus nurture debate goes on. However, as McGuffin and Thapar (2003: 215) report: 'The evidence pointing to a genetic contribution to antisocial personality comes from three main sources'.

These sources are first, studies on animals which point to a genetic component to some temperamental features such as aggression, second, genetic research in relation to twins which has suggested that certain traits (including antisocial ones) are hereditary, and third, studies of criminality within families which indicate an hereditary component to both juvenile delinquency and adult antisocial conduct. More recently, the study of molecular genetics is furthering understanding of the biological bases of inherited personality traits. One of the difficulties regarding the application of genetics to this area of study is that it remains uncertain as to whether psychopathy is a 'discrete entity', or whether it is a continuum of behaviour ranging from the blatantly pathological to the normal (see, for example, Roberts and Coid 2007). I would suggest that the latter is more likely, but given the difficulty of defining this condition, the application of research in relation to it remains uncertain and problematic. The study of molecular genetics may provide more certainty in the future. The work of Brunner et al. (1993) has gone some way in identifying a genetic marker associated with aggression which has helped to further our understanding of serious violent, unprovoked behaviour in some individuals. However, these conditions are rare and it remains difficult to generalize such findings to a wider population.

Cortical under arousal

Research in the field of neurobiology has also suggested that psychopathy may be linked with a defect or malfunction of certain brain mechanisms concerned with emotional activity and the regulation of behaviour. More specifically, cortical arousal refers to the situation where the brain is wide awake, attentive to stimulation and working at its maximum. Conversely, low cortical arousal refers to a lack of attention, tiredness and lack of interest. It has been suggested that psychopathy may be related to a lowered state of cortical excitability and to the attenuation of sensory input, particularly input that would, in ordinary circumstances, have disturbing consequences. This may partially explain the apparent callous and cold indifference to the pain and suffering of others which is demonstrated by some seriously psychopathically disordered individuals. This may also go some way to explain why certain psychopaths (particularly the seriously aggressive) may seek stimulation with arousing or exciting qualities and have reported that they derive a 'high' from their actions (see earlier discussion of Colin Pitchfork's case). McCord (1982: 28) stated that 'most psychopaths do not see security as a goal in itself; rather they crave constant change, whirlwind variety and new stimuli'. Further, he suggested that Ian Brady and Myra Hindley illustrated the psychopath's craving for excitement, since the ways in which they behaved were 'simply ways to attain new levels of excitement, a new "consciousness" and a temporary escape from boredom'. This craving may render the psychopath unaware of many of the more subtle cues required for the maintenance of socially acceptable behaviour and for adequate socialization – a failure to register.

Inability to learn/inconsequentiality

It has been postulated, since human behaviour is flexible and not fixed, that both criminal and non-criminal behaviours stem from the same general social-psychological processes and that, as such, many types of behaviour are learned, specifically through association with others. In the case of psychopathy however, it has been tentatively suggested that these individuals do not possess the same ability to learn what may be regarded as socially acceptable behaviour and, in particular, find it difficult to learn responses that are either motivated by fear or reinforced by fear reduction. There is experimental evidence to suggest that psychopaths are correspondingly less able to make connections between past events and the consequentiality of future behaviour.

Long-term substance abuse

It should be noted that the effects of long-term substance abuse often bear a close resemblance to SPD. Such secondary personality disordered individuals can usually be distinguished from true or primary personality disordered individuals by the presence of anxiety or guilt in the secondary group. This can normally be distinguished only by qualified medical clinicians, since the 'psychopathic' individual will demonstrate highly manipulative behaviour, making this distinction hard to make. The close interrelationship between psychopathy and substance abuse has been acknowledged for some time and issues of co-morbidity are ever present for researchers involved in clinical studies. A prospective longitudinal study carried out by Knop et al. (1993), in which an experimental cohort of 255 children with alcoholic fathers was identified, followed the children's development until the age of 30. At the conclusion of the study the social functioning of the group with substance dependence and/or antisocial personality disorder was significantly poorer than that of all other diagnostic groups. It may therefore be possible to utilize this type of research to predict those individuals who may be at a higher risk of developing substance abuse disorders and/or antisocial personality disorder later in life. What we do know is that those suffering from it or, perhaps more importantly, making others suffer from it, are extremely difficult to work with and manage (see later comments). Mann and Moran (2000) put the matter into perspective, as follows:

> Sadly, when looking for evidence to inform decision-making about the placement of personality disordered patients, our knowledge is lacking. Psychiatry has an unfortunate history of being characterized by opinions rather than facts, and in this regard, both the government and psychiatrists need to stand back from firm decisions until more is known . . . the whole diagnostic group of personality disordered patients is being judged by the difficulties and anxieties caused by one subgroup (the so-called 'severely personality disordered'). A sense of proportion is required.
>
> (Mann and Moran 2000: 16)

Some key characteristics

Although some of these have already been alluded to in the previous section, this issue merits some further comment. Sir Martin Roth (1990), a doyen of British psychiatry, once suggested (in summary form) that the key features of psychopathic disorder were egotism, immaturity in various manifestations, aggressiveness, low frustration tolerance and the inability to learn from experience so that social demands are never met. Roth's brief listing encapsulates many of the sixteen detailed characteristics suggested by Cleckley (1976) in various editions of *The Mask of Sanity*.[3] To these items I would add the following three elements. First, the curious *super-ego lacunae*, rather than the total lack of conscience suggested by some authorities. Second, the greater than usual need for excitement and arousal to which I have already referred. Third, a capacity to create chaos among family, friends, and those involved in trying to manage or contain them. I would suggest that this last characteristic is one of the most accurate indicators of the true, as distinct from the erroneously labelled, psychopath. It is often attested to by those who have extensive clinical experience in dealing with the psychopathically disordered. For example, the lack of true feeling (empathy) exhibited by the psychopath was stated graphically in the early 1960s by Johns and Quay (1962) in their comment that psychopaths 'know the words but not the music'. Rieber and Green (1988) add four salient characteristics in support of this, namely thrill-seeking, pathological glibness, antisocial pursuit of power and absence of guilt (quoted in Egger 1990: 82). The presence of such characteristics has led to many difficulties for academics, lawyers, psychiatrists and other health care and criminal justice professionals (see, for example, Gayford and Jungalwalla 1986).

In 1977 I made the following observations in an article that appeared in the *Prison Service Journal* (Prins 1977). The imaginary scenario I provided may give some indication of the scale of the problems involved in defining characteristics and management:

> Imagine, if you can, a top-level conference has been called to discuss the meaning of that much used and abused word *psychopathy*. You are privileged to be an observer at these discussions at which are present psychiatrists, psychologists, sociologists, lawyers, sentencers, theologians, philosophers, staff of penal establishments and special hospitals, social workers and probation officers. You have high expectations that some total wisdom will emerge from this well-informed and experienced group of people and that a definition will emerge that will pass the closest scrutiny of all concerned. After all, *this* is a gathering of *experts*. Alas, your expectations would have a quality of fantasy about them, for in reality you would find as many definitions as experts present. Let me just present one or two examples of this statement. There might be little agreement among psychiatrists; the term would be used to cover a very wide range of mental disorders, including those we might describe as 'neuroses' in this country; for some psychiatrists (for example, from the United States), the term might be synonymous with what we could describe as recidivism. The lawyers in the group would disagree also. Some might well accept the definition in the Mental Health Act 1959 [as it then was] which describes psychopathy as a 'persistent disorder or disability of mind (whether or not including subnormality of intelligence) which results in abnormally aggressive behaviour or seriously irresponsible conduct on the part of the patient and requires or is susceptible to medical treatment . . .' However, they would immediately begin to ask questions about the legal implications of the words 'disability of mind' and 'irresponsible conduct'. At this stage, the philosophers would no doubt chip in and also ask searching questions about the same terms. Later on in the discussion, a theologian might start asking awkward questions about the differences between 'sickness' and 'sin' and 'good' and 'evil'. The representative from the field of sociology in the group might usefully remind us that psychopaths lack what they describe as a capacity for role-taking, i.e. seeing yourself in an appropriate role in relation to others in their roles in [their] environment. And so the discussion would go on and on.

Don't ever assume that it has been different. For one hundred and fifty years the arguments have raged over definition, classification and management.

(Prins 1977: 8–9)

One might well ask, 'Have things changed much since that was written?' To which I would be forced to answer, 'Not all that much'. Moreover, a group such as the one described might need to be augmented to be more representative of today's thinking. For instance, we could usefully find a space for a geneticist, a developmental paediatrician, representatives from the Home Office and Department of Health, the voluntary sector (who do so much to cope with these 'hard to like' individuals) and – who knows in this progressive day and age – a consumer of the service and certainly a victim? A parallel to such a hypothetical group can perhaps be seen in the large conference prompted and attended by the Secretaries of State for Social Services and the Home Department in July 1999, when they highlighted for comment their joint proposals for dealing with the management of those persons exhibiting 'dangerous severe personality disorder' (DSPD) (see Home Office and Department of Health 1999; Prins 1999). It is of particular interest to note that the government ministers (perhaps wisely) provided only a loose definition of what they understood dangerous severe personality disorder to be and expressed the firm intention to fund major research into the problem – an intention now being put into practice. Personality disorder is referred to in this document as 'an inclusive term referring to a disorder of the development of personality . . . and is not a category of mental illness' (Home Office and Department of Health 1999: 5). Further, the document states that the phrase

> dangerous severely personality disordered (DSPD) is used to describe people who have an identifiable personality disorder to a severe degree, who post a high risk to other people because of serious anti-social behaviour resulting from their disorder.
>
> (Home Office and Department of Health 1999: 9)

These definitions can reasonably be regarded as 'loose' and reflect the reservations of experienced psychiatrists such as Sir Martin Roth (1990: 449), who commented that 'in its present state of development the concept of psychopathy is fuzzy at the edges and in need of refinement'. (For a useful commentary on some current concerns, see Laing 1999; see also a special issue on DSPD in *British Journal of Forensic Practice* 2006, 8(4).)

If we see psychopathic disorder as a process of disturbed psychological development (however caused) then we need not rely exclusively upon clinical descriptions. Its nature, early onset and manifestations are depicted clearly in the aged Duchess of York's reviling of her son Richard III in Shakespeare's play:

> Thou cam'st on earth to make the earth my hell.
> A grievous burden was thy birth to me;
> Tetchy and wayward was thy infancy;
> Thy school-days frightful, desp'rate, wild and furious;
> Thy prime of manhood daring, bold and venturous;
> Thy age confirm'd, proud, subtle, sly and bloody,
> More mild, but yet more harmful, kind in hatred:
> What comfortable hour canst' thou name
> That ever grac'd me with thy company?
>
> (*Richard III*, Act 4, Sc. 4)

Here we have the aged Duchess describing graphically some of the characteristics we regard as important in terms of possible aetiology and presentation. For example, an apparent difficult birth and long-standing antisociality – a requirement of the DSM-IVR-TM (APA 2005) and the ICD-10 (WHO 1992), which then becomes more marked in adulthood. All of this is accompanied by a veneer of charm and sophistication which only serves to act as a mask for the underlying themes of chaos and the potential for destructiveness. It should be re-emphasized that neither the DSM-IVR nor the ICD-10 refer to psychopathic disorder; the former refers only to antisocial personality disorder and the latter to dissocial personality disorder. As previously stated, neither description equates exactly with what has, up till now, been the legal description – psychopathic disorder. Although changing or deleting the name will not necessarily do away with our dislike for such patients, clients and offenders, describing and trying to delineate the disorder has the advantage of hopefully setting some boundaries to it. Creating typologies may also assist in management, even if the latter is very difficult. We should also note that a number of clinical and legal authorities considered that the espousal of the term 'psychopathic', and all that this entailed in practice, was unhelpful (see, for example, Blackburn 1988; Lewis and Appleby 1988; Solomka 1990; Cavadino 1998; Maden 1999).

Some problems of management

This section of the chapter is divided into two subsections; the first deals briefly with legal aspects as most of them have been dealt with in previous chapters and the second deals with clinical issues. The two elements are best seen as a whole. However, in an attempt to achieve clarity, I have chosen to split them. Some of my readers may consider that this is a largely artificial (and somewhat pedantic) distinction.

Legal implications

A brief history of the development of the law in relation to psychopathic disorder has been provided in earlier chapters and need not be repeated here. However, it seems important to make some comment on the legal wrangles that have occurred in relation to *treatability*, since this has been of significance in determining clinical management. There has been a great deal of discussion concerning whether psychopathy is an *illness* or a *disorder*. Certainly Cleckley (1976) seems to have considered it to be an illness, as did Henderson (1939). More recently, Professor Robert Kendall (1999) suggested:

> the historical reasons for regarding personality disorders as fundamentally different from mental illnesses are being undermined by both clinical and genetic evidence. Effective treatments for personality disorders would probably have a decisive influence on psychiatrists' attitudes.
>
> (Kendall 1999: 11)

Gunn (1999) has suggested an additional reason for the change of emphasis regarding treatability. This lies in the parlous state of general psychiatric provision, and most particularly in large conurbations such as London. The legal connotations of treatment have also resulted in a number of court rulings in England, Wales and in Scotland. In the case of *R. v. Canons Park Mental Health Review Tribunal ex parte A. [1995] QB 60*, the Court of Appeal held that the mere refusal of a patient to participate in group psychotherapy did not, of itself, indicate untreatability. A subsequent case in Scotland, *Reid v. Secretary of State for Scotland [1992] 2 WLR 28*, reopened the whole issue. In brief, this case concerned an offender-patient detained without limit of time under the provisions of the Scottish Mental Health Act 1984. In a ruling the Law Lords held that under Section 145(1) of the Act, medical treatment was to be given a broad meaning and that supervised care which endeavoured to prevent deterioration of the symptoms – but not the disorder itself – might justify liability to continued detention. In hearing this case the Law Lords appear to have decided *inter alia* that the Canons Park case had been wrongly decided. The then current view was summarized by Eldergill (1997):

> It can be seen that the treatability condition is satisfied if medical treatment in its broadest statutory sense – which includes nursing care – is eventually likely to bring some symptomatic relief to prevent the patient's mental health from deteriorating. There are few (if any) conditions which are not treatable in this sense.
>
> (Eldergill 1997: 225)

Unfortunately this saga did not end with that decision. There were continuing concerns about possible loopholes in the law that would allow dangerous psychopaths to obtain their freedom, and the case of Michael Stone illustrates this concern. Stone killed a mother, one of her daughters and their dog, and grievously injured her other daughter. His case is of interest because of the number of hearings it engendered, including a first trial and conviction, an appeal to the Court of Appeal and a second trial. He was subsequently also re-referred to the Court of Appeal. This further appeal failed and he was returned to prison to serve the life sentences originally imposed. Of importance was the *alleged* reluctance of the psychiatric services to 'treat' Stone. This seems to have prompted the political decision to introduce the concept of *dangerous severe personality disorder*. It is worth noting, however, that this move must be seen against a mounting background of political concern regarding dangerous behaviours engaged in by those showing various forms of mental disorder. (For the full judgment of the Stone case, see Citation no. (2005) EWCA Crim 105 no. 200300595/B3. 21.1.05; see also Francis 2007; Prins 2007.)

In Scotland, the case of Ruddle (*Ruddle v. Secretary of State for Scotland [1999]* GWD 29 1395) led the Scottish Parliament to pass, as a matter of urgency, the Mental Health (Public Safety and Appeals) (Scotland) Act 1999, which added public safety to the grounds for not discharging patients under Scottish mental health legislation. The main effect of this legislation had been to change the definition of mental disorder to 'mental illness (including personality disorder) or mental handicap however caused or manifested' and to require continued detention of a restricted patient 'if the patient is suffering from a mental disorder the effect of which is such that it is necessary in order to protect the public from serious harm'. Crichton et al. (2001) suggested that one of the 'incidental' effects of this enactment has been to clarify the fact that personality disorder [had] always been included (but by implication only) within the meaning of mental disorder in Scottish mental health legislation. Further, they also suggested that the 1999 Act merely plugged 'a loophole' and that further developments should wait upon any action that may be taken as a result of the two major reviews of Scottish mental health legislation and practice by the Millan (1999) and Maclean (2000) Committees (see also Darjee and Crichton 2002). For a discussion of some of the new arrangements under the recently implemented Scottish legislation, see Thomson (2005).

Clinical issues

From all that has been written so far, it should be obvious that those labelled as psychopathic present considerable psycho-socio-legal problems and that their day-to-day management causes the professionals involved both 'headache' and 'heart-ache'. Some aspects of mental health and criminal justice professionals' engagement in these encounters have already been touched upon, and the intention in this section is merely to highlight some of them further. Dr Peter Scott addressed some of these issues in the mid 1970s in a thought-provoking and under-referred-to report entitled *Has Psychiatry Failed in the Treatment of Offenders?* (Scott 1975). Scott suggested that we most frequently fail those who need us most. Such individuals often fall into two (perhaps overlapping) categories, the 'dangerous offender' and the 'unrewarding', 'degenerate' and 'not nice' offender. Of such 'embarrassing' patients Scott (1975) maintained that he or she is the patient who is

> essentially the one who does not pay for treatment, the coin in which the patient pays being (i) dependence – i.e. being manifestly unable to care for themselves, and thus appealing to the maternal part of our nature; (ii) getting better (responding to our 'life-giving' measures); (iii) in either of these processes, showing gratitude, if possible cheerfully.
>
> (Scott 1975: 8)

In other words, those patients, clients and offenders that Scott had in mind are just the ones who reject our 'best efforts', are manipulative, and delight in giving us a pretext for rejecting them so that they can continue on their 'unloved' and 'unloving' way. In Scott's terms, 'the "not nice" patients' are the ones who

> habitually appear to be well able to look after themselves but don't, and [as stated above] reject attempts to help them, break institutional rules, get drunk, upset other patients, or even quietly go to the devil in their own way quite heedless of nurse and doctor.
>
> (Scott 1975: 8)

Scott (1960) suggested other factors which are relevant to any consideration of the management of *so-called* psychopaths. I emphasize the word *so-called* because Scott did not feel there was much merit in distinguishing psychopaths from hardened chronic (recidivist) criminals – albeit a minority view (Scott 1960). Further, he stated that:

> There is a natural philanthropic tendency to extend help to the defenceless – probably an extension of parental caring . . . if this fails so that embarrassing people or patients are seen to accumulate, then anxiety is aroused and some form of institution is set up to absorb the problem . . . Not all embarrassing patients like being tidied up and these tend to be compulsorily detained . . . Within the detaining

institution two opposing aims begin to appear – the therapeutic endeavour to cure and liberate on the one hand, and the controlling custodial function on the other.

(Scott 1975: 9)

Scott (1975: 10) went on to suggest that although these functions should be complementary 'there is a tendency for them to polarise and ultimately, to split, like a dividing cell, into two separate institutions'. However, he also suggested that

neither of the two new institutions can quite eliminate the tendency from which it fled, so that the therapeutic institution now begins to miss the custodial function and tries hard to send some of its patients back to custody, and the custodial institution is unable to tolerate being unkind to people all the time and begins to set up a new nucleus of therapy.

(Scott 1975: 9)

His perceptive 'management' observations might well be considered carefully by those involved in implementing the institutional care programme for DSPD individuals now underway. These are the unlikeable clients, patients and offenders and often this dislike will operate at an unconscious level. Three, admittedly somewhat dated, quotations from the views of psychiatrists are useful in illustrating this problem, and their words are applicable to all professionals working in the field of criminal justice and forensic mental health. Maier (1990) suggested:

Could it be after all these Freudian years, that psychiatrists have denied the hatred they feel for psychopaths and criminals, and thus have been unable to treat psychopaths adequately because their conceptual bases for treatment have been distorted by unconscious, denied feelings from the start?

(Maier 1990: 776)

A somewhat similar view had been proffered earlier by Treves-Brown (1977), who stated that:

As long as a doctor believes that psychopaths are mostly 'bad', his successful treatment rate will be dismal. Since it takes two to form a relationship, an outside observer could be forgiven for suspecting that a doctor who describes a patient as unable to form a relationship, is simply trying to justify his own hostility to his patient.

(Treves-Brown 1977: 63)

Finally Winnicott (1949) – a doyen of child psychiatry, writing over half a century ago about the 'antisocial tendency' – gave further support for such views as follows:

> However much he loves his . . . [hard to like] . . . patients he cannot help hating them and fearing them, and the better he knows this the less will hate and fear be the motives determining what he does for his patients.
>
> (Winnicott 1949: 71)

These three quotations indicate that the mechanism of 'denial' is not merely the prerogative of patients and offenders, and for a very useful account of denial at a more general level, see Cohen (2001).

Despite the unattractiveness of such patients and the sometimes unconscious reactions of therapists, a number of forensic mental health and criminal justice professionals have expressed a degree of optimism about treatment. In the early 1990s Tennent et al. (1993) sought the opinions of psychiatrists, psychologists and probation officers about treatability. The survey was admittedly small, as was the response rate. However, there was reasonable evidence to suggest that although there were few clear-cut views as to the best treatment modalities, there *were* clear indications as to those felt to be helpful. For example, there were higher expectations of treatment efficacy with symptoms such as chronically 'antisocial', 'abnormally aggressive' and 'lacking control impulses' and much lower expectations for symptoms such as 'inability to experience guilt', 'lack of remorse or shame' and 'pathological egocentricity'. Support for the findings of this modest survey can be found in a much more extensive survey by Cope (1993) on behalf of the Forensic Section of the Royal College of Psychiatrists. Cope surveyed all forensic psychiatrists working in secure hospitals, units and similar settings in England and Wales. The majority of her respondents (response rate 91 per cent) were in favour of offering treatment to severely personality disordered (psychopathic) patients. Some confirmation of this optimism derives from another source. In an attempt to ascertain the motivations of consultant forensic psychiatrists for working in forensic psychiatric settings, I discovered that one of the attractions of the work was the challenge presented by 'psychopaths' (Prins 1998). Another fact that emerged from this survey was the need for forensic psychiatrists to work with and encourage their colleagues in general psychiatry to deal with such patients. This is a point emphasized very cogently by Gunn (1999); as he suggests, someone has to deal with such individuals and psychiatry should play its full part. For studies of work specifically with DSPD patients from the psychiatrists' point of view, see Haddock et al. (2001), Duggan (2007) and Langton (2007); from a forensic nursing perspective, see Bowers (2002), and more generally, see Harris and Rice (2007).

Some statements by a number of my survey respondents were very illuminating. One of them enjoyed the challenge presented by the severity and complexity of the cases which produced 'a kind of appalled fascination'. Another attraction was the chance to work with a wide range of agencies and disciplines and to pursue a more eclectic approach to patient care. Stimulation was another important factor (a factor shared with the psychopathic – see earlier discussion). Perhaps it takes one to recognize one! One stated: 'I could not envisage twenty years of listening to the neurotic and worried well'; 'after forensic psychiatry, other specialities seemed very tame and had much less variety and challenge'.

Whatever form of professional training is eventually formulated in order to deal more effectively with psychopathically disordered individuals, understanding and management will only be successful through the adoption of the need for a truly multidisciplinary approach (as implied in the 'imaginary' gathering quoted earlier). Such an approach would not only serve to take the broadest possible view of the topic but, at a narrower clinical level, should help to obviate potential missed diagnoses (for example, the importance of organic factors such as brain damage). Scott (1960) has some interesting observations to make on this matter. He stated that:

> This may be the point at which to acknowledge that, with psychopaths, highly refined psychotherapeutic procedures applied by medical men, are often no more successful, sometimes less successful, than the simpler and less esoteric approaches of certain social workers, probation officers, [and others] . . . some workers intuitively obtain good results with certain psychopaths; it should be possible to find out how they do it.
>
> (Scott 1960: 1645)

Sadly, no definitive research information is available to answer Scott's implied question about treatment success. However, what we do know is that severely dangerous and deviant behaviour requires calm and well-informed confrontation. In the words of George Lyward – a highly gifted worker with severely personality disordered older adolescents – 'Patience is love that can wait' (see Burn 1956). Coupled with this is the need to tolerate, without loss of temper, the hate, hostility, manipulation and 'splitting' shown by such individuals, together with an ability not to take such personal affronts as attacks. The psychiatrist and psychotherapist Penelope Campling (1996) has provided an excellent account of the management of such behaviours, and for a research-based exposition of the potential value of psychosocial therapy for severe personality disorders, see Chiesa and Fonagy (2003). It is also essential for professionals to have more than an 'intellectual' understanding of what the patient has done. Sometimes, this can be 'stomach-churning' and offers many opportunities for denial on the part of the professional. Such understanding also requires a degree of what has been described in another context as 'intestinal fortitude', an expression used by Michael Davies, leader of the BBC Symphony Orchestra, in relation to the playing of certain problematical orchestral works (BBC broadcast, 10 July 1999).

It is worth re-emphasizing the importance of the phenomenon of denial which is not the sole prerogative of our clients, patients and offenders. For, as Pericles says in Shakespeare's play of that name, 'Few love to hear the sins they love to act' (*Pericles*, Act 1, Sc. 1). The more troublesome and anxiety-making the relationship, the more the need not to go it alone. This is not an area of work that should be characterized by prima donna activities by professionals of either sex, for there are dangerous workers as well as dangerous clients, patients and offenders. In my view, there are three qualities that are of paramount importance in dealing with severely personality (psychopathically) disordered individuals. These are *consistence* (the capacity to take a firm line in dealing with deflecting activities by the client); *persistence* (expending efforts over very considerable periods of time, perhaps even years – a view that is supported by the belief in the occurrence of cortical maturation and the longer term benefits of team therapy in institutions such as those at Grendon Prison described by Taylor (2000) and Coughlin (2003)). Put in more vernacular terms, the capacity to hang in there, and finally, *insistence* (the capacity to give clear indications that requirements of supervision are to be met in spite of resistance on the part of the client). Such insistence must take priority when expectations of what supervision requires of the client are initially set out in the professional–client relationship. For some useful key 'tips', see Harris and Rice (2007: 367–368). For a small-scale study of the problems involved in providing services for a 'cluster' of personality disordered patients, see Lee et al. (2008). For a useful example of the 'ploys' used by the psychopathic when being interviewed, see Quayle (2008).

A final cautionary tale

The problems of trying to legislate for persons suffering from severe personality (psychopathic) disorder which may, from time to time, make them a danger to themselves and to others, are exemplified in the extra-ordinary Australian case of Garry David as told by Deidre Greig in her disturbing book, *Neither Bad nor Mad* (2002). Her account demonstrates the inability of both the criminal justice and mental health care systems to deal with such individuals, and Garry's story may be told here very briefly. Garry was born in November 1954 and had a disturbed family history. He died of complications arising from grievous self-inflicted injuries in June 1992. Garry's severe personality disorder gave rise to many years of dramatic and highly persistent disruptive and manipulative behaviours.

These included serious and highly bizarre episodes of both self-harm and harm to others. The inability of both systems to deal with him effectively led to numerous political manoeuvres to effect his indeterminate detention on the basis of his 'dangerousness'. *This included the passing of a single piece of legislation to deal solely with his case.* Over the years, numerous psychiatric professionals who had dealings with him could not agree on the nature and extent of his mental disorder or, in fact, whether or not he was mentally disordered at all. Limitations of space preclude a detailed discussion of the sad saga of the various commissions of inquiry, court hearings and appeals that dealt with this case, but what they do signify is the highly complex nature of the fluctuating relationships between health care and penal institutions which have already been referred to in this chapter. One of the more important (but unsurprising) findings in Greig's account (2002) is suggested by one of her commission sources:

> One lesson to be learned from legal history is that hard cases make bad law and that there is a risk that a hasty and ill-conceived response to one particular case . . . can seriously disturb a larger and well thought structure.
>
> (Greig 2002: 151)

The UK government is much concerned about 'Managing Dangerous People with Severe Personality Disorder' and has sponsored various possibilities, the most disquieting being the *apparent* possibility of detaining someone on the basis of what it is felt *they might do*. Other weaknesses include the expectation that criminal justice and mental health professionals have fool-proof skills in predicting future behaviour and its risks. At present, we are trying to treat or manage a problematic group of people with vast gaps in our knowledge base, coupled with a significant lack of capacity for self-examination when trying to engage with such people. Confronting one's own 'demons' is crucial in this respect. Psychopathic disorder is not going to go away whatever we call the condition in the future; and it has been rightly described as the Achilles Heel of criminal justice and psychiatry.

Concluding comments

I have emphasized in this chapter that the group of people we identify as 'psychopathic' arouse strong emotions in those who are charged with managing them. Discussion about these troubled and troubling individuals tends to generate more heat than light; I trust that the observations in this chapter will aid more considered discussion. The degree of success (or otherwise) of the four pilot DSPD centres (at HM Prisons Frankland and Whitemoor and the high security hospitals Broadmoor and Rampton) will be followed with much interest. Bowers et al. (2005) have already begun to identify some of the difficulties facing staff and an encouraging sign of the move to more 'joined up working' may be found in an article by Sizmur and Noutch (2005). For an interesting comparison between the Dutch and English systems of managing DSPD offender-patients, see Boer et al. (2008). In my opinion Gunn (1999) provides what is a useful and critical summary of the work which still needs to be done.

> In England and Wales we have an uphill struggle on our hands. We need to persuade our Home Office not to drop its interest (and we would add to this the Department of Health) and particularly [the] resource allocation for a needy, hitherto neglected group of patients, but at the same time to back away from new types of . . . preventive detention laws and focus instead on the well-tried arrangements we already have. It is true that our prisons can do with more psychiatric resources, we have secure hospitals that also need more resources . . . we certainly do not need new and restrictive laws. The United Kingdom has many laws which can be used imaginatively if we have sufficient and appropriate staffs. Politicians, many of whom are lawyers, rush to legislate; we need to provide them with resources.
>
> (Gunn 1999: 75–76)

Notes

1 When I was a student psychiatric social worker in the late 1950s at the (then) St George's Hospital Child Guidance Clinic (London), I recall a statement in conversation by the doyen child psychiatrist, Dr Emanuel Miller (father of Sir Jonathan Miller, the neurologist, playwright and producer). He described the severely personality disordered as 'Manfred'-like characters existing in their own time and space (Manfred was, of course, the poetic character depicted in Lord Byron's poem of that name, and in musical form by Schumann). Dr Miller's statement has remained with me ever since.

2 Some work by a neuro-scientist – Professor Stephen Swithenby of the Open University – would seem to support such a possibility. In laboratory-controlled experiments with young sufferers from the autistic spectrum disorder – Asperger Syndrome – he and his colleagues found that their subjects had problems in responding to facial images, but had less difficulty with inanimate objects (Annual Science Lecture entitled 'Imagining the Autistic Brain', given at Oakham School, 22 February 2008). This in no way suggests that Asperger sufferers are any more or less likely to be delinquent than non-sufferers. However, rare cases can occur as, for example, in the case of a York University student who, with an accomplice, was involved in a sophisticated cheating attempt in some university exams. The judge told the Asperger sufferer that 'I am persuaded that your underlying Asperger's condition has had a marked influence on your poor judgement as to what happened' (as reported in *The Independent*, 1 March 2008). For studies on autistic spectrum disorders, notably Asperger Syndrome, and the forensic mental health implications, see Deeley et al. (2006), Murphy (2007) and Tiffin et al. (2007).

3 Cleckley (1976: 362–363) identified sixteen characteristic points. While not suggesting that *all* of these characteristics would have to be present, in the chapters that follow his listing, he elaborates on each of them in turn. In my view those he lists as numbers 1–6, 8, 9, 11, 15 and 16 would continue to resonate powerfully with present-day professionals. I would emphasize the importance of the second and third of these alongside the capacity to create chaos, which is sometimes overlooked as an important 'marker'. Cleckley's original list is as follows:

1 Superficial charm and good 'intelligence'.
2 Absence of delusions and other signs of irrational thinking.
3 Absence of 'nervousness' or psychoneurotic manifestations.
4 Unreliability.
5 Untruthfulness and insincerity.
6 Lack of remorse or shame.
7 Inadequately motivated antisocial behaviour.
8 Poor judgement and failure to learn by experience.
9 Pathologic egocentricity and incapacity for love.
10 General poverty of major affective reactions.
11 Specific loss of insight.
12 Unresponsiveness in general personal relations.
13 Fantastic and uninviting behaviour with drink and sometimes without.
14 Suicide rarely carried out.
15 Sex life impersonal, trivial and poorly integrated.
16 Failure to follow any life plan.

Acts

Criminal Justice Act 1991
Criminal Justice Act 2003
Mental Deficiency Act 1913
Mental Deficiency Act 1927
Mental Health Act 1959
Mental Health Act 1983
Mental Health Act 2007
Mental Health (Patients in the Community) Act 1995
Mental Health (Public Safety and Appeal) (Scotland) Act 1999

Cases

R. v. Canons Park Mental Health Review Tribunal ex Parte A [1995] QB 60
R. v. M.J. Stone [2005] EWCA Crim 105
Reid v. Secretary of State for Scotland [1999] 2 WLR 28
Ruddle v. Secretary of State for Scotland [1999] GWD 29 1395

References

Ainsworth, M.D.S. (1962) 'The Effects of Maternal Deprivation: A Review of Findings and Controversy in the Context of Research Strategy', in *Deprivation of Maternal Care: A Reassessment of its Effects*, Public Health Papers no.14, Geneva: World Health Organisation.

American Psychiatric Association (APA) (2005) *Diagnostic and Statistical Manual of Mental Disorders*, 4th edn (text revision) (DSM-IV-TR), Washington, DC: APA.

Blackburn, R. (1998) 'On Moral Judgements and Personality Disorder: The Myth of Psychopathic Personality Revisited', *British Journal of Psychiatry* 153: 505–512.

—— (2007) 'Other Theoretical Models of Psychopathy', in C.J. Patrick (ed.) *Handbook of Psychopathy*, New York: Guilford Press.

Blair, J. and Frith, U. (2000) 'Neurocognitive Explanations of Anti-Social Personality Disorders', *Criminal Behaviour and Mental Health* (supplement) 10: S66–S81.

Blair, J., Mitchell, D. and Blair, K. (2005) *The Psychopath: Emotion and the Brain*, Oxford: Blackwell.

Board, B.J. and Fritzon, K. (2005) 'Disordered Personalities at Work', *Psychology, Crime and Law* 11: 17–32.

Boer, J. de, Whyte, S. and Maden, T. (2008) 'Compulsory Treatment of Offenders with Severe Personality Disorders: A Comparison of the English DSPD and Dutch TBS Systems', *Journal of Forensic Psychiatry and Psychology* 19: 148–163.

Bowers, L. (2002) *Dangerous and Severe Personality Disorders: Response and Role of the Psychiatric Team*, London: Routledge.

Bowers, L., Carr-Walker, P., Paton, J., Nijman, H.M., Callaghan, P., Allan, T. and Alexander, J. (2005) 'Changes in Attitude to Personality Disorder on a DSPD Unit', *Criminal Behaviour and Mental Health* 15: 171–183.

Bowlby, J. (1946) *Forty-Four Juvenile Thieves: Their Characters and Home-life*, London: Baillière, Tindall & Cox.

—— (1971) *Attachment*, Harmondsworth: Penguin.

—— (1979) *The Making and Breaking of Affectional Bonds*, London: Tavistock.

Brunner, H.G., Nelen, M., Breakfield, X.O., Ropers, H.H. and Van Oost, B.A. (1993) 'Abnormal Behaviour Associated with a Point Mutation in the Structure Gene for Monoamine Oxidase', *Science* 262: 578–586.

Burn, M. (1956) *Mr Lyward's Answer*, London: Hamish Hamilton.

Campling, P. (1996) 'Maintaining the Therapeutic Alliance with Personality Disordered Patients', *Journal of Forensic Psychiatry* 7: 535–550.

Cavadino, M. (1998) 'Death to the Psychopath', *Journal of Forensic Psychiatry* 9: 5–8.

Chiesa, M. and Fonagy, P. (2003) 'Psychological Treatment of Severe Personality Disorder: A 36-Month Follow-Up', *British Journal of Psychiatry* 183: 356–362.

Cleckley, H. (1976) *The Mask of Sanity*, 5th edn, St Louis, MO: C.V. Mosby.

Cohen, S. (2001) *States of Denial: Knowing About Atrocities and Suffering*, Oxford: Polity Press.

—— (2002) *Folk Devils and Moral Panics*, 3rd edn, London: Routledge.

Coid, J. (1989) 'Psychopathic Disorders', *Current Opinion in Psychiatry* 2: 750–756.

—— (1993) 'Current Concepts and Classification in Psychopathic Disorder', in P. Tyrer and G. Stein (eds) *Personality Disorder Reviewed*, London: Gaskell.

Cope, R. (1993) 'A Survey of Forensic Psychiatrists' Views on Psychopathic Disorder', *Journal of Forensic Psychiatry* 4: 214–235.

Coughlin, L. (2003) 'The Effects of Relocation of Staff Changes on Individuals with a Personality Disorder', *British Journal of Forensic Practice* 5: 12–17.

Crichton, J.H.M., Darjee, R., McCall-Smith, A. and Chiswick, D. (2001) 'Mental Health (Public Safety and Appeals) (Scotland) Act, 1999: Detention of Untreatable Patients with Psychopathic Disorder', *Journal of Forensic Psychiatry* 12: 647–661.

Curran, D. and Mallinson, P. (1944) 'Psychopathic Personality: Review of the Literature', *Journal of Mental Science* 90: 266.

Darjee, R. and Crichton, J.H.M. (2002) 'The Maclean Committee: Scotland's Answer to the "Dangerous People with Severe Personality Disorder" Proposals', *Psychiatric Bulletin* 26: 6–8.

Deeley, Q., Daly, E., Surgoladze, S., Tunstall, N., Mezey, G., Beer, D., Ambikapathy, A., Robertson, D., Giampietro, V., Brammer, M.J., Clarke, A., Dowsett, J., Fahy, T., Phillips, M.L. and Murphy, D.G. (2006) 'Facial Emotion Processing in Criminal Psychopathy: Preliminary Functional Magnetic Resonance Imaging Study', *British Journal of Psychiatry* 189: 533–539.

Department of Health (1999) *Review of the Mental Health Act, 1983: Report of the Expert Committee* (Chairman Professor Genevra Richardson), Cm 4480, London: TSO.

Department of Health and Home Office (1994) *Report of the Department of Health and Home Office Working Group on Psychopathic Disorder* (Chairman Dr John Reed, CB), London: Department of Health.

Department of Health and Social Security (DHSS) (1986) *Consultation Document: Offenders Suffering from Psychopathic Disorder*, London: DHSS and Home Office.

Dolan, M. (1994) 'Psychopathy: A Neurobiological Perspective', *British Journal of Psychiatry* 165: 151–159.

Duggan, C. (2007) 'To Move or Not to Move – That is the Question: Some Reflections on the Transfer of DSPD Patients in the Face of Uncertainty', *Psychology, Crime and Law* 13: 113–121.

East, N. (1949) *Society and the Criminal*, London: HMSO.

Egger, S.A. (ed.) (1990) *Serial Murder: An Elusive Phenomenon*, New York: Praeger.

Eissler, K.R. (ed.) (1949) *Searchlights on Delinquency: New Psychoanalytic Studies*, London: Imago.

Eldergill, A. (1997) *Mental Health Review Tribunals: Law and Practice*, London: Sweet & Maxwell.

Fallon, P., QC, Bluglass, R., Edwards, B. and Daniels, G. (1999) *Report of the Committee of Inquiry into the Personality Disorder Unit, Ashworth Special Hospital*, Volume 2, Cm 4195, London: TSO.

Fennell, P. (2007) *Mental Health: The New Law*, Bristol: Jordan.

Francis, R., QC (2007) 'The Michael Stone Inquiry: A Reflection', *Journal of Mental Health Law* 15: 41–49.

Gayford, J.J. and Jungalwalla, H.N.K. (1986) 'Personality Disorder According to the ICD 10 and DSM III and their Value in Court Reporting', *Medicine, Science and the Law* 26: 113–124.

Greig, D. (2002) *Neither Mad nor Bad: The Competing Discourses of Psychiatry, Law and Politics*, London: Jessica Kingsley.

Gunn, J. (1999) 'The Ashenputtel Principle', *Criminal Behaviour and Mental Health* 10: 73–76.

—— (2003) 'Psychopathy: An Elusive Concept with Moral Overtones', in T. Millon, E. Simondson, M. Birkett-Smith and R.D. David (eds) *Psychopathy: Anti-Social, Criminal and Violent Behaviour*, New York: Guilford Press.

Haddock, A., Snowden, P., Dolan, M., Parker, J. and Ress, H. (2001) 'Managing Dangerous People with Severe Personality Disorder', *Psychiatric Bulletin* 25: 293–296.

Hare, R.D., Harpur, T.J., Hakstian, A.R., Forth, A.E., Hart, S.D. and Newman, J.P. (1990) 'The Revised Psychopathy Checklist: Reliability and Factor Structure', *Psychiatric Assessment* 2: 338–341.

Harris, G.T. and Rice, M.E. (2007) 'Treatment of Psychopathy: A Review of Empirical Findings', in C.J. Patrick (ed.) *Handbook of Psychopathy*, New York: Guilford Press.

Henderson, D. (1939) *Psychopathic States*, New York: Norton.

Home Office and Department of Health (1999) *Managing People with Severe Personality Disorder: Proposals for Policy Development*, London: Home Office.

Home Office and Department of Health and Social Security (DHSS) (1975) *Report of the Committee on Mentally Abnormal Offenders* (Chairman Lord Butler of Saffron Walden), Cmnd 6344, London: HMSO.

Johns, J.H. and Quay, M.C. (1962) 'The Effect of Social Reward on Verbal Conditioning in Psychopathic and Neurotic Military Offenders', *Journal of Consulting Psychology* 26: 217–220.

Jones, M. (1963) 'The Treatment of Character Disorders', *British Journal of Criminology* 3: 276–282.

Kendall, R.E. (1999) 'The Distinction between Personality Disorder and Mental Illness', *British Journal of Psychiatry* 180: 110–115.

Knop, J., Goodwin, D.W., Jensen, P., Penick, E.C., Pollock, V., Gabrielli, W., Teasdale, T.W. and Mednick, S.A. (1993) 'A 30-Year Follow-up Study of Sons of Alcoholic Men', *Acta Psychiatrica Scandinavia* 75 (suppl. 37): 48–53.

Koch, J.W. (1891) *Die Psychopathischen Minderwertigkeiten*, Ravenburg: Maier.

Laing, J. (1999) 'An End to the Lottery: The Fallon Report on Personality Disordered Offenders', *Journal of Mental Health Law* 2: 87–104.

Langton, C. (2007) 'Assessment Implications of "What Works" Research for Dangerous and Severe Personality Disorder (DSPD) Service Evaluation', *Psychology, Crime and Law* 13: 97–111.

Lee, T., McLean, D., Moran, P., Jones, H. and Kumar, A. (2008) 'A Pilot Personality Disorder Outreach Service: Development, Findings and Lessons Learnt', *Psychiatric Bulletin* 32: 127–130.

Lewis, G. and Appleby, L. (1988) 'Personality Disorders: The Patients Psychiatrists Dislike', *British Journal of Psychiatry* 153: 44–49.

McCord, W. (1982) *The Psychopath and Milieu Therapy: A Longitudinal Study*, New York: Academic Press.

McGuffin, P. and Thapar, A. (2003) 'Genetics and Anti-Social Personality Disorder', in T. Millon, E. Simonson, M. Birkett-Smith and R.D. David (eds) *Psychopathy, Anti-Social and Violent Behaviour*, New York: Guilford Press.

Maclean, Lord (Chairman) (2000) *Report of the Committee on Serious Violent and Sexual Offenders*, Edinburgh: Scottish Executive.

Maden, T. (1999) 'Treating Offenders with Personality Disorder', *Psychiatric Bulletin* 23: 707–710.

Maier, G.J. (1990) 'Psychopathic Disorders: Beyond Counter-Transference', *Current Opinion in Psychiatry* 3: 766–769.

Mann, A. and Moran, P. (2002) 'Personality Disorder as a Reason for Action', *Journal of Forensic Psychiatry* 11: 11–16.

Millan, D. (Chairman) (1999) *Review of the Mental Health (Scotland) Act, 1984: First Consultation*, Edinburgh: Scottish Executive.

Millon, T., Simonsen, E. and Birkett-Smith, M. (2003) 'Historical Conceptions of Psychopathy in the USA and Europe', in T. Millon, E. Simonsen, M. Birkett-Smith and R.D. Davis (eds) *Psychopathy: Anti-Social and Violent Behaviour*, New York: Guilford Press.

Murphy, D. (2007) 'Hare Psychopathy Checklist Revised Profiles of Male Patients with Asperger's Syndrome Detained in High Security Care', *Journal of Forensic Psychiatry and Psychology* 18: 120–126.

National Institute for Mental Health in England (NIMHE) (2003) *Personality Disorder: No Longer a Diagnosis of Exclusion*, Leeds: Department of Health.

Patrick, C.J. (ed.) (2007) *Handbook of Psychopathy*, London: Guilford Press.

Pinel, P.H. (1806) *A Treatise on Insanity*, New York: Hafner.

Prichard, J.C. (1835) *Treatise on Insanity*, London: Gilbert & Piper.

Prins, H. (1977) 'I Think They Call Them Psychopaths', *Prison Service Journal* 28: 8–12.

—— (1998) 'Characteristics of Consultant Forensic Psychiatrists: A Modest Survey', *Journal of Forensic Psychiatry* 9: 139–149.

—— (1999) 'Dangerous Severe Personality Disorder: An Independent View', *Prison Service Journal* 126: 8–10.

—— (2001) 'Did Lady Macbeth Have a Mind Diseas'd? (A Medico-Legal Enigma)', *Medicine, Science and the Law* 41: 129–134.

—— (2005) *Offenders, Deviants or Patients?*, 3rd edn, London: Routledge.

—— (2007) 'The Michael Stone Inquiry: A Somewhat Different Homicide Report', *Journal of Forensic Psychiatry and Psychology* 18: 411–431.

Quayle, J. (2008) 'Interviewing a Psychopathic Subject', *Journal of Investigative Psychology and Offender Profiling* 5: 79–91.

Rieber, R.W. and Green, M.R. (1988) 'The Psychopathy of Everyday Life' (unpublished manuscript).

Roberts, A.D.C. and Coid, J.W. (2007) 'Psychopathy and Offending Behaviour: Findings from the National Survey in England and Wales', *Journal of Forensic Psychiatry and Psychology* 18: 23–43.

Robins, L.N. (1966) *Deviant Children Grown Up: A Sociological and Psychiatric Study of Sociopathic Personality*, Baltimore, MD: Williams & Wilkins.

Roth, M. (1990) 'Psychopathic (Sociopathic) Personality', in R. Bluglass and P. Bowden (eds) *Principles and Practice of Forensic Psychiatry*, London: Churchill Livingstone.

Rubin, M. (2005) *The Hollow Crown: A History of Britain in the Late Middle Ages*, London: Allen Lane.

Rutter, M. (1999) 'Psychosocial Adversity and Child Psychopathology', *British Journal of Psychiatry* 174: 480–493.

Schneider, K. (1958) *Psychopathic Personalities*, London: Cassell.

Scott, P.D. (1960) 'The Treatment of Psychopaths', *British Medical Journal* 2: 1641–1646.

—— (1975) *Has Psychiatry Failed in the Treatment of Offenders?*, London: Institute for the Study and Treatment of Delinquency (ISTD).

Shriver, L. (2005) *We Need to Talk about Kevin*, London: Serpent's Tail.

Sizmur, S. and Noutch, T. (2005) 'Dangerous and Severe Personality Disorder Services', *British Journal of Forensic Practice* 7: 33–38.

Snowden, P. and Kane, E. (2003) 'Personality Disorder: No Longer a Diagnosis of Exclusion', *Psychiatric Bulletin* 27: 401–403.

Solomka, B. (1990) 'The Role of Psychiatric Evidence in Passing Longer than Normal Sentences', *Journal of Forensic Psychiatry* 7: 239–255.

Spence, S., Hunter, A., Farrow, T.F.D., Green, R.D., Leung, D.H., Hughes, C.J. and Ganesan, V. (2004) 'A Cognitive Neuro-Biological Account of Deception: Evidence from Functional Neuro-Imaging', *Philosophical Transactions, Royal Society, London (B)* 359: 1755–1762.

Stein, G. (2009) 'Was the Scoundrel (Belial) of the Book of Proverbs a Psychopath? Psychiatry in the Old Testament', *British Journal of Psychiatry* 194: 33.

Taylor, R. (2000) *A Seven Year Reconviction Study of HMP Grendon Therapeutic Community*, Research Findings no. 115, London: Home Office Research, Development and Statistics Directorate.

Tennent, G., Tennent, D., Prins, H. and Bedford, A. (1993) 'Is Psychopathic Disorder a Treatable Condition?, *Medicine, Science and the Law* 33: 63–66.

Thomson, L.D.G. (2005) 'The Mental Health (Care and Treatment) (Scotland) Act, 2003: Civil Legislation', *Psychiatric Bulletin* 29: 381–384.

Tiffin, P., Shah, P. and Le-Couteur, A. (2007) 'Diagnosing Pervasive Developmental Disorders in a Forensic Adolescent Mental Health Setting', *British Journal of Forensic Practice* 9: 31–40.

Trethowan, W. and Sims, A.C.P. (1983) *Psychiatry*, 5th edn, London: Baillière Tindall.

Treves-Brown, C. (1977) 'Who is the Psychopath?', *Medicine, Science and the Law* 17: 56–63.

Tyrer, P. (1990) 'Diagnosing Personality Disorders', *Current Opinion in Psychiatry* 3: 182–187.

Tyrer, P., Casey, P. and Ferguson, B. (1990) 'Personality Disorder in Perspective', *British Journal of Psychiatry* 159: 463–471.

Tyrer, P., Duggan, C. and Coid, J. (eds) (2003) 'Ramifications of Personality Disorder in Clinical Practice', *British Journal of Psychiatry* 182: supplement 44.

Wambaugh, J. (1989) *The Blooding*, London: Bantam.

Whiteley, J.S. (1994) 'In Pursuit of the Elusive Category', *British Journal of Psychiatry Review of Books* 7: 7–14.

Winnicott, D.W. (1949) 'Hate in the Counter-Transference', *International Journal of Psychoanalysis* 30: 14–17.

World Health Organisation (WHO) (1992) *The ICD-10 Classification of Mental and Behavioural Disorders: Clinical Descriptions and Diagnostic Guidelines*, Geneva: WHO.

Further reading

Dolan, B. and Coid, J. (1993) *Psychopathic and Anti-Social Personality Disorders*, London: Gaskell.

Dowsett, J. and Craissati, J. (2008) *Managing Personality Disordered Offenders in the Community: A Psychological Approach*, London: Routledge.

Dowson, J.H. and Grounds, A.T. (1995) *Personality Disorders: Recognition and Clinical Management*, Cambridge: Cambridge University Press.

Moran, P. (1999) *Anti-Social Personality Disorder: An Epidemiological Perspective*, London: Gaskell.

Patrick, C.J. (ed.) (2007) *Handbook of Psychopathy*, London: Guilford Press (this is a very comprehensive conspectus).

All the journals cited in the text will repay consultation for further information:

Acta Psychiatrica Scandinavia
British Journal of Criminology
British Journal of Forensic Practice
British Journal of Psychiatry
British Medical Journal
Criminal Behaviour and Mental Health
Current Opinion in Psychiatry
International Journal of Psychoanalysis
Journal of Consulting Psychology
Journal of Forensic Psychiatry
Journal of Forensic Psychiatry and Psychology
Journal of Mental Health Law
Journal of Mental Science
Medicine, Science and the Law
Philosophical Transactions, Royal Society, London (B)
Prison Service Journal
Psychiatric Assessment
Psychiatric Bulletin
Psychology, Crime and Law
Science

Chapter 6

Grievous and other bodily harms

How oft the sight of means to do ill deeds
Makes deeds ill done!

(King John, in *King John*, Act 4, Sc. 2)

The title of this chapter can serve as the leitmotif for this and the following three chapters; for they are all concerned with aspects of violence, whether it occurs in violent assaults, homicide, sexual offences or arson (assault on property). It would be well-nigh impossible (indeed foolhardy) to attempt to encompass all aspects of violence in this chapter. Instead, I shall only deal with those aspects that 'fit' within the general framework of the rest of this book. The chapter is divided into the following sections. First, a brief contextual framework to set the scene. Second, comments on the size of the problem and some of the difficulties in determining this. Third, clinical aspects. Ideally readers may find that this chapter, and the three that follow, should be viewed as a whole. In previous editions I did not devote a separate chapter to homicide, but I have now decided (for reasons that I hope will become obvious) to deal with it in its own right.

A note on terms

The terms *aggression* and *violence* are seen, on occasion, to be used synonymously. This is not strictly correct, since people can behave aggressively without necessarily being violent. However, the distinction is not clear cut. Aggression is perhaps best regarded as denoting powerfully *assertive* behaviour, which most frequently expresses itself verbally. Aggression can be further divided into *manifest* aggression (physical aggression, verbal aggression) and *latent* aggression (aggressive fantasies, moods etc.). Three further distinctions can be made. First, aggression as evidenced in loss of control (as in some forms of crime and some psychiatric disorders). Second, planned aggression (sometimes known as instrumental aggression) or as goal seeking. Third, structural or institutionalized aggression (as a means of imposing control and/or sanctions). Violence is frequently regarded as destructive aggression – that is, aggression harnessed for harmful purposes. Archer and Browne (1989: 3) describe it as 'the exercise of physical force so as to injure or damage persons or property; otherwise to treat or use persons or property in a way that causes bodily injury and forcibly interferes with personal freedom'. (See also Hollin 1992: 147 et seq.; Blackburn 1993: Chapter 9.)

Newell (2007), a retired former senior prison governor, has complemented the foregoing definitions. He suggests usefully that:

> Unlike other crimes or offensive behaviours, certain aspects or levels of violence are tolerated, excused, justified or accepted, in the home, community and in the workplace. Everybody has their own threshold of acceptability of verbal, emotional and physical violence and different expectations of others in conflict situations.
>
> (Newell 2007: 227)

Newell (2007) adopts the Prison Service (2004) definition of violence – as follows:

> any incident in which a person is physically, emotionally or psychologically abused, threatened or assaulted. This includes an explicit or implicit challenge to their safety, well-being or health.
>
> (Newell 2007: 228)

In what follows I am concerned with those behaviours that are *marked by force, threats and, in most instances, a degree of premeditation.* The event or incident will usually have occurred over a short time-span, but not necessarily so (as, for example, in cases of so-called serial killing). The debate as to whether aggression and a propensity for violence are all pervasive, innate, or acquired, has continued over the centuries and is documented extensively. In the first edition of his book *Human Aggression* (1975), Dr Anthony Storr stated:

> that man is an aggressive creature will hardly be disputed. With the exception of certain rodents, no other vertebrate *habitually destroys members of his own species. No other animal takes positive pleasure in the exercise of cruelty upon another of his own kind* . . . there is no parallel in nature to our savage treatment of each other.
>
> (Storr 1975: 9, emphasis added)

In a revised and updated edition of this work, he added to this somewhat sombre comment on violence – as follows:

I think that *Homo Sapiens* has not altered very much in fundamental, physical or psychological characteristics since he first appeared upon the scene; and that the best we can hope for is some slight modification of his nastier traits of personality in the light of increased understanding. We cannot abolish man's potential for cruelty and destructiveness, but we may be partially able to control the circumstances which can lead to their overt expression.

(Storr 1991: 141–142)

In view of the acknowledged universality of the capacity to behave violently, it is of interest to observe that its overt *expression* appears to be shaped quite markedly by cultural influences. In their studies of so-called primitive societies, early anthropologists (such as Margaret Mead, Ruth Benedict, George Murdock and others) demonstrated the great variety that can be shown to exist in the display of aggressive and violent behaviour. In the late 1960s, the psychologist and psychoanalyst Erich Fromm attempted to synthesize some of their early work and to apply it to more developed societies. He found that three different and clearly delineated forms of society could be discerned: *life-affirmative societies, non-destructive-aggressive societies* and *destructive societies*. In life-affirmative societies, the main emphasis was upon the preservation and growth of life in all forms. 'There is a minimum of hostility, violence or cruelty among people, no harsh punishments, hardly any crime, and the institution of war is absent or plays an exceedingly small role' (Fromm 1977: 229). In non-destructive-aggressive societies, 'aggressiveness and war, although not central, are normal occurrences, and . . . competition, hierarchy and individualism are present' (Fromm 1977: 230). Destructive societies are 'characterized by much interpersonal violence, destructiveness, aggression and cruelty . . . pleasure in war, maliciousness and treachery' (Fromm 1977: 231). Fromm's view is admittedly very sweeping and some might consider it to be an oversimplification. Nevertheless, it may help us to understand the apparent overt differences in the phenomena of violence in various societies. It may also help us to understand what appears to be the ubiquitous phenomenon of violence in our own society, whether it be expressed in the home, the school or in those institutions established for the avowed purpose of the *protection* of the vulnerable (for example, establishments for children, elderly people and psychiatric hospitals of one kind or another), and in acts of terrorism and other global atrocities, both past and current.

I believe that whatever view we may take about the causes of violence in society, the following points would find a fairly general degree of acceptance:

- Violence, when shown by non-human animals, is usually purposive, self-protective, and conforms to certain ritualized patterns (Lorenz 1966).

- In the human species, violence may be sanctioned by a community (Fromm 1977).
- It appears to take little to disinhibit violence in human societies. As Storr (1991) suggests, it seems likely that men and women have always had the potential for the commission of a great deal of violence, but that this is usually kept in check by society's sanctions. These sanctions can, however, change over time; witness the enormity of the atrocities against millions of people during the Nazi regime in the 1930s and 1940s, and currently as a global phenomenon.

An explanation for such behaviour was provided by the psychologist Philip Zimbardo in an interview with McDermott (1993). Zimbardo (1973) was the originator of the famous (or infamous, depending upon your ethical standpoint) Stanford University prison experiment, in which quite ordinary students were able to inflict suffering and deprivation upon their fellows – to such an extent that the experiment had to be stopped prematurely because of its effect upon those who were the detainees. Zimbardo suggested three key factors that might be at work in bringing about the capacity for quite normal human beings to behave inhumanely towards others. These consisted of de-individualization (loss of personal identifiability and uniqueness); dehumanization (loss of a sense of personal value); and present-time orientation (engaging in current actions without concern for future consequences or past commitments). As with Fromm's views, Zimbardo's also have a broad sweep to them, but they have a certain credibility in the light of a great deal of theorizing about the aetiology and manifestation of violent behaviour.

In this and the following chapters we are most concerned with the situations in which *individual internal* mechanisms of control have broken down (though the broader canvas should not be dismissed). Internal control appears to be mediated by various psychological defence mechanisms – such as denial, repression and projection. Some early psychoanalysts (notably Melanie Klein 1963) claimed, on the basis of not inconsiderable clinical data, that even small infants possess highly destructive and violent urges. These may come to the fore in the face of hunger and frustration. Such urges normally find appeasement but, in the event of failure, serious distortions of personality may occur, as in the case of some of the psychopathically disordered persons described in Chapter 5.[1]

The rhetoric of violence

A topic frequently (and not always helpfully) debated, is the extent to which the level and frequency of violence are greater in contemporary society than in the past. Anthropological and historical perspectives tend to support the contention that we have a violent past and that although current scenarios may be fuelled allegedly by the more frequent ingestion of alcohol and other drugs, we have not, as Storr suggested, altered much in our capacity for violence since we emerged from the caves. From early times playwrights, philosophers and historians attested to this. Shakespeare, that shrewd observer of human nature, attested to the waywardness of youth, as the old Shepherd says in *The Winter's Tale*:

> I would there were no age between ten and three-and-twenty, or that youth would sleep out the rest; for there is nothing in the between but getting wenches with child, wronging the ancientry, stealing, fighting.
>
> (*The Winter's Tale*, Act 3, Sc. 3)

And the sombre seventeenth-century philosopher Thomas Hobbes wrote of humankind:

> No arts; no letters, no society; and which is worst of all, continual fear and danger of violent death. And the life of man, solitary, poor, nasty, brutish and short.
>
> (*Leviathan*, Part 1, Chapter 4: 13)

Interestingly, I find that when I use this quote with my clinical criminology and forensic psychology students, most recognize the last bit of the quotation but are not so familiar with the first. Hobbes also stated that 'all mankind [is in] a perpetual desire for power . . . that [stops] only in death'.[2]

The historian Edward Gibbon wrote of sixth-century Constantinople: 'It becomes dangerous to wear any gold buttons or girdles or to appear at a late hour in the streets of a peaceful capital' (quoted in Hankoff 1993: 1–3). Pearson (1983) has demonstrated very clearly that so-called modern 'hooliganism' has its origins in pre-Victorian England, and that serious crowd misbehaviour at, for example, football matches is as old as the game itself. Sharpe (1992), a University of York historian, has suggested that 'mugging' was as prevalent in London in the middle of the nineteenth century (in the very nasty guise of 'garrotting') as is alleged today.[3]

Finally, in this brief excursion into the rhetoric of violence, Sir Michael Day (1986) wrote the following in an attempt to give a sense of perspective:

> The world is steeped in the rhetoric of violence. The horror of international terrorism and the menacing of aggression acted out between factions and adherents of religious and political ideologies feed the media and in time may dull our senses. Perhaps it is no worse now than at any other period in man's history, but only seems so, because modern communication has shrunk the world and the modern armoury has enormously increased the consequences of violence. Even if somehow, we manage to distance ourselves from these, however, they

still provide a frightening backcloth to the violence and danger represented by some individuals in our society and expose the potential for
devastating aggression in all of us.

(Day 1986: xii)

In the light of events of 11 September 2001, and developments in the UK
and elsewhere since, Day's observation was prophetic.[4]

It was, I think, Alvin Toffler, in his book *Future Shock* (1970), who
coined the phrase 'disposable society' many years ago to indicate the short-
term life of many of our consumable and other items. Maybe, in today's
world, we need a new phrase to provide a short-hand description for the
possible mainspring of the violent phenomena that we deal with; perhaps
'over-reactive society' would be an appropriate term. Why do I say this? As
indicated in earlier chapters, we seem to use impulsive and not terribly well
thought out reactions to 'untoward' and 'unwanted' events. Politicians
seem to be the worst culprits (but one can perhaps understand their
motives) in their ever-increasing use of legislation to deal with 'private and
personal' ills (see, for example, Prins 1996). This is very evident in the
manner in which criminal justice and mental health legislation has placed
what appears to be undue emphasis on public protection and has made for
so much difficulty for sentencers and others. In education, we seem to swing
from one extreme to another in our searches for educational 'philosopher's
stones'; and the manner in which all forms of disaster are met by responses
calling for the often vengeful allocation of, and compensation for, blame
are yet further examples. One of the best (and tragic) examples of this trend
is the hounding of paedophiles (and, in the event, non-paedophiles, in some
cases; see Chapter 8). Nearly every major social problem these days seems
to arouse the media to call for a public inquiry; one must wonder just how
many trees have been consumed in the mountains of paper that both public
and private inquiries have taken place. Patience and thought do not seem to
be the order of the day. Just as King Richard II in Shakespeare's play of
that name declares that 'Patience is stale and I am weary of it' (*Richard II*,
Act 5, Sc. 5, line 103), before turning on his gaoler and beating him as his
killers arrive to dispatch him, so does impatience and lack of careful
thought seem to bedevil so much of our legislative and parliamentary
processes.[5]

The current volume of criminal violence

It is important to bear in mind the aphorism attributed to Mark Twain by
Benjamin Disraeli, 'There are three kinds of lies: lies, damned lies and
statistics'.[6] Although crimes of violence understandably receive the most
media coverage and cause the most concern, it is important to emphasize
that, taken as a whole, they represent less than 5 per cent of offences

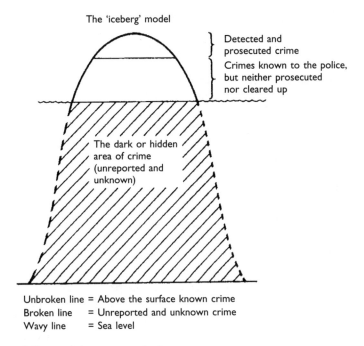

The 'iceberg' model

} Detected and
  prosecuted crime

} Crimes known to the police,
  but neither prosecuted
  nor cleared up

The dark or hidden
area of crime
(unreported and
unknown)

Unbroken line = Above the surface known crime
Broken line   = Unreported and unknown crime
Wavy line   = Sea level

Figure 6.1 An overall figure of the amount of crime

recorded by the police; and the more serious of these, for example those that endanger life and armed robbery, constitute only about one-third of 1 per cent of all recorded offences. However, a more comprehensive measure of the *real* extent of violent crime is that provided by the British Crime Survey (BCS), which involves face-to-face interviews with adults over 16 living in private households in England and Wales. In 2007 in the *Home Office Statistical Bulletin* (Home Office 2007) these consisted of 47,203 face-to-face interviews conducted between April 2006 and March 2007. The overall response rate for 2006/07 was 75 per cent. Interviewees were asked about their experiences of crime-related incidents in the twelve months prior to the interview. Violent crime represented 22 per cent of all crimes in the BCS in 2006/07, and 1 per cent of police recorded crime. The disparity between the two sources is, of course, very marked. I have endeavoured to highlight an overall picture of the amount of crime in Figure 6.1. Note that this figure is, of course, not to scale; it is merely intended as a pictorial representation.

Variations from year to year in the statistics gathered and presented by police forces are accounted for by variations in reporting procedures. However, in recent years, attempts have been made to rationalize these. Another confounding factor is the manner in which official designations of crime change from time to time (for example, child destruction is now termed intentional destruction of a viable unborn child – see also Chapter 7). For details of other offence reclassifications see Home Office (2007: 16). A further important recent development is the emphasis now being placed upon 'repeat victimization'. Interesting statistics for this important phenomenon between 1981 and 2006/7 may be found in the *Bulletin* (Home Office 2007: 22).

The statistics for recorded crime provide an incomplete picture, since they represent only the crimes that are brought to the attention of the police. The latter is estimated to be about 40 per cent of all crime. The BCS statistics indicate that this is more likely to be in the order of 50 per cent. The reasons for not reporting crime as given in the BCS are of interest. They include the following: trivial loss; police reluctance or could not take action; incident dealt with privately; inconvenient to report incident; reported to other authorities; common occurrence; fear of reprisal; bad experience of police in the past (Home Office 2007: 48, Table 2.11).

The Home Office statistics give the lie to some commonly held assumptions that crimes of violence against the person show a marked increase. In fact, the reverse would appear to be true. For example, police recorded crimes of violence against the person *fell* by 1 per cent in 2005/6 and 2005/7 – the first fall in eight years. The BCS findings also show a decrease – a fall of 41 per cent since a peak in 1995. This represents half a million fewer victims. However, for robbery there was a 3 per cent increase in the same period. Police-recorded sexual offences also showed a decline of 7 per cent between 2005/6 and 2006/7 (see also Chapter 8). Homicide figures indicate that 755 homicides were recorded by the police in 2006/7 – the smallest total for eight years. However, it should be remembered that such figures will fluctuate year on year according to the numbers of 'mass' killings by a single offender or by terrorist activity (see Chapter 7).

In Table 6.1 I have provided some figures for serious recorded violent crime. The very word *serious* can, of course, be questioned because the legal categorization of a crime may not necessarily give an accurate indication of its impact upon its victim. For example, an indecent assault may be anything from a light touch on the knee to a serious physical attempt at sexual penetration that may just fall short of attempted rape.

Who is most at risk of violent crime?

If we placed our trust solely in the media, the most likely victims of violent offences would appear to be elderly people. Although the impact of violent crimes on elderly people should never be underestimated, the statistics indicate that numerically they are *not* the most likely victims. Overall, the risk of being a victim of violent crime as revealed in the 2006/07 survey was

Table 6.1 Recorded crimes of serious violence 2002/3–2006/7

	2002/3	2003/4	2004/5	2005/6	2006/7
Homicide: murder, manslaughter, infanticide	1047	904	868	766	755
Attempted murder	822	888	740	920	636
Intentional destruction of viable unborn child	2	8	4	5	5
Causing death by dangerous driving, causing death by careless driving when under the influence of drink or drugs	414	445	441	432	462
More serious wounding or other acts endangering life	18,016	19,528	19,612	18,825	17,281
Threats or conspiracy to murder	18,132	22,299	23,758	18,683	12,829

Note: The range of offences I have selected is admittedly somewhat arbitrary. More detailed figures may be found in Home Office (2007: 36).

Source: Figures extracted from Crime in England and Wales 2006/07 (Home Office 2007).

3.6 per cent. Young males aged between 16 and 24 were most at risk with 13.8 per cent experiencing a violent crime of some sort in the year prior to being interviewed (Home Office 2007: 60). The risk of being a victim of violent crime was lower for older people. For men, the risk of suffering any violent crime decreased from 13.8 per cent for men aged 16–24 to 6.2 per cent for men aged 25–34 and to 0.5 per cent for men aged 75 and over, and 0.3 per cent for women aged 75 and over. Single persons are particularly at risk from stranger and acquaintance violence. However, a word of caution is needed in taking comfort from these figures. One needs to add in the fortunately rare cases of what I would call 'carer violence' committed against vulnerable groups, for example elderly people, individuals who are physically and mentally ill and handicapped, and children. One is mindful of the lethal activities of the GP Harold Shipman and nurse Beverley Allitt. Yorston (1999) suggests that with an increasingly older male and female population, crimes of violence (among others) may, for this group, begin to increase (Yorston 1999).

At one time it was thought that the risk of violent assault or behaviour was likely to be an exclusively urban phenomena; recent comments in the media seem to suggest that rural communities now face similar hazards. Currently concerns have increased about violence in the workplace and, in particular, in general hospitals as well as more specialist settings such as psychiatric units of varying degrees of security.

A small-scale survey I undertook a few years ago exemplifies current concerns about such violence. In 2001, the Department of Health issued a somewhat provocatively titled Resource Guide entitled *Withholding Treatment from Violent and Abusive Patients in NHS Trusts: 'We Don't Have to Take This'* (Department of Health 2001). The editor of the *Journal of Forensic Psychiatry* asked me to write a commentary on this document (Prins 2002).[7] In the course of my investigation I reviewed a selection of articles that had appeared in a number of forensic psychiatric and psychological journals for the period 1995–2002. I have now added to these and my current findings can be summarized as follows.

Psychiatric–patient violence: some selected aspects

The problem of predicting which patients would manifest violent behaviour was demonstrated in a small study by Eaton et al. (2000). They found prediction very difficult, but suggested (as others have done) that most violent and assaultive incidents are carried out by a small number of patients (Eaton et al. 2000; see also work by Grevatt et al. 2004; Doyle and Dolan 2006; Rutter et al. 2004). Crowding and density of patient populations have often been held to be important factors in the aetiology of patient violence. However, Hardie (1999), for example, did not find that patient density seemed to be associated with incidents of violence and self-harm in a medium-secure unit. The complex nature of interactions in understanding assaultive behaviour is to be found in an interesting article by Gudjonsson et al. (2000). They analysed some 2180 violent incident forms and found that nursing staff, followed by fellow patients, were the most likely victims of assault. They comment that 'gender, ethnic background, diagnosis and legal section were significantly related to the targets of assault . . . the findings show the importance of studying the interactions between different types of factors with regard to the characteristics and management of incidents' (Gudjonsson et al. 2000: 105; see also Watts et al. 2003; Wynn 2003; Hornsveld et al. 2007). Other papers reviewed also attested to the complex nature of the interactions between patients and staff. However, less attention seemed to have been devoted to the need for staff, particularly the less experienced, to examine their own reactions and the extent to which they *may* have unwittingly contributed to a violent incident. I am mindful here of the seminal work of Hans Toch (1992) in his US study of violent incidents involving the police. He discovered that in some areas, a small but identifiable number of police officers seemed to be involved, on a number of occasions, in violent incidents. What we do know is that threats to, and assaults by, patients on staff can have serious effects upon health professionals (see, for example, Shepherd 1994; Wykes 1994; Wildgoose et al. 2003; Dalton and Eracleus 2006; Dhumad et al. 2007).

This being the case, we could usefully ask what attempts are being made to help staff to understand such incidents and to promote their own awareness of the importance of their *possible* responsibility for them. Crichton and Calgie (2002) stress the importance of the 'moral' position taken by nurses. They suggest that 'a moral judgment about how blame-worthy a patient is perceived to be following an untoward incident, influences how staff respond' (Crichton and Calgie 2002: 32). O'Keefe (1999), in reviewing the guidelines on the management of imminent violence issued by the Royal College of Psychiatrists concluded that 'these guidelines . . . make an excellent attempt to give an overall current view of the management of imminent violence in the health service' (O'Keefe 1999: 398). For comment on the possible legal liabilities of staff in respect of episodes involving assault, see Miers (1996) and Andoh (2002). A less well researched area is that concerning the extent to which psychiatric and allied professionals suffer harassment and intimidation by dissatisfied parties *involved in litigation*. The topic has been usefully reviewed by Norris and Gutheil (2003).

A multidisciplinary 'public health' approach

Perhaps understandably, less seems to have been written about violence and abuse in non-psychiatric health facilities (see Dalton and Eracleus 2006). Schneiden et al. (1995), in commenting upon what they regard as an increase of violence in the general practice of clinical forensic medicine, stress the need for more training in this area for forensic medical examiners (formerly known as police surgeons). Crichton (1995) quotes a study by Walker and Caplan (1993) in which they compared psychiatric unit assault rates with violent crime rates in two health districts; they found that the level of inpatient violence reflected the district's level of violence at large. One has to ask to what extent there are cross-over points between assaults and abuse committed by those attending accident and emergency departments and those who have criminal records. In an interesting study by Shepherd and Farrington (1996) on the prevention of delinquency with particular refer-ence to violent crime, they noted the number of *victims* of violence attending Accident and Emergency (A and E) departments appeared to have increased threefold over the period 1974–91 (see also National Audit Office 2003). Shepherd and Farrington (1996: 331) pointed out that young male delin-quents are 'as much at risk of injury and other victimization as they are of committing offences'. They concluded that 'the need for doctors to join forces with social scientists . . . becomes obvious'. In support of this con-tention, they also make this interesting observation:

> independently of socio-economic variables, injury in violent crime is
> associated with a spectrum of disease in young adults comprising drug

abuse, assault, elective surgery and trauma which can be explained by underlying impulsivity. Preventing crime and violence should be a central issue in health care.

(Shepherd and Farrington 1996: 334)

In an earlier article dealing with the need for an integrated approach Shepherd (1995) suggests that 'further work is necessary to look for differing illness experience between offenders and the injured and to correlate offending, illness and injury with psychological, behavioural and developmental variables'. He uses the term *DATES* syndrome to describe these phenomena: 'It comprises drug abuse, assault, trauma and elective surgery' (Shepherd 1995: 351). Support for Shepherd's views also comes from a study by Junger and Wiegersma (1995) in that they found that 'social services in general (such as health services and correctional services) do, to a certain extent deal with the same [type of] individuals' (Junger and Wiegersma 1995: 144). A study by Raine and Liu (1998) also makes a plea for a new generation of biosocial health research. In a Norwegian study which set out to examine the true level of violence rather than sole reliance upon criminal statistics, Steen and Hunskaar (2001) found that

> most victims of violence who are taken care of by the health care system are treated in accident and emergency departments . . . and that [their] findings support the recommendation that combined police and accident and emergency department registrations should be used to monitor violence in a community.
>
> (Steen and Hunskaar 2001: 341)

The inference that one can draw from these studies is that violence, both personal, national and global, can be viewed very much as a 'public health' problem, a view given compelling impact by the publication of a groundbreaking document by the World Health Organization entitled *World Report on Violence and Health* (WHO 2002). In her preface to the report, the then Director-General of the World Health Organization, Gro Harlem Brundtland, had this to say:

> One theme that is echoed throughout this report is the importance of primary prevention. Even small investments here can have large and long-lasting benefits, but not without resolve of leaders and support for prevention efforts from a broad array of partners in both the public and private spheres, and from both industrialized and developing countries . . . Public health has made some remarkable achievements in recent decades, particularly in reducing rates of many childhood diseases. However, saving our children from these diseases only to let

them fall victim to violence or lose them later to acts of violence between intimate partners, to the savagery of war and conflict, or to self-inflicted injuries or suicide, would be a failure of public health.

(WHO 2002: xiii)

The complexity of the issues involved is further attested to in a commentary of the report by Soothill (2003). He concludes that:

Although the [Report] . . . provides an invaluable and welcome service in trying to strip away some of the myths about violence and to expose the facts about violence, this is – as the authors recognise – only a beginning . . . there are massive moral and political issues to confront in shaping our response to violence. Assuming that consensus is easily achieved – or even achievable – may be a way of burying our head in the sand and turning a blind eye to some very real issues.

(Soothill 2003: 14)

The public health implications have been emphasized more recently by Shepherd et al. (2006).[8] For a series of useful articles discussing various aspects of management, see Hornsveld (2005), Elbogen et al. (2006), Murphy (2006), Hodgins et al. (2007), Kaltiala-Heino et al. (2007), Newell (2007) and Blacker et al. (2008).

Because of increasing concerns about violence in the workplace, and in particular its best management, the Department of Health produced its Resource Guide in 2001. In doing so it included, as an appendix, a model policy and procedure adopted by Barts and the Royal London Trust – briefly summarized as follows.

'A model policy'

The policy document states that 'this policy will only apply to violent/abusive visitors and patients *who are aged 18 or over*' (Department of Health 2001: 2, emphasis in the original). Steps in the execution of the policy and procedures are set out in detail; these cover 'Expected Standards of Behaviour', and 'Sanctions', which include informal warning, formal written warning (a 'Yellow Card') and finally a 'Red Card' which will result in exclusion from the Trust. If we adopt the soccer terminology used in the document, the 'refereeing' will be undertaken by the clinical director, or nominated deputy. The policy section of the guidance ends with a stern warning – as follows:

Any patient behaving unlawfully will be reported to the police and The Trust will seek the application of the maximum penalties available in law. The Trust will prosecute all perpetrators of crime on or against Trust property, assets and staff.

(Department of Health 2001: 10)

One can envisage a situation arising where lawyers representing a defendant in such prosecutions would wish to argue points of interpretation of the law concerning such matters as definitions of trust property, assets and even possibly definitions of the word 'staff'.

Overall, the policy document (which won a Health and Social Care Award) seems to be a genuine and, for the most part, thoughtful attempt to get to grips with a troubling and troublesome area of health care and criminal justice practice. It occurred to me that it would be of interest to ascertain to what extent trusts in my own region had produced similar statements. To this end I circulated a letter of inquiry to the three main Leicestershire general hospitals, to the two similar hospitals in Nottingham and Derby, and to four secure – semi and low – establishments in the region. By definition the latter establishments would deal with potentially violent or violent patients and I thought it might be of interest to compare their procedures with those in general health care establishments, such as district general hospitals. What follows is a brief analysis of their responses. A copy of my letter of inquiry may be found as an appendix to the original article (Prins 2002).

The responses

Following one or two reminders, I obtained replies to my letters of inquiry from five trusts in the region, these being responsible for six 'general' hospitals and four secure establishments (one high security, two medium security and one low security). At the time of conducting my small inquiry no trust appeared to have formulated a *final* policy on violent and abusive patients and relatives, but all were working on producing them – and stated they were likely to implement them in the ensuing months. The population served by the secure, semi and low secure 'estate' is, by definition, likely to be a problematic one. As one of my forensic mental health respondents pointed out, 'I suppose in some ways our service is geared to understand that the environment we work within is likely to be of high risk and go prepared for this.' The same respondent noted the important constraints facing staff in their outpatient work.

> The potential risk for violence for those services undertaking triage and outpatient work on new patients without any known history is the more difficult area to assess and to manage. While we do undertake outpatient appointments for assessment, these are always managed

within environments in which there are appropriate health and safety and back-up facilities if an incident was to take place.

It was also noted by the same respondent that it was a very rare event indeed for their service to withhold treatment on the grounds of violence and/or abuse towards staff. Such a decision would be made only after the most careful consideration (and largely on the grounds of 'no further therapeutic treatment viability'). My respondent also noted that on only one occasion had this occurred in the three-year existence of their particular service. Most respondents also reported that there had, in fact, been little observed increase in violence or abuse by patients or relatives. However, one trust covering three large general hospitals reported a 'gradual increase', but as with all my respondents had no figures immediately available. One of my forensic mental health service respondents commented that 'we occasionally, but very rarely have a problem with visitors – verbal aggression – but we deal with this in a commonsense way'. One or two of my respondents remarked on the possible causes of alleged increases in hospital-based violence and abuse. For example, one thought there seemed to be less respect shown towards professionals in general these days. Purely anecdotally, there does seem to be something in this belief, for one can discern a general public lessening of confidence in professionals in a variety of spheres of activity, be they medicine, science, education or the civil service. It would be unwise to extrapolate too widely from such a very small sample of responses drawn from one health region (albeit a very large one). It seems likely that firmer evidence of disruptive and violent behaviour may exist in large conurbations such as London. This is exemplified by a sobering account that appeared in *The Independent* (23 February 2002). Apparently, drug-related violence is regarded as sufficiently serious to constitute 'Murder Mile' in the Hackney-Homerton area of London. 'Day in, day out, the hospital's medical team deals with more gunshot and knife-inflicted wounds than any other in Britain.' 'It is reported that the A and E department . . . treats an average of five gunshot cases a month and 50 stabbings.' It was suggested that the situation had become so serious in this part of the capital that a senior A and E consultant was actually travelling to Baragwanath Hospital in Soweto, South Africa, to further his expertise. Sadly, at this hospital, they have vast experience in dealing with the results of gang-related violence in their A and E department. And, of course, gun crime, particularly by young males, features as a continuing problem on the streets of large conurbations.

Since a number of my more informal soundings stressed the problem created by serious alcohol ingestion, it is interesting to note a contribution by a very thoughtful journalist, Fergal Keane. Writing in *The Independent*'s Review Section (2 March 2002), he identified the cost to the NHS of alcohol-induced illnesses, both in terms of violence and in terms of the long-term disastrous effects of alcohol abuse in individuals. He argued that, as a nation, we are in a state of 'denial' about the problem and what to do about it. As Keane said:

> Many find their way into the criminal justice system. Not just the street drunks banged away for being drunk and disorderly, but also the businessmen and women hauled off to the cells because they've trashed the house or committed an assault, [or] the man who kills in the middle of a blackout.

Like other authorities quoted earlier in this chapter, he calls for a coordinated healthcare and criminal justice approach to the problem.

Comment

As already suggested, it is difficult to ascertain the actual extent of violence in our society or the extent to which it may have increased in volume in recent times. What we can be somewhat uncomfortably aware of, is an increasing public and political concern about it and an ethos of 'something must be done', and that 'something' *must* provide an effective remedy. I have taken the view, rightly or wrongly, that such a trend is symptomatic of an 'over-reactive' society. The foregoing illustration is intended merely as one aspect of the problem of violence, but is an example capable of extrapolation to the problem more generally. Perhaps, more importantly, it will have helped to delineate possible cross-over points between those who create serious problems, for example in A and E departments, and those who are 'delinquent' in other respects. However, *impressionistically* it does not seem that those forensic mental health patients who have records for serious personal violence (such as homicide, arson and rape) will figure *very* largely in the populations of violent and abusive hospital patients as seen in A and E departments.

Some clinical examples: a mixture of motives and crimes

In introducing this chapter, I emphasized the somewhat arbitrary distinction being made between this one and the two that follow. I hope the following case illustrations will support my contention.

Case illustration 6.1

A young single man of 24 was convicted by the Crown Court of a series of indecent assaults on women. The facts were that, over a period of several weeks, he had gone out on his cycle at dusk and followed a number of young women along a lonely country lane. Coming up behind them, he attempted to pull them off their cycles, made various obscene suggestions to them, and attempted to put his hands up their skirts. He was of previous good character, but had suffered severe deprivation as a child and was of low intelligence. Because of these facts, the court, somewhat exceptionally, placed him under supervision. However, the seriousness of his premeditated assaultative attacks could have well earned him a prison sentence for what were, in effect, offences of violence.

Case illustration 6.2

A man in his late forties was charged with the attempted murder of his wife by cutting her throat while she lay asleep. He was normally an extremely docile and placid individual, a carpenter by trade and a very good workman. At his trial it transpired that for some years his wife had carried on 'business' as a prostitute. Despite all her husband's entreaties, she refused to give up her lifestyle; in a fit of despair and anger he attacked her. The case might, of course, have ended more tragically; his wife might have died from her injuries. In some cases, only the fact that the assailant had been interrupted during his or her assault may limit the harm caused. In others, the intention might not be to kill or seriously injure, but factors, unknown to the assailant, may render the course of events tragic – such as the victim being infirm or having a thin skull, or a delay in obtaining the medical emergency services.

Occasionally, the offence as charged may present, in disguised fashion, an underlying desire to perpetrate violence of a more personal kind. Charges of criminal damage (vandalism) can sometimes fall into this category.

Case illustration 6.3

I once had to prepare reports on three adolescent boys who were charged with what amounted to an 'orgy' of criminal damage to a number of railway carriages parked in a siding. They had systematically broken a large number of carriage windows by hurling fire extinguishers through them, removed dozens of electric light bulbs, threw them around the railway track, and urinated over the seats. Several thousands of pounds worth of damage had been caused. The history of each of these boys was revealing. The first lived with his elderly grandparents who, though concerned, were not particularly affectionate. His parents were separated and he rarely saw them. He was a boy with a chip on his shoulder. The second boy was illegitimate and came from a dysfunctional home background where his mother and sisters engaged in prostitution. He felt himself to be the odd one out. The third boy, a cousin of the second, was spending a holiday with the family. He was the orphaned child of a distant relative, and spent much of his time in a large children's home. It is not unrealistic to speculate that, unconsciously at least, the offences they committed may have been a symbolic manifestation of the aggression they felt towards their families and, by extension, to the wider community.

In other cases, the offender appears to have directed his or her violence from its original source to a more neutral one. I call this 'the innocent stranger in the street syndrome'. Scott (1977) cites the legendary Medea as an example who, wishing to get back at her husband, killed her baby saying 'that will stab thy heart'. He also quotes a clinical, now legendary, case which makes the point in graphic fashion:

Case illustration 6.4

A man of 47 asked a female storekeeper at his place of work for an item; she failed to produce it and treated him with scant respect. He picked up a hammer and beat her about the head in a manner which nearly killed her . . . [he was charged with inflicting grievous bodily harm] . . . When examined, he was not mentally ill, not depressed, not paranoid, and was distressed and perplexed by his behaviour. There was no previous crime of any sort. He was an excellent worker, employed beneath his capacity, but had never pressed for advancement. His wife was a somewhat dominant woman who nagged him and frequently expressed her dissatisfaction with his wages. He had not had a holiday away from home for 20 years. In the last few weeks he had had bronchitis, which kept him awake. He was tired, not feeling well, and taking a prescribed medication containing codeine. The storekeeper, he had hoped, would treat him with respect. She was an attractive and popular middle-aged woman whom he liked, but had never tried to make a relationship with. When she behaved like his wife, he reacted in a way which *could* be interpreted as venting all his suppressed resentment of his wife upon her.

(Scott 1977: 133, emphasis added)

Two further media reported examples of such displaced violence follow. The first is that of Frederic Blancke – the killer of the English school teacher, Fiona Jones, in France in 1989. Having quarrelled with his one-time girlfriend who, he alleged, had been seeing other men, he became enraged at seeing Fiona, who was looking so happy as she cycled through the French countryside. Having apparently failed in his first attempt to kill her, he returned to her body and finished her off with a knife. He claimed that his rage towards his girlfriend just welled up and this was directed to his hapless and innocent victim. In May 1993, some four years after the event, he was sentenced by a French court to fifteen years' imprisonment; the lightness of the sentence surprised many people (information derived from a *True Crimes* drama-documentary on British television on 9 January 1994).

The second case concerns a father who appears to have killed his two small sons aged 7 and 8 as a means of getting back at his recently estranged wife. Some six days after having been given two life sentences, he hanged himself in his prison cell. In sentencing him, the judge had said, 'You took those boys' lives to revenge yourself on your wife' (*The Independent*, 31 March 2003).

The following case comes from my own experience and is also illustrative of displaced aggression.

Case illustration 6.5

A youth of 16 was charged with causing grievous bodily harm to his elderly employer. Apparently he had attacked him from behind, struck him violently over the head and stolen a sum of money which he had subsequently abandoned. Of previous good character and background, he was remanded for psychiatric examination. He was found to be a youth who experienced great difficulty in countenancing any degree of frustration. There was evidence that on the morning of the offence he had been 'got at' by various people in authority and his offence was seen, in part, as a result of poor tolerance of frustration. His mother, who was also interviewed as part of the psychiatric assessment, was felt to have a certain cold detachment about her and she too seemed to have problems in coping with frustration. He was committed to local authority care, given intensive therapy, and subsequently did quite well.

Concluding comments

It will be obvious that I have been highly selective in my choice concerning those aspects of violence I have dealt with in this chapter. Some of my readers may find this not only disappointing, but also somewhat idiosyncratic. Significant gaps have been family violence, violence against elderly people and racially motivated violence. However, violence at the extreme end of the spectrum – homicide – is dealt with in Chapter 7, and I hope this will help to some extent to redress the balance. Those wishing to explore the topic of violence more widely should find the references cited and suggested further reading helpful.

Notes

1 The aetiology of violence is complex. Serious acts of violence as considered in this chapter would *appear* usually to have their origins in early childhood experiences, whether neurophysiological, psychological or close environmental (see comments in Chapter 5). For reviews and commentaries on various approaches to the topic, see Browne and Pennell (1998), Hyatt-Williams (1998), Cartwright (2002), Alsop (2003), Christoffersen et al. (2003), Fonagy (2003) and Mizen and Morris (2007).
2 I am grateful to my friend Dr John Moore for bringing this additional statement to my attention (personal communication, 28 March 2007).
3 For example, there is so much current concern about gun crime, that anti-gun crime tactics deployed by Scotland Yard were to be deployed throughout the UK in an attempt to curb the burgeoning menace of firearms and gang warfare. Whether this is an entirely new phenomenon or whether we are now more conscious of it following some distressing and dramatic incidents, for example the shooting to death of a woman shopkeeper in Nottingham and a subsequent

possible 'road rage' gun killing, is a moot point. To what extent 'road rage' is an entirely new phenomenon is also uncertain. In line with our current tendency to over-reaction, it may be that when our personal space is felt to be threatened on our ever busier highways in an era lacking a coherent transport policy, the phenomenon of 'road rage' *may* be more frequent.

4 Sir Michael Day, OBE, was Chief Probation Officer for the West Midlands before being appointed as chairman of the Commission for Racial Equality (CRE). His comments appeared in his Foreword to my book *Dangerous Behaviour, The Law and Mental Disorder*, London: Tavistock, 1986 (p. xi).

5 While acknowledging that exchanges in the House of Commons have always had a degree of 'ritual' intemperateness, recent exchanges seem to have gone beyond this, to the extent that they have become increasingly vitriolic and personally insulting in nature. Party political annual conferences have also witnessed a sad degree of personal muck-raking; and the dishonourable and illegal activities of some of our politicians do not provide good examples of conduct, particularly for the impressionable young. The media have a large part to play in these scenarios. *The Independent* (not in any respect an over-dramatic newspaper) had some trenchant comments to make in a leader of 11 October 2003:

> Not for the first time, a cursory reading of the press this week would suggest the country is going to hell in a hand-cart. This time, the rattling carriage contains a raucous payload of young people behaving badly. The case of characters includes professional footballers allegedly engaged in exploitative sex, professional footballers threatening to take their ball home because one of their number failed to take a drug test and professional hooligans trying to follow the hand-cart to Istanbul.

This somewhat scary and inflammatory seeming commentary is followed by the following more sensible paragraph.

> Welcome to the latest moral panic to grip the nation. This one is as specious as most of those that have gone before since medieval witch-hunts, the waves of hysteria often amplified by irresponsible reporting of asylum-seekers, predatory paedophiles, ecstasy, video nasties and many other modern ills.

6 Sometimes the attribution is solely to Twain (Samuel Langhorne Clemens). See *Oxford Dictionary of Quotations* (4th edn, A. Partington), Oxford: Oxford University Press, p. 249 (13).

7 In a report quoted by Jeremy Laurance in *The Independent* (27 March 2003), the National Audit Office (NAO) stated:

> 95,000 incidents of violence and aggression in hospitals were recorded in 2001–02, up from 84,000 in 1999–00. The rise was believed to be due, in part, to better reporting, but the NAO added: 'Many trusts consider that increased hospital activity and higher patient expectations particularly in relation to waiting times have also contributed to an increase in the actual level of violence' . . . the NAO estimate[d] that two out of five incidents are not reported, especially by doctors and in mental health units.

In the course of my survey, and on a purely anecdotal basis, I asked a practising neurologist, two retired physicians (a former paediatrician and a geriatrician) and my wife, a very experienced former nursing sister, what their recollections were of

A and E departments. All agreed that verbal abuse was not uncommon and there were incidents of *occasional* violence (loosely defined). There was some feeling that recourse to alcohol and other drugs might contribute to present-day problematic behaviour in A and E departments. My own unfortunate experience of a number of visits as a patient and patient's spouse to our local A and E department confirmed a picture of too many 'walking wounded', too many minor injuries that I consider could have been dealt with in GP practices and a general abuse of NHS facilities. The resulting overcrowding and a degree of serious under-staffing in some departments must, inevitably, contribute to an atmosphere of tension. This in turn *probably* increases the possibility of disruptive, abusive and occasionally violent conduct.

8 In an editorial in *Criminal Behaviour and Mental Health* 2005, 15(2), Shepherd notes that legislation in the previous decade has emphasized the need for 'joined up' working. He quotes provisions in the Crime and Disorder Act 1998, the Police Reform Act 2002 and the Domestic Violence and Victims Act 2004. Some useful work of coordination is being carried out by the voluntary sector. For example, a scheme to tackle domestic violence (which is said to affect 1.5 million women each year in the UK) sets out to coordinate services aimed at keeping the victim of such abuse safe in her own home, as reported by Jeremy Laurance in *The Independent* (3 December 2007). (However, some authors have detected flaws in some of these so-called partnership schemes. These are largely concerned with an apparent lack of commitment on the part of some State agencies to attending relevant meetings, despite an avowal that partnership schemes are very useful: see Welsh 2008.) Maybe it was the success of such schemes that led the president of the Family Division of the High Court, Sir Mark Potter, to seek a meeting with the Ministry of Justice in order to indicate his concern that recent legislation may, in fact, serve only to deter some women from reporting incidents of domestic violence on the grounds that over-ready recourse to legal proceedings may exacerbate an already potential dangerous situation (BBC Radio Four, News item, 14 April 2008).

Acts

Crime and Disorder Act 1998
Domestic Violence and Victims Act 2004
Police Reform Act 2002

References

Alsop, M. (2003) 'Attention Deficit Hyper-Activity Disorder (ADHD) and Crime', *Prison Service Journal* 149: 21–24.

Andoh, B. (2002) 'Legal Aspects of Mental Hospital Regimes', *Medicine, Science and the Law* 42: 14–26.

Archer, J. and Browne, K.D. (1989) 'Concepts and Approaches to the Study of Aggression', in J. Archer and K.D. Browne (eds) *Human Aggression: Naturalistic Approaches*, London: Routledge.

Blackburn, R. (1993) *The Psychology of Criminal Conduct: Theory, Research and Practice*, Chichester: Wiley.

Blacker, J., Watson, A. and Beech, A.R. (2008) 'A Combined Drama-Based and

CBT Approach to Working with Self-Reported Anger and Aggression', *Criminal Behaviour and Mental Health* 18: 129–137.

Browne, K. and Pennell, A.E. (1998) *The Effects of Video Violence on Young Offenders*, Research Findings no. 65, London: Home Office Research and Statistics Directorate.

Cartwright, D. (2002) *Psychoanalysis, Violence and Rage-Type Murder: Murdering Minds*, Hove: Brunner-Routledge.

Christoffersen, M.N., Francis, B. and Soothill, K. (2003) 'An Upbringing to Violence: Identifying the Likelihood of Violent Crime among the 1966 Birth Cohort in Denmark', *Journal of Forensic Psychiatry and Psychology* 14: 367–381.

Crichton, J.H.M. (ed.) (1995) *Psychiatric Patient Violence: Risk and Relapse*, London: Duckworth.

Crichton, J.H.M. and Calgie, T. (2002) 'Responding to In-Patient Violence in a Psychiatric Hospital of Special Security: A Pilot Project', *Medicine, Science and the Law* 42: 30–33.

Dalton, R. and Eracleus, H. (2006) 'Threats against Health Care Workers', (Part 1): 'A Review: Classification, Prevalence and Management'. (Part 2): 'The Characteristics of Those Who Make Threats: Threats and Predictors of Violence and Effects on the Victims', *British Journal of Forensic Practice* 8: 20–24 and 25–30.

Day, M. (1986) Foreword, in H. Prins, *Dangerous Behaviour: The Law and Mental Disorder*, London: Tavistock.

Department of Health (2001) *Withholding Treatment from Violent and Abusive Patients in NHS Trusts: 'We Don't Have to Take This'*, London: Department of Health.

Dhumad, S., Wijeratne, A. and Treasaden, I. (2007) 'Violence against Psychiatrists by Patients: A Survey in a London Mental Health Trust', *Psychiatric Bulletin* 31: 371–374.

Doyle, M. and Dolan, M. (2006) 'Predicting Community Violence from Patients Discharged from Mental Health Services', *British Journal of Psychiatry* 189: 520–525.

Eaton, S., Ghannan, M. and Hunt, N. (2000) 'Prediction of Violence on a Psychiatric Intensive Care Unit', *Medicine, Science and the Law* 40: 143–146.

Elbogen, E.B., Van Doren, R.A., Swanson, J.W., Swartz, M.S. and Monahan, J. (2006) 'Treatment Engagement and Violence Risk in Mental Disorders', *British Journal of Psychiatry* 189: 354–360.

Fonagy, P. (2003) 'Towards a Developmental Understanding of Violence', *British Journal of Psychiatry* 183: 190–192.

Fromm, E. (1977) *The Anatomy of Human Destructiveness*, Harmondsworth: Penguin.

Grevatt, M., Thomas-Peter, B. and Hughes, G. (2004) 'Violence, Mental Disorder and Risk Assessment: Can Structured Clinical Assessments Predict the Short-Term Risk of In-Patient Violence?', *Journal of Forensic Psychiatry and Psychology* 15: 278–292.

Gudjonsson, G., Rabe-Hesketh, S. and Wilson, C. (2000) 'Violent Incidents on a Medium Secure Unit: The Target and Management of Incidents', *Journal of Forensic Psychiatry* 11: 105–118.

Hankoff, L.D. (1993) 'Urban Violence in Historical Perspective', *International Journal of Offender Therapy and Comparative Criminology* 37: 1–13.

Hardie, T. (1999) 'Influence of Patient Density on Violence and Self Harming Behaviour in a Medium Secure Unit', *Medicine, Science and the Law* 39: 161–166.

Hodgins, S., Alderton, J., Cree, A., Aboud, A., and Mak, T. (2007) 'Aggressive Behaviour, Victimisation and Crime among Severely Mentally Ill Patients Requiring Hospitalisation', *British Journal of Psychiatry* 191: 343–350.

Hollin, C.R. (1992) *Criminal Behaviour: A Psychological Approach to Explanation and Behaviour*, London: Falmer.

Home Office (2007) *Statistical Bulletin 11/07: Crime in England and Wales 2006/07*, eds S. Nicholas, C. Kershaw and A. Walker, London: Home Office Research, Development and Statistics Directorate.

Hornsveld, R.H.J. (2005) 'Evaluation of Aggression Control Therapy for Violent Forensic-Psychiatric Patients', *Psychology, Crime and Law* 11: 403–410.

Hornsveld, R.H.J., Hollin, C.R., Nijman, H.L.I. and Kraaimatt, F.W. (2007) 'Violent Psychiatric Patients: Individual Differences and Consequences for Treatment', *International Journal of Forensic Mental Health* 6: 15–27.

Hyatt-Williams, A. (1998) *Cruelty, Violence and Murder: Understanding the Criminal Mind*, London: Jason Aronson.

Junger, M. and Wiegersma, A. (1995) 'The Relations between Accidents, Deviants and Leisure Time', *Criminal Behaviour and Mental Health* 5: 144–174.

Kaltiala-Heino, R., Berg, J., Selander, M., Työläjärvi, M. and Kahila, K. (2007) 'Aggression Management in an Adolescent Forensic Unit', *International Journal of Forensic Mental Health* 6: 185–196.

Klein, M. (1963) *Our Adult World and Other Essays*, London: Heinemann.

Lorenz, K. (1966) *On Aggression*, London: Methuen.

McDermott, M. (1993) 'On Cruelty, Ethics and Experimentation: Profile of Philip G Zimbardo', *The Psychologist* 6: 456–459.

Miers, D. (1996) 'Liabilities for Injuries Caused by Violent Patients', *Medicine, Science and the Law* 36: 15–24.

Mizen, R. and Morris, M. (2007) *On Aggression and Violence: An Analytic Perspective*, Basingstoke: Palgrave Macmillan.

Murphy, D. (2006) 'Homophobia and Psychotic Crimes of Violence', *Journal of Forensic Psychiatry and Psychology* 17: 227–238.

National Audit Office (NAO) (2003) *Press Notice*, 27.2.03. 'A Safe Place to Work – Protecting NHS Hospital and Ambulance Staff from Violence and Aggression', London: NAO.

Newell, T. (2007) 'Face to Face with Violence and Its Effects: Restorative Justice at Work', *Probation Journal: The Journal of Community and Criminal Justice* 54: 227–238.

Norris, D.M. and Gutheil, J.G. (2003) 'Harassment and Intimidation of Forensic Psychiatrists: An Update', *International Journal of Law and Psychiatry* 26: 437–445.

O'Keefe, G. (1999) 'Review of Management of Imminent Violence, Guidelines Issued by the Research Unit of the Royal College of Psychiatrists', *Journal of Forensic Psychiatry* 10: 391–398.

Pearson, G. (1983) *Hooligan: A History of Respectable Fears*, London: Macmillan.

Prins, H. (1996) 'Can the Law Serve as the Solution to Social Ills? The Mental Health (Patients in the Community) Act, 1995', *Medicine, Science and the Law* 36: 217–220.

—— (2002) 'Cui Bono? Witholding Treatment from Violent and Abusive Patients in NHS Trusts: "We Don't Have to Take This"', *Journal of Forensic Psychiatry* 13: 391–406.

Prison Service (2004) *Prison Service Order 2750: Reduction of Violence Strategy*, London: The Prison Service.

Raine A. and Liu, J.H. (1998) 'Biological Predispositions to Violence and their Implications for Biosocial Treatment and Prevention', *Psychology, Crime and Law* 4: 107–125.

Rutter, S., Gudjonsson, G. and Rabe-Hesketh, S. (2004) 'Violent Incidents in a Medium Secure Unit: The Characteristics of Persistent Perpetrators of Violence', *Journal of Forensic Psychiatry and Psychology* 15: 293–302.

Schneiden, V., Stark, M. and Payne-Jones, J. (1995) 'Violence and Clinical Forensic Medicine', *Medicine, Science and the Law* 35: 333–335.

Scott, P.D. (1977) 'Assessing Dangerousness in Criminals', *British Journal of Psychiatry* 131: 127–142.

Sharpe, J. (1992) 'Hard Times Revive Law and Order Panic', *The Independent*, 12 April.

Shepherd, J.P. (1994) *Violence in Health Care*, Oxford: Oxford University Press.

—— (1995) 'Injury and Illness Experience in Victims of Violence with Particular Reference to DATES Syndrome', *Criminal Behaviour and Mental Health* 5: 351–366.

Shepherd, J.P. and Farrington, D.P. (1996) 'The Prevention of Delinquency with Particular Reference to Violent Crime', *Medicine, Science and the Law* 36: 331–336.

Shepherd, J., Coid, J., Yang, M., Roberts, A., Ullrich, S., Moran, P., Bebbington, P., Brugha, T., Jenkins, R., Farrell, M., Lewis, G. and Singleton, N. (2006) 'Violence and Psychiatric Morbidity in the National Household Population in Britain: Public Health Implications', *British Journal of Psychiatry* 189: 12–19.

Soothill, K. (2003) 'A New Report on Violence: A Welcome and a Warning', *British Journal of Psychiatry* 182: 3–4.

Steen, V., and Hunskaar, S. (2001) 'Violence: A Prospective Study of Police and Health Care Registrations in an Urban Community in Norway', *Medicine, Science and the Law* 41: 337–341.

Storr, A. (1975) *Human Aggression*, Harmondsworth: Penguin.

—— (1991) *Human Destructiveness: The Roots of Genocide and Human Cruelty* (2nd edn of *Human Aggression*), London: Routledge.

Toch, H. (1992) *Violent Men: An Inquiry into the Psychology of Violence*, revised edn, Washington, DC: American Psychological Association.

Toffler, A. (1970) *Future Shock*, London: Bodley Head.

Walker, W.D. and Caplan, R.P. (1993) 'Assaultive Behaviour in Acute Psychiatric Wards and its Relationship to Violence in the Community: A Comparison of Two Health Districts', *Medicine, Science and the Law* 33: 300–304.

Watts, D., Leese, M., Thomas, S., Atakan, C. and Wykes, T. (2003) 'The Prediction of Violence in Acute Psychiatric Units', *International Journal of Forensic Mental Health* 2: 173–180.

Welsh, K. (2008) 'Partnership or Palming Off? Involvement in Partnership Initiatives on Domestic Violence', *Howard Journal of Criminal Justice* 47: 170–188.

Wildgoose, J., Briscoe, M. and Lloyd, K. (2003) 'Psychological and Emotional Problems in Staff Following Assault by Patients', *Psychiatric Bulletin* 27: 295–297.

World Health Organization (WHO) (2002) (1) *World Report on Violence and Health* (2) *World Report on Violence and Health: Summary*, eds E.G. Krug, L.L. Dahlberg, J.A. Mercy, A.B. Zwi and R. Lozano, Geneva: WHO.

Wykes, T. (1994) *Violence and Health Care Professionals*, London: Chapman & Hall.

Wynn, R. (2003) 'Staff's Choice of Formal and Informal Coercive Interventions in Psychiatric Emergencies', *International Journal of Forensic Mental Health* 2: 157–164.

Yorston, G. (1999) 'Aged and Dangerous: Old Age Forensic Psychiatry', *Psychiatric Bulletin* 174: 193–195.

Zimbardo, P.G. (1973) 'On the Ethics of Intervention in Human Psychological Research with Special Reference to the Stanford Prison Experiment', *Cognition* 2: 243–256.

Further reading

General

Cox, M. (ed.) (1999) *Remorse and Reparation*, London: Jessica Kingsley.

Discussion Meeting Issue (2008) 'The Neurobiology of Violence: Implications for Prevention and Treatment', organized by S. Hodgins, E. Viding and A. Plodowski, *Royal Socialty of Philosophical Transactions B* 363(1503): 2483–2622. See especially the articles by McGuire and Duggan.

Howells, K. and Hollin, C.R. (eds) (1989) *Clinical Approaches to Violence*, Chichester: Wiley.

Jones, D. (ed.) (2004) *Working with Dangerous People: The Psychotherapy of Violence*, Oxford: Radcliffe Medical Press.

Maden, A. (2007) *Treating Violence: A Guide to Risk Management in Mental Health*, Oxford: Oxford University Press.

Selected aspects

Brogden, M. and Nijhar, P. (2000) *Crime, Abuse and the Elderly*, Cullompton: Willan.

Knowles, S.F., Coyne, S.M. and Brown, S.L. (2008) 'Sex Differences in Aggressive Incidents towards Staff in Secure Services', *Journal of Forensic Psychiatry and Psychology* 19: 620–631.

Journals

Journal of Interpersonal Violence

Probation Journal: The Journal of Community and Criminal Justice, special issue on violence 2005, 52(4).

Psychology, Crime and Law, special issue on Working with Aggression and Violence 2005, 11(4).

See also suggestions for further reading listed in Chapter 7.

Chapter 7

Thou shall not commit murder

(Ten Commandments: Exodus 20: 13)

Murder most foul, as in the best it is;
But this most foul, strange, and unnatural.
(The Ghost, in Hamlet, Act 1, Sc. 5)

Murder will out; we see it day by day.
(Geoffrey Chaucer, Canterbury Tales: Nun's Priest's Tale,
Neville Coghill translation, Penguin Classics 1977)

One way of viewing murder is to see it at the extreme end of the spectrum of violence. This is essentially correct, but it is necessary to enter some caveats. For example, murder is not *unlawful* when committed in pursuance of warfare or in pursuance of judicial execution. Killing may be viewed in a more lenient light if the act was unintentional, or occurred in serendipitous fashion; for example, as referred to in Chapter 6, the victim succumbed because of an existing health problem, thin skull or failure of the para-medical services to arrive quickly enough. In addition, the severity of the penalty for unlawful killing may be mitigated by factors such as provocation and mental disturbance.

Nevertheless its primacy is attested to in biblical texts, in mythology and classical literature. The 'injunction' I am most familiar with is that contained in the Old Testament, most notably in the Book of Genesis with the description of Cain's fratricide. It is graphic in this respect.

Some of the material in this chapter appeared in my article 'Coke v. Bumble – Comments on Some Aspects of Unlawful Killing and its Disposal', *Medicine, Science and the Law* 2008, 48(1): 15–23, and is reproduced with the permission of the publishers.

The voice of thy brother's blood
Crieth unto me from the ground.

(Genesis 4: 10)

And the Lord set a mark upon Cain.

(Genesis 4: 15)

Elizabethan literature is replete with accounts of murder. Shakespeare and his contemporaries depict its horror, as for example in the Shakespeare's plays *Titus Andronicus*, with its gruesome and bizarre killings, the multiple murders in *Richard III* and the murder in *King Lear*. John Webster gives it primacy in his play *The Duchess of Malfi*: 'Other sins only speak, murder shrieks out' (Act 4, Sc. 2); and in the same play, the horror of what the killers have done to their sister (The Duchess) is contained in the chilling line, 'Cover her face, mine eyes dazzle'.[1] Not only does classical literature attest to the public's interest in murder, but also there is a virtual stream of later and contemporary fiction dealing with murder and an outpouring of film and television presentations of drama and documentaries. It is also of interest to note that British public lending libraries have recently witnessed the reading public's previous interest in romantic fiction turning to crime novels (Public Lending Right Statistics, quoted in *The Independent*, 10 February 2006). And a sombre (if somewhat gruesome) reminder of the heinous nature of murder is seen in the words that were used to impose the death penalty in the days before its abolition.

You shall be taken to the place from whence you came, and thence to a place of lawful execution, and there you shall be hanged by the neck until you be dead, and afterwards your body shall be buried in a common grave wherein you were last confined before your execution; and may the Lord have mercy upon your soul.

(quoted in McDermid 2006)

If the wording of the sentence of death was not a sufficient reminder, one notes the additional statement that burial among the general population is prohibited. The 'mark of Cain' lived on.

This interest might incline the unwary to the view that murder is a commonplace event. For a study of the media's role, see McKenna et al. (2007). Reference to the figures given in Chapter 6 do not support this view. More detailed statistics (for example, court disposals etc.) may be found in the Home Office (2008) *Statistical Bulletin* 03/08. However, as I shall show later, we do *not* know how many persons who disappear each year have suffered untimely deaths at the hands of others. The various descriptive terms used for homicidal acts may be found in Table 7.1.

Table 7.1 Common and some less common descriptive terms for homicidal acts[a]

Homicide	Generic term for murder, manslaughter and infanticide
Paricide[b]	Killing of a near relative or parent
Genocide	Extermination of a people or nation
Regicide	Killing of a male monarch
Reginacide	Killing of a female monarch (however, regicide may be taken to include monarchs of *both* sexes)
Femicide	Killing of females by males
Geronticide	Killing of elderly people
Uxoricide	Killing of a wife
Mariticide[c]	Killing of a husband
Sororicide	Killing of a sister
Fratricide	Killing of a brother[d]
Filicide	Killing of a son or daughter
Neo-naticide	Killing of new-born babies
Familicide	Killing of multiple family members[e]

Notes: (a) These descriptive terms have their roots largely in Latin and occasionally in Greek or old French. (b) Paricidal behaviour has often been viewed within a psychoanalytical framework, but this seems to carry less weight than in the past. Shon and Targonski (2003) suggest that paricides, as with homicidal behaviour more generally, seem to be disproportionately committed by males in late adolescence. They also suggest that 'fathers are likely to bear the brunt of lethal violence from sons and daughters alike' (Shon and Targonski 2003: 399; see also Marleau et al. 2003). (c) I am greatly indebted to Mrs Pauline West, a life-long student of Latin, for suggesting this term. (d) Sometimes also used to denote brother *and sister* killing, and for the accidental killing of one's own forces in war. (e) For an account of differences between those who commit multiple family homicides and those who commit filicide and uxoricide, see Liem and Koenraadt (2008b).

The rest of this chapter is divided into three sections. First, the current legal position, second, some clinical aspects, and third, proposals for reform of the present law.

The current law

It may come as a surprise to many people that currently there is no statutory definition of the crime of murder. It is punishable at common law. This derives from the seventeenth-century statement by Sir Edward Coke, in his treatise *The Institutes of the Laws of England*, and runs as follows:

> Murder is when a man of sound memory, and of the age of discretion, unlawfully killeth within any county of the realm any reasonable creature in *rerum natura* under the King's peace, with malice afore-thought, either expressed by the party, or implied by law, so as the party wounded, or hurt, etc. die of the wound or hurt within a year and a day after the same.
>
> (quoted in Blom-Cooper and Morris 2004: 15)[2]

Murder can be briefly described in the following more modern terms. The unlawful killing of another with malice aforethought (that is with criminal intention). Subject to certain exceptions, the crime of murder is committed when a person of sound mind and discretion unlawfully kills any reasonable creature in being and under the Queen's peace with intent to kill or cause grievous bodily harm (see Bowden 1990).

Present-day language is somewhat less archaic than Coke's; despite this, some further elaboration is needed. As already mentioned, killing the enemy in times of war is not murder; the office of public hangman was, of course, also exempt; 'reasonable creature' means a life in being; it is not murder to kill a child in the womb, now known as intentional destruction of a viable unborn child. And the requirement embodied in the 'year and a day rule' was abolished in 1996 (Law Reform (Year and a Day Rule) Act 1996).

Murder is currently reduced to manslaughter if the accused was

- provoked
- acting in pursuance of a suicide pact
- suffering from diminished responsibility (for discussion of some of the psycho-social problems of determining diminishment of criminal responsibility, see Chapter 2).

Other examples of unlawful killing include the following:

- *Manslaughter* is defined as unlawfully causing the death of another without malice aforethought. Currently, it includes *voluntary* manslaughter (i.e. provocation, diminished responsibility, and killing in pursuance of a suicide pact).
- *Involuntary manslaughter* covers cases where the killing was not intended, but where there was an intention to commit an unlawful or dangerous act, gross negligence, or disregard for the lives and safety of others.
- *Intentional destruction of a viable unborn child*: it is an offence to destroy the life of an unborn child; that is to say unless the provisions of current abortion legislation are complied with.
- *Causing death by dangerous or careless driving under the influence of drink or drugs*: these offences have gone through a number of classificatory revisions and now replace almost entirely the prosecution of motorists for manslaughter.
- *Infanticide*: although there had been a number of statutes dealing with the killing of infant children by mothers from very early times, current practice derives from twentieth-century statutes. (For a review of infanticide in England and Wales, see Marks and Kumar 1993; Law Commission 2004, 2005a, 2005b, 2006; Sharma 2006.) The specific

offence of *infanticide* was introduced because of an increasing reluctance on the part of the judges to pass the death sentence in cases where mothers killed their infant children and the fact that, when they had, the Home Secretary reprieved all mothers so convicted. The Infanticide Act 1922 referred to the killing of a 'newly born child'. Current legislation (Infanticide Act 1938) specifies a child of any age under 12 months. The 1938 Act also added a clause indicating that the effect of lactation consequent upon the birth could be considered (see also Chapter 2). The annual number of prosecutions for infanticide is very small – for example, in 2005/6 there were only two cases (Home Office 2008: 29).

Over-reliance on the criminal statistics for the true extent of murder is unhelpful. Many people (particularly children and young adults) and their fates remain unaccounted for. Biehal et al. (2003) examined the phenomena of those who go missing, their backgrounds, the reasons for their disappearance and, where known, their fates. Occasionally, their fates do come to light, sometimes many years after disappearance. Examples that readily come to mind being the victims of Fred and Rosemary West, Dennis Nilsen and a number of Harold Shipman's alleged victims.

Clinical aspects

Even making allowance for the very brief presentation of some legal definitions of homicide offences and their volume, it will be apparent that there are wide ranges of 'clinical' presentation.[3] I have attempted to summarize these in Table 7.2.

It is appropriate therefore to provide a brief discussion of these aspects before commenting on some areas of the law that are thought to be in need of change.

Normal and abnormal homicide

For many people, any form of homicide indicates a degree of mental abnormality. To the extent that life, for the most part, is held to be sacred, any activity that takes it away by unlawful and forceful acts departs from norms laid down by society. This is not to say that sometimes such acts may seem *understandable* which, of course, is not quite the same thing. For this reason (as I showed in Chapter 2) the law recognizes gradations of responsibility for such crimes and, as I shall endeavour to demonstrate later in this chapter, some of these 'gradations' are recognized as being in need of much needed reform. It is something of a truism that homicide is largely a 'domestic' affair and the family is certainly not the safe haven some have considered it to be (see, for example, Howitt 2006). As already indicated at various places in this text, certain forms of mental disorder are not

Table 7.2 Presentations of and motivations for homicide (unlawful killing)

1   Killing as a result of an unlawful or dangerous act, gross negligence or disregard for the lives and safety of others, for example, corporate manslaughter.[a]

2   Killing as a result of dangerous, careless and drunken driving.

3   'Political' and associated killings, for example, acts of genocide (Hitler, Stalin, Idi Amin, Saddam Hussein), sequential sacrificial killing (as in the Aztec civilization), 'cult' killings, including ritual killing for body parts (Muti killings: see Labuschagne 2004; Bhootra and Weiss 2006), killing in the course of warfare and terrorist activity. Some of the perpetrators in this category will show signs of severe personality (psychopathic) disorder and there will be inevitable overlap with some other categories. For a critical account of the extent to which mental disorder may or may not exist in terrorist offenders, see Dernevik et al. (2009).

4   Killing for clear motives of gain, or to punish adversaries or competitors, for example, 'gang' warfare, Mafia-type activities.

5   Killing associated with severe mental disorders, for example, schizophrenic and allied illnesses (such as the presence of 'dangerous obsessions'), manic-depressive illness, organic states, mental impairment. Some apparently 'motiveless' killings and the stalking and killing of 'celebrity' individuals could be included in this category.

6   'Domestic' killings: these are usually, but not always, one-off events, driven by stress and/or provocation, but excluding killing driven by identifiable mental illness (as in category 5). This category could include the 'mercy killing' of adult children, spouses or partners. It should also be noted that this category may involve several family members, as in the case of Jeremy Bamber, who was convicted of killing several of his family on the same day. We should also include so-called 'honour killings' and related 'forced marriages'.

7   Killing facilitated by the ingestion of substances of abuse such as alcohol, other drugs, solvents etc. (this category overlaps with categories 5 and 6).

8   'Carer' killings: these are sometimes committed by those with severe personality disorders such as the nurse Beverley Allitt and would include the activities of individuals like the GP Harold Shipman.

9   Multiple (mass) killings: these consist of large groups of individuals killed at the same location and at the same time. Examples are, in the UK, Michael Ryan at Hungerford and Thomas Hamilton at Dunblane. and in the USA, Charles Whitman in Texas, Richard Speck in Chicago, James Huberty in California and Seung-hui Cho in Virginia.

10 Parental or familial child killings: these may be subdivided in the following fashion (for further discussion, see Wilczynski 1997):
    • Intentional destruction of a viable unborn child
    • Neonaticide (killing of a newborn baby)
    • Killing of a child of more than one day old but under 12 months (infanticide)
    • Child killing as a result of non-accidental injury (previously known as 'battered child syndrome')

11 Killing of parents and/or siblings: overlaps with category 6.

12 Children as killers: these are rare, tragic and highly emotive events, as seen for example in the cases of Mary Bell and the two child killers of toddler James Bulger (see later comments).

13 So-called 'Serial Killing':
    • For gain, but not as in category 4, for example, Madame de Brinvilliers in seventeenth-century France, who killed various family members over a period of time for material gain.
    • For gain, but involving strangers, for example, the infamous Sawney Bean in fifteenth-century Scotland, who is said to have killed passers-by for their possessions; he then cannibalized some of them.

- Sexually motivated or control motivated serial killing: in my view this is best categorized as *sequential stranger killing*. Such killing is usually defined as needing at least three or four victims, not usually known to the perpetrator, with the killings being committed in different locations, usually over a considerable period of time. The emphasis is on repetition, the acts are not committed for gain, but seem to be compulsive in nature and are highly likely to rely on fantasy for their acting out.[b]

Examples of motivated serial killings are as follows:

  (i)   *Visionary*: motivated by delusional beliefs and sometimes by hallucinatory experiences (see category 5). For further discussion, see Chapter 4 in this book.

  (ii) *Missionary*: motivated by a need to exterminate a particular group of people – for example prostitutes, as in Peter Sutcliffe's case. This subclassification overlaps with the *Visionary* in (i) above; for example, Sutcliffe's history indicates that he could be said to fall into both categories.

  (iii) *Hedonistic*: this group will include so-called 'lust' killings, thrill seeking (for kicks), and for psychological and physical security – derived perhaps from the victim's property (but excluding those in category 13 'for gain').

  (iv) *Power and control*: these killers wish to exercise control over their victim's life and death. Although the motivation is not predominantly sexual, sexually deviant activity may form an important part of the scenario.[c]

Notes (a) In order to secure a conviction for corporate manslaughter, it needs to be demonstrated that there is a causal link between a grossly negligent act or omission by a person who is the 'controlling mind' of the company and the immediate cause of death. In most circumstances an individual can be a 'controlling mind' only if he or she is a director or other senior officer carrying out the functions of management. In order for proceedings for corporate manslaughter to be considered, the prosecution must be able to prove that at least one controlling mind is guilty of manslaughter. In larger corporations this may be difficult, in smaller bodies, less so. Current law is now embodied in the Corporate Manslaughter and Corporate Homicide Act 2007. The emphasis in the new legislation would seem to be on the implementation of adequate safety measures and the exercise of a 'duty of care'. It still remains possible to bring prosecutions for gross negligence under the common law; the new Act came into force on 8 April 2008 (I am most grateful to my colleague Dr Kate Brookes for bringing these provisions to my attention, personal communication, 13 November 2007; see also Berry 2006).

(b) The killing of large numbers of people over time may justify the label 'serial' killing, but as the table shows, it is too broad a term to have much diagnostic, prognostic and management significance. However, it is acknowledged that my own proposed classification is inevitably arbitrary; as will be seen, there are inevitable overlaps between the various categories and the motivation of individual offenders may change over time. In addition, Gresswell and Hollin (1994) make the important point that many classifications do not 'pick up the more subtle interactions between the killer, the victims and the environment. Nor do some of them appear flexible enough to accommodate a killer who may have different motives for different victims and changing motives over time' (Gresswell and Hollin 1994: 5).

(c) Note that the Domestic Violence, Crime and Victims Act 2004 creates the new offence of causing or contributing to the non-accidental death of a child or vulnerable adult. A *history* of domestic violence plays a worrying and prominent part in the killing of wives and female partners. It has been estimated that two women in England and Wales are killed every week by a current or former partner. Scotland Yard has developed a six-point 'early warning system' that is said to help identify 'domestic killers' before they commit murder. The six risk factors include the presence of pregnancy, stalking, sexual assault, increase in violence, custody disputes, and cultural restraint (i.e. restricted access to wider society and/or the police). Scotland Yard research indicates that these six factors will help to identify the perpetrators of domestic homicide *before* they kill. Other police forces are said to be implementing similar approaches (reported in *The Independent*, 11 February 2005).

continues overleaf

Table 7.2 *(continued)*

In an interesting and highly original study, Liu et al. (2008: 164) found that those involved in kidnapping 'are over 30 times more likely than males in the general population to be convicted of homicide'.

Large et al. (2008) examined the rates of homicide generally and the rates of homicides by mentally disordered people for a fifty-year period (1946–2004). From the mid-1970s onwards the rates of the latter declined steadily. Large et al. (2008: 130) suggest that this *might* be due to better early diagnosis and treatment and 'an informal change to the legal tests for the finding of homicide due to mental disorder'.

uncommonly associated with homicidal acts. There have been some important studies of so-called abnormal homicides and some of these merit our attention. The first was that carried out by West (1965) into 150 cases of murder followed by suicide in London for the years 1946–62. Not altogether surprisingly, one of West's main conclusions was that depression in various forms was a very common precipitating factor (West 1965). Another study by Mowat (1966) examined a highly selected group of abnormal homicides (forty male and six female patients) detained in Broadmoor Hospital. He found that a high proportion of them suffered from delusional jealousy (see Chapter 4). Mowat's findings are still of interest today, because they concentrated attention on the presence of delusions from a variety of causes. These have been the subject of more comprehensive investigation by later workers such as Mullen (1996). See also Belfrage and Rying (2004), Laajasolo and Häkkänen (2006) and Liem and Koenraadt (2007). Gillies (1976) carried out a comprehensive study in the west of Scotland. His findings contradict some of those contained in earlier studies in England. Gillies (1976) based his survey on his psychiatric examination of 400 murder cases undertaken for the prosecution between the years 1953 and 1974 (367 males and 33 females). The salient features he found were being male, youthfulness, the importance of alcohol, rarity of suicide and a high proportion of psychiatrically 'normal' persons. Furthermore, 47 per cent had histories of previous violence. Of the weapons used by the male accused, 56 per cent were sharp instruments, 37 per cent were blunt. Other methods used by both sexes included shooting and strangulation. Gillies (1976) found that most of the crimes in his sample appeared to be *unpremeditated*, apparently unintended and impulsive (for example precipitated over trifles, often when the parties involved were 'in their cups'. For a more recent two-city survey (Glasgow and Melbourne), see Lynch and Black (2008).

One of the largest studies into mentally abnormal violent offenders, including homicides, was carried out by Häfner and Böker (1982) in the former Federal Republic of Germany for the years 1955–64. They found that many of the offences occurred within a family setting, but some 9 per cent were strangers. Half of the attacks were planned in advance (compare this finding with that of Gillies 1976); in only about one-quarter of the cases was the crime impulsive. In about half of their cases a delusional relationship existed, but in about one-third there was no apparent motive. In their group, revenge constituted about one-third of the motives in the males; in some 40 per cent of the females the desire was to obtain release from feared distress or illness. Although somewhat dated now, Häfner and Böker's (1982) study of violence and homicide among mentally abnormal offenders is still regarded as thorough and methodologically sound. For more recent studies, see Brookman (2005: notably Chapters 3, 4 and 5), Shaw et al. (2006) and Swinson et al. (2007). The Shaw et al. (2006) study is of particular interest. They found that there was

> an association between schizophrenia and convictions for homicide. In addition, most perpetrators with a history of mental disorder *were not acutely ill or under mental health care at the time of the offence.* Some perpetrators received prison sentences despite having severe mental illness.
>
> (Shaw et al. 2006: 143, emphasis added)

(See also Chapter 4 of this volume.) Far less is known about the *mortality rate* of homicide offenders. However, the authors of a Swedish study suggest that the mortality among homicide offenders is about three times the rate for the general population, commonly suicide and self-neglect being important occurrences (Lindquist et al. 2007).

A recent short profile

The typical homicide perpetrator is stated by the Law Commission (2005a) to be white, male and between 21 and 40 years old. In 70 per cent of cases he will have killed a spouse, lover, relative, offspring or acquaintance, using either a sharp or blunt instrument (50 per cent of cases). Firearms are rarely used, compared with the United States, where in 2003 67 per cent of all murders involved the use of firearms compared with 5–10 per cent in the UK. The typical victim is white (78 per cent of cases) and male (68 per cent of cases). The proportion of female victims (32 per cent of cases) is much higher than the proportion of female perpetrators (10 per cent of cases). In 62 per cent of cases victims were over 30 years of age. Only 2 per cent of perpetrators were over 60, whereas 12 per cent of victims were over that age. It is also of interest to note the much higher proportion of women charged with murder where the victim was their partner (35 per cent of women defendants) as compared with 19 per cent of male defendants. The Law Commission, in addition to providing the above information (which I have condensed) also provides information about the legal defences being offered.

- Lack of intent   Males 25 per cent; females 29 per cent
- Provocation   Both males and females: 18 per cent
- Self-defence   Males 14 per cent; females 10 per cent
- Diminished responsibility Males 8 per cent; females 14 per cent.

The Law Commission also observes that generally speaking at least 5 per cent of all murder trials are preoccupied by claims that the police have got the wrong person. In 10–15 per cent of cases, there are guilty pleas or no apparent defence (source for all above figures is Law Commission 2005a: 325–326).

The 'serial killer': a suggested misnomer

In the prosecution of the GP Harold Shipman, he was described in the media as a 'serial killer'. Such a description seemed to me to be somewhat erroneous in the light of what (admittedly little) we know about the behavioural and other characteristics of so-called serial killers (see, for example, Table 7.2, Note 13). The unlawful killing of single individuals over prolonged periods of time has a very long history (examples may be found in Egger 1990; Gresswell and Hollin 1994; Holmes et al. 1998). Attempts at explaining the phenomenon have included studies into the background and personal pathology of some so-called serial killers (see, for example, Holmes and De Burger 1988). Claims have been made for socio-cultural explanations, notably by Leyton (1989), more generally by Seltzer (1998) and more recently by Wilson (2007). Seltzer (1998) locates serial killing within what he describes as the 'wound culture' in the United States: 'a public fascination with torn and open bodies and torn and open persons, a collective gathering around shock, trauma and the wound' (Seltzer 1998: 1). I suggest that much of this interesting theorizing would be helped by more clarity about the different phenomena we are trying to describe; hence my proposed formulation in *Table 7.2*. Opinions also vary as to whether or not there has been an increase in recent times in those killings categorized as 'serial'. There does not appear to be any clear consensus. The public's understanding (or perhaps *misunderstanding*) of the phenomenon has no doubt been fed by various media presentations (literary and audio-visual) such as the works of Thomas Harris, Patricia Cornwell, Kathy Reichs, Mo Hayder, Val McDermid, Tess Gerritsen and Simon Beckett. The UK television series *Prime Suspect, Waking the Dead, Silent Witness* and some of the US productions such as *CSI Miami* and *Law and Order (Criminal Intent)* all have their place in the current scenario. In addition, the names of certain notorious 'serial killers' have attained household provenance – examples being Peter Sutcliffe, Dennis Nilsen and Steve Wright in the UK, Andrei Chikatilo and Anatoly Onoprienko in the Ukraine, Jeffrey Dahmer,

Ted Bundy, David Berkowitz, Albert deSalvo, Edmund Kemper and Susan Atkins in the United States. All the foregoing tend to feed and distort public assumptions and fears concerning what is regarded frequently as an all-pervasive menace. Most serial killers are male. For a review of the literature on female serial killers, see Frei et al. (2006). For a study of consistency among serial homicide offenders, see Salfati and Bateman (2005).

Some further clinical observations

Parents who kill their children

Although I indicated earlier in this book that I was not attempting to include violence in the family more generally, it would be wrong if I did not include some reference to those situations where parents killed their children. Such killings have been classified in a variety of ways. Scott (1973), in an early contribution, discerned five types of behaviour:

- Killing of an unwanted child by parents (most frequently the mother).
- As a result of aggression due to mental abnormality.
- Behaviour due to displacement anger (sometimes referred to as the Medea Syndrome – see Chapter 6).
- Cases in which the stimulus seems to arise from the victim, as is sometimes found in cases of non-accidental injury (NAI).
- For altruistic reasons – 'mercy killings'.

In a more recent empirical study, Wilczynski (1997) elaborated on the classifications by Scott (1973) and others; she suggested some ten sub-divisions (Wilczynski 1997: 44–62). Dr Patrick McGrath, sometime medical director of Broadmoor Hospital, examined a fifty-year (1919–69) cohort of 280 female filicide admissions to the hospital from England and Wales (McGrath 1992; see also Oberman 2003). From his survey he concluded that:

[T]hat the modal maternal filicide committed to Broadmoor was a white Anglo-Saxon Protestant, aged 31–5, married, suffering from an affective psychosis, altruistically motivated (there is only one 'baby batterer' in the cohort) and not influenced by drink or drugs. She has a previous history of psychiatric referral. The modal victim was the youngest child, of either sex, healthy, the sole victim. The age of the victim was 2–5 years, ranging from 1–29 years. The offence was carried out by readily available domestic means (suffocation, strangulation, gassing, drowning).

(McGrath 1992: 271)

Finally, three more recent studies of the phenomenon should be mentioned. Dolan et al. (2003) describe the histories of 64 men accused of killing a single child victim:

> They were characterised by relatively young age and a lack of long-term stable relationships. Previous psychiatric contact and/or history was noted in one third of cases. Over half the group had a criminal record and previous violence to children was noted in 28% of cases. Fathers or surrogate fathers, accounted for nearly two thirds of the accused. In terms of the victims, children under six months were at greatest risk . . . sexually motivated homicide accounted for approximately 18.7% of deaths. Victim behaviours and domestic disharmony acted as precipitants in 64% of the cases, with 54% of the victims dying as a result of physical beatings. Alcohol consumption at the material time was more common that noted in previous studies of child homicide.
>
> (Dolan et al. 2003: 153)

On the basis of their research, Dolan et al. (2003: 167) suggest that: 'There is clearly a need for on-going research into child homicide, both to monitor trends and evaluate motives and precipitants, particularly in view of the higher than expected frequency of sexually motivated homicides in [our] series'. It is interesting to note that many of their findings would seem to fit well with those reported in *The Independent* article, quoted earlier.

Romain et al. (2003) conducted a retrospective study in Switzerland of forty-one cases of childhood homicide for the years 1990–2000. They discerned two 'common profiles':

> In the first, one of the parents shot all the children and then committed suicide afterwards. The second profile they defined as 'fatal child abuse' and concerned younger victims whose cause of death was the result of cranio-cerebral trauma from battering or shaken baby syndrome.
>
> (Romain et al. 2003: 203)

Dolan et al. (2003), Romain et al. (2003) and a more recent study by Liem and Koenraadt (2008a) demonstrates not only the range of behaviours leading to such homicides but also the possibility of unsafe convictions as a result of mistaken diagnoses, as some recent high profile cases have attested to.

Children who kill

The trial and convictions of the 10-year-old boys Robert Thompson and Jon Venables for the killing of the toddler James Bulger in 1993 reawakened interest in the fairly rare phenomenon of young children who kill.[4]

Gunn and Taylor (1993: 517) commented that 'there are only two or three cases each year in Britain'. Even with this worrying figure one has to ask whether or not some cases involving serious violence, and maybe homicide, are not reported because the children are below the age of criminal responsibility and thus not open to prosecution.[5] However, figures obtained by the BBC under the Freedom of Information Act show that there were about 1300 incidents of criminal damage and arson and over 60 sex offences where suspects were under 10 in England and Wales (reported by Robert Verkaik, Law Editor, *The Independent*, 3 September 2007).

Gunn and Taylor (1993) quote a journalist, Wilson (1973), who identified and described some 57 incidents of homicide involving children under the age of 16 between the years 1943 and 1972. Of the 75 children involved (12 girls and 63 boys) 48 were British. Although Wilson (1973) described 15 of the children as mentally abnormal, and several as being of low intelligence, no cases of frank severe mental illness were recorded. It may be that with advances in psychiatric and psychological knowledge some of these youngsters *might* have been diagnosed as having attention deficit disorders or Asperger Syndrome.[6] Wilson's (1973) series included older children (for example adolescents); a report by another journalist, Richard Grant, describes the alleged torturing and killing of a 12-year-old girl by four teenage girls in the United States (*The Independent* Saturday Review, 22 August 1992). Similar instances have occurred in more recent years in the UK. Two fairly recent accounts by highly responsible journalists have appeared concerning the lives of children who kill. Gitta Sereny's (1998) book *Cries Unheard* charts the history and subsequent care and management of Mary Bell who, when 11 years old, killed two small boys. Her case received further media interest when, some years after her return to the community and her rehabilitation, she and her adolescent daughter were the subject of media-fuelled critical comment, because Mary was said to have been in receipt of a sum of money from Gitta Sereny for her help in compiling her life story (Sereny 1998). The other work is Blake Morrison's (1997) coverage of the Thompson and Venables trial. Both books provide sensitive depictions of the social and family circumstances of these three child killers. In 1960, the distinguished American child psychiatrist, Lauretta Bender, made an important statement concerning the need to make a distinction between pre-pubertal and adolescent killers:

> The psychodynamic of a pre-puberty child who has caused a death is that he experiments in fantasy and by acting out to determine if irreparable death is possible. An adolescent makes an effort to deny both guilt for his part in the act that caused the death and to claim amnesia or other repressive defences. Both are usually misunderstood and dangerous.
>
> (Bender 1960: 511)

Bender's (1960) statement has implications for our understanding of the age at which children develop a moral sense. Early workers such as Jean Piaget and Arnold Gesell and others paved the way for our understanding of this problem. In more recent times, one of my postgraduate criminology students at Leicester's Department of Criminology conducted a comprehensive review of the literature and conducted, in a primary school, a small-scale empirical study of children's understanding of right and wrong behaviour at different ages of development (Hefford 2005).

Bender (1960) found a considerable degree of social deprivation and family pathology. Follow-up revealed continuing deterioration and, for some, the need for psychiatric hospital placement. In studying homicides committed by *older* children, she found that

> a constellation of factors was required for a boy or girl to cause a death. This needed to be a disturbed, poorly controlled impulsive child, a victim who acted as an irritant, an available lethal weapon, and *always* a lack of protective supervision by some person who could stop the fatal consequences.
>
> (Bender 1960: 41)

Bender's findings of social deprivation and personal pathology are echoed by Bailey (2000) in a valuable contribution comparing and contrasting juvenile homicides in the United States and UK (see also McNally 1995; Dolan and Smith 2001).

> It may be inferred tentatively that in the UK killings by children or adolescents . . . may be likely to reflect serious personal pathology, although rarely illness such as schizophrenia, than is the case with most other serious crime committed by young people.
>
> (Bailey 2000: 151)

Bender's (1960) observations are important in connection with the speculations as to causation in the James Bulger case. I have suggested elsewhere (Prins 1994) that, as adults, we find it very difficult to comprehend that during the age of so-called innocence very young children can engage in homicidal acts. As indicated earlier in this book, even very small infants seem capable of intense rage when frustrated (Klein 1963). For example, experienced primary school teachers are aware of the vigilance needed to prevent mayhem in school playgrounds. An acquaintance with contemporary non-specialist literature reveals the capacity of children to act murderously, as evidenced in William Golding's book *Lord of the Flies* (1954) and, in more recent times, Jonathan Trigell's book *Boy A* (2004).

Perhaps in the light of the preceding comments, we shall have to learn to confront the uncomfortable notion that the killing, or attempted killing, of children by children *may* be more frequent than the available records show, and that, as Bender (1960) suggested, vigilance and active preventive measures are needed to avert its more frequent occurrence.

A brief note on offender profiling

I debated at length where I should include some brief notes on the topic of offender profiling. Because it is probably most frequently employed in homicide cases (but not exclusively so), I have decided to include it here. The choice is, admittedly, somewhat arbitrary.

With the apparent number of so-called 'serial killers', notably in the United States, there has developed an interest in building profiles of such individuals. Such profiles (usually the work of forensic psychologists or psychiatrists) can sometimes assist police investigators in building up a picture of common psychological, social and environmental characteristics in cases where the killers may have managed to evade detection over a prolonged period of time.

Interest in profiling in the UK developed sharply in the wake of the Peter Sutcliffe case and the setting up of sophisticated computer-based retrieval systems (see, for example, Doney 1990; Bilton 2003). Attempts to build profiles in both homicide and non-homicide cases are not new and all good detectives operate through their own 'computer base' (their brain) a means of forming pictures based upon their stored experience. Fictionalized accounts of more primitive forms of profiling abound; writers such as Edgar Allan Poe, with his detective Auguste Dupin, and Wilkie Collins in *The Woman in White* and in *The Moonstone*. We should not ignore the approach taken by Sherlock Holmes in many of his cases. Recent fiction as referred to in Chapter 6 has carried forward this tradition into the modern era. Modern technology merely makes this more sophisticated and more readily available to others. In an interesting article Boon and Davies (1992) trace the history of profiling techniques in the United States. They credit its first major use to the work of a psychiatrist, James A. Brussel, who accurately pinpointed the characteristics of a hard-to-catch bomber. In the UK, work on profiling has been taken ahead very much by the activities of Canter and his co-workers at Liverpool University (Canter 1989, 1994, 2004, 2007). Boon and Davies (1992), from Leicester University, also noted workers in this field, report that Canter and his colleagues:

> have found five aspects of the criminal and his or her behaviour to be of help to investigators; residential location, criminal biography, personal characteristics, domestic and social characteristics, and occupational and education history. Not all of these have been found to be of equal utility, with the researchers reporting that most help is

derived from analysis of details relating to residential location and criminal offence history.

(Boon and Davies 1992: 4)

See also Copson (1996), Oleson (1996) and Canter (2004).

For a review of the literature, see Gregory (2005). For critical evaluative contribution, see Alison et al. (2003), Keppel et al. (2005),[7] Marshall and Alison (2007) and Woodhams et al. (2007).

It is difficult to know what attributes make for a competent profiler. One suggestion is that competence in critical thinking is an essential ingredient. However, Bennell et al. (2008) indicate that this has not been subjected to adequate assessment. In the course of an interesting study in which participants were given a 'mock' scenario, 'no significant relationship was found between critical thinking ability and profile accuracy' (Bennell et al. 2008: 143).

Finally, a crime novelist, who also has professional experience of criminal and forensic investigative techniques, makes a poignant suggestion of what needs to be in the profiler's mind, whatever system he or she uses:

If violent, aggressive behaviour, dominates your thinking, your imagination, you're going to start acting out in ways that move you closer to the actual expression of these emotions. Violence fuels more violent thoughts and more violent thoughts fuel more violence. After a while, violence and killing are a natural part of your adult life and you see nothing wrong in it.

(Cornwell 1992: 327)

Proposals for reform

There is general agreement that the law relating to homicide is unsatisfactory. This has been expressed by the judiciary, the legal profession, mental health professionals and politicians. For example, the complexities relating to pleas of diminished responsibility are evident in numerous well-known cases (see Chapter 2 in this volume). One much debated issue is the degree to which psychiatrists should opine on the question of legal diminishment of responsibility as a moral, as distinct from a forensic mental health, issue. In a very stimulating article, Hardie et al. (2008) consider this issue in some detail.

Hardie et al. (2008) examined 143 psychiatric reports out of 156 cases. In 93 per cent of 118 cases in which there was a diminished verdict, this was achieved without trial of the issue. Half of the reports examined by the researchers gave a clear opinion on diminished responsibility, one-third invited the court to draw a particular conclusion and only 11 per cent provided relevant evidence without answering the legal question. In cases when there was an opinion or an invitation to make a finding on the legal question, a trial was less likely. A trial was also less likely if reports agreed on what the verdict should be (Hardie et al. 2008: 117). The researchers concluded that 'Psychiatrists frequently answer the legal question of diminished responsibility. The judiciary and medical experts should join in research to examine the consequences of different styles or approaches in presentation of essentially similar evidence' (Hardie et al. 2008: 118).

Attempts to reform the law of homicide, and in particular that of murder, are not new. As Blom-Cooper and Morris (2004: 33) observe, 'Between 1867 and 1908 no fewer than six Bills came before Parliament, none of which would be enacted'.[8] In a Law Commission Report of 2004, it was acknowledged that the present law was 'a mess' and highly respected academic criminal lawyers have also seriously criticized the law of homicide. Professor John Smith of Nottingham University's School of Law once described the law relating to intent in murder cases as 'a muddle'. Professor Edward Griew (latterly also of Nottingham University) stated in relation to diminished responsibility that the wording of Section 2 of the Homicide Act 1957 'is altogether a disgrace' and as being 'quite shockingly elliptical' (quoted in Law Commission, 2205a: 152 and 153).

A trenchant judicial statement of the current law's weaknesses is that made by Lord Justice Mustill:

> Murder is widely thought to be the gravest of crimes. One would expect a developed system to embody a law of murder clear enough to yield an unequivocal result on a given set of facts, a result which conforms with apparent justice and has a sound intellectual base. This is not so in England, where the law of homicide is permeated by anomaly, fiction, misnomer and obsolete reasoning . . . One conspicuous anomaly is the rule which identifies the 'malice aforethought' (a doubly misleading expression) required for the crime of murder not only with a conscious intention to kill, but also with an intention to cause grievous bodily harm. It is therefore, possible to commit a murder not only without wishing the death of the victim but without the least thought that this might be the result of the assault. Many would doubt the justice of this rule, which is not the popular conception of murder and (as I shall suggest) no longer rests on any intellectual foundation. The Law of Scotland does very well without it, and England could perhaps do the same.
>
> (Judgment of Lord Justice Mustill 1998)

The Law Commission was charged with reviewing the current law. Its proposals for reform are based upon an initial consultation exercise (Law Commission 2005a, 2005b) and are then formulated in their final proposals (Law Commission 2006). Both are lengthy documents and reflect the Law

Commission's highly detailed approach to its task. The Law Commission was charged specifically with reviewing 'the various elements of murder, including the defences and partial defences to it, and the relationship between the law relating to homicide, in particular manslaughter' (Law Commission 2006: 1). However, the Commission's review would 'only consider the areas of euthanasia and suicide inasmuch as they form part of the law of murder . . . abortion will not be part of the review' (Law Commission 2005a: 1). Other issues excluded were justification for killing: abortion, necessity and self-defence; child destruction, defences of insanity and intoxication; aggravating factors 'such as an especially evil malice or the fact that a child or law officer on duty was intentionally targeted'. The justification for these exemptions by the Commission was that there was existing legal guidance on some of these matters in the Criminal Justice Act 2003, Section 269 and Schedule 21 (notably the presence of aggravating or mitigating factors in considering mandatory life sentences). The Law Commission proposed a distinction between 'first degree' and 'second degree' murder which would be elaborated into a 'ladder' or 'hierarchy' of culpability. Any Act replacing the Homicide Act 1957 should redefine in more modern language the criteria for findings of diminished responsibility. The Law Commission proposed the retention of the partial defences of diminished responsibility, provocation and infanticide. In respect of the latter it advocated the deletion of the criterion of 'lactation consequent upon the birth' and suggested the substitution of two years for twelve months as the relevant period in which prosecutions might be brought. There was a large number of responses (both in concurrence and disagreement) to these proposals. It is clear from the Law Commission's final proposals that it has had to work hard to reconcile some highly conflicting views. It is commendable that it has done so.

The Law Commission's final proposals

(Note: for purposes of brevity I have been very selective in summarizing some of the final proposals.) The Law Commission published its final proposals in late November 2006 (Law Commission 2006). The title of its final report, *Murder, Manslaughter and Infanticide*, neatly encapsulates its main concerns. It incorporates a number of research findings, particularly papers by Professor Mitchell – on defences to murder in a sample of 93 cases for the years 1995 and 1996, and a study by Professor Mackay into a sample of infanticide cases for the period 1990–2003. It is apparent from the Law Commission's final proposals that they have been framed on the (undoubtedly correct) assumption that the mandatory sentence of life imprisonment for murder will continue (see my earlier comments). In a covering letter with the report, the current chairman Mr Justice Etherton states: 'The Government will consider our recommendations *in the light of a public consultation which it will undertake in order to take account of the broader areas of public policy.* We anticipate that the public consultation will take place in the course of 2007' (letter accompanying the Report, 29 November 2006, emphasis added). It seems, therefore, that any changes in the law are unlikely to take place in the immediate future. The results of the consultation exercise were published in July 2008 (Ministry of Justice et al. 2008). Minor modifications are currently being considered.

1   A new Homicide Act should replace the 1957 Act. Such an Act would provide clear and comprehensive definitions of the proposed homicide offences and their partial defences.

2   The structure of a new homicide law would contain a three-tier structure to replace the current two-tier structure of murder and manslaughter. Murder would be divided into two tiers – first degree and second degree murder (as in their consultation proposals).[9]

3   First degree murder should encompass:
    (i)   intentional killings; and
    (ii) killings with intent to cause serious injury, where the killer was aware that his or her conduct involved a serious risk of causing death.

4   Second degree murder should encompass:
    (i)   killings intended to cause serious injury; or
    (ii) killings intended to cause injury or fear or risk of injury where the killer was aware that his or her conduct involved a serious risk of causing death; or
    (iii) killings intended to kill or to cause serious injury where the killer was aware that his or her conduct would involve a serious risk of causing death but successfully pleads provocation, diminished responsibility or that he or she killed pursuant to a suicide pact.

5   Manslaughter should encompass:
    (i)   killing another person through gross negligence ('gross negligence manslaughter'); or
    (ii) killing another person,
          (a) through the commission of a criminal act intended by the defendant to cause injury; or
          (b) through the commission of a serious criminal act that the defendant was aware involved a serious risk of causing some injury ('criminal act manslaughter').

6   Provocation
    Provocation should remain a partial defence, and if successful would reduce first degree to second degree murder (see also Kerrigan 2006).

7   Diminished responsibility
    The partial defence of diminished responsibility is to be maintained. A successful plea would reduce first degree to second degree murder. The

1957 Act definition of diminished responsibility would be modernized to replace the somewhat archaic language currently in use. The notion of developmental immaturity would also be incorporated into the new definition.

8 Mercy and consensual killings

The Law Commission recommend a public consultation as to the extent to which the law should recognize either an offence of 'mercy killing' or a partial defence of mercy killing.

9 Infanticide

In contrast to its initial consultation proposals, the Law Commission does not recommend any change in the existing law. However, the commission suggests that where infanticide is not raised as an issue at trial, and the defendant is convicted by a jury of first or second degree murder, the trial judge should have the power to order a medical examination and, if evidence is adduced, that at the time of the killing the requisite elements of a charge of infanticide were present, on the production of such evidence, and if the defendant wishes to appeal, then the judge should have power to postpone sentence while her case was determined by the Court of Appeal.

An alternative proposition

In their book, Blom-Cooper and Morris (2004) state in powerful terms that:

It is our unequivocal view that the unsatisfactory state of the law of murder *per se* is beyond cure, whether by statute or judicial development. It is an anachronistic legacy from a bygone age that serves only as an impediment to justice. Yet it has remained intact for 400 years.

(Blom-Cooper and Morris 2004: 171)

Blom-Cooper and Morris (2004) therefore propose a Criminal Homicide Act – along the following lines:

Clause 1

(1) A person* who, by any act or omission, intends to cause, or by behaviour manifesting recklessness, gross negligence or by reason of serious failure of corporate management, causes serious physical harm to another person resulting in that person's death, commits the offence of criminal homicide.

* By virtue of the Interpretation Act 1978, Section 3, Schedule 1 unless the contrary intention appears, 'person' shall include a body of persons corporate or incorporate.

(2) A person convicted of criminal homicide shall be liable to a sentence of life imprisonment, or a fine, unlimited in amount, or

both, or such other non-custodial penalty, including a hospital order as the court might deem appropriate.

(3) Life imprisonment shall constitute the maximum penalty and all custodial sentences of determinate length shall be equally available to the court.

(4) Life imprisonment shall mean liability to incarceration for the period of the offender so sentenced and not a sentence of incarceration determinable upon the life of the offender.

(5) In the case of a Child or Young Person convicted of criminal homicide the same penalties shall be available to the court, save the maximum penalty shall be an order of detention at Her Majesty's Pleasure substituted for a sentence of life imprisonment.

Blom-Cooper and Morris's proposed Criminal Homicide Act has much to commend it in terms of its simplicity (but not simplisticness) and its flexibility. The Law Commission did not dismiss Blom-Cooper and Morris's proposals out of hand, stating that 'There is powerful force [in their] argument'. It noted that a similar proposal for a single offence of unlawful homicide was also put forward by Victim Support (Law Commission 2005a: 32–33). However, the proposals did not find acceptance in the Law Commission's final report.

Despite the disappointment that will have been felt by many people working in the criminal justice and forensic mental health systems, the Law Commission is to be congratulated on producing its very detailed and informative reports. Its task was doubtless made the more difficult by its recognition that there is little hope in the immediate future of the abolition of the mandatory life sentence for murder. Thus judicial discretion still remains fettered.[10]

In a lecture to the Judicial Studies Board (as reported in *The Independent*, 23 March 2007) the Lord Chief Justice (Lord Phillips of Worth Maltravers) expressed his own concern over the present unsatisfactory state of affairs. Alongside disappointment we should also recognize that the Law Commission's attempts to clarify homicide law have much to commend them and deserve very careful consideration. The extent to which its suggested frameworks and definitions will encompass satisfactorily the considerable variations and presentations for some forms of homicidal behaviour as outlined in Table 7.2 remains to be seen.[11]

Notes

1 Some readers may recall that P.D. James used the first three words of this quotation as the title of one of her crime novels.

2 Blom-Cooper and Morris (2004) draw attention to the numerous high legal offices held by Edward Coke; for example, Solicitor General, Recorder of

London, Attorney General and Lord Chief Justice. He had also prosecuted in the treason trials of the Earl of Essex, Sir Walter Raleigh and the conspirators in the Gunpowder Plot. Despite some unpleasant personal characteristics (Blom-Cooper and Morris 2004: 23), he was pre-eminent as a jurist and no other commentator seems to have come near him since Henry de Bracton in his seminal thirteenth-century treatise, *De Legibus et Consuetudinibus Angliae* (On the Laws and Customs of England).

3 The term 'clinical' is used here as a form of shorthand for psychiatric, psychological and socio-psychological aspects.

4 It will be recalled that there was a considerable media-fuelled interest, not only concerning the crime committed by these two children, but also considerable ill-judged comment on the eventual decision to release them after they had been in detention for about ten years. In an interesting and thought-provoking article, Rowbotham et al. (2003) compared public reactions to the James Bulger case with those that occurred in respect of two 8-year-old child killers, Peter Barratt and James Bradley, in 1861. The authors discovered that, somewhat contrary to expectation, the reactions of the Victorian public were more temperate than expected and, in both instances, the media seemed less influential in actually shaping public opinion than one would have supposed.

5 In the aftermath of the Thompson and Venables case, and acting upon a direction from the European Court of Human Rights, the manner in which such cases are heard in the Crown Courts has now been made considerably more 'user friendly' in the interests of the welfare of such young defendants.

6 It should be noted that although children under 10 cannot be dealt with through criminal proceedings, it might be that, in some cases, they could be dealt with as being in need of care and control within the child care legislation.

7 In their article, Keppel et al. (2005) review the methods of killing used by the nineteenth-century killer 'Jack the Ripper' in six of his eleven victims. They identify eleven elements which led Keppel et al. (2005) to postulate that six of the attacks were unique to one person. They distinguish between the *MO (modus operandi)* that defines the actions necessary to commit such killings and the *signature* which concerns details of the actual behaviour (Keppel et al. 2005).

8 Blom-Cooper and Morris (2004) revisit the debates and discussions that took place in Parliament. In doing so, they examine critically the so-called bargaining that is said to have occurred in order to gain acceptance in 1965 for the abolition of the death penalty (Murder (Abolition of the Death Penalty) Act 1965) (see Blom-Cooper and Morris 2004: Chapter 6).

9 In my written submission to the Law Commission, I expressed a degree of concern about the use of the terms 'first degree' and 'second degree' as being somewhat unfortunate importations from United States practice. Many of the laws relating to homicide and other serious criminality in the United States do not commend themselves to me.

10 However, illustration of a sensible extension of the exercise of judicial discretion may be seen in the abolition of the jury's decision-making in cases of 'unfitness to plead' (being under disability in relation to the trial). The resolution of this issue is, in future, to be decided by the judge. However, a 'trial of the facts' will continue to require consideration by a jury (Domestic Violence, Crime and Victims Act 2004, Section 22, effective from 31 March 2005).

11 The government published its responses to the Law Commission's proposals in the form of a Consultation Paper (Ministry of Justice et al. 2008). Following the consultation period, it had intended to include legislative provision in a Law Reform, Victims and Witness Bill in the next parliamentary session (2008–2009).

Some of the main proposals are summarized as follows. Note: I have not included the extended recommendations on complicity in acts of homicide.

1 It recommends the abolition of the partial defence of provocation and the use of that word and replace it with new partial defences of:

- killing in response to a fear of serious violence:
- killing in response to words and conduct which caused the defendant to have a justifiable sense of being seriously wronged (to apply only in exceptional circumstances).

2 A new partial defence of diminished responsibility based on the concept of a 'recognized medical condition'.
3 Amendment of the law relating to infanticide to make it clearer that infanticide cannot be charged in cases that would not be regarded as homicide.

The government does not accept the Law Commission's proposal for a notion of developmental immaturity (in relation to defendants under the age of 18) since it considers that this would be covered under the provision of recognized medical condition.

The proposals outlined above are *now* to be included in a Coroners and Justice Bill (introduced 14 January 2009) as follows

- Abolition of the existing partial defence of provocation and its replacement with two new partial defences of killing in response to a fear of serious violence, and killing in response to words or conduct which caused the defendant to have a justifiable sense of being seriously wronged.
- Modernization of the partial defence of diminished responsibility based on the concept of a 'recognized medical condition'.
- Clarification of the offence of infanticide.

(Criminal Law Policy Unit (Murder Review Team), Ministry of Justice, London, personal communication, 19 January 2009; see also Ministry of Justice 2009.)

See also Chapter 2, this volume, note 9.

Acts

Corporate Manslaughter and Homicide Act 2007
Criminal Justice Act 2003
Domestic Violence, Crime and Victims Act 2004
Homicide Act 1957
Infanticide Act 1922
Infanticide Act 1938
Interpretation Act 1978
Law Reform (Year and a Day Rule) Act 1996
Murder (Abolition of the Death Penalty) Act 1965

Cases

Judgment of Lord Mustill, Attorney General's Reference [1998] AC 245 at 250 2 DF.
R. v. Sutcliffe. *The Times* and *Guardian*, various dates, May 1981.

References

Alison, L., Smith, M.D. and Morgan, K. (2003) 'Interpreting the Accuracy of Offender Profiles', *Psychology, Crime and Law* 9: 185–195.

Bailey, S. (2000) 'Juvenile Homicide', *Criminal Behaviour and Mental Health* 10: 149–154.

Belfrage, H. and Rying, M. (2004) 'Characteristics of Spousal Homicide Perpetrators: A Study of All Cases of Spousal Homicide in Sweden 1990–1999', *Criminal Behaviour and Mental Health* 14: 121–133.

Bender, L. (1960) 'Children and Adolescents Who Have Killed', *American Journal of Psychiatry* 116: 510–513.

Bennell, C., Corey, S., Taylor, A. and Ecker, J. (2008) 'What Skills are Required for Effective Offender Profiling? An Examination of the Relationship between Critical Thinking Ability and Profile Accuracy', *Psychology, Crime and Law* 14: 143–157.

Berry, C. (2006) 'Corporate Manslaughter', *Medicine, Science and the Law* 46: 2–6.

Bhootra, B.L. and Weiss, E. (2006) 'Muti Killing: A Case Report', *Medicine, Science and the Law* 46: 255–259.

Biehal, N., Mitchell, F. and Wade, J. (2003) *Lost from View: Missing Persons in the UK*, Bristol: Policy Press.

Bilton, M. (2003) *Wicked Beyond Belief: The Hunt for the Yorkshire Ripper*, London: HarperCollins.

Blom-Cooper, L., QC and Morris, T. (2004) *With Malice Aforethought: A Study of the Crime and Punishment for Homicide*, Oxford: Hart.

Boon, J. and Davies, G. (1992) 'Fact and Fiction in Offender Profiling', *Newsletter of the Division of Legal and Criminological Psychology* 32: 3–9. Leicester: British Psychological Society.

Bowden, P. (1990) 'Homicide', in R. Bluglass and P. Bowden (eds) *Principles and Practice of Forensic Psychiatry*, London: Churchill Livingstone.

Brookman, F. (2005) *Understanding Homicide*, London: Sage.

Canter, D. (1989) 'Offender Profiles', *The Psychologist* 2: 12–16.

—— (1994) *Criminal Shadows: Inside the Mind of the Serial Killer*, London: HarperCollins.

—— (2004) 'Offender Profiling and Investigative Psychology', *Journal of Investigative Psychology and Offender Profiling* 1: 1–15.

—— (2007) *Mapping Murder: The Secrets of Geographical Profiling*, London: Virgin.

Copson, G. (1996) 'At Last Some Facts about Offender Profiling in Britain', *Forensic Up-Date* 46: 4–9. Leicester: British Psychological Society.

Cornwell, P. (1992) *All That Remains*, London: Little, Brown.

Dernevik, M., Beck, A., Grann, M., Hogue, T. and McGuire, J. (2009) 'The Use of Psychiatric and Psychological Evidence in the Assessment of Terrorist Offenders', *Journal of Forensic Psychiatry and Psychology* 20(4): 508–515.

Dolan, M. and Smith, C. (2001) 'Juvenile Homicide Offenders: 10 Years Experience of an Adolescent Forensic Psychiatry Service', *Journal of Forensic Psychiatry* 12: 313–329.

Dolan, M., Guly, O., Woods, P. and Fulham, R. (2003) 'Child Homicide', *Medicine, Science and the Law* 43: 153–169.

Doney, R.H. (1990) 'The Aftermath of the Yorkshire Ripper: The Response of the United Kingdom Police', in S.A. Egger (ed.) *Serial Murder: An Elusive Phenomenon*, London: Praeger.

Egger, S.A. (ed.) (1990) *Serial Murder: An Elusive Phenomenon*, London: Praeger.

Frei, A., Völm, B., Graaf, M. and Dittmann, V. (2006) 'Female Serial Killing: A Review and Case Report', *Criminal Behaviour and Mental Health* 16: 167–176.

Gillies, H. (1976) 'Murder in the West of Scotland', *British Journal of Psychiatry* 128: 105–127.

Gregory, N. (2005) 'Offender Profiling: A Review of the Literature', *British Journal of Forensic Practice* 7: 29–34.

Gresswell, D.M. and Hollin, C.R. (1994) 'Multiple Murders: A Review', *British Journal of Criminology* 34: 1–14.

Gunn, J. and Taylor, P.J. (eds) (1993) *Forensic Psychiatry: Clinical, Legal and Ethical Issues*, London: Butterworth-Heinemann.

Hardie, T., Elcock, S. and Mackay, R.D. (2008) 'Are Psychiatrists Affecting the Legal Process by Answering Legal Questions?', *Criminal Behaviour and Mental Health* 18: 117–128.

Häfner, H. and Böker, W. (1982) *Crimes of Violence by Mentally Abnormal Offenders*, Cambridge: Cambridge University Press.

Hefford, A. (2005) *Youthful Killers: Evil or Incapable of Assuming Criminal Responsibility?* Unpublished M.Sc. Dissertation, Department of Criminology, Leicester: University of Leicester.

Holmes, R.M. and De Burger, J. (1988) *Serial Murder*, London: Sage.

Holmes, R.M., De Burger, J. and Holmes, S.T. (1998) 'Inside the Mind of the Serial Murderer', in R.M. Holmes and S.T. Holmes (eds) *Contemporary Perspectives on Serial Murder*, London: Sage.

Home Office (2008) *Statistical Bulletin: Homicides, Firearms Offences and Intimate Violence 2006/07*, Supplementary Volume 2 to *Crime in England and Wales, 2006/07*, London: Home Office Research, Development and Statistics Directorate.

Howitt, D. (2006) 'Paedophilia Prevention and the Law', in K. Moss and M. Stephens (eds) *Crime Reduction and the Law*, London: Routledge.

Keppel, R.D., Weiss, J.G., Brown, K.M. and Welch, K. (2005) 'The Jack the Ripper Murders: A Modus Operandi and Signature Analysis of the 1888–1891 Whitechapel Murders', *Journal of Investigative Psychology and Offender Profiling* 2: 1–21.

Kerrigan, K. (2006) 'Provocation: The Fall (and Rise) of Objectivity', *Journal of Mental Health Law* 14: 44–52.

Klein, M. (1963) *Our Adult World and Other Essays*, London: Heinemann.

Laajasolo, T. and Häkkänen, H. (2006) 'Excessive Violence and Psychotic Symptomatology among Homicide Offenders with Schizophrenia', *Criminal Behaviour and Mental Health* 16: 242–253.

Labuschagne, S. (2004) 'Features and Investigative Implications of Muti-murder in South Africa', *Journal of Investigative Psychology and Offender Profiling* 1: 191–206.

Large, M., Smith, G., Swinson, N., Shaw, J. and Nielssen, O. (2008) 'Homicide due to Mental Disorder in England and Wales over 50 years', *British Journal of Psychiatry* 193: 130–133.

Law Commission (2004) *Partial Defences to Murder: Report no. 290*, London: Law Commission.

—— (2005a) *A New Homicide Act for England and Wales? A Consultation Paper*, no. 177, London: Law Commission.

—— (2005b) *A New Homicide Act for England and Wales: An Overview*, London: Law Commission.

—— (2006) *Murder, Manslaughter and Infanticide*, Law Commission no. 304, HC 30, London: TSO.

Leyton, E. (1989) *Hunting Humans: The Rise of the Modern Multiple Murderer*, Harmondsworth: Penguin.

Liem, M.C.A. and Koenraadt, F. (2007) 'Homicide-Suicide in the Netherlands: A Study of Newspaper Reports: 1992–2005', *Journal of Forensic Psychiatry and Psychology* 18: 482–493.

—— (2008a) 'Filicide: A Comparative Study of Maternal versus Paternal Child Homicide', *Criminal Behaviour and Mental Health* 18: 166–176.

—— (2008b) 'Familicide: A Comparison with Spousal and Child Homicide by Mentally Disordered Perpetrators', *Criminal Behaviour and Mental Health* 18: 303–318.

Lindqvist, P. Leifman, A. and Eriksson, A. (2007) 'Mortality Among Homicide Offenders: A Retrospective Population-based Long-term Follow-up', *Criminal Behaviour and Mental Health* 17: 107–112.

Liu, J., Francis, B. and Soothill, K. (2008) 'Kidnapping Offenders: Their Risk of Escalation to Repeat Offending and Other Serious Crime', *Journal of Forensic Psychiatry and Psychology* 19: 164–179.

Lynch, M. and Black, M. (2008) 'A Tale of Two Cities: A Review of Homicide in Melbourne and Glasgow in 2005', *Medicine, Science and the Law* 48: 24–30.

McDermid, V. (2006) *A Place of Execution*, London: HarperCollins.

McGrath, P.G. (1992) 'Maternal Filicide in Broadmoor Hospital – 1919–1969', *Journal of Forensic Psychiatry* 3: 271–297.

McKenna, B., Thom, K. and Simpson, A.I.F. (2007) 'Media Coverage of Homicide Involving Mentally Disordered Offenders: A Matched Comparison Study', *International Journal of Forensic Mental Health* 6: 57–63.

McNally, R. (1995) 'Homicidal Youth in England and Wales: 1982–1992: Profile and Policy', *Psychology, Crime and Law* 1: 333–342.

Marks, M.N. and Kumar, R. (1993) 'Infanticide in England and Wales', *Medicine, Science and the Law* 33: 329–339.

Marleau, J.D., Millaud, F. and Auclair, N. (2003) 'A Comparison of Parricide and Attempted Parricide: A Study of 39 Psychotic Adults', *International Journal of Law and Psychiatry* 26: 269–279.

Marshall, B.C. and Alison, L.J. (2007) 'Stereotyping, Congruence and Presentation Order: Interpretative Biases in Utilizing Offender Profiles', *Psychology, Crime and Law* 13: 285–303.

Ministry of Justice (2009) *Homicide Reform Bulletin No. 1* (March 2009), London: Ministry of Justice.

Ministry of Justice, Attorney General's Office and Home Office (2008) *Murder, Manslaughter and Infanticide: Proposals for Reform of the Law*, Law Commission Consultation Paper CP19/08, London: Ministry of Justice.

Morrison, B. (1997) *As If*, London: Granta.

Mowat, R.A. (1966) *Morbid Jealousy and Murder*, London: Tavistock.

Mullen, P. (1996) 'Jealousy and the Emergence of Violent and Intimidatory Behaviours', *Criminal Behaviour and Mental Health* 6: 194–205.

Oberman, M. (2003) 'Mothers Who Kill: Cross-Cultural Patterns and Perspectives on Contemporary Maternal Filicide', *International Journal of Law and Psychiatry* 26: 493–514.

Oleson, J.C. (1996) 'Psychological Profiling: Does It Actually Work?', *Forensic Up-Date* 46: 11–14.

Prins, H. (1994) 'Psychiatry and the Concept of Evil: Sick in Heart or Sick in Mind?' *British Journal of Psychiatry* 165: 297–302.

Romain, N., Michaud, K., Horisberger, R., Brandt-Casadevall, C., Krompecher, T. and Mangin, P. (2003) 'Childhood Homicide: A 1990–2000 Retrospective Study at the Institute of Legal Medicine in Lausanne, Switzerland', *Medicine, Science and the Law* 43: 203–206.

Rowbotham, J., Stevenson, K. and Pegg, S. (2003) 'Children of Misfortune: Parallels in the Cases of Child Murderers Thompson and Venables, Barratt and Bradley', *Howard Journal of Criminal Justice* 42: 107–122.

Salfati, C.G. and Bateman, A.L. (2005) 'Serial Homicide: An Investigation of Behavioural Consistency', *Journal of Investigative Psychology and Offender Profiling* 2: 121–144.

Scott, P.D. (1973) 'Parents Who Kill their Children', *Medicine, Science and the Law* 13: 120–125.

Seltzer, M. (1998) *Serial Killers: Death and Life in America's Wound Culture*, London: Routledge.

Sereny, G. (1998) *Cries Unheard: The Story of Mary Bell*, London: Macmillan.

Sharma, B.R. (2006) 'Historical and Legal Aspects of Infanticide', *Medicine, Science and the Law* 46: 152–156.

Shaw, J., Hunt, I.M., Flynn, S., Meehan, J., Robinson, J., Bickley, H., Parsons, R., McCann, K., Burns, J., Amos, T., Kapur, N. and Appleby, L. (2006) 'Rates of Mental Disorder in People Convicted of Homicide: National Clinical Survey', *British Journal of Psychiatry* 188: 143–147.

Shon, P.C.H. and Targonski, J.R. (2003) 'Declining Trends in US Parricides, 1976–1998: Testing the Freudian Assumptions', *International Journal of Law and Psychiatry* 26: 387–402.

Swinson, N., Bettadapura, A., Windfuhr, K., Kapur, N., Appleby, L. and Shaw, J. (2007) 'National Confidential Inquiry into Suicide and Homicide by People with Mental Health Illness: New Directions', *Psychiatric Bulletin* 31: 161–163.

West, D.J. (1965) *Murder Followed by Suicide*, London: Macmillan.

Wilczynski, A. (1997) *Child Homicide*, London: Greenwich Medical Media.

Wilson, D. (2007) *Serial Killers: Hunting Britons and their Victims*, Winchester: Waterside Press.

Wilson, P. (1973) *Children Who Kill*, London: Michael Joseph.

Woodhams, J., Hollin, C.R. and Bull, R. (2007) 'The Psychology of Linking Crimes: A Review of the Evidence', *Legal and Criminological Psychology* 12: 233–249.

Further reading

Selected aspects

Birch, H. (ed.) (1993) *Moving Targets: Women, Murder and Representation*, London: Virago.

Brookman, F. (2005) *Understanding Homicide*, London: Sage (this book provides a useful wide-ranging coverage of the topic).

Cavadino, P. (ed.) (1996) *Children Who Kill*, Winchester: Waterside Press.

Cox, M. (ed.) (1999) *Remorse and Reparation*, London: Jessica Kingsley.

Doctor, R. (ed.) (2008) *Murder: A Psychotherapeutic Investigation*. London: Karnac (an interesting collection of contributions on psychoanalytic approaches to homicide).

Masters, B. (1997) *The Evil that Men Do: From Saints to Serial Killers*, London: Black Swan.

Putkonen, H., Weizmann-Henelius, G., Lindberg, N., Rovamo, T. and Häkkänen, H. (2008) 'Changes Over Time in Homicides by Women: A Register-Based Study Comparing Female Offenders from 1982 to 1992 and 1993 to 2005', *Criminal Behaviour and Mental Health* 18: 268–278.

Radford, J. and Russell, D.E.H. (eds) (1992) *Femicide: The Politics of Woman Killing*, Buckingham: Open University Press.

Ressler, R.K., Burgess, R.W. and Douglas, J.E. (1988) *Sexual Homicide: Patterns and Motives*, Oxford: Lexington/Macmillan.

Profiling

Ainsworth, P.B. (2001) *Offender Profiling and Crime Analysis*, Cullompton: Willan.

Britton, P. (1997) *The Jigsaw Man*, London: Corgi.

—— (2000) *Picking Up the Pieces*, London: Corgi (these two books by Britton offer personal accounts by a forensic psychologist).

Holmes, R.M. and Holmes, S.T. (1996) *Profiling Violent Crimes: An Investigative Tool*, London: Sage.

Jackson, J.C. and Bekerian, D.A. (1997) *Offender Profiling: Theory Research and Practice*, Chichester: Wiley.

Suicide bombing

Although terrorist activity is not dealt with in this chapter, two useful articles deal with the psychological and psychiatric aspects of this behaviour:

Gordon, H. (2002) 'The "Suicide Bomber": Is it a Psychiatric Phenomenon?', *Psychiatric Bulletin* 26: 285–287.

Soibelman, M. (2004) 'Palestinian Suicide Bombers', *Journal of Investigative Psychology and Offender Profiling* 1: 175–190.

Biographical accounts

Burn, G. (1984) *Somebody's Husband, Somebody's Son: The Story of Peter Sutcliffe*, London: Heinemann.
—— (1998) *Happy Like Murderers*, London: Faber & Faber.
Masters, B. (1985) *Killing for Company*, London: Cape.
—— (1993) *The Shrine of Jeffrey Dahmer*, London: Hodder & Stoughton.
—— (1996) *She Must Have Known: The Trial of Rosemary West*, London: Transworld.
Wansell, G. (1996) *An Evil Love: The Life of Frederick West*, London: Headline.

Journals

The following journals will be found to contain helpful material:

British Journal of Forensic Practice
British Journal of Psychiatry
Criminal Behaviour and Mental Health
Homicide Studies
Howard Journal of Criminal Justice
International Journal of Forensic Mental Health
Journal of Forensic Psychiatry and Psychology
Journal of Interpersonal Violence
Journal of Investigative Psychology and Offender Profiling
Journal of Mental Health Law
Legal and Criminological Psychology
Psychology, Crime and Law

Chapter 8

Sex – lawful and unlawful

> so shall you hear
> Of carnal, bloody, and unnatural acts
>
> (Horatio, in *Hamlet*, Act 5, Sc. 2)

Horatio's statement serves as a compelling reminder of the powerful emotions and attitudes that are aroused when sexuality is described and discussed and, in particular, deviant sexuality. Thus, the material in a chapter such as this is not the easiest to write about, for the following reasons. First, emotion often obscures objectivity (most notably when sexual offences within a family context are being dealt with and those against children and young persons more generally). Second, the 'borderline' between so-called normal and deviant sex is not always easy to delineate. And as I have tried to demonstrate earlier in this book, legislative proscription can (and does) change over historical time. Third, persistent sexual offending is not easy to eradicate, partly because patterns of sexual preference and expression are likely to be laid down early in life. A good deal of success or otherwise in management will often depend upon the capacity of those given the task of dealing with such individuals to engage in what I can best describe as 'dispassionate compassion'. Fourth, although recent substantial changes in the law have gone some way to reflect changes in the light of clinical experience, the success or otherwise of such changes is still to be determined (see later). Finally, in writing about all these matters, it is not always easy to steer a clear path between unambiguous description and being accused of indulging in a degree of vicarious pruriency and indeed voyeurism. Emotive responses have long historical roots in religious texts such as the English Bible. For example, homosexuality is described in the Book of Leviticus as an 'abomination' and intercourse with animals as 'a violation of nature' (18: 23 and 24). In a short but excellent survey of historical perspectives on sexual deviation, Gordon (2008) reminds us that:

While it is almost certainly the case that all human societies through history have imposed limits on the types of sexual behaviour regarded as acceptable, a degree of variation across cultures has occurred, while within certain cultural traditions, change in sexual mores may occur over time. Religious interest tends to be more associated with moral condemnation of sexual deviance and the secular with greater liberalism.

(Gordon 2008: 79)

For a detailed critical account, for example of homosexual practices in ancient Greek civilization, see Davidson (2007).

These less liberal attitudes found vehement expression in the opposition demonstrated against the appointment of the openly gay American clergyman Gene Robinson to the office of Bishop of New Hampshire, and the withdrawal from the appointment of Canon Jeffrey John as Bishop of Reading in the UK. A little thought concerning the numbers of homo-sexuals in the community and, by implication, within the church would tend to support the view that being gay is OK as long as you don't go public about it if you are a clergyman. This chapter includes, first, a brief context-setting background. Second, there is a brief description of sexual offences (clinical and legal). Third, comments are made on what the statistics tell us. Fourth, the rest of the chapter comprises a discussion of some of the more common sexual offences and briefer reference to a selection of rarer sexual misbehaviours that come within the purview of the criminal law.

Background and context

Sexual behaviour depends for its expression upon a number of factors, biological (for example, hormonal and neuroendocrinal influences) and those best described as social and familial. In the human species, although hormonal and allied influences have always been considered to be of some importance, there is some evidence that this influence may be increasing as, for example, in the recently somewhat controversial view that there may be neurochemical factors in the development of male and female homosexu-ality. See, for example, an early but important article by MacCulloch and Waddington (1981). A more wide-ranging overview of the totality of sexual behaviour and misbehaviour may be found in the third volume of the *Encyclopaedia of Criminology and Deviant Behaviour* (Davis and Geis 2001). The highly divergent patterns of sexual behaviour have been described by Kaul (1993), a forensic psychiatrist, in the following terms:

Sexual behaviour in humans does not necessarily conform to any single pattern. People differ in the type as well as the frequency of preferred activity. The attitudes that different cultures have towards types of sexual behaviour differ as do the attitudes of the same society over a period of time . . . Sexual preference is varied, not only with regard to the physical or other attributes of the partner one chooses, but also the type of sexual activity engaged in.

(Kaul 1993: 207)

We have seen how such variations are reflected in the criminal law and the manner in which it penalizes some behaviours and not others (as, for example, in the gradual extension of the decriminalization of consenting adult male homosexual behaviour). Five further points can usefully be made by way of introduction. First, as already suggested, sexual behaviour and, in particular, sexual misbehaviour are emotive topics; it will be seen just how emotive when I discuss paedophilia. Attitudes towards the physical expression of sexuality – even among professionals – are still sometimes based upon a degree of ignorance and anxiety. Although there is a great deal more talk about, and open portrayal of, sexual activity of all kinds than in the past, it is by no means certain that such public portrayal has done very much to remove anxieties and inhibitions. Concerns about HIV infection and AIDS have revived fears and taboos about sexual activity; they are reminiscent of those that used to be prevalent in discussions about other sexually transmitted diseases such as syphilis and gonorrhoea. The so-called 'Aids industry' and its attendant features have been graphically described by the journalist Elizabeth Pisani (2008), in her book *The Wisdom of Whores*. Such taboos and proscriptions may also have their origins in the fact that the sexual and procreative organs (particularly in the female) are closely associated anatomically with the elimination of bodily wastes – hence the importance attached to this conjunction by the early practitioners of psychoanalysis. And it is worthy of note that seminal emissions were once described as 'pollutions'. Second, we should note that sexual *attractiveness* is often at the heart (either implicitly or explicitly) of much media advertising. The promotion of sexual prowess and attractiveness as highly desirable attributes may, in fact, serve only to make people more anxious about their sexual *performance* than about sexual expression as part of caring adult relationships – be they heterosexual or homosexual. Third, changes in our attitudes towards women in what is still a highly male-sex dominated society are of great importance. With a continuing degree of ignorance and prejudice we continue to place women in a very ambiguous position which leads to much confusion concerning our expectations of them. Fourth, we should note a number of changes in our references to sexual behaviour and misbehaviours. For the most part, we no longer use euphemisms for certain forms of sexual activity. In my youth (some 65 plus years ago!) buggery (anal sex) was never referred to as such, but a well-known Sunday newspaper, which always carried quite detailed account of sex offence trials, always referred to such activities as 'serious or unnatural offences'. In similar terms, oral sexual practices (such as fellatio, cunnilingus, anilingus) were never referred to publicly; now it is commonplace, both in court reporting, publicity about sexually transmitted diseases and in the various media.[1] Although such practices are now much more openly acknowledged in the light of more liberated views about the legitimacy of a variety of forms of sexual activity, the law still seems somewhat capricious in this respect. This was evidenced some years ago when a group of adult sado-masochists were prosecuted and sentenced to imprisonment for engaging in mutually consenting private activity in which various injuries were inflicted on their genitalia. Appeals to the High Court in the UK and to the European Court of Human Rights failed; the courts held that in certain circumstances people should be protected even from their own consensual activities. The question of consent is vitally important in the area of sexual activity – as I shall show when we come to consider serious sexual assaultative behaviour such as rape. Fifth, any discussion of sexual deviation (and particularly that also adjudged to be criminal) must take into account the idea that sexual feelings and expression are not as dichotomous as some people imagine, for we all have physical and emotional elements of the opposite sex within us – some more than others. In this respect, it is important to be sure that when we discuss overt sexuality, we endeavour to be clear about physically endowed sex on the one hand and what might be called gender sex (what we feel about our sexuality) on the other. Bancroft (1989) once put the matter succinctly (see also Bancroft 1991):

> We tend to take our gender for granted: 'Of course you are male if you have a penis'. Usually we can afford to do so, but the processes leading to the ascription of gender identity are so complex it is little wonder they occasionally go wrong.
>
> (Bancroft 1989: 153)

The complex web of factors that go to determine sexual *offending* behaviour has been usefully reviewed by Lanyon (1991). Having made the above points, can we determine to what extent we can make any helpful distinctions between so-called 'normality' and 'deviation' in relation to sexual behaviour? I suggest that the answer has to be a carefully qualified 'Yes'. The qualification is important because, as we have seen, any distinctions will have to be culture bound; they may change over time and can therefore be seen only as broad contemporary generalizations. They will also be heavily dependent upon different aesthetic preferences. I think the qualified 'Yes' can therefore be best expressed as follows. Sexual behaviour encompasses those forms of sexual activity between two adults (and the age of achieving adulthood may vary of course over historical time) which are acceptable to both parties, do not involve coercion, exploitation or degradation, and do not affront notions of public propriety prevailing at the time. Finally, in this general introduction, it is very important to avoid the all too common stereotyping of the sex offender; the 'dirty mac' image still holds much sway and, as we shall see when we consider paedophilia, is very prevalent in this particular connection.

Clinical and legal descriptions

I now consider clinical and legal descriptions. In presenting these I must emphasize that they will often overlap and should not therefore be considered as discrete entities.

Clinical descriptions

The following clinical description is partly derived from Scott (1964) and Prins (2005) (see also Briggs 1994; Grubin and Kennedy 1991; Gayford 1997).

- Sexual activity not requiring a human partner – the use of animals (for example bestiality, zoophilia, zooerasty) or objects (fetishism).
- Sexual activity not involving a *willing* partner – for example, rape (hetero- and homosexual), voyeurism ('Peeping Tom' activities), exhibitionism (indecent exposure), necrophilia, scatologia (obscene phone calls). These categories overlap very closely with those in the next one.
- Sexual activity under *unusual* conditions – and here, matters of consent may be all important and continue to occupy a grey area. Some examples are sexual activity with elderly people (gerontophilia) (see Kaul and Duffy 1991, Brogden and Nijhar 2000 and Jeary 2004, 2005), with children of both sexes (paedophilia), consanguinous sexual activity (incest), sexual activity requiring excessive punishment or suffering (sado-masochistic activities), non self-induced sexual asphyxia (eroticized repetitive hanging) – which sometimes results in death (see Knight 1979; Prins 1991: 90–93).
- Certain other sexually motivated activities which may present in *masked* form. For example, some types of stealing (underclothes or similar garments from clothes-lines), some rare types of fire-raising (see Chapter 9), sexual gratification from the sight of, or contact with, certain human bodily secretions (for example vampirism), excrement (coprophilia) or urine (urolagnia – "golden shower"), smells of bodily secretions (mysophilia). For example, Napoleon is said to have told Josephine not to wash before he returned from battle (about three weeks) (Gayford 1997).

It will be obvious that many of these activities will overlap and that the paraphilias (to give them their generic title) cover a very wide range of behaviours. Gayford (1997) has provided a very useful definitional statement of the latter. He suggests that the paraphilias can be defined as disorders of sexual preference. More pejorative titles used to be sexual perversions, sexual deviations or anomalies. Sometimes terms used have been 'fringe sex', 'pervy' or 'kinky sex'. Gayford (1997: 303) suggests that more polite terms might be minority sexual practices, or alternative sexual practices.

The *Diagnostic and Statistical Manual of Mental Disorders* (DSM-IV (TR)) describes them as follows:

> The essential features of a paraphilia are recurrent, intense sexual arousing fantasies, sexual urges, or behaviours generally involving 1) non-human objects, 2) the suffering or humiliation of oneself or one's partner, or 3) children or other non-consenting persons that occur over a period of at least 6 months. For some individuals, paraphiliac fantasies or stimuli are obligatory for erotic arousal and are always included in sexual activity. In other cases, the paraphiliac preferences occur only episodically (e.g. perhaps during periods of stress), whereas at other times the person is able to function sexually without para-philiac fantasies or stimuli. The behaviour, sexual urges, or fantasies cause clinically significant distress or impairment in social, occupa-tional, or other important areas of functioning.
>
> (American Psychiatric Association (APA) 2005: 523)

Perkins (1991), in an earlier review of classification, suggested the following:

1 *Compensatory* – as a result of social or sexual relationship problems.
2 *Displaced aggression* – motivated by anger or hatred; here the concentration is upon degrading or defiling the victim and the use of more force than is necessary to overpower the victim; particular victims may be sought out – for example, prostitutes.
3 *Sadistic* – more violence than is necessary – as in (2) but it is also cold and deliberate; sexual gratification is derived from the infliction of pain and from the fear shown by the victim.
4 *Impulsive or opportunistic* – such offenders have histories of various other forms of antisocial behaviour; obtaining sex by force is just another aspect of this lifestyle.

Legal descriptions

There are some areas of overlap and the choice of offences to be included is, to some extent, idiosyncratic. Some former descriptive terms have now been replaced under the Sexual Offences Act 2003 (see Table 8.1, p. 250).

Rape and attempts (on males and females); indecent assault (on females and males); buggery and attempts (on males and females); unlawful sexual intercourse with females under age; procuration for sexual purposes; abduction; indecency with children; gross indecency; indecent exposure; bestiality; soliciting for prostitution; importuning; trading in, or possession of, obscene publications; use of children for pornographic purposes (e.g. in order to make films, videos, or to take still or computerized images); making obscene phone calls; sexual interference with a cadaver (corpse); homicide committed for purposes of sexual gratification; conspiracy to corrupt public morals. To this list we would add some less obvious 'sexual' crimes where an apparently non-sexual offence may be sexually motivated. Examples would be some forms of larceny (stealing women's underclothing from clothes-lines); certain forms of burglarious activity (where the goods stolen may have sexual connotations, for example, the shoes belonging to the female occupier of the premises), or where the behaviour of the burglar appears unusual (for example, slashing bedsheets with a knife).

It is worth noting that, contrary to general assumption, the more serious sexual offences are almost always punished by immediate imprisonment. This is particularly noticeable in rape cases. Where sentences for sexual offences have been regarded as too lenient, the Court of Appeal has not been reluctant to increase them, as a number of recent cases have demonstrated (see Stone 2003a).

Finally, it is important to observe that the legal descriptions of sexual offences do not necessarily adequately describe the severity or importance of the offence to the victim. For example, an indecent assault may be as severe for the victim as an attempted rape; the decision to charge for one or other offence may sometimes be somewhat arbitrary. As I shall show shortly, the offence of indecent exposure (often regarded quite lightly by some males) can have a marked and traumatic effect upon some victims.

What do the statistics tell us?

Contrary to much public opinion, sexual offences constitute a very small proportion of all recorded crimes, something in the order of 2 per cent of all offences and about 1.75 per cent of all persons found guilty of indictable (the more serious) offences. This is not to deny that this small proportion will contain a number of very serious incidents causing much physical and psychological harm to victims, and although the reconviction rate for most sexual offenders is comparatively low, those who do reoffend may commit very serious offences (Hood et al. 2002). One also needs to be aware of the considerable discrepancy between the numbers of actual sexual offences *known to the police* and the number actually *dealt with or prosecuted*. Reasons for this discrepancy are not hard to find. Victims and witnesses may be reluctant to come forward; corroboration may thus prove problematic. This is a particular concern in cases of alleged child sexual abuse which may come to light (or in some cases *appear* to come to light) long after the events complained of. In a very small number of recent institutional sex abuse cases, such allegations have proved to be unfounded. There is also much debate concerning the truth of allegations made by adults who claim to have been abused by family members in childhood (for example false, or recovered, memory syndrome) (see Brewin 1996; Gudjonsson 1997; Brandon et al. 1998). Consenting parties may be reluctant to admit to having engaged in unlawful sexual activity and it may therefore prove difficult to show that an offence has occurred. It is also well known that many more sexual offences (among others) are committed than are ever reported to the police (see Chapter 6 in this volume). For example, the 1998 and 2000 *British Crime Surveys* attempt to provide the 'most accurate ever estimates of the extent and nature of sexual victimisation in England and Wales . . . questions were asked of both men and women aged 16–59' (Myhill and Allen 2002: 1). In relation to female victims, in the year preceding the survey, it was estimated that 61,000 victims reported they had been raped and 0.9 per cent of women said they 'had been subject to some form of sexual victimization (including rape) in this period' (Myhill and Allen 2002: 2). In some cases (notably rape for example) victims may not wish to suffer the trauma of medical and police enquiries, followed by a public court appearance, in which, despite more recent safeguards, both fact and reputation may be challenged and impugned. Parents and other guardians of sexually assaulted children may wish to spare them a similar experience. Males who have been the subject of serious sexual assault are often very reluctant to report the alleged offence because of the humiliation they may feel and, like their female counterparts, exposure to public scrutiny. The factors described above should be borne in mind when considering the figures provided for the years 2002–07 in Table 8.1.

Although the majority of sexual offences are committed by males, there would appear to have been an increasing trend for women to be involved in sexual crimes in recent years. In an admittedly small-scale study of the criminal statistics for a ten-year period (1978–87), O'Connor (1987) indicated that 0.95 per cent of all sexual offences were committed by women. He made a detailed study of nineteen women convicted of indecency and sixty-two convicted of other sexual offences. Within the group he found a high incidence of psychopathology. A sizeable proportion were convicted of gross indecency and sexual assaults on children or (in the company of male assailants) aiding and abetting such assaults.

A more recent study of thirty female sex offenders by Matravers (2005) carries O'Connor's (1987) work further. She distinguished three types of sex-offending women: women who were lone offenders, women who committed their offences with a single male co-offender and women who offended as part of a group. She suggests that her findings 'underline the necessity of looking beyond stereotypes when developing theoretical

Table 8.1 Selection of sexual offences (recorded crime) 2002–07

	2002/3	2003/4	2004/5	2005/6	2006/7[a]
Rape of a female	11,445	12,378	12,869	13,327	12,630
Rape of a male	850	894	1,144	1,116	1,150
Indecent assault on females[b]	25,275	27,240	24,630	23,020	21,403
Abuse of children through prostitution and pornography[c]	—	—	99	124	101
Incest[d] or familial sexual offences	99	105	713	966	1,344
Abduction of females[e]	291	403	86	36	21
Other sexual offences including indecent exposure (now classified as exposure under the 2003 Act)	13,573	13,810	15,320	14,917	13,787

Notes: (a) Police recording of offences has improved following changes in recording practices since 2002. (b) Includes under-age children. Includes the new offences under the 2003 Act of *assault by penetration* and *sexual assault*, which replace the old offence of indecent assault, thus adding a degree of greater specificity to the offence. (c) New categorization introduced under the 2003 Act. (d) The 2003 Act extended the range of 'incest'-related offence behaviours. (e) Previously categorized as abduction.

Source: Extracted from Home Office (2007: 37, Table 2.04).

explanations of women's involvement' . . . 'The offending of convicted women sex offenders is best understood as the result of an interacting range of individual, situational and structural factors' (Matravers 2005: 13).

Having briefly considered the size of the problem, I now go on to examine certain sexual offences in detail. There are obvious problems in singling out specific categories. For example, an offender not infrequently commits more than one type of sexual offence (or a non-sexual offence for that matter); some of the offence categories will therefore overlap. For example, a rape may end in homicide, either because the killing was planned as part of, or a sequel to, the rape, or the victim may have died as a result of the attack. Death may also have resulted in the assailant's wish to silence the victim to avoid subsequent identification. As we saw in Chapter 6, the borderline between sexual and violent offences is a debatable one. It is therefore very important to emphasize that *every case is different* and great care needs to be taken before reaching any generalized conclusions. Despite this caveat, it seems helpful to divide the categories of sexual offences in a fairly crude way. I deal first of all with *indecent exposure*; second, with *sexual offences against children* (paedophilia) and *consanguinous sex* ('incest'). I include 'incest' with more general sexual offences against children because incestuous behaviour (particularly with young victims) may be regarded as a highly specific form of serious sexual assault. Third, I deal with *rape*, and fourth, with certain aspects of *sexual homicide* and other more rare sexual offences such as *bestiality and necrophilia*.

Indecent exposure: now known simply as exposure and voyeurism[2]

Indecent exposure would appear to be the commonest of all sexual offences, though the actual number of prosecutions is but a minute proportion of its actual incidence. This is because many offences are never reported and even when prosecutions take place the number of other offences of exposure that a defendant may ask to be taken into consideration (TIC) is unlikely to be a true record of the actual number of acts of exposure committed. It is almost exclusively a male offence, though a few women will indulge in such behaviour. Changes in the law have made the offence non-gender specific (Sexual Offences Act 2003). Throughout history, the display and emphatic presentation of the male genitals and buttocks have been commonly recorded and demonstrated. Examples may be found in the ruins of Pompeii and the use of the codpiece in Tudor times. Chaucer, in his bawdy *Miller's Tale*, has one of the characters putting his 'ers' (backside) out of the window. The practices of 'mooning' (exposing male buttocks) and 'streaking' by both sexes have become fairly commonplace. A descriptive term is 'dogging', described by Dalzell and Victor (2006: 619) as '*al fresco* sexual activities such as exhibitionism or voyeurism (with multiple partners) in parked vehicles generally in the countryside'. Until 2003, the male form of the offence of indecent exposure was dealt with under the somewhat antiquated provisions of the Vagrancy Act 1824 (as amended by the Criminal Justice Act 1925, Section 42). The offence was dealt with summarily, but repeated offenders could be remitted to the Quarter Sessions (later the Crown Court) for greater punishment as incorrigible rogues. Section 66 of the Sexual Offences Act 2003 now provides that:

1   A person commits an offence if –
    (a) he intentionally exposes his genitals, and
    (b) he intends that someone will see them and be caused alarm or distress. (This does not include the buttocks or female breasts) (see Stevenson et al. 2004).
2   A person found guilty of an offence under this section is liable –
    (a) on summary conviction, to a term of imprisonment not exceeding six months or a fine not exceeding the statutory maximum or both
    (b) on conviction on indictment, to imprisonment for a term not exceeding two years.

Voyeurism

It is of interest to note here that Section 67 of the Act creates the new offence of voyeurism ('Peeping Tom') as follows. A person commits an offence if

(a) for the purpose of obtaining sexual gratification, he observed another person doing a private act, and

(b) he knows that the other person does not consent to being observed for his sexual gratification. A person also commits an offence if he installs or operates equipment (such as a camera for example) or constructs or adapts a structure or part of a structure with the intention of enabling himself or another person to commit an offence under Section 1 of Section 67 of the Act.

For examples of Court of Appeal approaches to both non-aggravated and aggravated forms of voyeurism, see Stone (2008). Stevenson et al. (2004) indicate that opinion was divided as to the appropriateness of making this form of behaviour a criminal offence. For example, the human rights body, Liberty, considered that such behaviour should not be a matter for the criminal law. However, the government reviewing bodies not only considered that could such behaviour cause considerable distress to the parties being spied upon, but also received evidence that in some cases perpetrators went on to commit more serious sexual crimes, as was the case with some exposers (Home Office 2000; Stevenson et al. 2004: 138).

The penalties that can be imposed are the same as for indecent exposure.

Clinical aspects

(Indecent) exposure can be regarded as an illegal form of exhibitionism. This latter term is, as Gayford (1981) reminds us, somewhat ambiguous since clinically it covers many aspects of exhibitionistic behaviour. Various other clinical terms have been suggested such as sexual exhibitionism, or male genital exhibitionism, thus emphasizing the genital element involved (Gayford 1981). It is unwise to treat the offence behaviour lightly; some exposers are likely to go on to commit more serious sexual contact offences. In the case of the latter exposers, the behaviour may be aggressive, exposing to the victims where there is little chance of 'escape', making angry gestures and masturbating in front of them (for further discussion see Sugarman et al. 1994; MacPherson 2003). Most victims tend to be adult females and children of either sex and the perpetrators youngish males. Gittleson et al. (1978) surveyed 100 nurses; of their sample, 44 of the subjects had been the female victims of exposure, one-third of these on two or more occasions. One-third of all incidents had not been reported to anyone. Interestingly, in over one-fifth of the episodes, 'the reaction of family and friends in whom the victim confided had been more distressing to the victim than the episode itself' (Gittleson et al. 1978: 61) (see later discussion of paedophilia). A slightly later study in the United States of a group of female college students largely confirmed the findings of the Gittleson study (Cox and McMahon 1978). In a more recent study carried out by Sharon Riordan, a former postgraduate student of mine, 72 women were surveyed (Riordan 1999). The incidence of exposure was fairly similar to the two earlier studies quoted above. However, the survey revealed that the victims found the experience somewhat more traumatic than in the earlier studies and it had greatly increased their more general fear of sexual crime. They also considered that the police and men in general tended to 'trivialize' the offence (Riordan 1999; see also Bennetto 1995, quoting from Beck n.d.). In his book about Jeffrey Dahmer, Masters (1993) comments upon the former's repeated acts of indecent exposure and suggests that had these activities been acted upon at an earlier stage, Dahmer's career as a serial killer *might* have been halted. He also suggested that, for Dahmer, indecent exposure represented a 'wish for sensuality without involvement' (Masters 1993: 71); in other words, a form of love-making at a safe distance.

Various attempt have been made to classify the behaviour and personality types of indecent exposers (see, for example, MacDonald 1973; Rooth 1975; Gayford 1981, 1997; Yap et al. 2002). The following classification, which readers may find helpful, is my own synthesis of some of those quoted above. It therefore makes no claims to great originality.

1 The inhibited (and in some cases latently homosexual) young man who struggles against his impulses to expose himself. He usually exposes with a flaccid (unerect) penis and feels anxious about his behaviour. When such behaviour occurs in adolescence against a family background of prudery or reticence in discussing sexual matters, sex education and simple supportive counselling may be helpful.

2 Situational exposure: here the exposure may take place against a background of marital or other stress (such as the wife or partner's unavailability or due to pregnancy). Simple counselling may also be helpful in such cases.

3 The less inhibited type described earlier who exposes with an erect penis and who may accompany his exposure with masturbation and aggressive and sexually explicit language. Intervention in such cases *may* help to prevent a progression to more serious sex offending. For this reason, it is very important for professional workers to ascertain the circumstances of the exposure *in as much detail as possible* (see, for example, Sugarman et al. 1994; MacPherson 2003).

4 Exposure occurring in a setting of clear mental illness, such as depression, hypomania, schizophrenia or dementia. In such cases medical intervention aimed at alleviating the illness may bring about a subsequent cessation of the behaviour.

5 Exposure committed by those with moderate to severe learning difficulties. In such cases, the exposure is most likely to be due to lack of social skills and against a background of mounting need for sexual expression. Counselling in such cases can also be helpful. (It is a

mistake to assume that even quite seriously mentally impaired people cannot be helped by counselling, provided it is tailored to their particular levels of need and understanding.)

6   Cases in which the exposure is facilitated by substance abuse (such as alcohol) reactive depression or simple loneliness.

The classification suggested above will, it is hoped, provide some clues to aetiology. Additional explanations include a need to assert a wavering or undeveloped masculinity. In some cases (as in 3 above) there may be a need to assert power over, or to insult or shock, women. The exposure may be a suppressed desire to commit a seriously violent sexual contact offence such as rape. Treatment (best seen as management) has already been briefly touched upon. Counselling of various types and intensity may be helpful, though some cases are of such long-standing severity that they have an addictive quality and are very resistant to treatment in the sense of 'cure'. As with all sexual offenders, the communication of genuine interest and warm concern on the part of the counsellor and a degree of unshockability are more important than the school of thought or mode of practice espoused. Treatment by whatever mode should have as its aim the facilitation of the offender in managing his life in such a way that temptation and possible relapse are avoided. For two early but useful illustrations of approaches to management see Jones and Frei (1977) and Snaith and Collins (1981). I now provide two case illustrations demonstrating some aspects of the foregoing.

Case illustration 8.1

A was an 18-year-old male who was made the subject of a probation order as a result of being convicted of a number of acts of indecent exposure. It transpired that these acts had taken place over a period of several months. His victims were young teenage girls. His exposure took place in lanes in vicinity of the village where he lived. His acts of exposure were un-aggressive, and took place without erection or accompanying masturbation or speech. Inquiry into his background revealed him to be the only child of elderly parents. Sexual matters had never been a topic of conversation in the household and sex education consisted of that gleaned from school friends. For some time he had wanted to make contact with the opposite sex, but found it extremely difficult to engage with girls. During his period of probation he began to discuss his difficulties and, in particular, his guilty feelings about his offences. Some simple counselling, notably in the area of sexual behaviour and subsequent enhancement of his social skills, helped him to be more comfortable about sex. In the course of time he formed a good relationship with a girl of about his own age. His progress under the probation order was sufficiently good for the probation officer to ask that it be discharged on the grounds of good progress.

Case illustration 8.2

B was a 30-year-old man with a long history of offences of exposure which had resulted in numerous court appearances. These had usually been dealt with by either fines or probation orders. However, on one occasion the magistrates considered that their sentencing powers were insufficient and remitted him to the Crown Court where he received a sentence of twelve months' imprisonment. In contrast to A, his exposures were highly aggressive in nature. He selected his victims, usually young women, with considerable planning, taking care that they would not be able to evade his confrontations easily. He exposed with an erect penis, was often masturbating and accompanied this behaviour by making obscene and aggressive comments. His behaviour just stopped short of progression to a sexual contact offence. Over the years a number of attempts had been made to help him modify his behaviour, mainly by behavioural psychological means, but these attempts had met with very little success. During a spell under probation supervision, he committed a violent sexual assault on a young woman. For this offence he received a substantial term of imprisonment. His case illustrates the possibility of escalation from exposure to more serious sexual offending as referred to earlier.

Paedophilia

In what follows I am concerned predominantly with sexual assaults on children outside the family (other than incest, which I deal with separately). Child sexual abuse within the family is a topic in its own right and space constraints preclude its treatment here. However, it is important to emphasize that a number of the characteristics shown by those who sexually abuse children outside the family are very similar to those who do so within it. For example, some men who commit incestuous acts with their offspring have a number of convictions for sexually assaulting children outside the family. In Dennis Howitt's (1995) book *Paedophiles and Sexual Offences against Children*, my colleague at Loughborough University makes (as usual) a trenchant statement in the introduction to his book:

> Being face to face with a paedophile is not a comfortable situation. Most of us harbour a catalogue of beliefs and emotions about such people, which structures our perceptions of what to say, think and do. Rarely are our feelings built entirely on factual knowledge . . . Images such as satanic abuse, paedophile rings, bogus social workers, dirty old men in rain coats and sado-masochistic or perverted child sex killers may dominate.
>
> (Howitt 1995: 1)

It is only fair to relate that some surveys of public attitudes to paedophiles show a greater degree of sensitivity than selective reporting by the media would suggest (see McCartan 2004; see also a larger scale survey by Brown et al. 2008). With this cautionary note in mind we can begin to attempt to extend our knowledge of this problematic group of individuals.

Sexual offences against children have been widely prevalent throughout history and it also seems to be the case that sexual assaults on children both within and outside the family have been, and are, much more common than is often supposed. In this connection it is useful to recall why Freud had to revise his original theory of the neuroses. This was based on his view that some neurotic conditions in his female patients had their origins in sexual abuse within their families. Fear of the opprobrium that such a view might fall upon him for stating this openly, it has been suggested that he then revised his theory to suggest that the events unearthed during psycho-analysis were of 'hysterical' and not factual origin (Masson 1985).

Those who sexually molest children span the social spectrum; for example, from the notorious fifteenth-century Marshal of France, Gilles de Rais (a colleague of Joan of Arc), to the most lowly itinerant. Contrary to public opinion, most paedophilic activity is carried out by those placed in positions of trust towards children – for example parents, friends, teachers, clergy, social workers, doctors and nurses. In clinical terms, the *Diagnostic and Statistical Manual of Mental Disorders* (APA 2005) gives the following criteria for paedophilia:

A. Over a period of at least six months, recurrent, intense sexually arousing fantasies, sexual urges, or behaviours involving sexual activity with a prepubescent child *or* children (*generally* age 13 years or younger) (emphasis added).
B. The fantasies, sexual urges or behaviour cause clinically significant distress or impairment in social, occupational, or other important areas of functioning.
C. The person is at least age 16 years and at least 5 years older than the child or children in Criterion A.

(APA 2005: 528)

Assessors are also asked to specify if the person is

- sexually attracted to males
- sexually attracted to females
- sexually attracted to both.

(APA 2005: 528)

Note the proviso in A (*generally* aged 13 years or younger). Paedophilic activity can, of course, involve young persons of more mature years.

In another thoughtful contribution, West (2000) places the problem in perspective. He indicates that media activity has hyped up fears about sexual abuse of children; although there is a very small number of highly dangerous predatory paedophiles, these constitute a very small proportion of the total picture (see also Soothill et al. 2002, 2004). West (2000) sums up the position in the following fashion:

> A punitive socio-legal policy towards sexual offenders against minors has been driven by public demand. The perception of an appallingly high incidence of serious abuse by incorrigible men has been encouraged by press sensationalism, but criminal statistics and recidivist studies fail to confirm either an escalation of sex crimes against minors or the inevitability of recidivism.
>
> (West 2000: 511)

West (2000) goes on to make the very important point that:

> Exaggerated perception of risk produces undue restrictions on children's freedom and on their interactions with teachers and other adults. Assumptions of incorrigibility impede the rehabilitation of offenders through vigilantism, stigmatization and barriers to employment. This amplifies deviance and does not protect children.
>
> (West 2000: 511)

(See also Silverman and Wilson 2002: notably Chapter 2.)[3]

West's remarks bring a sense of balance to our consideration of the problem. Bearing these in mind, we can now refer to the possible effect of such abuse in *individual* cases. There is evidence to suggest that the physical and emotional trauma that is caused as a result of sudden, unexpected or coercive sexual relationships with children may be considerable (Mullen 1990; Dare 1993; Lincoln 2001; Spataro et al. 2004; Saint-Martin et al. 2007). The following would seem to be the most significant determinants of trauma (see also West 2000: 522–525):

- the victim's previous and current social and psychological environment
- the anxiety engendered by being forced to keep a 'guilty secret' (particularly in incest cases)
- the opportunities, or lack of them, for offloading this guilt
- the nature of the pre-existing or current relationship with the assailant or the avenues of escape from it, if any
- the reactions of those having care of the victim; these reactions are arguably more important in determining later guilt or trauma than any of the foregoing factors.

It is important to take a cautious approach to the classification of paedophiles since pigeon-holing individuals is seldom a very satisfactory aid to understanding. However, some professionals suggest that some distinctions may be made between *homosexual* and *heterosexual* paedophiles, though of course such individuals may assault victims of both sexes. Bluglass (1982) considers that *homosexual paedophiles* are more likely to have had past involvement with children, to prefer them as sexual partners and to show deviant patterns of sexual arousal. *Heterosexual* paedophiles are somewhat more likely to be situationally motivated, usually to prefer adult women, and to seek out a child only at times of social and environmental stress. A somewhat crude (and perhaps oversimplified) form of classification is to divide paedophiles into *youthful* and *adult* offenders. Youthful offenders may be divided into two rough sub-categories:

- Inadequate adolescents who may bribe young children into engaging in deviant sexual practices.
- Rather more dangerous adolescent offenders who have a history of being sexually abused themselves and who have shown sexually inappropriate behaviour from an early age (see Bagley 1992). They may progress to becoming highly sexually deviant adults (see Pithers et al. 2002; Janes 2007; Vizard et al. 2007; Oxnam and Vess 2008). Such offenders appear to be a fairly heterogenous group in terms of personality characteristics and psychopathology, 'while also suggesting different aetiological pathways and different treatment needs' (Oxnam and Vess 2008: 228).

Adult paedophiles may be divided roughly into:

- Middle-aged heterosexual paedophiles, socially isolated and incompetent; they may seek the company of children for comfort.
- Predominantly homosexual paedophiles, whose sexual preferences are by no means dulled by age, even though their sexual capacity may be. *It is very unwise to think that as such individuals become older that they necessarily become less dangerous.* In fact, they may become more easily frustrated and feel less in command (powerful). Any feeling that their young victims (or would-be victims) find them no longer attractive and who rebuff their overtures, may serve to remind them of their waning 'powers'. In aggressive frustration they may resort to violent means to achieve their ends. However, it is true to say that not all older paedophiles behave in this fashion. Clark and Mezey (1997) describe a group of thirteen child sex abusers *over the age of 65*. They found them to be similar in most respects to sex offenders against children in other age groups, but that they differed in being of higher socio-economic status and more stable backgrounds. They suggest, in respect of offenders of this age and background, that the courts tended to seek non-custodial disposals, viewing them as *less risky*. Clark and Mezey

(1997) also suggest that courts were hesitant to use imprisonment because of the physical frailty of some offenders in this age group. It is, of course, the more general case that, with an ageing population, sexual as with other offenders will present management problems of increasing magnitude. For the importance of taking age-at-release into account in the prediction of recidivism, see Barbaree et al. (2008).

- Paedophiles of impaired intellect: social ineptitude and a lack of 'moral' sense may contribute to their offending.
- A group that can be described as multi-antisocial: these men are lacking in general social conformity and are likely to have convictions for non-sexual offences.
- Paedophiles who are exclusively homosexual and who exert a powerful and coercive influence over their victims. They sometimes see themselves as the 'protectors' of disadvantaged youths and are highly resistant to treatment measures.

Finally, it is important to attempt to distinguish between those who use force as a means of gaining cooperation in the act and those offenders for whom the infliction of pain and terror is an end in itself (see also later discussion of rapists). It is also very important to note that recidivism may occur after long periods of time; the longer the time for exposure, the greater the risk of further offending (see Cann et al. 2004).

Management

Although it is a recurring truism that every case will be different, it is possible to make some observations about management which have a general applicability. In my view, the first and perhaps most important point to make is that one should not talk of 'curing' sexual offenders. This is because, as suggested earlier, most available evidence supports the view that sexual preferences are usually laid down very early in life and may be highly resistant to change. The problem is exacerbated because, as we have seen, only an uncertain picture of the respective contributions made by biological, genetic and wider familial and environmental influences to sexual conduct is possible. It is more realistic to talk about 'management' or attitude change and prevention of relapse. This may be facilitated by intensive individual or group psychotherapy of different schools, by powerful behavioural techniques of one kind or another that aim to produce gradual change in sexual orientation or by limited and carefully controlled use of chemotherapeutic methods. Whichever technique is used, it is best to avoid thinking of 'cure' and to concentrate upon helping sex offenders make more satisfactory adjustments to their behaviour and its consequences. In other words, the prevention of relapse. No *single* method of management is likely to be successful; it is best to espouse a multi-method approach (for example, judicious use of chemotherapy is more successful when allied to counselling). It is best not to think globally about sexual offence behaviour, but to try to break the behaviour down into manageable segments and typologies. But perhaps of most importance is the need to remember that all persistent sex offenders (and some less persistent ones) are *highly reluctant to admit to their role in sexual offending and will persistently use evasion and denial.*[4]

The phenomenon of denial is vital in dealing with sex offenders. In an important paper, Mezey et al. (1991) suggest that there are six aspects of denial: denial of the act itself, denial of the child as a person, denial of the child as a victim, denial of adult responsibility, denial of consequences for the child and denial of consequences for the offender. Denial will, of course, hold a very prominent place in the mind of the sexual offender sentenced to imprisonment; fear of reprisal from fellow inmates may be uppermost in mind. Attempts have been made to introduce special 'treatment' programmes in some prisons and limited success has been reported (see Beech et al. 1998; West 2000; Friendship et al. 2002). Community treatment programmes implemented by the probation service have met with a small but encouraging degree of success (see, for example, Hedderman and Sugg 1996; Manderville-Norden et al. 2008). For additional information on the use of and accreditation of prison and probation management programmes, see Rex and Bottoms (2003). One method that has been used to supplement an offender's own account of his sexual preferences and practices is that of phallometric assessment. This involves the measurement of erectile tumescence by a gauge attached to the penis. The offender is then shown a variety of arousing situations by means of videos or audio tapes and the degree to which he continues to be aroused when aversive stimuli are introduced or suggested can thus be measured. Such testing is by no means fool-proof, since it has been shown that offenders can 'fake' their responses. However, such measures may prove useful as adjuncts to reliance upon self-reports and the observations of penal and mental health professionals. For a review of the 'state of the art', see Launay (1994, 1999). For the use of polygraphy ('lie detection') in the management of sex offenders, see Grubin (2002) and Grubin and Madsen (2005, 2006). For a recent survey, see also Fowles and Wilson (2008).

Case illustration 8.3

I have selected this example of paedophilic behaviour in order to demonstrate its intractability and the manner in which even very skilled and experienced professionals can be deceived. It concerns a 50-year-old male offender-patient originally detained in a (special) high security hospital under the then Mental Health Act 1959. After some six years in hospital, he was discharged conditionally by the Home Secretary, but recalled to hospital by the Home Secretary some five years later. He had been convicted of further offences and made the subject of another hospital order with restrictions under the 1983 Act. He was classified as suffering from psychopathic disorder. Periodic appeals to the Mental Health Review Tribunal for discharge were unsuccessful. He first came to the attention of the courts for sexual offences against children when aged about 20. He had a disturbed childhood, having been in care, was of dull normal intelligence and had no regular employment. His continuing powerful homosexual paedophilic tendencies had been treated with anti-libidinal drugs, but to little effect. A subsequent court appearance led to his con-viction for further sexual assaults on young boys and the imposition of the hospital order referred to above. During his time in hospital, he received psychological treatment and, despite continuing denial of sexual interest in young people, he made progress on other fronts; and like many similar high security offender-patients was considered to be a 'model' resident. In view of his overall progress a tribunal decided to authorize his discharge, but not without some obvious misgivings. His very experienced community supervisors (psychiatrist and probation officer) expressed themselves very pleased with his progress. However, it emerged that over the ensuing months he had been actively engaged in paedophilic behaviour with a range of young people – aged from about 12 to 17. Moreover, *he had committed further offences while on bail* for the first offences that had come to light. A subse-quent further appearance before a Crown Court resulted in yet another hospital order with restrictions, an order imposed solely on the grounds of alleviating or preventing a deterioration in his continuing psychopathic condition. His prognosis was, understandably, considered to be extremely poor and it seems highly unlikely that he will be released again. His capacity for deception and denial would reinforce such a decision.

Incest: familial child sex offence, Section 2, Sex Offences Act 2003

Incest (consanguinous sexual relationships) is the sexual crime that probably provokes the most emotive reactions. Taboos and injunctions against it have existed since time immemorial and the Book of Leviticus contains the injunction that 'no man shall approach a blood relation for intercourse' (Chapter 18: 6). Indeed, as Bluglass (1979: 152) writes, 'In England and Wales incest, like witchcraft, bestiality and adultery [incest] . . . was in earlier times considered an offence against God'. However, history reveals that there have been notable exceptions; for example, in the cultures of ancient Egypt and Greece. Mythology and literature are also replete with allusions to incestuous conduct and to incestuous themes. There are a number of reasons for the strict injunctions against consanguinous conduct. First, there are the religious injunctions already referred to. Second, there appears to be a deeply held and primitive horror of consanguinous rela-tionships between parents and their offspring. Third, Freud suggests in his work *Totem and Taboo* (1960) that in primitive societies the incest taboo was erected to preserve the power of the paternal tyrant in order that he might prevent the younger males from banding together to deprive him of his sexual rights over the females. Fourth, taboos are said to be powerful because of the serious role confusion that can occur when close kin have sexual relationships. Fifth, there is the view that incestuous relationships may produce a higher incidence of genetic weakness than those found in non-incestuous unions. However, the committee reviewing the then current law did not regard this as the most cogent reason, preferring to rely more heavily on the breach of trust involved and society's disapproval of such behaviour (as quoted in Stevenson et al. 2004: 102). It should also be noted that it is probably the combination of poor antenatal and postnatal care, poor nurturing, adverse social environment *and* the incestuous relationships that occur in socially dysfunctional families that produce these results and not the effects of genetic transmission alone. It may surprise readers to learn that incest did not become a criminal offence until 1908, and then only after two failed attempts in Parliament (Bluglass 1979). Hitherto, it had been dealt with by the ecclesiastical courts. The Punishment of Incest Act 1908 (repealed and re-enacted in the Sexual Offences Act 1956) has now been superseded by the Sexual Offences Act 2003. Under Section 27 of the Act consanguinous relationships are now described as being that of parent, step-parent, grandparent, brother, sister, half-brother, half-sister, aunt, cousin or uncle and foster parent. Thus the new Act broadens the relationships that were contained in earlier legislation and specifically includes step-relationships and foster-relationships. Such a broadening of inclusion reflects, as Stevenson et al. (2004: 102) suggest, 'the looser struc-ture of modern families'. The maximum penalty on indictment is fourteen years' imprisonment; on summary conviction a sentence of six months' imprisonment or a fine not exceeding the statutory maximum, or both. Cases of incest are not prosecuted frequently. Generally a veil of secrecy is preserved within the family. Sometimes the case may come to light only due to pregnancy, because of an attempt at blackmail, through the investigation of some non-related alleged criminal conduct, or as a result of a confession by one of the parties. The most outstanding characteristics in the back-grounds in a large proportion of incestuous families are those of social and emotional dysfunction. The following is a somewhat simplified classifica-tion of the conditions that can obtain in incestuous families. My previous cautionary comments concerning category overlap are also relevant in incest cases (I use the word 'incest' as a shorthand term while recognizing its emotive meaning; no doubt others will continue to do the same).

I have made an attempt to classify incestuous situations as follows:

- Incest occurring in large, overcrowded families, where the participants almost slip into an incestuous pattern of behaviour. Sibling incest may be a feature of such cases (see, for example, Gibbens et al. 1978; Batten 1983).

- Very rarely, incestuous relationships may develop because of mental impairment or psychotic illness in either or both parties.
- Cases where the wife (or partner) is absent through death or separation and where the daughter(s) may take over the wife's or partner's role. It may also occur in cases where she is still physically present but where she has abrogated her sexual role. In a few cases, not only is she aware of what is occurring, but also she appears prepared to collude in the practice.
- Cases in which the father is a dominating and coercive individual who uses threats and/or violence to get his way in the full knowledge that such behaviour is wrong. Such men may have histories of serious alcohol abuse and have convictions for non-sexual offences (see Bluglass 1979; Cooper and Cormier 1990).
- Rare instances of the parties not knowing that they are in a consanguinous relationship. For example, a brother and sister who have been separated from each other very early in life may meet much later and *unknowingly* enter into a sexual relationship. Prior to the 2003 Act, the position seemed somewhat ambiguous. However, Section 28 appears to preclude criminal proceedings in such instances.

The emotive nature of incestuous behaviour means that professionals have to come to terms with their own incest anxieties and fears. On the whole, the courts take a serious view of incest committed by adult males with their female children; the abhorrence felt for the offence may, as indicated above, to some extent be vitiated by removing its name from statute since the behaviour is now subsumed under the title of Familial Child Sex Offences. This *may* have the helpful effect of enabling all concerned to see the offence for what it is – an offence connected with adverse family attitudes and living conditions, calling for social and other intervention rather than punitive wrath borne of irrational feelings. In addition, the use of the term 'incest' meant that we linked together all its variants and treated all cases alike (see Studer et al. 2000). Courts are now being encouraged to take a more flexible approach to sentencing and to make distinctions between cases of severity and those of a less serious nature. In the latter cases, the use of immediate custody may serve to make matters worse. The family will not be helped by further breakdown and the victim may harbour feelings of guilt for having informed the authorities (for, contrary to common belief, some daughters remain fond of their abusive parent). Supervision of the offender with a prohibition placed on immediate contact may be more effective than immediate removal from the family home. However, in some cases of long-term coercive and sometimes violent forms of incestuous abuse of several children, imprisonment may be the only option. A dispassionate view of the problem is still needed. In the early 1980s, Batten (1983) wrote:

> The incestuous child is readily placed in the role of victim and all the pressures from society and the legal system reinforce this. However, the child is still left with the break-up of the family and a distrust of adults. What is really needed is care and support.
>
> (Batten 1983: 252)

It will be of interest to note, as time goes by, whether the widening of 'consanguinity' increases the previous very low rate of 'incest' prosecutions.

Rape on females

Henry Fielding, in *Jonathan Wild* (Book III, Chapter 7), says this:

> He in a few minutes ravished this fair creature, or at least would have ravished her, if she had not, by a timely compliance, prevented him.

Sadly, many women do not manage to avoid the seriously assaultative and predatory attention of males as described by Fielding. The quotation also demonstrates some of the difficulties and ambiguities surrounding consent and compliance that have made convictions for rape problematic. However, since the early 1990s, court decisions have, belatedly, tended to support the view that when a woman says 'No' she means it; this has not always been the case. Prosecutions for rape and other sexual assault cases have also been difficult, partly because of the very small number of cases in which false accusations have been proved.

Rape cases constitute a fairly sizeable proportion of serious sexual assaults. However, the very low rate of convictions for rape in Britain (some 5.7 per cent of reported cases) has been said to be partly the fault of the police for not taking allegations seriously enough and not being trained sufficiently well in rape investigative procedures. There has also been evidence to suggest that the circumstances in which rape has been carried out have been becoming more violent. Lloyd and Walmsley describe three main trends. First, a slight increase in the number of offences involving the use of excessive violence; second, an increase in sexual acts in addition to the rape (for example, anal and/or oral sex); third, an increase in the length of time that victims were under the coercion of the offenders (Lloyd and Walmsley 1989; Lloyd 1991). The official (statistical) classification of a sexual offence may not give an accurate indication of its severity. For example, there are many gradations of rape and indecent assault, from fairly minor (but perhaps no less traumatic) attempts at rape to serious indecent assaults that may just fall short of it. The belief on the part of certain males that some women may enjoy the experience of 'a bit of rough' and being sexually subdued fails entirely to recognize the terror and distress endured by women in such an experience. Since the late 1990s, women have been somewhat more willing to report rape to the authorities, but progress in this area is still slow. The reasons are not hard to discern. A woman may be understandably reluctant to go through the ordeal of a searching medical examination; some women have described a degree of clumsiness and lack of sensitivity by inexperienced examiners in the past. Some may be reluctant to report the behaviour to their partners, other family members or friends; this may result in their carrying a quite unnecessary burden of guilt and added torment. The physical consequences of rape, apart from any vaginal, anal or other injuries that may have been caused, are very important. The victims may have become pregnant, have contracted a sexually transmitted disease such as syphilis or gonorrhoea, HIV infection or AIDS. These added traumas will serve to compound their distress. Many women feel so defiled by the experience that they may go to extreme lengths to 'cleanse' themselves, for example repeatedly scrubbing their genitalia with powerful disinfectants. Since the late 1990s, society has begun to recognize the real trauma involved for rape victims and the need for rape counselling, sometimes over prolonged periods. Much of the good work in this area was promoted by the women's movement and the introduction of rape crisis centres throughout the UK. However, much more needs to be done, since there are still those who take a less than sensitive view of females' experience of rape (for example in comments such as 'she must have asked for it', or 'she was giving out the wrong signals').

One of the most significant and disturbing contributions to establishing the reasons for the low prosecution and conviction rates in rape cases is the report by HM Crown Prosecution Service Inspectorate and HM Inspectorate of Constabulary (HMCPSI and HMIC 2007) entitled *Without Consent*. This excellent report should be read by all concerned with the investigation and prosecution of rape allegations.

Legal aspects

It is only in fairly recent times that the ingredients of the offence of rape have been afforded full definition, the first *statutory* reference to these ingredients being in the Sexual Offences Act 1956. Increasing concerns about consent were reflected in the Sexual Offences (Amendment) Act 1976 and the current legal position is now contained in the Sexual Offences Act 2003. Section 1 of the Act now defines rape in the following terms:

A person (A) commits an offence if –
(a) he intentionally penetrates the vagina, anus or mouth of another person (B) with his penis,

(b) B does not consent to the penetrations, and

(c) A does not reasonably believe that B consents.

The Act leaves it to the courts to determine the issues of reasonable belief as follows:

> Whether a belief is reasonable is to be determined having regard to all the circumstances, including any steps A has taken to ascertain whether B consents.

Sections 74, 75, 76 and 77 provide more details concerning the determination of consent. Despite these specific provisions there will doubtless be continuing debates in court as to whether consent was, or was not, freely given.[5] It should also be noted here that the sections of the Act are not gender specific so that male rape is included within the definition, having first been defined as a specific offence in the Criminal Justice and Public Order Act 1994 (see later discussion of male rape). In a guideline judgment given on 9 December 2002, the Court of Appeal provided revised guidelines for sentencing in rape cases (see Stone 2003c). The maximum sentence for rape remains life imprisonment. For further details of the new law, see Stevenson et al. (2004: 34–38, 39–48).

Classification

There have been a number of studies of what might loosely be described as the epidemiology of rape, an early study carried out by Amir (1971) being one of the most comprehensive. Amir (1971) found that, contrary to common belief, about one-third of the victims had been in previous contact with their assailants. Much of Amir's early work has been confirmed by more recent studies, such as those by Myhill and Allen (2002) and Muir and Macleod (2003). In many cases the rape had been planned and some half of the victims had failed to resist their attackers (a hardly surprising finding given the terror that such attacks will induce). Other findings (Hood et al. 2002) also indicate that over fairly long periods of time (in one study six years) rapists and other serious sexual offenders were relatively infrequently reconvicted, in the region of less than 10 per cent; however, those who *were* reconvicted, committed very serious crimes (Hood et al. 2002).

The arbitrary nature of *classification* must again be acknowledged. In particular, in attempting any form of classification, problems arise because we are sometimes describing the offence by the nature of the behaviour displayed (for example, aggressive or over-inhibited), sometimes by the choice of victim (for example, children) and sometimes by the presence of other features such as mental disorder (disturbance) (see, for example, Grubin and Kennedy 1991; Fisher and Mair 1998). If, for a moment, we disregard those rapes that arise out of *allegedly* mistaken consent, we find that key features underlying, or associated with most rapes, are anger, a desire to control and aggression. As suggested in Chapter 6, in most cases female rape seems best regarded as a crime of extreme personal violence rather than as an offence aimed at achieving sexual satisfaction per se (see Löbmann et al. 2003). For this reason, a classification proposed by Groth and Hobson (1983) seems a useful starting point. Their typology suggests three clear-cut but overlapping classes of rape.

- *Anger rape*: motivated by feeling 'put down' or by retribution for perceived wrongs.
- *Power rape*: engaged in as a means of denying deep feelings of inadequacy and insecurity.
- *Sadistic rape*: victims are usually complete strangers; they may be subjected to torture, bondage, and other deviant sexual practices.

Taking Groth and Hobson's (1983) classification a little further, a slightly more detailed typology can be proposed:

1 The sexually virile young man, out for what he can get, whose exploitative hedonism is not counterbalanced by finer scruples or concern – the 'opportunistic' rapist. Perhaps we should include here husbands who rape their wives, although its inclusion here is not altogether satisfactory.

2 The more inhibited, shy young man, who is trying to overcome his feelings of sexual inferiority. He may misinterpret the responses of his victim and not register that 'No' means 'No'. It is thought by some that such rapists may be latently homosexual and their behaviour could be seen as a defence against their homosexuality (see also my classification of indecent exposers).

3 The sexually violent and aggressive man. Such offenders have records of other forms of violence, alcohol often plays a large part in narcoticizing inhibition and they may hold the mistaken belief that it may improve their performance; the reverse is, of course, the case, as the porter in *Macbeth* demonstrated so graphically.

4 A group who are potentially highly dangerous, in that they need to gain reassurance by a show of force. West et al. (1978) studied a group of incarcerated rapists who were undergoing group psychotherapy. One of the main features that emerged was that these men suffered severe feelings of inferiority concerning their masculinity (West et al. 1978). Confirmation for this finding may be found in later work by Perkins (1991). This group includes those who set out to defile and denigrate their victims, forcing them to participate in acts of vaginal, anal and

oral sex. Many of these men appear to be women haters and some may eventually commit sadistic sexual murder (see later).

5   A sub-group of (4) above. These men, also potentially highly danger-ous, seem to have insatiable sexual appetites and may need the resistance of their victims to arouse their potency. Such offenders may obtain sexual pleasure from their sadistic activities (true sadists).

6   Rapists who are found to be suffering from a definable form of mental disorder such as psychosis or mental impairment. Such cases are com-paratively rare. However, Smith and Taylor (1999: 233) suggest that 'when a man with schizophrenia commits a serious sex offence the illness is, more commonly than not, relevant to the offence even though a direct symptom relationship may be relatively unusual'.

7   A predominantly young group, who rape in groups or packs ('gang-bangs'). They are likely to have previous convictions for violence and other offences. They may engage in deviant sexual practices with their victims and subject them to forms of defilement, such as urinating on them. Unlike some of the other typologies presented above, they are not, in the main, characterized by gross personal psycho-pathology.

Management

Much of what has been said earlier about other forms of sexual offending can be applied to cases of female rape. The formulation of some kind of typology based upon an in-depth assessment will afford clues as to the most appropriate form of management. Brief counselling and training in sexual and social skills may be of help with the first two groups. Those in group (3) may respond to measures aimed at improving their life styles and in helping them with their drinking problems. Those in groups (4) and (5) are much harder to manage and may need long-term incarceration in order that psychotherapeutic treatment programmes may take effect. Some success with programmes designed to develop social competence and to modify deviant sexual preferences by various means has been reported in custodial settings (see Hedderman and Sugg 1996; Beech et al. 1998; Friendship et al. 2002). The use of anti-androgen medication linked with counselling has already been referred to in the discussion of paedophilia. Those in group (7) may outgrow their unpleasant proclivities, but they need to be removed from circulation for a time, for the protection of a society, for purposes of retribution and deterrence, and to allow their consciences to develop. No *single* form of management is likely to be effective. It is highly dangerous to espouse with Messianic enthusiasm any one theory or treatment model. A multidisciplinary approach, based upon a full assessment of the personal and situational factors in the rapist's life is essential. For discussion of a variety of approaches, see, for example, Matravers (2003), Craissati (2004), Bilby et al. (2006) and Brooks-Gordon et al. (2006).

Having said this, it is important to emphasize again that almost without exception, rape offenders will be sentenced to immediate imprisonment, sometimes for long periods. During such time they may be afforded the opportunity to participate in sexual offending treatment programmes of one kind or another. Such approaches seem to have met with a moderate degree of success, but long-term follow-up and supervision are essential in these cases. This is because research tends to show that in the *long term*, reoffending is more common than was once thought to be the case (see, for example, Soothill et al. 2002).

Male rape

As already indicated, male rape is now designated as a specific offence, having parity with female rape. As with female victims, males may be very reluctant to disclose the attack to family, friend or professional helpers. The trauma, both physical and mental, is no less severe than those suffered by their female counterparts. For accounts see, for example, King et al. (2002) and Huckle (1995). For recent comprehensive reviews of male rape in prisons, see Knowles (1999) and Banbury (2004).

Bestiality (zoophilia)

In early modern England, those committing bestiality were liable to the death penalty, as Gayford (1997: 313) indicates 'often for the animal as well as the human'. Until 2003, the offence of bestiality was dealt with under the Sexual Offences Act 1956, and those convicted could be awarded a life sentence. It is now dealt with under Section 69 of the Sexual Offences Act 2003 as *Intercourse with an animal*.

> A person commits an offence if –
> (a) he intentionally performs an act of penetration with his penis,
> (b) what is penetrated is the vagina or anus of a living animal, and
> (c) he knows that, or is reckless as to whether, that is what is penetrated . . .
> on summary conviction, [an offender can be sentenced] to imprisonment for a term not exceeding 6 months or a fine not exceeding the statutory maximum or both;
> on conviction on indictment, to imprisonment for a term not exceeding 2 years.

Fudge (2000), in a study of bestiality in the sixteenth century, suggests that it was only then that it became a heavily proscribed and punished form of behaviour. She surmises that this was due to concerns about the pollution of the human species and what might best be described as cross-mating between animals and humans. Having studied early records of the behaviour, she provides descriptions of sex with a variety of farm and other animals. In her article Fudge (2000) cites a number of other texts which throw light upon this 'oddity' of behaviour. The clinical literature on the topic is somewhat sparse, and prosecutions rare. However, it is reasonable to assume that its occurrence is probably more common than is generally believed. Duffield et al. (1998) describe and discuss the cases of seven young patients referred to an adolescent psychiatric service dealing with sex abusers. On the basis of their own study and the work of others, Duffield et al. (1998) concluded that bestiality was frequently accompanied by other paraphilias. In summary, the behaviour is most likely to occur mainly in males who may be mentally disturbed or impaired, be socially isolated, have difficulties in making relationships and showing other forms of sexually deviant behaviour. Although the behaviour is now dealt with under the 2003 Act, many people maintain that it could more appropriately have been dealt with under the legislation covering cruelty to animals. However, such a view was not favoured by the Criminal Law Revision Committee, who considered that abolishing the offence would not meet with public approval and legally proscribing it would enable offenders to be afforded treatment under mental health legislation. Against this, one could put forward the view that if the behaviour was dealt with under the cruelty to animals legislation, offenders might still be afforded mental health treatment if this were to be deemed appropriate.

Necrophilia

Necrophilia, sexual excitement aroused by the dead, or performed with cadavers (corpses) has a long history. Examples may be found in ancient Egyptian records where it is recorded that embalmers were sometimes prone to sexually interfere with the corpses they were preserving. In order to prevent this, an edict was handed down ordering that the bodies should be in a degree of putrefaction before embalming activities started. Gayford (1997) suggests that necrophilia can be clinically sub-divided in three ways. *Pseudonecrophilia* derives from a psychoanalytic notion of fascination with, or fantasy involving, the dead. *Necrophilous character* consists of 'a passionate attraction to all that is dead or decaying' (Gayford 1997: 312). Necrophilia has also been associated with vampiristic and cannibalistic activity in the form of necrophagy (see Hucker 1990; Prins 1991). In *symbolic necrophilia*, specially designated brothels cater for those who wish to indulge their predilections for substitute necrophilic activity. Here, a prostitute plays the part of a corpse, 'complete with shroud and coffin'. It will be recalled that Dennis Nilsen (see Chapter 2) indulged in necrophilic activity. For obvious reasons, prosecutions are rare and the true incidence of necrophilic activity is not known. Certain occupations may facilitate indulgence in the practice, for example, those who work in mortuaries and at undertakers. Until the passing of the Sexual Offences Act 2003, there was no statutory basis for prosecutions for interference (sexual or otherwise) with corpses. In rare instances, prosecutions might be brought for criminal damage (to graves, coffins, etc.) or 'outrages on public decency'. The new Act now makes specific provision. Section 70 provides for *Sexual penetration of a corpse*:

(1) A person commits an offence if –
   (a) he intentionally performs an act of penetration with a part of his body or anything else,
   (b) what is penetrated is a part of the body of a dead person,
   (c) he knows that, or is reckless as to whether, that is what is penetrated, and
   (d) the penetration is sexual.
(2) A person found guilty of an offence under this section is liable –
   (a) on summary conviction, to imprisonment for a term not exceeding 6 months or a fine not exceeding the statutory maximum or both;
   (b) on conviction on indictment, to imprisonment for a term not exceeding 2 years.

Sexual murder

If we exclude crimes of passion and murder committed as a result of sexual jealousy, sexual murder is, fortunately, a rare event. As noted elsewhere, it is sometimes difficult to determine whether a killing has occurred as a result of the pursuit of sadistic pleasure, as a means of keeping the victim quiet (unable to give evidence) or as a result of an unintentional act of violence that has become lethal during some form of sexual activity; for example, the occurrence of manual strangulation during some forms of anal intercourse. Incidents have been described in which death has occurred in the course of fellatio due to aspiration of ejaculate or from impaction of the penis in the hypo-pharynx (Rupp 1970). Other possible victims include indiscriminate and cruising homosexuals who may be at risk from so-called 'queer bashers'; sometimes a homosexual overture towards the wrong person may result in a murder. Those engaged in both male and female prostitution may also be at considerable risk from those seeking deviant practices (see West 1992). Grubin (1994), in an article on sexual murder, suggests that the incidence of sexual murder of women is unknown and quotes criminal statistics which indicate that about one-third of female homicide victims are killed by their spouses (Grubin 1994: 624). He makes the important point that statistics of the true incidence of sexual murder are difficult to obtain, both in the UK and North America. This is because the offence is classified as homicide and not as a sexual offence. The motivation for sexual murder may be very complex. MacCulloch et al. (1983) pointed out in their study of thirteen sadistic offenders in a British high security hospital (not all of them killers) that fantasy played a very important part in the motivation and the preparation leading up to the eventual offence (see also Grubin 1997). In an older but often quoted article, Brittain (1970) (who was qualified as a forensic pathologist and psychiatrist) provided a clinical composite picture of the sadistic sexual killer. It is important to emphasize that Brittain (1970) suggested a *composite* picture and that we should not expect to find all the many features he described in any *single* case (see also Grubin 1994). I have merely selected a few of them for purposes of demonstrating the diversity of psychopathological factors (for a useful critique of Brittain's views, see MacCulloch et al. 2000).

Brittain (1970) suggests that such killers are often withdrawn, introverted, over-controlled, timid and prudish, for example taking offence at 'dirty jokes'. The killer is likely to be over 30 and come from any occupational status, but an unusual number seem to have been employed as butchers or as workers in abattoirs. They often seem to be remarkably ambivalent towards their mothers and their personality profiles appear to show a mass of contradictions with many unresolved psychological conflicts. Their mothers tend to be gentle, over-indulgent, but not particularly maternal. Fathers are notably either absent or, if present, rigidly strict. Such offenders tend to have a keen interest in depictions of torture, atrocities, Nazi activities and regalia, the occult and the more bizarre type of horror film. They frequently keep such materials locked away in a room or a shed. They are said to show an irrational preoccupation with the size of their genitalia, which they unrealistically regard as excessively small. Their sex lives are poor or non-existent. In the course of the offence, the offender may insert articles such as a torch, milk bottle or poker with great force into the victim's vagina or rectum. Their murders, usually carefully planned, are ferocious and bizarre in their execution. Sexual intercourse does not necessarily accompany the murder but they might masturbate beside the corpse. It has been suggested that 'the brutal and murderous assaults actually are a substitute for the sexual act' (Schlesinger and Revitch 1983: 214; see also Revitch and Schlesinger 1981). The prognosis for such offenders is not good and some of them seem to welcome the control afforded by incarceration because they are troubled by their sadistic impulses and activities. However, those in charge of them and who share the responsibility for making recommendations about future dangerousness have to guard against being misled by *appearances* of good behaviour and apparently sincere protestations of reform (see Chapter 10 in this volume).

Cautionary concluding comments

The range of behaviours that constitute sexual offending is vast and complex. It is necessary to reiterate the need for professionals to try to overcome their misconceptions and prejudices so that we may 'hear' what such offenders are saying as non-judgementally as possible. This is very important because the behaviour of some sex offenders not only is bizarre but also may well fill us with revulsion. However, demonstrations of 'dispassionate compassion' should not blind us to the manner in which such offenders or offender-patients may engage in various forms of denial of their behaviour. On the credit side, some sex offenders (and sometimes those convicted of the more serious sex crimes) are distressed and disturbed by their behaviour and its effects upon others; they may have a desire to change. Although there is an undoubted need for the development of sensible typologies, there is also a need to avoid stereotyping and to maintain an open mind. To achieve this, a multi-method and multidisciplinary approach is likely to be the most effective. Sexual offending appears in many guises, and sometimes the most disguised forms may be the most ominous prognostically. In my view, it is premature to talk about 'cure'; in the 'management' of the offender, the work must be towards helping him deal with his impulses in a more acceptable way; the provision of viable alternative forms of behaviour, are perhaps the most we can hope to achieve. Despite the recently established complex systems of registration and other control devices, things can continue to go seriously wrong, as the case of Ian Huntley demonstrated in 2002.

Following his conviction for the murder of two 10-year-old girls, Jessica Chapman and Holly Wells, it became clear that Ian Huntley's previous history rendered him highly unsuitable for work that would bring him into contact with children. His history contained several allegations of unlawful sexual intercourse with under-age girls, an accusation of indecent assault on a 12-year-old girl and four allegations of rape. It was stated that lack of evidence prevented prosecution in nearly all these cases. However, in one of the rape cases, a prosecution was brought but the charges subsequently withdrawn. It emerged that the lines of communication between the Humberside and Cambridgeshire police forces were unsatisfactory, data that should have been retained were prematurely discarded and the provisions of the data protection legislation misinterpreted. It is apparent that even when systems are set up to prevent such eventualities, communication problems and inadequacies in recording (including a certain degree of dilatoriness in initiating adequate records) and inconsistent recording procedures between the various authorities involved, may vitiate best intentions (see also Chapter 10). The decision when to keep information on record, and at what stage to destroy it, is not always easy, but wisdom (and maybe hindsight) would seem to dictate that allegations such as those in the Huntley case would have been singled out for indefinite retention.

Notes

1 Various terms in the vernacular are used to describe these activities and certain others. Some examples are:

- *Fellatio:* giving head, going down on, giving a blow job, sucking off.
- *Cunnilingus:* 'tipping the velvet' – as in Sarah Waters' novel *Tipping the Velvet* (1998) in which she depicts aspects of Victorian lesbianism.
- *Anilingus:* rimming, apposition of the mouth to the anal area, more especially in the gay community.
- *Fisting:* insertion of the fist into the anus – mainly in male homosexual intercourse.
- *Flashing:* indecent exposure.
- *Cottaging:* practice in the male gay community of frequenting public toilets to engage in sexual encounters.

2 Detailed explanations and interpretations of the sections relating to indecent exposure and voyeurism may be found in Stevenson et al. (2004).

3 Unfortunately, there have been a number of instances of vigilantism; the most notable was probably the demonstration in 2001 at Paulsgrove, a suburb of Portsmouth, following the sexual abuse and killing of Sarah Payne. Moves to introduce a form of 'Megan's Law', based on the practice in some US states, have fortunately not been successful. This form of 'outing' was promoted largely by the *News of the World.* In a short but powerful commentary on the long-standing harassment and subsequent alleged murder of a 73-year-old paedophile in the north of England, Paul Vallely emphasizes the importance of 'scapegoating'. He reminds us that in Leviticus (Chapter 16, v. 10) the 'scapegoat was an animal which was symbolically laden with the sins of the community and then driven out into the wilderness'. He continues, 'Societies also do this with people; we make them the Other; offer them up and send them out. The process of demonization is about denying the full humanity of an individual and reducing him to his offence' (*The Independent*, 12 December 2003). The sex offenders registration scheme introduced by the Sex Offenders Act 1997 does not allow public access to those required to be registered within its terms. However, such access is permitted in the United States. In a thoughtful contribution Thomas (2003) gives cogent reasons why the adoption of 'open access' in the UK would raise a number of problematic issues (see also Winick 2002). The sex offenders registration scheme was supplemented by the Crime and Disorder Act 1998. It allows magistrates to impose certain restrictions on a sex offender (such as control of their movements) whose behaviour indicates they might do serious harm. There is also provision under the Police Act 1997 for the issue, in certain circumstances, of certificates indicating a person's previous convictions (or lack of them). One of the aims of such certification is to prevent sex offenders from securing employment which would bring them into contact with children (for critical comment, see West 2000; Home Office 2007a; Thomas 2008).

4 Advances in communication technology have many benefits, but they have also produced hazards, some of which could not perhaps have been readily foreseen. In recent times there have been a number of cases where paedophiles have been able to 'groom' children and young people via the Internet. In September 2003, one Internet provider, *Microsoft*, announced that it was closing its 'chatrooms' to 'curb [the] paedophile threat' (*The Independent*, 24 September 2003). The manner in which paedophiles may use the Internet to 'fuel' their fantasies is described by Wilson and Jones (2008; see also Laulik et al. 2007; Sheldon and Howitt 2008). More general concerns regarding grooming have now been reflected in the

provisions of the Sexual Offences Act 2003. The associated problem of making indecent images of children is dealt with under Sections 45 and 46 of the Act and the Court of Appeal has issued detailed guidelines on sentencing in such cases (see Stone 2003b). In 2009 the government introduced further proposed safeguards, not only in respect of Internet safety but also, as already mentioned in this chapter, somewhat Draconian restrictions upon those having almost any kind of innocent activity with children, for example, escorting them to sports activities.

5 Some readers might consider it a moot point as to whether young women might contribute to their situation by allowing themselves to become intoxicated by alcohol or other drugs. This would apply, of course, to non-surreptitious consumption. It might certainly have a considerable bearing on the issue of consent; some prosecutors might even suggest a degree of what the civil law would describe as 'contributory negligence'. This, of course, in no way excuses the assailant. In an interesting article Horvath and Brown (2007) explore some of these issues. Less attention seems to have been paid to the psychological effects of being accused of sexual offences (see Aslan 2008).

Acts

Crime and Disorder Act 1998
Criminal Justice Act 1925
Criminal Justice and Public Order Act 1994
Mental Health Act 1959
Mental Health Act 1983
Police Act 1997
Punishment of Incest Act 1908
Sexual Offences Act 1956
Sexual Offences (Amendment) Act 1976
Sexual Offences Act 2003
Sexual Offenders Act 1997
Vagrancy Act 1824

References

American Psychiatric Association (APA) (2005) *Diagnostic and Statistical Manual of Mental Disorders*, 4th edn (text revision) (DSM-IV-TR), Washington, DC: APA.

Amir, M. (1971) *Patterns of Forcible Rape*, Chicago, IL: University of Chicago Press.

Aslan, D. (2008) 'Psychological Aspects of Coping with Being Accused of Sexual Offences', *British Journal of Forensic Practice* 10: 19–35.

Bagley, C. (1992) 'Characteristics of 60 Children and Adolescents with a History of Sexual Assault against Others: Evidence from a Comparative Study', *Journal of Forensic Psychiatry* 3: 299–309.

Banbury, S. (2004) 'Coercive Sexual Behaviour in British Prisons as Reported by Adult Ex-Prisoners', *Howard Journal of Criminal Justice* 43: 113–130.

Bancroft, J. (1989) *Human Sexuality and its Problems*, 2nd edn, London: Churchill Livingstone.

—— (1991) 'The Sexuality of Offending: The Social Dimension', *Criminal Behaviour and Mental Health* 1: 181–192.

Barbaree, H.F., Langton, C.M., Blanchard, R. and Boer, D.P. (2008) 'Predicting Recidivism in Sex Offenders Using the SVR-20: The Contribution of Age-at-Release', *International Journal of Forensic Mental Health* 7: 47–64.

Batten, D.A. (1983) 'Incest: A Review of the Literature', *Medicine, Science and the Law* 23: 245–253.

Beck, R. (n.d.) *Rape from Afar: Men Exposing to Women and Children* (unpublished study), University College of Wales, Cardiff.

Beech, A., Fisher, D., Beckett, R. and Scott-Fordham, A. (1998) *An Evaluation of the Prison Sex Offender Treatment Programme*, Research Findings no. 79, London: Home Office Research, Development and Statistics Directorate.

Bennetto, J. (1995) 'Victims of Flashing "Perceive Threat of Rape or Murder"', *The Independent*, 24 July.

Bilby, C., Brooks-Gordon, B. and Wells, H. (2006) 'A Systematic Review of Psychological Interventions for Sexual Offenders – II Quasi-Experimental Data', *Journal of Forensic Psychiatry and Psychology* 17: 467–484.

Bluglass, R. (1979) 'Incest', *British Journal of Hospital Medicine* 22: 152–157.

—— (1982) 'Assessing Dangerousness in Sex Offenders', in J.R. Hamilton and H. Freeman (eds) *Dangerousness: Psychiatric Assessment and Management*, London: Gaskell.

Brandon, S., Boakes, J. and Glaser, D. (1998) 'Recovered Memories of Childhood Sexual Abuse: Implications from Clinical Practice', *British Journal of Psychiatry* 172: 296–307.

Brewin, C.R. (1996) 'Scientific Status of Recovered Memories', *British Journal of Psychiatry* 169: 131–134.

Briggs, D. (1994) 'Assessment of Sexual Offenders', in M. McMurran and J. Hodge (eds) *The Assessment of Criminal Behaviour in Clients in Secure Settings*, London: Jessica Kingsley.

Brittain, R.P. (1970) 'The Sadistic Murderer', *Medicine, Science and the Law* 10: 198–208.

Brogden, M. and Nijhar, P. (2000) *Crime, Abuse and the Elderly*, Cullompton: Willan.

Brooks-Gordon, B., Bilby, C. and Wells, H. (2006) 'A Systematic Review of Psychological Interventions for Sexual Offenders I: Randomised Control Trials', *Journal of Forensic Psychiatry and Psychology* 17: 442–466.

Brown, S., Deakin, J. and Spencer, J. (2008) 'What People Think about the Management of Sex Offenders in the Community', *Howard Journal of Criminal Justice* 47: 259–274.

Cann, J., Falshaw, L. and Friendship, C. (2004) 'Sexual Offenders Discharged from Prison in England and Wales: A 21-Year Reconviction Study', *Legal and Criminological Psychology* 9: 1–10.

Clark, C. and Mezey, G. (1997) 'Elderly Sex Offenders against Children: A Descriptive Study of Child Sex Offenders Over the Age of 65', *Journal of Forensic Psychiatry* 8: 357–369.

Cooper, I. and Cormier, B. (1990) 'Incest', in R. Bluglass and P. Bowden (eds) *Principles and Practice of Forensic Psychiatry*, London: Churchill Livingstone.

Cox, D.J. and McMahon, B. (1978) 'Incidents of Male Exhibitionism in the United

States of America as Reported by Victimised Female College Students', *International Journal of Law and Psychiatry* 1: 453–457.

Craissati, J. (2004) *Managing High Risk Sex Offenders in the Community: A Psychological Approach*, Cullompton: Willan.

Dalzell, T. and Victor, T. (eds) (2006) *Dictionary of Slang and Unconventional English*, Volume 1, London: Routledge.

Dare, C. (1993) 'Denial and Childhood Sexual Abuse', *Journal of Forensic Psychiatry* 4: 1–4.

Davidson, J. (2007) *The Greeks and Greek Love: A Radical Re-Appraisal of Homosexuality in Ancient Greece*, London: Weidenfeld & Nicolson.

Davis, N. and Geis, G. (eds) (2001) *Sexual Deviance*, Volume 3 of *Encyclopaedia of Criminology and Deviant Behaviour*, Hove: Brunner-Routledge.

Duffield, G., Hassiotis, A. and Vizard, E. (1998) 'Zoophilia in Young Sex Abusers', *Journal of Forensic Psychiatry* 9: 294–304.

Fisher, D. and Mair, G. (1998) *A Review of Classification for Sex Offenders*, Research Findings no. 78, London: Home Office Research, Development and Statistics Directorate.

Fowles, T. and Wilson, D. (2008) 'Penal Policy File 118', *Howard Journal of Criminal Justice* 48: 92–104.

Freud, S. (1960) *Totem and Taboo*, London: Routledge & Kegan Paul.

Friendship, C., Blud, L., Erikson, M. and Travers, R. (2002) *An Evaluation of Cognitive Behavioural Treatment for Prisoners*, Research Findings no. 161, London: Home Office Research, Development and Statistics Directorate.

Fudge, E. (2000) 'Monstrous Acts: Bestiality in Early Modern England', *History Today* 50: 20–25.

Gayford, J.J. (1981) 'Indecent Exposure: A Review of the Literature', *Medicine, Science and the Law* 21: 233–242.

—— (1997) 'Disorders of Sexual Preference: A Review of the Literature', *Medicine, Science and the Law* 37: 303–315.

Gibbens, T.C.N., Way, C. and Soothill, K.L. (1978) 'Siblings and Child Incest Offenders', *British Journal of Criminology* 18: 14–52.

Gittleson, N.L., Eacott, S.E. and Mehta, B.M. (1978) 'Victims of Indecent Exposure', *British Journal of Psychiatry* 132: 61–66.

Gordon, H. (2008) Editorial: 'The Treatment of Paraphilias: An Historical Perspective', *Criminal Behaviour and Mental Health* 18: 79–87.

Groth, A.N. and Hobson, W.F. (1983) 'The Dynamics of Sexual Assault', in L.B. Schlesinger and E. Revitch (eds) *Sexual Dynamics of Anti-Social Behaviour*, Springfield, IL: Charles C. Thomas.

Grubin, D. (1994) 'Sexual Murder', *British Journal of Psychiatry* 165: 624–629.

—— (1997) 'Predictors of Risk in Serious Sex Offenders', in C. Duggan (ed.) *Assessing Risk in the Mentally Disordered, British Journal of Psychiatry* 170 (suppl. 32).

—— (2002) 'The Potential Use of Polygraphy in Forensic Psychiatry', *Criminal Behaviour and Mental Health: Special Supplement* 12: S45–S53.

Grubin, D. and Kennedy, H.G. (1991) 'The Classification of Sexual Offenders', *Criminal Behaviour and Mental Health* 1: 123–139.

Grubin, D. and Madsen, L. (2005) 'Lie Detection and the Polygraph: A Historical Review', *Journal of Forensic Psychiatry and Psychology* 16: 357–369.

—— (2006) 'Accuracy and Utility of Post-Conviction Polygraph Testing of Sex Offenders', *British Journal of Psychiatry* 188: 479–483.

Gudjonsson, G. (1997) 'Members of the British False Memory Society: The Legal Consequences of the Accusations of the Families', *Journal of Forensic Psychiatry* 8: 348–356.

Hedderman, C. and Sugg, D. (1996) *Does Treating Sex Offenders Reduce Offending?*, Research Findings no. 45, London: Home Office Research, Development and Statistics Directorate.

HM Crown Prosecution Service Inspectorate and HM Inspectorate of Constabulary (HMCPSI and HMIC) (2007) *Without Consent: A Report on the Joint Review of the Investigation and Prosecution of Rape Offences*, London: HM Inspectorate of Constabulary.

Home Office (2000) *Setting the Boundaries: Reforming the Law on Sexual Offences and Review of Part I of the Sex Offenders Act, 1997 (Vols. I and II)*, London: Home Office Communications Directorate.

—— (2007a) *Review of the Protection of Children from Sex Offenders*, London: Home Office.

—— (2007b) *Statistical Bulletin 11/07: Crime in England and Wales 2006/07*, London: Home Office Research, Development and Statistics Directorate.

Hood, R., Shute, S., Feilzer, M. and Wilcox, A. (2002) *Reconviction Rates of Serious Sex Offenders and Assessments of Their Risk*, Research Findings no. 164, London: Home Office Research, Development and Statistics Directorate.

Horvath, M. and Brown, M. (2007) 'Alcohol as a Drug of Choice: Is Drug Assisted Rape a Misnomer?', *Psychology, Crime and Law* 13: 417–429.

Howitt, D. (1995) *Paedophiles and Sexual Offences against Children*, Chichester: Wiley.

Hucker, S. (1990) 'Necrophilia and Other Unusual Philias', in R. Bluglass and P. Bowden (eds) *Principles and Practice of Forensic Psychiatry*, London: Churchill Livingstone.

Huckle, P.L. (1995) 'Male Rape Victims Referred to a Forensic-Psychiatric Service', *Medicine, Science and the Law* 35: 187–192.

Janes, L. (2007) 'Children Who Commit Sexual Offences: Some Legal Anomalies and Practical Approaches to the Law', *Howard Journal of Criminal Justice* 46: 493–499.

Jeary, K. (2004) 'Sexual Abuse of Elderly People: Would We Rather Not Know the Details?', *Journal of Adult Protection* 6: 21–30.

—— (2005) 'Sexual Abuse and Offending against Elderly People: A Focus on Perpetrators and Victims', *Journal of Forensic Psychiatry and Psychology* 16: 328–343.

Jones, I.H. and Frei, D. (1977) 'Provoked Anxiety as a Treatment of Exhibitionism', *British Journal of Psychiatry* 131: 295–300.

Kaul, A. (1993) 'Sex Offenders – Cure or Management?', *Medicine, Science and the Law* 33: 207–212.

Kaul, A. and Duffy, S. (1991) 'Gerontophilia: A Case Report', *Medicine, Science and the Law* 31: 110–114.

King, M., Coxell, A. and Mezey, G. (2002) 'Sexual Molestation of Males: Association With Psychological Disturbance', *British Journal of Psychiatry* 181: 153–157.

Knight, B. (1979) 'Fatal Masochism – Accident or Suicide?', *Medicine, Science and the Law* 19: 118–120.

Knowles, G.J. (1999) 'Male Prison Rape: A Search for Causation and Prevention', *Howard Journal of Criminal Justice* 38: 267–282.

Lanyon, R.I. (1991) 'Theories of Sex Offending', in C.R. Hollin and K. Howells (eds) *Clinical Approaches to Sex Offenders and their Victims*, Chichester: Wiley.

Laulik, S., Allan, J. and Sheridan, L. (2007) 'An Investigation into Maladaptive Personality Functioning in Internet Sex Officers', *Psychology, Crime and Law* 13: 523–535.

Launay, G. (1994) 'The Phallometric Measurement of Sex Offenders: Some Professional and Research Issues', *Criminal Behaviour and Mental Health* 4: 48–70.

—— (1999) 'The Phallometric Assessment of Sex Offenders: An Up-Date', *Criminal Behaviour and Mental Health* 9: 254–274.

Lincoln, C. (2001) 'Genital Injury: Is It Significant? A Review of the Literature', *Medicine, Science and the Law* 41: 206–216.

Lloyd, C. (1991) 'Changes in the Pattern and Nature of Sex Offences', *Criminal Behaviour and Mental Health* 1: 115–122.

Lloyd, C. and Walmsley, R. (1989) *Changes in Rape Offences and Sentencing*, London: Home Office Research and Planning Unit.

Löbmann, R., Greve, W., Wetzels, P. and Bosold, C. (2003) 'Violence against Women: Consequences and Coping', *Psychology, Crime and Law* 9: 309–331.

McCartan, K. (2004) 'Here There Be Monsters: The Public's Perception of Paedophiles with Particular Reference to Belfast and Leicester', *Medicine, Science and the Law* 44: 327–342.

MacCulloch, M.J. and Waddington, J.L. (1981) 'Neuroendocrine Mechanisms and the Aetiology of Male and Female Homosexuality', *British Journal of Psychiatry* 139: 341–345.

MacCulloch, M.J., Snowden, P.R. and Wood, P.J.W. (1983) 'Sadistic Fantasy, Sadistic Behaviour and Offending', *British Journal of Psychiatry* 143: 20–29.

MacCulloch, M., Gray, N. and Watt, A. (2000) 'Brittain's Sadistic Murderer Syndrome Revisited: An Associative Account of the Aetiology of Sadistic Sexual Fantasy', *Journal of Forensic Psychiatry* 11: 401–418.

MacDonald, J.M. (1973) *Indecent Exposure*, Springfield, IL: Charles C. Thomas.

MacPherson, G.J.D. (2003) 'Predicting Escalation in Sexually Violent Recidivism: Use of the SYR-20 and PCL 54 to Predict Outcome with Non-Contact Recidivists and Contact Recidivists', *Journal of Forensic Psychiatry and Psychology* 14: 615–627.

Manderville-Norden, R., Beech, A. and Hayes, F. (2008) 'Examining the Effectiveness of a UK Community-Based Sexual Offender Treatment Programme for Child Abusers', *Psychology, Crime and Law* 14: 493–512.

Masson, J. (1985) *The Assault on Truth: Freud's Suppression of the Seduction Theory*, Harmondsworth: Penguin.

Masters, B. (1993) *The Shrine of Jeffrey Dahmer*, London: Hodder & Stoughton.

Matravers, A. (2003) *Sex Offenders in the Community: Managing and Reducing the Risk*, Cullompton: Willan.

—— (2005) 'Understanding Women Sex Offenders', *Criminology in Cambridge: Newsletter of the Institute of Criminology* May: 9–13.

Mezey, G., King, M., Vizard, E., Hawkes, C. and Austin, E. (1991) 'A Community Treatment Programme for Convicted Child Sex Offenders: A Preliminary Report', *Journal of Forensic Psychiatry* 2: 11–25.

Muir, G. and Macleod, M.D. (2003) 'The Demographic and Spatial Patterns of Recorded Rape in a Large UK Metropolitan Area', *Psychology, Crime and Law* 9: 345–355.

Mullen, P. (1990) 'The Long-term Influence of Sexual Assault on the Mental Health of Victims', *Journal of Forensic Psychiatry* 1: 14–34.

Myhill, A. and Allen, J. (2002) *Rape and Sexual Assault of Women: Findings from the British Crime Survey*, Research Findings no. 159, London: Home Office Research, Development and Statistics Directorate.

O'Connor, A. (1987) 'Female Sex Offenders', *British Journal of Psychiatry* 150: 615–620.

Oxnam, P. and Vess, J. (2008) 'A Typology of Adolescent Sexual Offenders: Millon Adolescent Clinical Inventory Profiles, Developmental Factors and Offence Characteristics', *Journal of Forensic Psychiatry and Psychology* 19: 228–242.

Perkins, D. (1991) 'Clinical Work with Sex Offenders in Secure Settings', in C.R. Hollin and K. Howells (eds) *Clinical Approaches to Sex Offenders and their Victims*, Chichester: Wiley.

Pisani, E. (2008) *The Wisdom of Whores: Bureaucrats, Brothels and the Business of AIDS*, London: Granta.

Pithers, W.D., Gray, A. and Davis, M.E. (2002) 'Investing in the Future of Children: Building Programs for Children or Prisons for Adult Offenders', in B.J. Winick and J. LaFond (eds) *Protecting Society from Sexually Dangerous Offenders: Law Justice and Therapy*, Washington, DC: American Psychological Association.

Prins, H. (1991) *Bizarre Behaviours: Boundaries of Psychiatric Disorder*, London: Routledge.

—— (2005) *Offenders, Deviants or Patients?*, 3rd edn, London: Routledge.

Revitch, E. and Schlesinger, L.B. (1981) *Psychopathology of Homicide*, Springfield, IL: Charles C. Thomas.

Rex, S. and Bottoms, A. (2003) 'Evaluating the Evaluators: Researching the Accreditation of Offender Programmes', *Probation: The Journal of Community and Criminal Justice* 50: 359–368.

Riordan, S. (1999) 'Indecent Exposure: The Impact Upon the Victim's Fear of Sexual Crime', *Journal of Forensic Psychiatry* 10: 309–316.

Rooth, F.G. (1975) 'Indecent Exposure and Exhibitionism', in T. Silverstone and B. Barraclough (eds) *Contemporary Psychiatry*, Ashford: Headley Brothers.

Rupp, J.C. (1970) 'Sudden Death in the Gay World', *Medicine, Science and the Law* 10: 189–191.

Saint-Martin, P., Bouyssy, M. and O'Byrne, P. (2007) 'Analysis of 756 Cases of Sexual Assault in Tours (France)', *Medicine, Science and the Law* 47: 315–324.

Schlesinger, L.B. and Revitch, E. (eds) (1983) *Sexual Dynamics of Anti-Social Human Behaviour*, Springfield, IL: Charles C. Thomas.

Scott, P.D. (1964) 'Definition, Classification, Prognosis and Treatment', in I. Rosen (ed.) *The Pathology and Treatment of Sexual Deviation*, London: Oxford University Press.

Sheldon, K. and Howitt, D. (2008) 'Sexual Fantasy in Paedophilic Offenders: Can

Sex – lawful and unlawful 281

Any Model Explain Satisfactorily New Findings from a Study of Internet and Contact Sexual Officers?', *Legal and Criminological Psychology* 13: 137–158.
Silverman, J. and Wilson, D. (2002) *Innocence Betrayed: Paedophilia, the Media and Society*, Cambridge: Polity Press.
Smith, A. and Taylor, P.J. (1999) 'Serious Sex Offending Against Women by Men with Schizophrenia: Relationship of Illness and Psychotic Symptoms to Offending', *British Journal of Psychiatry* 174: 233–237.
Snaith, R.P. and Collins, S.A. (1981) 'Five Exhibitionists and a Method of Treatment', *British Journal of Psychiatry* 138: 126–130.
Soothill, K., Francis, B., Ackerley, E. and Fligelstone, R. (2002) *Murder and Serious Sexual Assault: What Criminal Histories Can Reveal about Future Serious Offending*, Police Research Series Paper 144, London: Home Office Research, Development and Statistics Directorate.
Soothill, K., Peelo, M., Pearson, J. and Francis, B. (2004) 'The Reporting Trajectories of Top Homicide Cases in the Media: A Case Study of *The Times*', *Howard Journal of Criminal Justice* 43: 1–14.
Spataro, J., Mullen, P.E., Burgess, P.M., Wells, D.L. and Moss, S.A. (2004) 'Impact of Child Sexual Abuse on Mental Health: Prospective Study in Males and Females', *British Journal of Psychiatry* 184: 416–421.
Stevenson, K., Davies, A. and Gunn, M. (2004) *Blackstone's Guide to the Sexual Offences Act, 2003*, Oxford: Oxford University Press.
Stone, N. (2003a) 'In Court: Rape: New Guidelines', *Probation Journal: The Journal of Community and Criminal Justice* 50: 182–183.
—— (2003b) 'In Court: Indecent Images of Children', *Probation Journal: The Journal of Community and Criminal Justice* 50: 315–319.
—— (2003c) 'In Court: Generic Application of Rape Guidelines', *Probation Journal: The Journal of Community and Criminal Justice* 50: 413–414.
—— (2008) 'In Court: Sentencing for Exposure', *Probation Journal: Journal of Community and Criminal Justice* 55: 212–213.
Studer, L.H., Clelland, S.R., Aylwin, A.S., Reddon, J.R. and Monro, A. (2000) 'Rethinking Risk Assessment for Incest Offenders', *International Journal of Law and Psychiatry* 23: 15–22.
Sugarman, P., Dumughn, C., Saad, K., Hinder, S. and Bluglass, R. (1994) 'Dangerousness in Exhibitionists', *Journal of Forensic Psychiatry* 5: 287–296.
Thomas, T. (2003) 'Sex Offender Community Notification: Experiences from America', *Howard Journal of Criminal Justice* 42: 217–228.
—— (2008) 'The Sex Offender Register: A Case Study in Function Creep', *Howard Journal of Criminal Justice* 47: 227–237.
Vizard, E., Hickey, N., French, L. and McCrory, E. (2007) 'Children and Adolescents Who Present with Sexually Abusive Behaviour: A UK Descriptive Study', *Journal of Forensic Psychiatry and Psychology* 18: 59–73.
West, D.J. (1992) *Male Prostitution: Gay Services in London*, London: Duckworth.
—— (2000) 'Paedophilia: Plague or Panic', *Journal of Forensic Psychiatry* 11: 511–531.
West, D.J., Roy, C. and Nicols, F.L. (1978) *Understanding Sexual Attacks*, London: Heinemann.
Wilson, D. and Jones, T. (2008) 'In My Own World: A Case Study of a Paedophile's

Thinking and Doing and his Use of the Internet', *Howard Journal of Criminal Justice* 47: 107–120.

Winick, B. (2002) 'A Therapeutic Analysis of Sex Offender Registration and Community Notification Laws', in B.J. Winick and J. LaFond (eds) *Protecting Society from Sexually Dangerous Offenders: Law, Justice and Therapy*, Washington, DC: American Psychological Association.

Yap, A.K., Lim, L.E., Ong, S.H. and Chan, A.O.M. (2002) 'Personality of Males Charged with Outrages of Modesty', *Medicine, Science and the Law* 42: 167–171.

Further reading

It is hoped that the works cited in the text will afford useful additional reading. The implications arising from the implementation of the Sexual Offences Act 2003 are described thoroughly in Stevenson, K., Davies, A. and Gunn, M. (2004) *Blackstone's Guide to the Sexual Offences Act 2003*. Oxford: Oxford University Press.

A very readable and well researched socio-historical account of rape from 1860 to the present day is provided in Bourke, J. (2007) *Rape: A History from 1860 to the Present Day*, London: Virago.

One of the most important official publications to appear recently concerning rape is HM Crown Prosecution Service Inspectorate and HM Inspectorate of Constabulary's (2007) joint report *Without Consent*. I have referred to it only briefly in this chapter, but the entire report merits the most careful study: HMCPSI and HMIC (2007) *Without Consent: A Report on the Joint Review of the Investigation and Prosecution of Rape Offences*, London: HMIC.

For a very recent account of perspectives on sex offending and its management, see Special Issue of *Psychology, Crime and Law*, Vol. 16, Nos. 1–2 January–February, 2010. (Eds Woodhams, N. and Hatcher, R.).

See also the Stern Review of Rape Cases. Stern, Baroness Vivien (2010). *Rape Review*, London: Government Equalities Office.

Chapter 9

No smoke without fire

> What an immense stack of timber can be set ablaze by the tiniest spark.
> (Letter of James, *New English Bible*, 3: 5)

> Fire is a good servant but a bad master.
> (*Seventeenth-century proverb*)

Both the above quotations emphasize the damage that can be caused by the improper and illegal use of fire. In this chapter I shall use the term arson (the legal term in the UK), but in other jurisdictions arson is often described as fire-raising, fire-setting, incendiarism, and clinically as pyromania and pathological fire-raising. I use the term arson for purposes of simplicity since it can be used to cover all the aforementioned descriptive terms. Arson is correctly viewed as a very serious form of offending. The reasons are not hard to discern. First, its detection (even by the most modern forensic science methods) can be extremely difficult. Second, it may involve numerous victims; sometimes these may be in addition to those originally intended as such. Third, it may be committed at one remove by the offender. This chapter contains, first, a brief historical context; second, a short exposition of the law in the UK; third, some brief statistics on the size of the problem, and fourth, a discussion of some aspects of classification and management.

The motivations of arsonists are complex, and courts are inclined to call for psychiatric reports in all but the most *apparently* straightforward of cases. I emphasize the word *apparently* because even what appear to be the clearest of motives (such as setting a fire in order to claim insurance compensation for a failing business) may be associated with an underlying psychiatric problem (see Prins 1994, 2001). However, Soothill (1991) has wisely suggested caution against seeking psychiatric explanations in cases where the behaviour is merely baffling, since this tends to 'medicalize' socially problematic behaviour.

Context

As is well known, fire may be both used and abused. The phenomenon has played a prominent part both in biblical texts and in mythology. Examples include the legend of the Phoenix, which lived for hundreds of years, burned itself to death and then rose again from its ashes; of Prometheus, who stole fire from the Gods and who became the origin of much later psychoanalytic theorizing about fire-raising; the neophyte youth Phaeton who, having lost control of his father's (Helios) chariot, was killed by Zeus with a thunderbolt before he could cause further harm. In the more factual pages of history, we can find many references to incendiary mixtures and devices. MacDonald (1977) alludes to interesting sketches of mortars made by Leonardo da Vinci. In the sixteenth century there are descriptions of various complex 'noxious engines' that made use of explosive devices to cause horrifying injuries to those within range. In more recent times (and notably in the mid-nineteenth century) it appears that the medical profession began to turn its attention to explanations of fire-raising behaviour and, at a later date, psychoanalysts put forward various complex if somewhat controversial explanations linking fire-raising behaviour to sexual dysfunction of one kind or another. Although classical psychoanalytic explanations of fire-raising behaviour (based largely on Freudian interpretation of the myth of Prometheus) do not find much favour nowadays, it is fair to say that sexual *dysfunction* is found not infrequently in the backgrounds of some persistent fire-raisers (see Hurley and Monahan 1969; MacDonald 1977; A. Barker 1994; Prins 1994; for a more detailed account of the relationship between arson and sexuality, see Prins 2001). It is of more than passing interest to note the extent to which the phenomenon of fire is often linguistically linked to aggression and sexuality. For example, we speak or write of 'white hot' rage, 'heated arguments', 'enflamed passions', to have the 'hots' for someone of the opposite (or same) sex, 'to burn with desire' – and so on. Language represents cultural values and can be very influential in our modes of thinking about the existence of fire in its many powerful forms.[1]

The law in the UK

Arson

The law relating to arson would appear to have a lengthy history. Geller (1992) states that:

> Ancient Roman legal texts recognized arson and defined penalties for this offence. In France, prior to the French Revolution, deliberate arson was punished by death – hanging for commoners and

decapitation for nobles. Under some circumstances, arsonists were burned alive . . . In Britain, during the reign of George II convicted arsonists . . . were banished from the country.

(Geller 1992: 283)

The legal definition of arson varies from one country to the next; no attempt is made to define it internationally. Other jurisdictions have comparable statutes and penalties. The word itself is derived from Anglo and old French and from medieval Latin *ardere – ars* to burn (*Concise Oxford English Dictionary*). In England and Wales, prior to 1971, the offence of arson was dealt with under Common Law. Currently, it is dealt with under the provisions of the Criminal Damage Act 1971. Similar provisions apply in Northern Ireland. In Scotland, it is dealt with currently under a number of Common Law offences such as 'wilful fire-raising' and 'culpable and reckless fire-raising'. Section 1 of the Criminal Damage Act 1971 states as follows:

(1) A person who without lawful excuse destroys or damages any property belonging to another intending to destroy or damage any such property or being reckless as to whether any such property would be destroyed or damaged shall be guilty of an offence.
(2) A person who without lawful excuse destroys or damages any property, whether belonging to himself or another –
  (a) intending to destroy or damage any property or being reckless as to whether any such property would be destroyed or damaged; and
  (b) intending by the destruction or damage to endanger the life of another or being reckless as to whether the life of another would be thereby endangered;
  shall be guilty of an offence.
(3) An offence committed under this section by destroying or damaging property by fire *shall be charged as arson* (italics added).[2]

Under Section 4 of the Act, the offences of both arson and endangering life are punishable with maximum penalties of life imprisonment, the latter being used most frequently in cases of persistent fire-raising behaviour where severe personality disorder associated with vengeful feelings may be in evidence. In addition, similar cases and those in which clearly definable mental disorder may be involved, are sometimes dealt with in England and Wales by way of the mental health legislation (Mental Health Act 1983, Hospital Order with Restrictions, Sections 37/41, as amended by the Mental Health Act 2007).

How much of a problem

I have already made reference to the problems involved in determining whether a fire has been caused 'maliciously by deliberate ignition', or by accident. This accounts for the seemingly wide disparity between the figures recorded in the annual *Fire Statistics* issued by the Department of Communities and Local Government (2008a, 2008b) and the number of offences of arson brought before the courts. Some brief statistics may help to inform this picture. In 2006, Local Authority Fire and Rescue Services (Fire Brigades) attended 862,100 fires and false alarms in the UK; 79 per cent of all fires were outdoors and 13 per cent in side dwellings. Despite these large numbers, the latest *Fire Statistics* show the number of deliberate fires (including arson) decreased by 9 per cent and deaths from fires showed a continuing downward trend, being the lowest since 1959. As did non-fatal road vehicle fires – the lowest number of road vehicle fires in a twelve-year period from 1995. There was also a 6 per cent fall in the number of arson offences recorded by the police (see Table 9.1).

Although the above trends give cause for a degree of optimism, the financial and other costs involved in fire incidents of all types is enormous. These place huge demands upon financial institutions such as the insurance industry. One notable feature in this respect has been the huge cost of fires in schools and in the deliberate firing of discarded motor vehicles. These activities seem to be mainly due to the activities of disaffected young people. However, not all motor vehicle fires can be laid at the door of such disaffected youth. Insurance companies are well aware of cases where a motor vehicle may be fired in order to claim on an insurance policy, or used as a means of ending a hire-purchase liability. Readers interested in pursuing these particular phenomena should consult the regular Arson Intelligence Newsletters issued by the Arson Prevention Bureau under the auspices of the Association of British Insurers (address given under Further Reading at the end of this chapter). In addition, the newsletters contain very useful descriptions of the pioneering preventive liaison work among young people, into the hazards of fires and its possible consequences, being undertaken by social services, fire, police and psychology departments.

Why do they do it? Classification and management

Numerous attempts have been made to provide typologies of arsonists; the first large-scale attempt being the well-known early study by Lewis and Yarnell (1951). (For an account of this study, and of some later attempts to provide typologies during recent years, see Prins 1994: 99). Two broad, useful groupings were proposed by Faulk (1994). Group I consisted of those cases in which the fire served as a means to an end (for example, revenge, fraud, or a plea for help); Group II consisted of those cases where

Table 9.1 Recorded offences of arson for the years 2002–07

2002/3	2003/4	2004/5	2005/6	2006/7
53,552	57,546	43,368	45,731	43,103

Note: The *actual* number of *prosecutions and convictions* for arson year on year stands between 2500 and 3000.

Source: Home Office (2007: 39)

Table 9.2 A suggested classification of arsonists

• Arson committed for financial reward (insurance, fraud, etc.)
• Arson committed to cover up another crime (for example, burglary or homicide)
• Arson committed for political purposes (terrorist and associated activities)
• Self-immolation as a political gesture (strictly speaking, not arson as such, but included here for completeness: see Prins 1994)
• Arson committed for mixed motives (for example, during a phase of minor depression, as a cry for help, or under the influence of alcohol or other drugs)
• Arson due to the presence of formal mental disorder (for example, severe affective disorder, schizophrenic illness, organic mental disorder, learning disability)
• Arson due to motives of revenge, against either an individual or individuals, or society, or others, more generally
• Arson committed as an attention-seeking act (but excluding the mixed motives set out above and arson committed as a means of deriving sexual satisfaction and/or excitement (for example, pyromania); these forms of arson are described by some authorities as 'pathological'
• Fire-raising by young adults ('vandalistic')
• Arson by children

Note: In a retrospective study of 153 adult arsonists, who had been referred to him for psychiatric examination, Rix (1994) broadened our original classification to include: *desire for rehousing, carelessness, antidepressant* (to relieve feelings of depression) and *proxy*, in which the offender had acted on behalf of another who had borne a grudge. Jayaraman and Frazer (2006) conducted a follow-up study of Rix's (1994) work, reaching similar conclusions. They recommended that comparative studies be made of arsonists in prisons, hospitals and the community.

the *fire itself* was the phenomenon of interest. In 1985, two psychiatrist colleagues and I examined the files of 113 imprisoned arsonists eligible for parole (Prins et al. 1985). From this small-scale and highly selected sample, we derived the classification shown in Table 9.2.

Although this rudimentary classification has been adopted over the years by a number of workers, it has certain weaknesses. For example, it collates the *behavioural* characteristics of fire-raisers, various *types* of fire-raisers and their *motives*. In a very comprehensive and critical review of the psychiatric literature on arson, Ann Barker (1994) underlines some of the weaknesses of our classification. For example, where we categorised in sub-heading (f) fire-raising due to formal mental disorder, she suggests that this relies heavily upon 'a description of mental states, which may merely affect motivation, rather than being in themselves motives' (Barker 1994: 16–17). She favours future classifications being 'elaborated in terms of multi-axial systems of description, analogous to that found in DSMIII(R)' (Barker 1994: 20). She goes on to suggest that

> such a system emphasizes the notion of arson merely as a symptom to be viewed in the context of the whole person, not only to delineate different syndromes of arsonists, but also to identify individual points of therapeutic intervention and future dangerousness.
>
> (Barker 1994: 20)

In another important contribution, Canter and Fritzon (1998) have suggested that more will be gained from concentrating upon the *settings* in which arson takes place as a means of sharpening typologies. They suggest four 'themes to arson'.

> *Two* relate to expressive acts (a) those that are realized within the arsonist's own feelings, being analogous to suicide, and (b) those that are acted on objects, like the burning of symbolic buildings. The other two relate to instrumental acts (c) those that are for personal indulgence, similar to personal revenge, and (d) those that have an object focus, such as hiding evidence from a crime.
>
> (Canter and Fritzon 1998: 73)

Subsequent work by Fritzon and colleagues has confirmed the usefulness of the approach: see, for example, Almond et al. (2005) and Miller and Fritzon (2007).

Such research (which seems to derive to some extent from recent work on offender profiling), would seem to have considerable potential for future developments in classification.

Characteristics and motivation

Arsonists appear to be *mostly* young adult males and many of them have considerable relationship difficulties. A large proportion have problems with alcohol and some of them are of below average intelligence (see Murphy and Clare 1996; Taylor et al. 2002; Devaprian et al. 2007). When women commit repeated acts of fire-raising and have some accompanying degree of mental disorder, however slight, they are more likely than their male counterparts to be given a psychiatric disposal (see Coid et al. 1999; Noblett and Nelson 2001; Dickens et al. 2007; Wachi et al. 2007).

Studies of arsonists indicate considerable evidence of abuse and unstable childhoods and serious psychological disturbance, particularly among females. However, despite media presentations to the contrary, and as already indicated, a *direct* sexual motivation for arson is rare, though many arsonists have problems in making satisfactory personal and sexual relationships. Those who engage in arson for purposes of revenge are likely to be potentially the most dangerous. Such persons are like the monster in Mary Shelley's *Frankenstein*, who says 'I am malicious because I am miserable'. These are the arsonists who have problems in dealing with their feelings of anger and frustration at real or imagined wrongs. I now provide a short account of some of the main motivational aspects. For a more detailed presentation with accompanying case illustrations, see Prins (1994).

Arson committed for financial or other reward

In these cases the aim of the arsonist is to gain some financial or similar reward. The apparent increase in the burning of vehicles referred to earlier would fall into this category. However, the motives may not be so clear cut, as some individuals who set fires for apparent gain in this fashion may, for example, also be suffering from a degree of depression due to overwhelming financial or other difficulties.

Case illustration 9.1

A woman set fire to her one-bedroomed flat causing the destruction of not only her own home but also two neighbouring flats. As a result of the fires, an elderly neighbour, who lived two flats away, sustained injuries from which he died. In court it was alleged that the defendant had doubled her insurance on her home contents and set the fire in order to deal with increasing debts. It was also alleged that on the night before the fire, she had removed some of her own property to a relative's home. The judge told the defendant that although she did not intend to cause injury, she knew there were elderly residents nearby and that the risk of injury would be high. She was sentenced to seven years' imprisonment. (*The Independent*, 16 June and 30 June 1992).

Arson to conceal other crimes

Sometimes acts of arson will be committed in order to conceal a variety of offences. These may range from theft to murder. Such activities may be engaged in order to remove the means of DNA identification. These acts may cause enormous damage, particularly if they are set to cover offences such as burglarious activities in large and well-stocked warehouses. Woodward (1987) cited two instances of this kind of fire-setting. A warehouse of a shipping company was destroyed by fire. The goods stored there included television sets, car tyres and other goods that would catch fire quickly. From the forensic examination at the scene of the fire, it was apparent that burglarious activity had taken place before the fire had been set.

Arson committed for political purposes

There are two main motives for arson committed by political activists. The first concerns the desire to destroy the property of those they are against; the second is the publicity gained for the activists' cause. The one-time alleged destruction of second homes by Welsh activists and animal rights organizations would be illustrative of the first, and the previous activities of the work of the Irish Republican Army (IRA) and other paramilitary and fascist organizations would be illustrative of the second. A disturbing trend is the number of outbreaks of arson and similar attacks on so-called 'foreigners'. Although the main motives are often seen to be political, there are also sometimes psychopathological elements, such as the feeling of power such activities may provide. To this extent, the motivation may be mixed as, for example, in the case of other offences such as serious sexual assault.

Cases of self-immolation

These are not cases of arson as such. However, an act of self-immolation may have serious consequences for the lives of others as the following example shows.

Case illustration 9.2

A young woman in the north of England tried to kill herself in her bedroom by dousing her body in petrol and then attempting to ignite it. This having failed, she subsequently tried to blow herself up (and the other residents of the house) by turning on the gas taps and striking matches. Fortunately, this attempt also failed. However, the legal ingredients of a charge of endangering life through arson were sustainable and the defendant was admitted compulsorily to a psychiatric hospital under the Mental Health Act 1983. At the time she was found to have been suffering from a serious depressive illness, but subsequently made a reasonably good recovery. This example also illustrates the problem of trying to pigeon hole people since the young woman's problem could have been classified under the heading of mental disorder.

Ritualized self-destruction

Ritualized self-destruction – mainly for political reasons – sometimes occurs. A report in *The Independent* (21 May 1991) described the ritual suicide of Kim Ki Sol, who wrote, 'There are many meanings to my act today' before 'setting himself alight and jumping in flames from the roof of a seven-storey building at Seoul's Sogang University'. Culture-based self-immolation is not of course a new phenomenon as, for example, in the phenomenon of Suttee. Eileen Barker (1989) describes a number of young members of a group known as Ananda Marga, 'who immolated themselves' as a protest 'against the imprisonment in India of their leader.' Two of them said that their 'self-immolation is done after personal and independent decision. It is out of love for all human beings, for the poor, for the exploited, the suffering' (Barker 1989: 54–55). Topp (1973), an experienced prison doctor, drew attention to the extent to which self-destruction by fire seemed to have shown a slow but steady increase in penal establishments. He suggested that such individuals who choose an obviously very painful method of death are likely to be those who have some capacity for splitting off feelings from consciousness. Some may be epileptics in a disturbed state of consciousness. However, in all such cases of self-immolation, people probably vary enormously in their pain thresholds. Some would succumb very quickly to such an agonizing method of self-destruction. Most likely shock and asphyxiation would occur within a very short space of time so that the severe pain caused by the burning of vital tissues would not have to be endured for long. Such may have been the fates of some of the early martyrs who chose to suffer death at the stake. Occasionally, such sufferers were 'granted the merciful privilege . . . of having a small bag of gunpowder hung around [the] neck in order to speed their demise and so reduce [their] suffering' (Abbot 1991: 167).

Arson committed for mixed and unclear reasons

These are cases in which it is difficult to ascribe a *single specific* motive. Such cases may include the presence of a degree of mild (reactive) depression which may lead the fire-raiser to direct anger at a spouse or partner, thus revenge may also play a part. This group will also include cases in which the fire-raising may be a disguised plea for help, or a reaction to sudden separation or bereavement; in some of these cases alcohol appears to be relevant and may lead to befuddled activity on the part of the individual, who may unwittingly cause a conflagration.

Arson due to serious mental disorder

Functional psychoses may play a part in some acts of fire-raising, notably the schizophrenias. Such cases will most likely be accommodated in secure or semi-secure hospitals of one kind or another. Manic-depressive psychosis features occasionally, the classic case being that of Jonathan Martin, the early-nineteenth-century arsonist who set fire to York Minster (see Prins 1994; Enayati et al. 2008).

Arson associated with 'organic' disorders

Occasionally, brain tumour, injury, epilepsy, dementia or metabolic disturbance may play a part. For example, although epilepsy is not commonly associated with fire-raising, one should always be on the lookout for the case in which such a crime has been committed, when the person appeared not to be in a state of clear-consciousness or when onlookers were present. For examples of brain damage and other organic states and their relationship to fire-raising, see Hurley and Monahan (1969).

Arson motivated by revenge

Those incidents motivated by revenge are potentially the most dangerous. However, in considering the link between motives of revenge and arson, it is important to stress that it is hazardous to try to place motivations for fire-raising behaviour in discrete categories; the vengeful fire-raiser may show clear signs of identifiable mental illness, may be mentally and/or physically impaired, or may not be 'ill' in any formal psychiatric sense. However, their dangerous potential is considerable, as the following case illustration demonstrates.

Case illustration 9.3

A man aged about 30 had developed a passionate and quite unshakeable belief that a young woman was in love with him. His passions were not reciprocated; in fact they were actively resisted on several occasions. So obsessive were this man's amorous desires that they had a delusional quality. As a means of gaining attention to his plight and of getting back at the young woman concerned, he placed an incendiary device in her home with the avowed intention of killing her and her family. Fortunately, a family member spotted it and dealt with it before the fire took too great a hold. Many years after this event, the offender (detained in hospital on a hospital order without limit of time) still harboured vengeful feelings and seemed quite without insight into what he had done or compassion for his intended victim. It important to stress here that the vengeful arsonist is likely to harbour his or her destructive desires over a very long period (see also Sugarman and Dickens 2009).

Pyromania

Pyromaniacs are arsonists who do not appear to be suffering to any significant extent from formal mental disorder or to be operating from motives of gain or revenge. They appear to derive a pathological excitement from, and involvement in, setting the fire, attending the scene, busying themselves at it, or having called out the fire brigade in the first instance. The DSM-IV (TR) (APA 2005) lists six differential criteria for the diagnosis of the condition (see also Barnett and Spitzer 1994):

1   Deliberate and purposeful fire setting on more than one occasion.
2   Affective arousal and tension prior to the act.

3   Fascination with, and attraction to, fire and its situational context.
4   Pleasure, gratification or relief when setting fires or witnessing or involvement in their aftermath.
5   The exclusion of other causes (see above).
6   The fire setting is not 'better accounted for' by conduct disorder, or antisocial personality disorder.

(Paraphrased from DSM-IV-TR (APA 2005: 614–615))

Sexually motivated arson

Fras (1983) has summarized much of the history of the posited relationship between sexual satisfaction or excitement and arson (see also Prins 2001). The infrequency of the relationship in practice should not blind professionals to the possibility of its existence in certain cases, or its similarity to sex offending. As Fras (1983: 199) states, 'In its comparative, stereotyped sequence of mounting pressure . . . it resembles the sexual perversions, as it may parallel them in its imperviousness to treatment'. It is noteworthy that Hurley and Monahan (1969) found 54 per cent of the arsonists they studied in Grendon had clear psychosexual difficulties and marital problems, and that 60 per cent reported difficulties in social relationships with women (see also Prins 2001, 2009).

Young adult vandalism and arson

The backgrounds and motivations of adolescent and young adult arsonists appear to be rather different from those characterizing children who set fires. The adolescents and younger adults we looked at in our prison sample seemed to have been motivated more specifically by boredom and to have engaged in the behaviour for kicks. It is not unknown for bored and disaffected young employees to set fire to their places of work. For example, such instances have been reported in the hotel and catering industry. As with school and vehicle arson, there was often an accompanying element of getting back at a society that did not appear to care about them. Unlike child fire-raisers, their backgrounds seemed less socially and psychologically disturbed. It is also important to note that the arson offences committed by this age group are often closely associated with the ingestion of alcohol. The following case illustration shows how some of these elements may be combined.

Case illustration 9.4

A group of five unemployed older teenagers (ages ranging from 16 to 19) had been to a disco where they had imbibed a fair amount of alcohol, although they were not drunk. They had waited for a considerable time for the last bus home only to find they had missed it. They had been whiling away their time at the bus stop indulging in a fair amount of horse-play. As they became more impatient, their horse-play escalated into more aggressive activity. They smashed the windows of a large outfitter's shop nearby, entered it, and began damaging the contents. In the course of this activity, one of them lit some waste paper while others looked on encouraging him. A fire soon took hold, engulfing the premises, rapidly destroying the shop and its contents.

Child arsonists

The literature on children as arsonists suggests that they come, predominantly, from disturbed and dysfunctional family backgrounds and exhibit a range of conduct disordered behaviours from an early age. Some of the earlier studies lack control group populations, thus making the results somewhat inconclusive. However, a fairly large-scale study of fire-raising in a 'normal' population was conducted by Kafry (1980). She studied the fire behaviour and knowledge in a random sample of 99 boys of approximately 8 years of age. Kafry (1980) found that interest in fire was almost universal; 'fire-play' was carried out by 45 per cent of the boys studied, and interest in fire began at a very early age. An ominous finding was that although the children's parents seemed aware of the risks of fires, a large percentage did not provide any adequate instruction and warning to their children. Those children who played with matches and raised fires seemed to be more mischievous, aggressive, exhibitionistic and impulsive than those who expressed no such curiosity. The findings are of interest because these characteristics seem to be similar to those demonstrated in a number of adult arsonists, particularly those of aggression and impulsiveness. Later studies seem to be consonant with Kafry's (1980) findings; see, for example, Vandersall and Weiner (1970), Strachan (1981), Stewart and Culver (1982), Wooden and Berkey (1984), Jacobson (1985a, 1985b), Perrin-Wallqvist and Norlander (2003), Santtila et al. (2003) and Kennedy et al. (2006). See also Wooden and Berkey (1984) for a more extended account. Two quotations make a fitting conclusion to this section. The first is from John Dryden's *The Hind and the Panther* (III: 389) 'And thus the child imposes on the man', and 'Tall oaks from little acorns grow' (David Everett, 1769–1813).

Management

It should be obvious from the foregoing and Table 9.2 that no *single* form of management is likely to be effective. Because fire-raising behaviour is so diverse and, as Barker (1994) suggests, best treated as a 'symptom', every case deserves painstaking analysis, however 'obvious' the motivation may seem. The classifications already outlined, even with their acknowledged deficiencies, will (it is hoped) facilitate the process of management. The latter can be highlighted in the following fashion.

1 Distinguish the fraudulent arsonist.
2 Distinguish the politically motivated. However, it is wise to remember that some politically motivated arsonists may also have mental health problems.
3 Distinguish the vandalistically motivated.
4 Distinguish those who are driven to arson by clear evidence of mental disorder, notably functional psychosis, organic disorder, and learning disability.
5 Distinguish those who appear to be pyromaniacs as defined in DSM-IV-TR.
6 Distinguish those comparatively rare cases in which sexual disorder of one kind or another seems to play a significant role.
7 Distinguish those driven by motives of revenge. This group may include a number of arsonists classifiable as being psychopathically disordered.

Successful management must rest on a multifaceted approach and the ability of all members of forensic psychiatric and criminal justice teams to cooperate in the interests of the arsonist and the community. The management of arsonists has no place for 'prima donna' activity. A helpful example of a multidisciplinary approach may be found in an article by Clare et al. (1992). The authors describe in detail their management of a case that required an understanding of both physical and learning disabilities and a capacity to work intensively using eclectic behavioural techniques over a prolonged period of time. Despite minor setbacks, the patient, who had been subject at one time to containment in a high security hospital, remained free of his long-standing fire-raising behaviour at four-year follow-up. It would be mistaken to believe that psychoanalytically based psychotherapy had no place in the management of psychotic and seriously personality disordered arsonists. Dr Murray Cox (1979) described some of his very useful group work with such patients in Broadmoor. In doing so, he made the important point that 'the almost limitless range of clinical presentations means there is no neat unitary hypothesis which can underlie the behaviour of all patients convicted of arson' (Cox 1979: 344). Interesting exploratory work is currently being undertaken in the high security (special) hospitals, though the long-term benefits of such work have yet to be assessed. Vengeful arsonists may do so because they feel wronged or misunderstood. Any attempts that can be made to help them find ways in which they may achieve more satisfaction from their life experiences are to be welcomed. Many of them are socially inept; they set fires as a means of communication and to draw attention to themselves, so that techniques aimed at improving their self regard, self-image and social competence should help to minimize the risk of future offending. Thus social skills training has an important part to play with this group of arsonists. (For a study of learning-disabled fire-raisers, see Dickens et al. 2008.)

Summary

Not only is arson a very worrying offence, but also its causes are complex, and various attempts at classification have not been entirely successful. The recidivistic nature of fire-raising is emphasized in an important contribution by Soothill et al. (2004), whose article replicates an earlier study of the criminal careers of arsonists (Soothill and Pope 1973). They compared their original small sample of arsonists with three new series convicted in all courts in 1963, 1980 and 2000–01. Soothill et al. (2004) found an increasing number of females and a rise in the average age of both sexes. In this later series previous convictions for violence and criminal damage (including arson) were also much more in evidence. Within what is a twenty-year follow-up period the proportion reconvicted for arson has *more than doubled*. They conclude that 'the situation in relation to arson has deteriorated significantly over the past forty years' (Soothill et al. 2004: 27; see also Barnett et al. 1999). Recent attempts to view arson as a 'symptom' appear to offer the hope of more successful modes of management. In this chapter I have merely outlined the problems. The references cited and the suggestions for further reading should enable those who wish to pursue this important topic in greater depth to do so.

Notes

1 The degree to which flames may excite passion, and notably sexual passion, is well described in Walt Whitman's 'A Song of Joys' (1882):

> I hear the alarm at dead of night,
> I hear the bells – shouts! I pass the crowd – I run!
> *The sight of the flames maddens me with pleasure.*
>   (emphasis added)

2 The House of Lords, in allowing the appeals of two boys aged 11 and 12 against their convictions for arson, clarified the definition to be used where recklessness was invoked by the prosecution. As follows:

> A person acts recklessly within the meaning of Section 1 of the 1971 Act with respect to (i) a circumstance where he was aware of a risk that it exists or will exist; (ii) a result when he is aware of a risk that will occur; and it is, in the circumstances known to him, unreasonable to take the risk. (*Regina v G and another* (2003) UKHL 50).
>   (Reported in *The Independent Law Report* by Kate O'Hanlon,
>   *The Independent*, 22 October 2003, judgment delivered 22 October)

Acts

Criminal Damage Act 1971
Mental Health Act 1983
Mental Health Act 2007

References

Abbot, G. (1991) *Lords of the Scaffold: A History of the Executioner*, London: Robert Hale.

Almond, L., Duggan, L., Shine, J. and Canter, D. (2005) 'Test of the Arson Action Model on an Incarcerated Population', *Psychology, Crime and Law* 11: 1–15.

American Psychiatric Association (APA) (2005) *Diagnostic and Statistical Manual of Mental Disorders*, 4th edn (text revision) (DSM-IV-TR), Washington, DC: APA.

Barker, A.F. (1994) *Arson: A Review of the Psychiatric Literature*, Maudsley Monograph no. 35, Oxford: Oxford University Press.

Barker, E. (1989) *New Religious Movements: A Practical Introduction*, London: HMSO.

Barnett, W. and Spitzer, M. (1994) 'Pathological Fire-Setting 1951–1991: A Review', *Medicine, Science and the Law* 34: 4–20.

Barnett, W., Richter, P. and Renneberg, B. (1999) 'Repeated Arson: Data from Criminal Records', *Forensic Science International* 101: 49–54.

Canter, D. and Fritzon, K. (1998) 'Differentiating Arsonists: A Model of Fire-Setting Actions and Characteristics', *Legal and Criminological Psychology* 3: 73–96.

Clare, I.C.H., Murphy, D. and Chaplin, E.H. (1992) 'Assessment and Treatment of Fire-Setting: A Single Case Investigation Using a Cognitive Behavioural Model', *Criminal Behaviour and Mental Health* 2: 253–268.

Coid, J., Wilkins, J. and Coid, B. (1999) 'Fire-Setting, Pyromania and Self Mutilation in Female Remanded Prisoners', *Journal of Forensic Psychiatry* 10: 119–130.

Cox, M. (1979) 'Dynamic Psychotherapy with Sex Offenders', in I. Rosen (ed.) *Sexual Deviation*, 2nd edn, Oxford: Oxford University Press.

Department of Communities and Local Government (DCLG) (2008a) *Fire Statistics UK, 2006*, London: DCLG.

—— (2008b) *Summary Report: Statistical Release 1*, London: DCLG.

Devaprian, J., Raju, L.B., Singh, M., Collacott, R. and Bhavnik, S. (2007) 'Arson: Characteristics and Predisposing Factors in Offenders with Intellectual Disabilities', *British Journal of Forensic Practice* 9: 23–27.

Dickens, G., Sugarman, P., Ahmad, F., Edgar, S., Hofberg, K. and Tewari, S. (2007) 'Gender Differences amongst Adult Arsonists at Psychiatric Assessment', *Medicine, Science and the Law* 47: 233–238.

—— (2008) 'Characteristics of Low IQ Arsonists at Psychiatric Assessment', *Medicine, Science and the Law* 48: 217–220.

Enayati, J., Grann, M., Lubbe, S. and Dazel, S. (2008) 'Psychiatric Morbidity in Arsonists Referred for Forensic Psychiatric Assessment in Sweden', *Journal of Forensic Psychiatry and Psychology* 19: 139–147.

Faulk, M. (1994) *Basic Forensic Psychiatry*, 2nd edn, Oxford: Blackwell Scientific.

Fras, I. (1983) 'Fire-Setting (Pyromania) and its Relationship to Sexuality', in L.B. Schlesinger and E. Revitch (eds) *Sexual Dynamics of Anti-Social Behaviour*, Springfield, IL: Charles C. Thomas.

Geller, J.L. (1992) 'Pathological Fire-Setting in Adults', *International Journal of Law and Psychiatry* 15: 283–302.

Home Office (2007) *Statistical Bulletin 11/07: Crime in England and Wales 2006/07*, eds S. Nicholas, C. Kershaw and A. Walker, London: Home Office Research, Development and Statistics Directorate.

Hurley, W. and Monahan, T.M. (1969) 'Arson, the Criminal and the Crime', *British Journal of Criminology* 9: 4–21.

Jacobson, R. (1985a) 'Child Fire-Setters: A Clinical Investigation', *Journal of Child Psychology and Psychiatry* 26: 759–768.

—— (1985b) 'The Sub-Classification of Child Fire-Setters', *Journal of Child Psychology and Psychiatry* 26: 769–775.

Jayaraman, A. and Frazer, J. (2006) 'A Growing Inferno', *Medicine, Science and the Law* 46: 295–300.

Kafry, D. (1980) 'Playing with Matches: Children and Fire', in D. Canter (ed.) *Fires and Human Behaviour*, Chichester: Wiley.

Kennedy, P.J., Vale, E.L.E., Kahn, S.J. and McAnaney, A. (2006) 'Factors Predicting Recidivism in Child and Adolescent Fire-Setters: A Systematic Review of the Literature', *Journal of Forensic Psychiatry and Psychology* 17: 151–164.

Lewis, N.D.C. and Yarnell, H. (1951) *Pathological Fire-Setting (Pyromania)*, Nervous and Mental Disease Monographs no. 82, New York: Coolidge Foundation.

MacDonald, J.M. (1977) *Bombers and Firesetters*, Springfield, IL: Charles C. Thomas.

Miller, S. and Fritzon, K. (2007) 'Functional Consistency across Two Behavioural Modalities: Fire Setting and Self Harm in Female Special Hospital Patients', *Criminal Behaviour and Mental Health* 17: 31–44.

Murphy, G.H. and Clare, I.C.H. (1996) 'Analysis of Motivation in People with Mild Learning Disabilities (Mental Handicap) Who Set Fires', *Psychology, Crime and Law* 2: 153–164.

Noblett, S. and Nelson, B. (2001) 'A Psycho-Social Approach to Arson: A Case Controlled Study of Female Offenders', *Medicine, Science and the Law* 41: 325–330.

Perrin-Wallqvist, R. and Norlander, T. (2003) 'Firesetting and Playing with Fire during Childhood and Adolescence: Interview Studies of 18-year-old Male Draftees and 18–19-year-old Female Pupils', *Legal and Criminological Psychology* 8: 151–158.

Prins, H. (1994) *Fire-Raising: Its Motivation and Management*, London: Routledge.

—— (2001) 'Arson and Sexuality', in C.D. Bryant, N. Davis and G. Geis (eds) *Encyclopaedia of Criminology and Deviant Behaviour*, Volume 3, Hove: Brunner-Routledge.

—— (2009) 'The Special Problems of Arson (Fire-Raising)', in M.G. Gelder, J.J. Lopez-Ibor, N.C. Andreasen and J.R. Geddes (eds) *New Oxford Textbook of Psychiatry*, Volume 2, 2nd edn, Oxford: Oxford University Press.

Prins, H., Tennent, G. and Trick, K. (1985) 'Motives for Arson (Fire-Setting)', *Medicine, Science and the Law* 25: 275–278.

Rix, K.J.B. (1994) 'A Psychiatric Study of Adult Arsonists', *Medicine, Science and the Law* 34: 21–34.

Santtila, P., Häkkänen, H., Alison, L. and Whyte, C. (2003) 'Juvenile Firesetters: Crime Scene Actions and Offender Characteristics', *Legal and Criminological Psychology* 8: 1–20.

Soothill, K. (1991) 'Arson', in R. Bluglass and P. Bowden (eds) *Principles and Practice of Forensic Psychiatry*, London: Churchill Livingstone.

Soothill, K. and Pope, P.J. (1973) 'Arson: A Twenty-Year Cohort Study', *Medicine, Science and the Law* 13: 127–138.

Soothill, K., Ackerley, E. and Francis, B. (2004) 'The Criminal Careers of Arsonists', *Medicine, Science and the Law* 44: 25–40.

Stewart, M.A. and Culver, K.W. (1982) 'Children Who Set Fires: The Clinical Picture and a Follow-Up', *British Journal of Psychiatry* 140: 357–363.

Strachan, J.G. (1981) 'Conspicuous Fire-Setting in Children', *British Journal of Psychiatry* 138: 26–29.

Sugarman, P. and Dickens, G. (2009) 'Dangerousness in Firesetters: A Survey of Psychiatrists' and Others' Views on Risk of Such Offenders', *Psychiatric Bulletin* 33: 99–101.

Taylor, J.L., Thorne, I., Robertson A. and Avery, G. (2002) 'Evaluation of a Group Intervention for Convicted Arsonists with Mild and Borderline Intellectual Disabilities', *Criminal Behaviour and Mental Health* 12: 282–293.

Topp, D.O. (1973) 'Fire as a Symbol and as a Weapon of Death', *Medicine, Science and the Law* 13: 79–86.

Vandersall, T.A. and Weiner, J.M. (1970) 'Children Who Set Fires', *Archives of General Psychiatry* 22: 63–71.

Wachi, T., Watanabe, K., Yakota, K., Suzuki, M., Hoshino, M., Sato, A. and Fujita, G. (2007) 'Offender and Crime Characteristics of Female Serial Arsonists in Japan', *Journal of Investigative Psychology and Offender Profiling* 4: 29–52.

Wooden, W.S. and Berkey, M.L. (1984) *Children and Arson: America's Middle Class Nightmare*, London: Plenum Press.

Woodward, C.D. (1987) 'Arson: The Major Fire Problem of the 1980's', *Journal of the Society of Fellows, The Chartered Insurance Institute* (Part 1), 2: 55–86.

Further reading

The Arson Prevention Bureau publishes regular newsletters and other materials dealing with arson in all its aspects. The address of the Arson Prevention Bureau is: 51 Gresham Street, London EC2V 7HQ. Website: www.arsonpreventionbureau.org.uk

Barker, A.F. (1994) *Arson: A Review of the Psychiatric Literature*, Maudsley Monograph no. 35, Oxford: Oxford University Press.

Dickens, G., Sugarman, P., Edgar, S., Hofberg, K., Tewari, S. and Ahmed, F. (2009) 'Recidivism and Dangerousness in Arsonists', *Journal of Forensic Psychiatry and Psychology* 20: 621–639.

Prins, H. (1994) *Fire Raising: Its Motivation and Management*, London: Routledge.

Chapter 10

'The malady of not marking'

It is the disease of not listening, the malady of not marking, that I am troubled withal.

(Falstaff, in *Henry IV (Part 2)*, Act 1, Sc. 2)

How dangerous is it that this man goes loose?

(King Claudius, in *Hamlet*, Act 4, Sc. 3)

Never predict anything, particularly the future.

(attributed to Samuel Goldwyn, film producer)

If my readers have persisted so far in this book they will, I am sure, have discovered that a large proportion of the individuals described will have committed very serious offences indeed, that they generate a great deal of anxiety, both for the general public and for those given the responsibility of dealing with them. A significant by-product of this latter obligation is the dilemma facing many professionals in balancing the rights of such individuals against the protection of society.[1] There is a further balancing act to contend with, namely that of over-predicting or under-predicting 'dangerous' behaviour. I will deal with this in some detail later in this chapter, but three mental health inquiries I chaired illustrate the problem. My points can be made very briefly. The first inquiry concerned the death of Orville Blackwood, a young African Caribbean offender-patient detained in Broadmoor. As his death occurred following a period of seclusion, an independent inquiry was established. We took the view that in Orville Blackwood's case the dangers he posed had been to some extent *over-estimated*. The second case concerned that of a paedophilic offender-patient

Some of the material in this chapter is derived from my article 'Taking Chances: Risk Assessment and Management in a Risk Obsessed Society', *Medicine, Science and the Law* 2005, 45(2): 93–109. It is reproduced here with the permission of the editor and publishers of the journal.

in a medium secure unit. He had been allowed to go on escorted day-leave (with only one nurse) to a theme park and zoo popular with children. He absconded from this excursion and it was not until the next day that he was recovered. Here, taking into account his past history, we considered his risk to children had been *underestimated*. My third example concerned a young adult male who killed an innocent itinerant in a Leicester street. Because he had been known to the mental health (and various other services) an independent inquiry was established in accordance with central government prescription. Our investigation revealed that the young man in question appeared to have given a number of 'warning signs' of escalating violence; these appeared to have been ignored. (Full details of the three inquiries may be found in Prins et al. 1993; Prins et al. 1997; Prins et al. 1998.) For further special comments on mental health inquiries, see later in this chapter. More general material on risk assessment in forensic mental health and criminal justice may be found in my book on this topic (Prins 1999). An updating of this and related material is provided in this chapter, which includes the following sections: first, a brief examination of the climate and the context in which the assessment and management of risk currently takes place. Second, brief reference to legal and administrative aspects. Third, some semantic issues. Fourth, clinical matters including homicide inquiries. I have divided the material into these sections for clarity of presentation, but ideally it should be seen as a whole.

The culture of risk and blame

In the early 1990s the Royal Society (1992) made a sobering comment: 'Risk is ubiquitous and no human society can be considered risk free'. As already suggested in this book, we know that human beings are made anxious about ambiguity and uncertainty and will sometimes engage in dubious and harmful practices to avoid them. Much recent and current concern about so-called 'dangerous' people has its roots in these phenomena: unless they are properly understood, many of our efforts aimed at dealing with such people will fail. Beck (1998) puts an eloquent gloss on the matter, as follows:

> Calculating and managing risks which nobody really knows has become one of our main preoccupations. That used to be a specialist job for actuaries, insurers and scientists. Now we all have to engage in it, with whatever rusty tools we can lay our hands on – sometimes the calculator, sometimes the astrology column.
>
> (Beck 1998: 12)

Crucial to our understanding is the uncertainty of risk prediction (see later). This is particularly important at the present time when blame is so quickly apportioned in a variety of hazardous and tragic circumstances, be they homicides, train, air or sea disasters, flood damage or BSE.

The example of the Hampstead winter swimmers

Sometimes our concerns about risk-avoidance assume such ludicrous proportions that it requires the courts to bring an element of good sense into the situation. The Hampstead Heath Winter Swimming Club in London took the Corporation of London to court against its decision to close their three ponds on safety grounds when the ponds were not being supervised by lifeguards. Apparently changes to the lifeguards' duty hours meant that club members were not allowed to swim at their own risk. The doughty swimmers took their case to the High Court. The presiding judge – Mr Justice Burnton – decided in their favour, stating that in this case the law would 'protect individual freedom of action . . . and avoid imposing a grey and dull safety regime on every one'. His Lordship relied in part upon a previous judgment in an earlier case in which the House of Lords found against a man injured when diving into a quarry pit. 'If people want to . . . dive into ponds or lakes that is their affair' (as reported by Jonathan Brown, *The Independent*, 27 April 2005).

One could of course quote many other examples of this excessive preoccupation with risk-avoidance. Teachers are now reluctant to comfort children physically for fear of being accused of paedophilic inclinations, and reluctant to engage in adventure-type school trips for fear of being taken to court if accident befalls. Far fewer children gain from the healthy exercise of walking to school for parental fear of accident or assault. Overprotection of this kind ill prepares children for the Hobbesian view of life as 'nasty, brutish and short'. In the United States it is said that it is becoming increasingly difficult to recruit doctors to the practice of obstetrics and gynaecology for fear of litigation when and if things go wrong. Terence Blacker goes as far as to suggest in an article in *The Independent* (21 October 2005) that such preoccupations are turning us all into mindless wimps. He describes our plight as one of terror. He states: 'fear is habit-forming, weakening. The more we allow various vested interests to frighten us with their apocalyptic warnings, the less capable we shall be of dealing with a real global crisis, if, when it comes along'. Sobering thoughts indeed.

Much concern about risk is, of course, media driven; if mental health, criminal justice and legal professionals are forced into making predictions, there may be an assumption on the part of the public that such professionals are capable of getting it right every time. The latter will then assume (no doubt unwittingly) a mantle of infallibility and will have to count the cost when they get it wrong, as from time to time they assuredly will. It is worthwhile emphasizing that homicide inquiries (which I discuss later) are a good example of this problem and one that needs placing in perspective.

We know factually that the number of homicides committed by persons with mental disorders (particularly mental illness) is very small (and has, in fact, contrary to public opinion, actually declined since the late 1990s), but the media seem to have vastly influenced the politicians in their somewhat frenetic search for solutions (see, for example, Taylor and Gunn 1999; Cohen 2007; Department of Health 2008). It is also worth remembering (as a means of gaining historical perspective) that fashions in criminal justice and mental health come and go. Soothill (1993) has demonstrated very usefully the manner in which this may occur. He cites as examples our almost ten-year cyclical preoccupations with, for example, homosexuality and prostitution, with rape, with physical child abuse and with so-called 'satanic' child sexual abuse etc. As I showed in Chapter 7, recent preoccupation has been with so-called 'serial killing' – a much ill-used and abused term which often serves to obfuscate rather than illuminate. In 2001 it was pointed out to me that our recent 'folk devils' (as described by Cohen 2007) appear to be 'stalkers' (cyber and others) and 'errant doctors' (Dr Edward Petch, personal communication, 13 June 2001).

Reference has been made to the hazards of prediction; it is worthwhile commenting on this aspect in a little more detail. The sometime science correspondent of *The Independent* – William Hartston – once expressed our inadequacies very well:

> Such are the risks we all run every day that, if you are an adult aged between 35 and 54, there is roughly a one-in-400 chance you will be dead within a year. Homo sapiens is a bit of a twit about assessing risks. We buy lottery tickets in the hope of scooping the jackpot, with a one-in-14 million chance of winning, when there's a one-in-400 chance that we won't even survive the year . . . the evidence suggests that our behaviour is motivated by panic and innumeracy.
>
> (William Hartston, *The Independent*, 19 September 1997)

The realities of our being involved in a hazardous event can be seen in Table 10.1 and the notes accompanying it.

The perceptions of risk as outlined in Table 10.1 have very important implications for risk assessment and management. Measures to reduce risks may have unseen (and sometimes hazardous) consequences. For example, as William Hartston suggested in his article,

> wearing seat belts may make drivers more reckless because they feel safer; and marking a road as an 'accident black spot' may reduce accident figures so successfully that it ceases to be a black spot – it was only dangerous in the first place because people didn't know how dangerous it was.

Table 10.1 Likelihood of involvement in a hazardous event

Being struck by lightning[a]	one in 10 million
Contracting CJD by eating beef on the bone	one in 6 million
Drowning in the bath	one in 800,000
Death from homicide	one in 100,000
Death playing soccer	one in 25,000
Dying in a plane crash	one in 20,000
Dying from being involved in a road accident	one in 8,000
Dying from 'flu	one in 5,000
Dying from smoking ten cigarettes a day	one in 200[b]

Source: Daily Telegraph, 5 December 1997.

Notes (a) Compared with the risk of death from being struck by lightning or eating beef on the bone, the other risks quoted are far more substantial; as the author of the article from which these figures are extrapolated states, the risk is 'so small that it almost tips off the scale' (R. Uhlig, *Daily Telegraph,* 5 December 1997). (b) Statistical odds can be expressed in the following fashion:

Negligible risk is	less than one in 1,000,000
Minimal risk is	one in 100,000 to one in 1,000,000
Very low risk is	one in 10,000 to one in 100,000
Moderate risk is	one in 100 to one in 1,000
High risk is	greater than one in 100

Source: Sir Kenneth Calman, Former Chief Medical Officer of Health, Department of Health as quoted in *Guardian,* 3 October 1996).

I have sometimes wondered if the introduction of speed humps and speed tables will, over time, have the intended desired effect. Many drivers become frustrated by them and they may, in fact, demonstrate their frustration by acts of careless or negligent driving immediately *after* traversing them. An example drawn from earlier times tends to lend support to these contentions. Adams (1995) cites the introduction of the Davy lamp which was intended to save lives in the mining industry; but, as Adams suggests, it actually resulted in an *increase* in explosions and fatalities because the lamp permitted mining activity to be carried out at deeper levels where the explosive methane content was much higher (Adams 1995: 211).

Professional perceptions of risks

There can be little doubt that there has been a massive growth in what can best be described as the 'risk industry'. This is exemplified in well-publicized concerns about safety in the home, safety at work, the development of casualty services and those associated with child care.

Adams (1995) suggests that we may all tend to overdo the risk-prevention business. He cites as examples, overestimates of household risks lead to unnecessary expenditure on insurance; the design of buildings which take into account hazards which can be rated as almost zero, such as earthquakes in areas where these are unlikely; over-zealous safety measures on the railways leading to increases in passenger costs which, in turn, may drive people away from the railways on to the roads, thus creating greater driving hazards; abnormal fears of mugging and similar attacks may lead elderly people and other vulnerable people to lead unnecessarily isolated lives. Adams (1995: 17) suggests that there are two types of human beings. The first is the zero-risk individual *homo prudens*, personifying 'prudence, rationality and responsibility'. He describes this creature as 'a figment of the imagination of the safety profession'. The second is a type of being within every one of us, a creature he describes as *homo aleatorius*: 'dice man, gambling man, risk-taking man'. Adams' descriptions give further credibility to the importance of *irrationality* in human risk-taking behaviour or abstention from it.

Definitions of risk

In 1983, the Royal Society produced a report on *Risk*. This was subsequently revised in the light of development in knowledge and practice and nine years later a further version appeared (Royal Society 1992). In their introduction to this later report, the authors concentrated their minds on a range of terms used in the literature on risk. Some of them are quoted below:

- *Risk* is defined in terms of the probability 'that a particular adverse event occurs during a stated period of time, or results from a particular challenge'.
- A *hazard* is defined as 'the situation that in particular circumstances could lead to harm'.
- *Risk assessment* is used to 'describe the study of decisions subject to uncertain circumstances'. The Royal Society working group divided risk assessment into *risk estimation* and *risk evaluation*.
- *Risk estimation* 'includes: (a) the identification of the outcomes; (b) the estimation of the magnitude of the associated consequences of these outcomes; and (c) the estimation of the probabilities of these outcomes'.
- *Risk evaluation* is 'the complex process of determining the significance or value of the identified hazards and estimated risks to those concerned with or affected by the decision'.
- *Risk management* is 'the making of decisions concerning risks and their subsequent implementation, and flows from risk estimation and risk evaluation'.

(Royal Society 1992: 2–3)

The authors of the report cautioned against equating *risk* with *danger*. To put it simply, I see *risk* as the probability of an event occurring, and *danger* as the extent of the hazard or harm likely to accrue. The term 'acceptable risk' is frequently used by decision takers and policy makers. The authors of the Royal Society Report, in support of the views expressed by Sir Frank Layfield (1987) in his report of the Sizewell B nuclear plant inquiry, prefer the term 'tolerable'. Layfield considered that the use of the term 'acceptable' did not reflect the seriousness of the problems involved in risk-taking activities; he suggested the term 'tolerable' as being a more accurate description of what was involved. Following Layfield's report, the Health and Safety Executive (1988) defined 'tolerable risk' in the following fashion:

> 'Tolerability' does not mean 'acceptability'. It refers to the willingness to live with a risk to secure certain benefits and in the confidence that it is being properly controlled. To tolerate a risk means that we do not regard it as negligible or something we might ignore, but rather as something we need to keep under review and reduce still further if and as we can.
>
> (Health and Safety Executive 1988, quoted in Royal Society 1992)

Risk prediction

There is a vast and ever growing literature on the prediction of risk (see, for example, Adams 1995; Royal Society 1992; Monahan and Steadman 1994; Monahan et al. 2001: especially Chapters 1 and 7). If, by prediction, we mean the capacity to get it right every time, the short answer has to be 'No'. If we have more modest goals, and ask if there are measures that could be taken to attempt a possible reduction in dangerous behaviour, then it is possible to give a qualified 'yes'. Pollock and Webster (1991) put the matter very succinctly: 'From a scientific perspective [the question] is impossible to answer since it is based upon an unscientific assumption about dangerousness, namely that it is a stable and consistent quality existing within the individual' (Pollock and Webster 1991: 493). They suggest that a translation into more appropriate terms would produce the following question:

> What are the psychological, social and biological factors bearing on the defendant's . . . behaviour and what are the implications for future [behaviour] and the potential for change?
>
> (Pollock and Webster 1991: 493)

Over the years there has been much debate concerning *actuarial* versus *clinical* prediction. Not all of this debate has been helpful. However, one of the most important (and modest) enterprises in the field of criminal justice was the pioneering work of Mannheim and Wilkins (1955) with their prediction scales in relation to the (then) sentence of Borstal Training. I use the term modest because the authors stated that their scales could never *replace* individual assessment, largely because predictions based upon retrospective studies of case records could never take sufficiently into account subtle factors that might have been relevant at the time of sentence. We have, of course, made significant progress since those early pioneering days. However, as Fitzgibbon (2008) has shown, much depends upon the abilities of those using such scales and measurements to 'input' the relevant data. For commentary on Fitzgibbon's article, see Mehta (2008). Professor Tony Maden's (2007) book does much to clarify the usefulness of an actuarial approach. The message I take from his work is that predictive scales can alert one to the need to focus one's efforts and resources on particular *classes* of offenders-patients (see also Gray et al. 2008).

For some years, workers in the criminal justice and mental health fields have taken comfort from the oft-quoted statement by the American psychologist William Clement Kvaraceus (1966) that 'nothing predicts behaviour like behaviour'. However, as commentators such as Gunn (1996), have pointed out, such statements may rest upon statistical error and reinforce the fallacious view that risk is a static phenomenon and unaffected by changes in social and other circumstances (Gunn 1996). As MacCulloch et al. (1995) stated:

> Predicting and preventing violence is a fundamental part of clinical practice . . . forensic psychiatrists, psychologists and clinical criminologists are asked to assess cases to make a prediction of the likelihood of harm to others in the future.
>
> (MacCulloch et al. 1995: 61)

(See also Kettles et al. 2003; Krauss and Lee 2003; Maden 2007.)

Legal and administrative aspects

A number of legislatures, notably in some of the states on the continent of North America, have made attempts to define dangerousness for the purposes of incarceration of individuals adjudged to be dangerous, be this incarceration in penal or mental health care institutions. Currently in the UK, the Criminal Justice Act 2003 makes it possible to impose specific sentences that take account of an offender's potential for future dangerousness. Since the late 1990s, there has been an increase in the use of the 'life' (indeterminate) sentence for cases not involving homicide. This has been justified in various court of appeal decisions on the grounds that by such means offenders considered to be dangerous (but not necessarily mentally abnormal within the meaning of the current mental health legislation) can be incarcerated until such time as the authorities (for example, the Parole Board) consider, on the basis of expert advice, that they may be safely released. However, it should also be noted that decisions based solely on concerns about dangerousness appear to have recently become 'contaminated' by considerations based on political expediency. This would appear to have occurred in the case of Myra Hindley and some others. So far as those formally judged to be mentally disordered are concerned, current mental health legislation recognizes the concept of potential dangerousness. Thus, the Mental Health Act 1983 (England and Wales) (as amended by the Mental Health Act 2007), makes provision, *inter alia*, for the compulsory detention of an individual with a view to the 'protection of other persons' and, as I showed in earlier chapters, Section 41 of the Act makes provision (subject to certain criteria being satisfied) for placing an order restricting discharge upon a person made the subject of a hospital order to protect the public from 'serious harm'; and, as I also indicated, the proclivities of some offender-patients are recognized in the setting up and maintenance of the three high security hospitals in England and Wales (Broadmoor, Rampton and Ashworth) for those patients who 'exhibit dangerous, violent or criminal propensities' (National Health Service and Community Care Act 1990, Section 4). From the 1970s onwards, the law and practice relating to both mentally abnormal and dangerous offenders have been examined by five different groups – the Butler Committee, the Scottish Council on Crime, the 'Floud' Committee, the Reed Committee and, most recently, in the joint Home Office and Department of Health (1999) report on *Managing People with Severe Personality Disorder* (see Prins 1999; see also Chapter 5 this volume).

What's in a name?

The words 'danger', 'dangerousness' and 'risk' have little real meaning on their own. It is only when placed in context that they become useful, but any interpretation must, to some extent, be subjective. Walker (1983) made a useful point when he suggested that

> dangerousness is not an objective quality, but an *ascribed* quality like trustworthiness. We feel justified in talking about a person as dangerous if he has indicated by word or deed that he is more likely than most people to do serious harm.
>
> (Walker 1983: 24, emphasis added)

The Butler Committee, in examining the notion of *dangerousness in relation to mentally abnormal offenders*, considered it to be

> a propensity to cause serious physical injury or lasting psychological harm. Physical violence is, we think, what the public are most worried about, but the psychological damage which may be suffered by some victims of other crimes is not to be underrated.
>
> (Home Office and DHSS 1975: 59)

Practising clinicians and others who have day-to-day contact with those deemed to be dangerous, generally agree with Dr Peter Scott's definition that dangerousness is 'an unpredictable and untreatable tendency to inflict or risk irreversible injury or destruction, or to induce others to do so' (Scott 1977: 128). Some clinicians, for example Dr David Tidmarsh (1982), suggested that Scott's (1977) inclusion of unpredictability and untreatability can be questioned, since the anticipation and modification of a danger does not necessarily minimize the risk. Scott (1977) also stressed another very important element, namely that the use of dangerousness as a label might contribute to its own continuance – a point that could usefully be heeded by lawyers, sentencers and criminal justice and forensic mental health professionals. For our purposes, it is worth noting Floud's statement that 'risk is in principle, a matter of fact, but danger is a matter of judgement or opinion' (Floud 1982: 214).[2] Thus, the notion of dangerousness implies a prediction, a concern with future conduct. Most authorities agree that apart from a very small group of individuals who may be intrinsically dangerous because of some inherent physical or other defect (which may make them particularly explosive), the general concern is with the *situation* in which the combination of the *vulnerable* individual with a *provoking incident* may spark off explosive and dangerous behaviour. As noted by the Butler Committee,

> the individual who spontaneously 'looks for a fight' or feels a need to inflict pain or who searches for an unknown sexual victim is fortunately rare, although such people undoubtedly exist. Only this last category can be justifiably called: 'unconditionally' dangerous.[3]
>
> (Home Office and DHSS 1975: 58)

Risk and *danger* may be distinguished in the following somewhat over-simplified fashion.

Risk may be said to be the *likelihood* of an event occurring, and danger may be said to be the *degree of damage (harm)* that may occur should the event take place. Dr Adrian Grounds (1995) makes the important additional point that both of these also need to be distinguished from worry.

> They are not well correlated and judgements and decisions based on worry may not be well founded. The problem is that feelings of worry are expressed by professionals in the vocabulary of risk. The feeling 'I am very worried about X' is likely to be translated into 'X is a high risk' in written and spoken communications. Worry may, however, be excessive or insufficient in relation to the risk. The test is the same as for risk: how well grounded is it in [the offender's] history?
>
> (Grounds 1995: 54–55)

'Dangerousness' of course means different things to different people. If I asked my readers to rank the following people in order of their dangerousness, they would probably find themselves in some difficulty. Of the following who, for example, would be considered the more dangerous? The bank robber, the persistent paedophile, the person who peddles dangerous drugs to children, the person who drives when knowingly unfit to do so, the swimmer who has a contagious disease, but continues to use the public baths, the bigoted patriot, national leader or politician who believes they are always right, the computer hacker, the person who is HIV positive or has AIDS who persists in having unprotected sexual intercourse with a variety of partners,[4] the consortium which disposes of toxic waste products without safeguards, forensic mental health or criminal justice professionals who always act on their own initiative without adequate consultation with colleagues and who believe that their 'personality' will 'get them by' in dangerous situations? All of these persons present hazards of one kind or another, depending upon the situation in which they find themselves.

Clinical issues including inquiries

Sentencers (both professional and lay) and forensic mental health and criminal justice professionals have to carry out their work of limiting mayhem within the constraints of the complex legislative and administrative frameworks referred to earlier in this book. This legislative framework has become so complex that even experienced sentencers find some of the legal requirements difficult to interpret. Professionals not only have to deal with these legal complications but also (as stated earlier) have to carry out their work within the current 'blame culture' and to endeavour to balance offenders' and offender-patients' needs against the need to protect the public. The current political climate continues to place a premium on the latter, and this has been re-enforced with the implementation of the Criminal Justice Act 2003 (see Bickle 2008). I now point out some of the pitfalls for professionals and suggest ways in which practice might be improved. I begin by providing four case illustrations (which I use with my postgraduate students) in order to demonstrate some of the dilemmas involved.

Case illustration 10.1

Paul was in the community on conditional discharge from hospital (Mental Health Act 1983, Sections 37/41). The order had been imposed for killing his wife. He had been detained in hospitals for some ten years before being conditionally discharged by a Mental Health Review Tribunal. The facts of his original offence were that, having killed his wife (by manual strangulation) he had secreted her body, and it was some months before it was discovered. At the time of his arrest he had been seeing another woman on a regular basis. A year after being conditionally discharged into the community, he informed his supervising probation officer that he had been seeing a woman and hoped to marry her. In this case the probation officer's responsibilities seemed quite clear. In the first instance, the development would have to be reported to the Ministry of Justice Mental Health Unit. Second, the officer would have needed to ascertain from Paul more details of this new relationship. In the course of such a discussion Paul would have to be advised that he should inform the woman of his past history (given the particular circumstances of his original offence). Should Paul be unwilling to do so, his probation officer (having taken advice from his line management, and maybe the Mental Health Unit) would need to inform Paul that in the light of his refusal to do so, he would have to inform her himself.

To some, perhaps, this might seem like an intrusion into an offender-patient's personal liberty, but the broader issue of the protection of the public, in this case the woman he is seeing and maybe others, necessitates such action (see earlier discussion). The issues seem clear cut. In other cases there are grey areas that require careful consideration of who else might need to be involved – as illustrated in Case 10.2.

Case illustration 10.2[5]

Tom was a 60-year-old offender released on life licence for killing a child during a sexual assault. He had been convicted on a previous occasion of indecent assault and had then been made the subject of a hospital order without restrictions (Mental Health Act 1983, Section 37). He had been living in the community on life licence for about two years, and had so far not given his probation officer any cause for concern.[6] His probation officer has just received a phone call stating that Tom had been seen 'loitering' by the bus stop outside a local primary school. What should his probation officer do about this development? There would appear to be several steps that need to be taken. First, further information is required as to the source and reliability of the information received. This is of particular importance at a time when both public and political concerns about paedophilic behaviour are highly emotive (see Chapter 8).

Did this information come via the school or, for example, from a bystander who knew Tom's history and was perhaps out to make trouble for him by deliberately misconstruing a quite innocent piece of behaviour? (After all, he *could* have been waiting for a bus quite legitimately.) The second step in trying to elucidate the problematic behaviour would be to arrange a very urgent appointment to see Tom. Why, for example, was he at this particular bus stop? His responses would have to be judged in the light of details about his previous offences. It would be very ominous if, for example, the circumstances of the offence for which he received his life sentence were similar to his present behaviour. Third, the probation officer would have to consider the pros and cons of contacting the school and/or the local police to ascertain if any complaints or comments had been received concerning similar conduct by Tom. Whatever steps the probation officer takes, *the offender is entitled to be told of the action proposed and the reasons for it.* Such information will be likely to be received and accepted more easily had Tom been given very clear indications at the start of his life licence (or conditional discharge, if he had been dealt with through the forensic mental health care system) concerning his obligations under their terms. Tom needs to be made aware of his supervisor's responsibilities to report any apparently untoward conduct. Sadly, there have been occasions in the past when mutual expectations and obligations have not been shared openly. In such cases an offender or offender-patient can feel legitimately surprised when speedy and sometimes apparently condign action is taken. Some other aspects of the 'need to tell' are illustrated in the next two case examples.

Case illustration 10.3

A psychiatrist had been seeing a male patient on a regular informal outpatient basis over a period of several months. In the past, the patient had undergone a number of compulsory admissions to hospital for a paranoid psychosis (Mental Health Act 1983, Sections 2 and 3, as amended). During a recent session with his psychiatrist, he revealed a powerful belief that a former girlfriend had been unfaithful to him, that he has been following her, and that he felt like killing her. What should the psychiatrist do? In the first instance he needs to check back over past records to see if similar beliefs have been expressed on other occasions and what the outcomes were. Second, he would need to make a careful appraisal of the quality of the patient's intended actions, discussing the case with other professionals and/or his professional bodies. For example, the circumstances of the self-reported 'stalking' require careful and detailed evaluation, as does the quality of his expressed feelings about killing her. *Feeling* like killing someone is not quite the same as expressed threats to kill (which in law constitute a criminal offence). If his past history reveals similar threats and his *current* threats have a delusional intensity, then the psychiatrist would be exercising appropriate professional responsibility if he arranged for the patient's former girlfriend to be warned about his feelings.

Case illustration 10.4

My fourth example concerns a case in which the offender-patient had given clear indication of possible intended harm. This concerned events uncovered during a homicide inquiry which I chaired. The perpetrator of the homicide, who had been known to the mental health and a number of other social and educational agencies, had given a clear written warning to his supervising social worker of his possible intentions. He wrote a letter from the prison in which he was then being held – as follows:

> I think that jail is the Best place for me at the moment because it sort's my head out. If I was on the street I would put peples life at risk, so that's over with [original spelling].

We commented as follows:

> Although in retrospect, everyone [now] considered that this letter was important and significant, at the time, its content and import were not communicated [by social services] to the Probation Service . . . With hindsight, it would appear that the content of this letter might have prompted a referral for further psychiatric assessment.
>
> (Prins et al. 1998)

It is hoped that the above short case examples illustrate some of the dilemmas faced by professionals and will serve as an introduction to four following sections of this chapter:

- Aspects of communication
- Vulnerability
- Establishing an effective baseline
- Improving practice and lessons from homicide inquiries.

Aspects of communication

A non-mental-health and criminal justice professional once wisely stated that 'All tragedy is the failure of communication' (Wilson 1974). Such a statement embraces several relevant aspects of communication.

First, there is the need for good interprofessional communication. For example, case conferences and public protection committees sometimes fail to work as effectively as they could because of the mistaken belief that multi-agency is synonymous with multidisciplinary when, in terms of role perceptions and territorial boundaries, it clearly is not. For an account of an imaginary case conference see Prins (1999: 127–129). Multi-Agency Public Protection Arrangements (MAPPA) were given a statutory foundation by Sections 67 and 68 of the Criminal Justice and Court Services Act 2000 and implemented in April 2001. Bryan and Doyle (2003) outline the legal responsibilities now placed upon police and probation services in England and Wales as follows:

- Establish arrangements for assessing and managing the risk of serious harm posed by certain sexual, violent and other dangerous offenders;
- Review these arrangements with a view to monitoring their effectiveness [and] prepare and publish an annual report on the discharge of these arrangements within the Area.

    (Bryan and Doyle 2003: 29; see also Kemshall 2003; Tancredi 2005)

For a more recent and comprehensive account of MAPPA, see Young et al. (2005). They make the important point that 'a challenging task that faces mental health teams is how to integrate forensic services effectively and ethically with the criminal justice system in such a manner that dangerous offenders can be managed with *safety and dignity*' (Young et al. 2005: 312, emphasis added). Some of the problems in achieving these desirable outcomes have been identified by Ansbro (2006a, 2006b). Issues of confidentiality are prominent in relation to inter-agency functioning and often impede it. For a useful account of this problem, see Morris (2003). Multi-Agency Public Protection Arrangements have been established anew under the Criminal Justice and Court Services Act 2000.

Second, there is the need for adequate communication between worker and offender or offender-patient and an understanding of the impediments to this. These include ambivalence, hostility, fear and denial, not only on the part of the offender-patient, but also on that of the worker. Denial is by no means the sole prerogative of offenders and offender-patients. Maybe offenders, offender-patients and their professional workers should heed Banquo's advice to his fellows:

> And when we have our naked frailties hid,
> That suffer in exposure, let us meet,
> And question this most bloody piece of work
> To know it further.
>
> (*Macbeth*, Act 2, Sc. 3)

Third, how well do professionals 'hear' the concerns of the carers of their charges? In the Andrew Robinson inquiry, it became clear that Andrew's parents had tried to draw attention repeatedly to their fear of his continued psychotically motivated aggression and violence towards them. Their home had become a place of terror and accounts of their fears appear to have gone unheard (Blom-Cooper et al. 1995). Similar accounts of lack of family and junior staff members' involvement may be found in a number of other homicide inquiries (for further examples, see Prins 1999: Chapter 5).

Fourth, there is the need for professionals to be in touch with the warring and less comfortable parts of themselves. This need may show itself for example in misperceptions of race and gender needs; in our inquiry into the death of Orville Blackwood in Broadmoor, we considered that perceptions of young African Caribbeans as always being 'big, black and dangerous' might seriously have handicapped some of the staff's handling of this group of offender-patients (Prins et al. 1993).

Finally, there may also be unresolved and professionally limiting personal conflicts about certain specific forms of conduct, notably those involving extreme sexual deviation. Perhaps professionals working in this field might usefully heed the statement by Pericles in Shakespeare's play of that name that 'Few love to hear the sins they love to act' (*Pericles*, Act 1, Sc. 1). (See also Chapter 8 in this volume.)

Vulnerability

The assessment and management of dangerous behaviour and the risk factors involved are concerned, essentially, with the prevention of vulnerability, namely taking care not to place the offender or offender-patient in a situation in which they may be highly likely to re-enact their previous pattern(s) of dangerous behaviour. The recognition of this reduces the vulnerability of both the public to the commission of unfinished business and the vulnerability of the offender or offender-patient (Cox 1979).

Establishing an effective baseline

All the research and clinical studies in the area of risk assessment and management in criminal justice and forensic mental health attest to the importance of obtaining the basic facts of the situation. It is this kind of evidence that decision-making bodies, such as courts, Mental Health Review Tribunals, the Parole Board and the Ministry of Justice require in order to make the most effective decisions. This necessitates having an accurate and full record of, for example, the index offence, or other incident and, in addition, the person's previous history, especially their previous convictions. A bare legal description tells us nothing about seriousness of intention at the time of the offence, or its prognostic significance. This has become of increasing importance today when plea bargaining and advocates' attempts to persuade courts to down-grade offences have become more frequent. An incident that may well have had the ingredients to justify an original charge of attempted murder may eventually end up, by agreement, as one of unlawful wounding. Neither do the bare details of an offence give any real indication of motivation. For example, burglary may take the form of a conventional break-in, or it may have more ominous prognostic implications if, say, the only items stolen were the shoes belonging to the female occupant of the premises. As indicated in Chapter 8, those males who expose themselves to women in an aggressive fashion associated with erection and masturbatory activity need to be distinguished from those who are more passive and who expose from a distance without erection; the former group are those who are sometimes more likely to go on to commit serious sexually assaultive offences. In his seminal article on assessing dangerousness in criminals, Scott (1977) stressed the need for a longitudinal view of the offender's 'career-path' and a careful scrutiny of *all* the facts.

Useful guidance on the basic requirements for risk assessment was issued in the Department of Health's (1994) *Guidance on the Discharge of Mentally Disordered People and their Continuing Care in the Community*. The advice emphasized the following points, among others, advocated by the Panel of Inquiry into the case of Kim Kirkman:

past history of the patient; self reporting by the patient at interview; observation of the behaviour and mental state of the patient; *discrepancies between what is reported and what is observed*; statistics derived from studies of related cases and prediction indicators derived from research.

(West Midlands Health Authority 1991: 7, emphasis added)

Similar points were made by the former Association of Chief Officers of Probation (ACOP 1994) in its *Guidelines on the Management of Risk and Public Protection*. For example, ACOP suggests such questions as:

Who is likely to get hurt? How seriously and in what way? Is it likely to happen right now, next week or when? How often? In what circumstances will it be more rather than less likely to occur? Is the behaviour that led to the offending continuing? What is he/she telling you, not only by words but also by demeanour/actions?

(ACOP 1994: 5)

High hopes had once been placed upon various procedures for risk *registration*. However, some of the evidence I once gathered from the fields of child care and probation seemed to indicate that risk registration did not *necessarily* ensure good practice (Prins 1995). Some of us might be forgiven for thinking that we live in the age of the tick box and the protocol. 'Audit' is the order of the day, but whether its somewhat obsessional hold on administrators and others aids practice is by no means clear. One consultant psychiatrist has gone so far as to coin a new word for this preoccupation – 'Formarrohoea' (Hardwick 2003).

Improving practice and lessons from homicide inquiries

There is no doubt that many professionals carry out very high-quality work in cases requiring risk assessment and management. However, there have been instances when the quality of work has shown deficiencies; some of these deficiencies have been highlighted in various inquiries, such as those into the cases of Andrew Robinson (Blom-Cooper et al. 1993) and others (see later). I now illustrate why this might be and how such deficiencies might be remedied. Basically, it has to do with asking 'unaskable', 'unthinkable' and 'uncomfortable' questions. I have tried to group these questions under seven headings in order to describe them as seven possible 'sins of omission'. Before doing so, one or two preliminary general observations may be helpful. Professionals in this difficult and often highly charged area need two types of supervision and support. The first is the support and supervision that hold them accountable to their organization for what they do. The second, and equally important, is the degree of supervision from line management that enables them to do more effective and empathic work. It is very important for workers to have the chance to share perspectives with their peers. This may assist in the development of knowledge and confidence. The following seven areas of questioning may go some way to providing more effective engagement.

Have past precipitants and stresses in the offender or offender-patient's background been removed? If still present, are they amenable to further work and, more importantly, has the worker the courage to deal with them?

A period of long-term work with an offender or offender-patient may induce in the worker a form of 'familiarity', which may blind them to subtle changes in the individual's social and emotional worlds. If they have worked very hard to induce change through the establishment of a 'good' relationship, they may not wish to do anything that may challenge that; they may prefer not to know. Genders and Player (1995), in their study of Grendon Prison, stated that they were often reminded of the words of the old song 'I wish I didn't know now what I didn't know then'.

What is the person's current capacity for dealing with provocation?

It is useful to remind ourselves of Scott's (1977) advice that aggression may be deflected from a highly provoking source to one that may be scarcely provoking at all (see Chapter 6 in this volume). As suggested earlier in this book, some of our most perplexing cases are those in which serious violence has been caused to the 'innocent stranger' in the street. Careful scanning of the immediate environment may enable us to sense (and perhaps help the individual to avoid) potentially inflammatory situations. For example, to what extent has the over-flirtatious wife or partner of a jealous husband or partner courted a potentially dangerous situation by sarcasm, making denigrating remarks about sexual prowess, been otherwise contemptuous, or worn provocative clothing? The same is true of course with the male in the provocative role, as is the case from time to time, in male homosexual relationships. Detailed accounts of previous provoking incidents are therefore vital in order to assess future risk and provide effective continuing management (see Craissati and Sindall 2009; Matthews 2009).

How does this offender-patient continue to view him or herself?

The need for a macho self-image in a highly deviant male sex offender is often based upon unresolved past conflicts with women. This may make him likely to continue to take his revenge by way of serious sexual assaults accompanied by extreme violence and degradation of his victims.

To what extent have we been able to assess changes for the better in this person's capacity to feel empathy for others? Does this individual still treat others as objects rather than as persons upon whom to indulge their deviant desires and practices?

As I showed in Chapter 5 the true, as distinct from the pejoratively labelled, psychopath tends to see all those around him (or her) as malevolently disposed.

To what extent does the behaviour seem person-specific, or as a means of getting back at society in general?

I showed this in the case of some arsonists (see Chapter 9). The person who says with continuing hatred in their voice, 'I know that one day I'm going to kill somebody', has to be taken very seriously. To what extent are thoughts of killing or injury still present? Is there a pleasurable feel to their talk about violent acts? Is there continuing interest in such material as violent pornography, horror videos, the occult, atrocities, torture, etc.? Sometimes the 'evidence' is less tangible and 'hunches' need to be relied upon, but always carefully followed up and checked out. Thus, Commander Adam Dalgliesh in P.D. James' *Original Sin* described his 'instinct' as something which he sometimes distrusted, but had learned not to ignore (James 1994).

How much continuing regard has been paid to what the offender/ offender-patient actually did at the time of the offence? Was it so horrendous that they blotted it out of consciousness?

For example, did they wander off in a semi-amnesic state or, upon realizing what they had done, summon help immediately? Or did they, having mutilated the body, go off happily to a meal and a good night's sleep? How much are they still claiming it was a sudden and spontaneous crime, when the evidence shows careful planning and considerable premeditation? What was the significant role of substance abuse of one kind or another? Prisons and, to a lesser extent, secure hospitals are not ideal places for testing out future proclivities in such people. However, escorted periods of leave with close supervision may enable alcohol intake and its effects to be assessed. The persistent paedophile on an escorted group outing to the seaside may alert observant nursing staff to continuing abnormal sexual interest by having eyes only for the semi-naked children playing on the beach. In similar fashion, staff may report patients' interest (and arousal) when in the presence of the children of visitors to the ward, or to pictures of children on the television. How much is known about what 'aids' to sexual fantasy they are storing in their rooms or cells (for example, newspaper clippings, graphic details from court depositions)? The offender-patient who says he is writing his life history in a series of exercise books could well be asked to show them to us; somewhat surprisingly, they are very often willing to do so. We may find detailed descriptions of continuing violent and/or sadistic fantasies, which are being used as rehearsal for future activity. All these indicators, coupled with psychophysiological measures, may help us to obtain a better, if not conclusive, perception of likely future behaviour (for some further illustrative material, see Prins 1999: 141 et seq.).

Can we discern to what extent has this individual begun to come to terms with what they did?

It is important for all professionals and decision-makers to regard protestations of guilt and remorse with a degree of caution. As Russel and Russel (1961) state:

> A person who expresses guilt is to be regarded with vigilance. His next move may be to engineer a situation where he can repeat his activities (about which he expresses guilt), but this time with rationalization and hence without guilt. He will therefore try to manipulate his victim into giving him a pretext.
>
> (Russel and Russel 1961: 141)

Sometimes, an offender or offender-patient may be reluctant to acknowledge the truth of what they have done for fear of causing hurt to relatives and others close to them. Dr Patrick McGrath, sometime medical superintendent at Broadmoor, cited the case of a paedophilic sadistic killer who consistently denied his guilt in order to spare his 'gentle devoted parents who could not believe his guilt'. When they died, within a fairly short while of each other, he willingly admitted his guilt, and in due course was released (McGrath 1989). Neither should we forget that in relation to confession and guilt, offender or offender-patients may, in fact, not be guilty of any crime, as a number of causes célèbres have so sadly demonstrated.

When things go wrong: homicide inquiries

I hope it will have become fairly obvious that sometimes the desirable outcomes just outlined do not appear to have taken place, and perhaps most notably in relation to homicides committed by those known to the mental health and allied services. Inquiries into mental health service deficiencies are, of course, not new. During the 1960s and 1970s a number of inquiries took place into institutional provision such as care homes (both child and adult) and psychiatric hospitals. Following the increasing use of community provision, such inquiries began to focus more frequently upon the latter. Nowadays we live in the 'Age of the Inquiry' – a term used by two colleagues in their book on the subject (Stanley and Manthorpe 2004). A tradition of inquiries is now well entrenched. Whenever 'ill' befalls, there are (often strident) calls for an inquiry, whether these ills consist of disasters at sea, in the air or on land, the mass killing of school children, defaulting doctors, the murder of their patients, or the defaulting activities of some of our political representatives. Limitations of space precludes a detailed discussion of this important aspect of forensic-psychiatric and criminal justice management. I shall deal with the topic only briefly; further detailed discussion may be found in Peay (1996) and Prins (2004a, 2004b). As a result of a small number of high-profile cases (and no doubt having in mind the earlier lethal activities of the St Alban's poisoner, Graham Young, the nurse Beverley Allitt and one or two others) the government took two steps. The first was the establishment of the *Confidential Inquiry into Homicides and Suicides by Mentally Ill People* (Department of Health and Royal College of Psychiatrists 1992), and subsequently a circular in 1994 which directed that there should be an independent inquiry into homicides committed by those in contact with the mental health services (Department of Health 1994). Since that time, a very large number of such inquiries have taken place. Partly as a result of the events unravelled by the team inquiring into the Michael Stone case, the 1994 remit was amended in 2005 (Department of Health 2005). This revision clarified certain matters, largely concerning the scope of inquiries, the role of the media and the preparatory work needed prior to the establishment of an inquiry.[7] (For details of the revised remit, see Prins 2007.)[8]

Some issues

Over the years a number of issues have arisen. I now identify some of those that I consider to have been (and still are) of some importance.

The 'in public' or 'in private' debate

There are those who consider that in most cases inquiries should be in public. Sir Louis Blom-Cooper and I have debated this matter elsewhere. He favours public hearing and I, with very limited exceptions, favour private hearings (see, for example, Prins et al. 1993; Blom-Cooper 1999). Sir Cecil Clothier (1996) makes a sensible mid-way comment when he suggests that inquiries could, if appropriate, be held partly in public and partly in private. When discussing this he also makes the trenchant comment that 'the media will always be in favour of a public inquiry, piously exclaiming that the sole purpose is to inform an anxious readership. But of course a public inquiry affords exciting copy and often ready-made headlines' (Clothier 1996: 51).

Getting at the truth

Louis Blom-Cooper has wisely stated that the purpose of inquiries is 'to examine the truth . . . what happened, and who if anyone was responsible, culpably or otherwise, for it having happened?' (Blom-Cooper 1993: 20). So far so good, but are there not problems in such a definition of purpose, and are there not indeed other purposes, explicit or implicit? The search for truth is admirable, but is it as readily ascertainable as might be inferred from his remarks? All who work in this difficult field agree that it is all to easy to be wise after the event and that hindsight bias may lead us to draw facile or indeed quite erroneous conclusions. The balance that needs to be struck has been put into a very useful context by Coonan et al. (1998) when they suggest that:

> The essential requirement is that the Inquiry should be fair and just, and at the same time provide answers to the fundamental questions: 'How?' and 'Why?' the death occurred. A balance must be struck between the competing demands of the inquisitorial nature of the inquiry and the requirement to provide some degree of protection to individuals whose credibility and competence is strongly impugned . . . Provided the correct balance is struck, the requirements of seeking the truth, making recommendations, and at the same time identifying individual failure, where appropriate is both reconcilable and achievable.
>
> (Coonan et al. 1998: 3)

For whose benefit?

In aiming to ascertain the truth we need to ask ourselves – for whose benefit is the inquiry taking place? There are a number of players to be considered here. First, there are the professionals involved, who may well see themselves as on trial. The inquiry team has to handle their feelings with a great deal of sensitivity but, at the same time, not hesitate to ask some penetrating questions. This is not an easy balance to strike. Second, there are the views of (often grieving) relatives to consider. Their grief may, of course, be expressed in angry recrimination towards the professionals involved, and may indeed also explode occasionally against the inquiry team. Third, a group that is somewhat neglected in my experience: it consists of the relatives of the perpetrator. They may have a heavy burden to carry – a mixture of guilt for their own part in the drama and anger towards the various agencies who they may feel have let them down. Such issues have been explored by Rock (1996, 1998) and, more recently, by Malone (2007).

The perpetrator

Although it is likely that the perpetrator of the homicide may have been interviewed by one or two members of the inquiry team, it is not always clear to what extent the findings of such an interview will be made available for those having the future management of the offender. Provided consent is obtained, I would suggest that such information might be very useful to those concerned. The medical colleague and I who interviewed the perpetrator in my own homicide inquiry attempted to make sure that our findings were passed on in our final report to those concerned (Prins et al. 1998).

The inquiry team

Inquiry teams vary in size from a threesome to as many as six or seven members. Little attention appears to have been paid to the emotional and physical impact of the work involved on team members. I therefore decided to undertake a small-scale survey of the views of some thirteen inquiry chairs. The results of this study may be found in Prins (2004a, 2004b).

Publication and distribution of the report

The official view expressed in the Department of Health's amending directive to the 1994 Circular is that decisions concerning publication and distribution are in the hands of the commissioning authority – usually the Strategic Health Authority. On occasion, in the past, an authority has restricted the distribution of the report – to the extent that bona fide inquirers have had difficulty in accessing it. We found this to be the case with our report on Orville Blackwood's death (Prins et al. 1993). Reports have also been of varied 'print' quality. Some have been produced in house and have not looked very impressive. However, some in-house reports have been produced to a high standard. Others have been published as Command Papers and by The Stationery Office (TSO). In future, it seems likely that a more uniform style of production and presentation will be the norm.

Comment

Whereas in the past there seems to have been an automatic recourse to an independent external inquiry in all cases, it now seems that the adoption of these will be more selective. Investigation of what are now described as adverse events will have as their starting point a detailed primary internal investigation. What this reveals will determine whether an external inquiry is needed. It is to be hoped that these more uniform procedures will enable the lessons to be learned from both types of investigations more effectively. For a very helpful commentary on the need to streamline the inquiry process, see Pearson et al. (2009). In this respect, Michael Howlett, Director of the Zito Trust, has wisely pointed out a number of homicide inquiry reports have indicated that maybe a homicide could have been prevented, if not predicted. Not quite the same thing (personal communication, 5 January 2009).

Finally, a trenchant comment by Professor Jill Peay: 'Do inquiries after homicide explain, expose, expiate or merely excoriate?' (Peay 1996: 11). Readers of this book must make up their own minds.

Concluding observations

In this chapter I have endeavoured to place notions of dangerousness and risk within recent contexts. I have tried to offer some examples of ways in which the supervision of potentially high-risk serious offenders might be made more effective. Although the advent of sophisticated computational techniques has undoubtedly provided a platform for actuarial advances, it is still the worker at the *individual* level who has to make prognostic judgements and undertake the hazards of ongoing supervision (see Mullen 2002; Maden 2003). It is comparatively easy and safe to predict what someone will do two weeks or even a month hence; much more hazardous to predict what they might do in a year's time.

Central to the task of the criminal justice or mental health professional in high-risk cases is a commitment to detail and to tracing connections between behaviour patterns. In a review of Gail Bell's (2001) book *The Poison Principle*, Forrester (2003), a forensic psychiatrist, makes the following very apposite comment:

> Detail forms the substance of forensic psychiatry in the same way that the investigations of a physician might invoke various [tests], so the investigative forensic-psychiatrist must put together a fully corroborated personal narrative, or be charged with pitiful neglect.
>
> (Forrester 2003: 467)

For an informative account by an academic chemist concerning the use and constitution of poisons in homicide cases, see Emsley (2008). It involves a great deal of personal soul-searching in order to come to grips with behaviour that is frequently anxiety-making and sometimes horrifying. It also calls for operating with a greater degree of surveillance and close monitoring than is customary in some other areas of counselling. It certainly involves a capacity not to attempt to go it alone and in this area of work there is no place for 'prima donna' activities. Despite the difficulties (or maybe because of them), many workers enjoy the challenge presented by those who have shown, or are adjudged likely to show, dangerous behaviour towards others. Such was the view of a small group of consultant forensic psychiatrists when asked for the reasons why they chose to specialize in forensic psychiatry (see Prins 1998).

Sadly, but perhaps understandably, politicians and the general public have very high expectations that mental health and criminal justice professionals can get it right every time. Professionals can give of their best only on the understanding that they are not infallible; and if society has ordained that risks through legislation will be taken, then occasional failures are inevitable. Decision-making is often not only complex but also emotive. Maybe if professionals are occasionally found wanting, it is because as Rumgay and Munro (2001) suggested they feel powerless to 'intervene effectively'. In other instances it may be that people cannot take on board the notion that killers like Harold Shipman, for example, could behave as they did since such behaviour defies all expectations (Smith 2003a, 2003b).

Notes

1 The dilemmas involved in balancing rights and obligations is perhaps well illustrated in two Home Office inquiry reports into the criminal conduct of three offenders under supervision at the time of their crimes. The first, Anthony Rice, committed murder while on life licence for attempted rape. The second concerned the joint activities of Damien Hanson and Elliot White, who murdered a man and attempted to murder his wife. Hanson was on parole from a sentence for attempted murder and conspiracy to rob. White was subject to a Drug Treatment and Testing Order (DTTO). The latter had been imposed for breaching a community treatment order imposed for being in unlawful possession of 2.8 grams of cocaine. Both inquiries revealed the dilemmas involved in balancing human rights against issues relating to public protection (HM Inspectorate of Probation 2006a, 2006b).

2 A large number of pronouncements have been made in the High Court in recent times concerning sentencing aspects of risk determination. Readers are directed to the quarterly 'In Court' sections of the *Probation Journal*, particularly for the years 2007 and 2008. Readers should note that the Criminal Justice Act 2003 has been amended by the Criminal Justice and Immigration Act 2008.

3 In the 1970s and early 1980s the words 'danger' and 'dangerousness' were more in evidence than today. Gradually, it has become more common (and sensible) to speak and write about 'risk'. Risk *assessment* and *management* are sometimes viewed as discrete entities. In my view they should be seen as part of seamless practice, since *management* should entail continuing *reassessment*.

4 A man was convicted and sentenced to a substantial term of imprisonment for inflicting 'biological' grievous bodily harm by such means. It was said to be the first instance of this kind in England and Wales. However, there had been an earlier conviction for such an offence in Scotland.

5 The situation in Case 10.5 arose and was dealt with *before* the current sex offender registration and associated procedures were in force.

6 It should be noted here that the probation service has undergone major changes in both organization and practice in recent times. It became the National

Probation Service in 2001 and currently consists of forty-two Probation Areas. Probation Boards have replaced Probation Committees and central government now funds the full costs of the Probation Service. There has been a decided shift to law enforcement and public protection as significant aims of the service's work. The service is also increasingly involved in work with victims, but this work has developed with some degree of inconsistency. A further reorganization of the service has followed the reorganization of the structure of the Ministry of Justice. The National Probation Service will be brought even closer together with the Prison Service – a 'Correction Service' perhaps (see Penal Policy File no. 115, *Howard Journal of Criminal Justice* 2008, 47: 317–318). A further interesting development has seen the involvement of psychologists in the work of the service; for example the appointment of trainee psychologists to *both* prison and probation areas. Under the provisions of the Criminal Justice Act 2003, the Probation Service is likely to be involved increasingly in the assessment of potentially 'dangerous offenders', particularly those sentenced for serious sexual and violent crimes.

7. Michael Stone was convicted and sentenced to life imprisonment for the murder of Lin Russell and her younger daughter Megan, and the grievous injury of her older daughter Josie. His case went to what in effect amounted to three trials. Because of this prolonged trial process, the mandatory inquiry was not published until some six years after his crimes. The inquiry, conducted by Robert Francis, QC, and colleagues, was also unusual in that it explored in some detail the role of the media and made a number of recommendations to improve such involvement. It also dealt comprehensively with the anonymity of witnesses and other matters concerning confidentiality (see Francis et al. 2000; Francis 2007). Such matters had, of course, been dealt with in other inquiries, but perhaps in not such detail. The findings and recommendations of the Stone Inquiry were doubtless influential in the framing and promulgation of some aspects of the 2005 revision of the 1994 Guidance.

8 I am reliably informed my Michael Howlett of the Zito Trust that the number on inquiries is now closer to 400 (personal communication, 5 January 2009).

Acts

Criminal Justice Act 2003
Criminal Justice and Court Services Act 2000
Mental Health Act 1983
Mental Health Act 2007
National Health Service and Community Care Act 1990

References

Adams, J. (1995) *Risk*, London: University College London Press.
Ansbro, M. (2006a) 'What Can We Learn from Serious Incident Reports?', *Probation Journal: The Journal of Community and Criminal Justice* 53: 57–70.
—— (2006b) 'Serious Further Offence Inquiry', *Probation Journal: The Journal of Community and Criminal Justice* 53: 167–177.
Association of Chief Officers of Probation (ACOP) (1994) *Guidelines on the Management of Risk and Public Protection*, London: ACOP.

Beck, U. (1998) 'Politics of Risk Society', in J. Franklin (ed.) *The Politics of Risk Society*, Cambridge: Polity Press.

Bell, G. (2001) *The Poison Principle*, Sydney: Picador.

Bickle, A. (2008) 'The Dangerous Offender Provisions of the Criminal Justice Act 2003 and their Implications for Psychiatric Evidence in Sentencing Violent and Sexual Offenders', *Journal of Forensic Psychiatry and Psychology* 19: 603–619.

Blom-Cooper, L., QC (1993) 'Public Inquiries', in M. Freeman and B. Hepple (eds) *Current Legal Problems*, Oxford: Oxford University Press.

—— (1999) 'Public Inquiries in Mental Health Care (With Particular Reference to the Blackwood Case at Broadmoor and the Patient Complaints at Ashworth Hospital)', in D. Webb and R. Harris (eds) *Mentally Disordered Offenders: Managing People Nobody Owns*, London: Routledge.

Blom-Cooper, L., QC, Hally, H. and Murphy, E. (1995) *The Falling Shadow: One Patient's Mental Health Care: 1978–1993*, London: Duckworth.

Bryan, T. and Doyle, P. (2003) 'The "MAPPA"', *Prison Service Journal* 147: 29–36.

Clothier, C., QC (1996) 'Ruminations on Inquiries', in J. Peay (ed.) *Inquiries After Homicide*, London: Duckworth.

Cohen, S. (2007) *Folk Devils and Moral Panics*, 3rd edn, London: Routledge.

Coonan, K., QC, Bluglass, R., Halliday, G., Jenkins, M. and Kelly, O. (1998) *Report into the Care and Treatment of Christopher Edwards and Richard Lindford*, Essex: North East Essex Health Authority, Essex County Council, HM Prison Service and Essex Police.

Cox, M. (1979) 'Dynamic Psychotherapy with Sex Offenders', in I. Rosen (ed.) *Sexual Deviation*, 2nd edn, Oxford: Oxford University Press.

Craissati, J. and Sindall, O. (2009) 'Serious Further Offences: An Exploration of Risk and Typologies', *Probation: The Journal of Community and Criminal Justice* 56(1): 9–27.

Department of Health (NHS Executive) (1994) *Guidance on the Discharge of Mentally Disordered People and their Continuing Care in the Community*, HSG/94/27, London: Department of Health.

Department of Health (2005) *Independent Investigation of Adverse Events (Memorandum Replacing Paras 33–36 in HSG (94) 27 (LASSL (94) 4)*, London: Department of Health.

Department of Health (NHS London) (2008) *A Review of 26 Mental Health Homicides in London Committed between January 2002 and December 2006*, London: Department of Health.

Department of Health and Royal College of Psychiatrists (1992) *Confidential Inquiry into Homicides and Suicides by Mentally Ill People: Preliminary Report*, London: Department of Health.

Emsley, J. (2008) *Molecules of Murder: Criminal Molecules and Classic Cases*, Cambridge: Royal Society of Chemistry Publishing.

Fitzgibbon, D.W. (2008) 'Fit for Purpose? OASys Assessments and Parole Decisions', *Probation Journal: The Journal of Community and Criminal Justice* 55: 55–69.

Floud, J. (1982) 'Dangerousness and Criminal Justice', *British Journal of Criminology* 22: 213–223.

Forrester, A. (2003) 'Review of G. Bell, *The Poison Principle: A Memoir of Family Secrets and Literary Poisonings*', *Journal of Forensic Psychiatry* 14: 465–468.

Francis, R., QC (2007) 'The Michael Stone Inquiry: A Reflection', *Journal of Mental Health Law* 15: 41–49.

Francis, R., QC, Higgins, J. and Cassam, E. (2000) *Report of the Independent Inquiry into the Care and Treatment of Michael Stone*, Horley, Sussex: South East Coast Strategic Health Authority (formerly West Kent Health Authority).

Genders, E. and Player, E. (1995) *Grendon: A Study of a Therapeutic Prison*, Oxford: Clarendon Press.

Gray, N.S., Taylor, J. and Snowden, R.J. (2008) 'Predicting Violent Convictions Using the HCR-20', *British Journal of Psychiatry* 192: 384–387.

Grounds, A.T. (1995) 'Risk Assessment and Management in Clinical Context', in J. Crichton (ed.) *Psychiatric Patient Violence: Risk and Response*, London: Duckworth.

Gunn, J. (1996) 'The Management and Discharge of Violent Patients', in N. Walker (ed.) *Dangerous People*, London: Blackstone.

Hardwick, P. (2003) 'Formarrhoea', *Psychiatric Bulletin* 27: 388–389.

Health and Safety Executive (1988) *The Tolerability of Risks from Nuclear Power Stations*, London: HMSO.

HM Inspectorate of Probation (Home Office) (2006a) *An Independent Review of a Serious Further Offence Case: Anthony Rice*, London: Home Office.

—— (2006b) *An Independent Review of a Serious Further Offence Case: Damien Hanson and Elliot White*, London: Home Office.

Home Office and Department of Health (1999) *Managing People with Severe Personality Disorder: Proposals for Policy Development*, London: Home Office.

Home Office and Department of Health and Social Security (1975) *Report of the Committee on Mentally Abnormal Offenders* (Butler Report), Cmnd 6244, London: HMSO.

James, P.D. (1994) *Original Sin*, London: Faber & Faber.

Kemshall, H. (2003) 'The Community Management of High-Risk Offenders: A Consideration of "Best Practice" – Multi-Agency Public Protection Arrangements (MAPPA)', *Prison Service Journal* 46: 2–5.

Kettles, A.M., Robson, D. and Moody, E. (2003) 'A Review of Clinical Risk and Related Assessments in Forensic-Psychiatric Units', *British Journal of Forensic Practice* 5: 3–12.

Krauss, D.A. and Lee, D.H. (2003) 'Deliberating on Dangerousness and Death: Jurors' Ability to Differentiate between Expert Actuarial and Clinical Predictions of Dangerousness', *International Journal of Law and Psychiatry* 26: 113–137.

Kvaraceus, W. (1966) *Anxious Youth: Dynamics of Delinquency*, Columbus, OH: Charles E. Merrill.

Layfield, F. (1987) *Sizewell B Public Inquiry*, Volumes 1–8, London: HMSO.

MacCulloch, M., Bailey, J. and Robinson, C. (1995) 'Mentally Disordered Attackers and Killers: Towards a Taxonomy', *Journal of Forensic Psychiatry* 6: 41–61.

McGrath, P. (1989) Book Review, *British Journal of Psychiatry* 154: 427.

Maden, A. (2003) 'Standardised Risk Assessment: Why All the Fuss?', *Psychiatric Bulletin* 27: 201–204.

—— (2007) *Managing Violence: A Guide to Risk Management in Mental Health*, Oxford: Oxford University Press.

Malone, L. (2007) 'In the Aftermath: Listening to People Bereaved by Homicide', *Probation Journal: The Journal of Community and Criminal Justice* 54: 383–393.

Mannheim, H. and Wilkins, L. (1955) *Prediction Methods in Relation to Borstal Training*, London: HMSO.

Matthews, J. (2009) 'People First: Probation Officer Perspectives on Probation Work', *Probation: The Journal of Community and Criminal Justice* 56(1): 61–67.

Mehta, A. (2008) 'Fit for Purpose: OASys Assessments and Parole Decisions – A Practitioner's View', *Probation Journal: The Journal of Community and Criminal Justice* 55: 189–194.

Monahan, J. and Steadman, H. (1994) *Violence and Mental Disorder: Developments in Risk Assessment*, Chicago, IL: University of Chicago Press.

Monahan, J., Steadman, H.J., Silver, E., Appelbaum, P.S., Robbins, P.C., Mulvey, E.P., Roth, L.H., Grisso, T. and Banks, S. (2001) *Rethinking Risk Assessment: The MacArthur Study of Mental Disorder and Violence*, Oxford: Oxford University Press.

Morris, F. (2003) 'Confidentiality and the Sharing of Information', *Journal of Mental Health Law* 9: 38–50.

Mullen, P.E. (2002) 'Response to Professor Tony Maden's Training in Standardised Risk Assessment, in *Forum* (June 2002)', *Forum: Newsletter of the Forensic Faculty of the Royal College of Psychiatrists* 5: 1 (November).

Pearson, A., Swinson, N. and Shaw, J. (2009) 'Independent Investigations after Homicide', *Mental Health Today* February: 25–29.

Peay, J. (ed.) (1996) *Inquiries After Homicide*, London: Duckworth.

Pollock, N. and Webster, C. (1991) 'The Clinical Assessment of Dangerousness', in R. Bluglass and P. Bowden (eds) *Principles and Practice of Forensic Psychiatry*, London: Churchill Livingstone.

Prins, H. (1995) '"I've Got a Little List" (Koko, Mikado), But Is It Any Use? Comments on the Forensic Aspects of Supervision Registers for the Mentally Ill', *Medicine, Science and the Law* 35: 218–224.

—— (1998) 'Characteristics of Consultant Forensic Psychiatrists: A Modest Survey', *Journal of Forensic Psychiatry* 9: 139–149.

—— (1999) *Will They Do It Again? Risk Assessment and Management in Criminal Justice and Psychiatry*, London: Routledge.

—— (2004a) 'Mental Health Inquiries: "Cui Bono?"', in N. Stanley and J. Manthorpe (eds) *The Age of the Inquiry: Learning and Blaming in Health and Social Care*, London: Routledge.

—— (2004b) 'Mental Health Inquiries: Views from the Chair', *Journal of Mental Health Law* 10: 7–15.

—— (2007) 'The Michael Stone Inquiry: A Somewhat Different Homicide Report', *Journal of Forensic Psychiatry and Psychology* 18: 411–431.

Prins, H., Backer-Holst, T., Francis, E. and Keitch, I. (1993) *Report of the Committee of Inquiry into the Death in Broadmoor Hospital of Orville Blackwood and a Review of the Deaths of Two Other Afro-Caribbean Patients: 'Big, Black and Dangerous'?*, London: Special Hospitals Service Authority (SHSA).

Prins, H., Marshall, A. and Day, K. (1997) *Report of the Independent Panel of Inquiry into the Circumstances Surrounding the Absconsion of Mr Holland from the Horizon NHA Trust on 19 August 1996*, Harperbury, Herts.: Horizon NHS Trust.

Prins, H., Ashman, M., Steele, G. and Swann, M. (1998) *Report of the Independent*

Panel of Inquiry into the Treatment and Care of Sanjay Kumar Patel, Leicester: Leicester Health Authority.

Rock, P. (1996) 'The Inquiry and Victims' Families', in J. Peay (ed.) *Inquiries After Homicide*, London: Duckworth.

—— (1998) 'Murders, Victims and Survivors', *British Journal of Criminology* 18: 185–200.

Royal Society (1992) *Risk: Analysis, Perception, Management*, London: Royal Society.

Rumgay, J. and Munro, E. (2001) 'The Lion's Den: Professional Defences in the Treatment of Dangerous People', *Journal of Forensic Psychiatry* 12: 357–378.

Russel, C. and Russel, W.M.S. (1961) *Human Behaviour*, Boston, MA: Little, Brown.

Scott, P.D. (1977) 'Assessing Dangerousness in Criminals', *British Journal of Psychiatry* 131: 127–142.

Smith, J. (2003a) *The Shipman Inquiry: Second Report: The Police Investigation of March, 1998*, Cm 5853, London: TSO.

—— (2003b) *The Shipman Inquiry: Third Report: Death Certification and the Investigation of Deaths by Coroners*, Cm 5854. London: TSO.

Soothill, K. (1993) 'The Serial Killer Industry', *Journal of Forensic Psychiatry* 4: 341–354.

Stanley, N. and Manthorpe, J. (eds) (2004) *The Age of the Inquiry: Learning and Blaming in Health and Social Care*, London: Routledge.

Tancredi, T. (2005) 'Multi-Agency Public Protection Arrangements', in D. Crighton and G. Towl (eds) *Psychology in Probation Services*, Oxford: Blackwell.

Taylor, P. and Gunn, J. (1999) 'Homicides by People with Mental Illness: Myth and Reality', *British Journal of Psychiatry* 174: 9–14.

Tidmarsh, D. (1982) 'Implications from Research Studies', in J. Hamilton and H. Freeman (eds) *Dangerousness: Psychiatric Assessment and Management*, London: Gaskell.

Walker, N. (1983) 'Protecting People', in J. Hinton (ed.) *Dangerousness: Problems of Assessment and Prediction*, London: Allen & Unwin.

West Midlands Health Authority (1991) *Report of the Panel of Inquiry Appointed to Investigate the Case of Kim Kirkman*, Birmingham: West Midlands Health Authority.

Wilson, J. (1974) *Language and the Pursuit of Truth*, Cambridge: Cambridge University Press.

Young, S., Gudjonsson, G.H. and Needham-Bennett, K. (2005) 'Multi-Agency Protection Panels for Dangerous Offenders: One London Forensic Team's Experience', *Journal of Forensic Psychiatry and Psychology* 16: 312–327.

Further reading

Books

Casement, P. (1985) *On Learning from the Patient*, London: Tavistock.

—— (1990) *Further Learning from the Patient: The Analytic Space and Process*, London: Routledge.

—— (2006) *Learning from Life: Becoming a Psycho-Analyst*, London: Routledge.

(These three books, although written from a psychoanalytic perspective, offer very useful insights into psychotherapy with troubled people.)

Kemshall, H. (2003) *Understanding Risk in Criminal Justice*, Maidenhead: Open University Press (provides helpful focus on risk in relation to the criminal justice system).

Moss, K. (2009) *Security and Liberty: Restriction by Stealth*, Basingstoke: Palgrave Macmillan (a very compelling discussion of the erosion of liberties in the name of protection).

Tyrer, P. (ed.) (2007) *Assessment, Risk and Outcome in Severe Personality Disorder. British Journal of Psychiatry* 190 (suppl. 49), London: Royal College of Psychiatrists.

Articles – statistical aspects

Douglas, K.S. and Ogloff, J.R.P. (2003) 'Multiple Facets of Risk for Violence: The Impact of Judgemental Specificity on Structured Decisions about Violence Risk', *International Journal of Forensic Mental Health* 2: 19–34.

Doyle, M., Dolan, M. and McGovern, J. (2002) 'The Validity of North American Risk Assessment Tools in Predicting In-Patient Violent Behaviour in England', *Legal and Criminological Psychology* 7: 141–154.

Gale, T.M., Hawley, J. and Sivakumaran, T. (2003) 'Do Mental Health Professionals Really Understand Probability? Implications for Risk Assessment and Evidence-Based Practice', *Journal of Mental Health* 12: 417–430.

Holdsworth, N. and Dodgson, G. (2003) 'Could a New Mental Health Act Distort Clinical Judgement? A Bayesian Justification of Naturalistic Reasoning about Risk', *Journal of Mental Health* 2: 451–462.

Krauss, D.A., Sales, B.D., Becker, J.V. and Figueredo, A.J. (2000) 'Beyond Prediction to Explanation in Risk Assessment Research', *International Journal of Law and Psychiatry* 23: 91–112.

Loza, W., Villeneuve, D.B. and Lozo-Fanous, A. (2002) 'Predictive Validity of the Violence Risk Appraisal Guide: A Tool for Assessing Violent Offender's Recidivism', *International Journal of Law and Psychiatry* 25: 85–92.

Szmukler, G. (2003) 'Risk Assessment: "Numbers and Values"', *Psychiatric Bulletin* 27: 205–207.

Envoi[1]

'The end is forbidden'[2]

The length of this book is not to be taken as an indication of its comprehensiveness. As I stated in the Preface, I decided upon the sub-title *Explorations in Clinical Criminology* to indicate that what followed in the book was just that – my own explorations, and (I hope) what would also be those of my readers. Perhaps a more appropriate sub-title would have been *An Introduction to*, or even *Encounters in Clinical Criminology*. I think that the content of the book will possibly be of greatest interest and use to newcomers in the field. However, it may be that some aspects of the material will be of interest to more experienced practitioners who may, who knows, find things they were unaware of, or had perhaps forgotten! One thing I wish to make very clear, namely the book is not intended as a handbook. To suggest that it was would be an unwarranted presumption on my part. Finally, I repeat some lines I used in the Epilogue of the third edition (Prins 2005: 309–310).

> [The individuals] described in this book defy ready categorization . . . they require a degree of calm reflectiveness and emotional distancing (but not coldness); a degree of dispassionate compassion. Over-reaction to some admittedly appalling crimes is to be avoided . . . [not least] . . . by politicians, the media in all its forms, and public alike. It is the individual who should be at the core of our endeavours . . . a quote from the essayist Alexander Pope . . . makes a fitting conclusion: 'Know then thyself, presume not God to scan, the proper study of mankind is man' (*An Essay on Man:* Epistle 2, 1733).

Notes

1 Envoi is an archaic word, meaning author's concluding words.
2 Quoted by Sir Norwood East (1949) *Society and the Criminal*, London: HMSO, from Rudyard Kipling's poem *The Palace*.

Reference

Prins, H. (2005) *Offenders, Deviants or Patients?*, 3rd edn, London: Routledge.

Author index

Smartt, U. 83
Smith, A. 268
Smith, C. 226
Smith, H. 142
Smith, J. 63, 64, 324
Smith, R. 24
Snaith, R.P. 254
Snow, P. 75
Snowden, P. 161
Solomka, B. 170
Soothill, K. 199, 257, 269, 284, 296
Spataro, J. 257
Spence, S. 162
Spencer, S. 32, 33, 34
Spitzer, M. 292
Stanley, N. 10, 320
Steadman, H. 116, 306
Steen, V. 198
Steuve, A. 115
Stevenson, K. 251, 252, 262, 274n2
Stone, J.H. 133
Stone, N. 77, 86, 252, 275n4
Storr, A. 188, 189, 190
Strachan, J.G. 294
Street, R. 75
Studer, L.H. 263
Sugarman, P. 90, 252, 253, 292
Sugg, D. 260, 268
Swanson, J.W. 115
Swinson, N. 221
Szasz, T. 29, 54, 104

Tancredi, T. 313
Tantam, D. 134
Targonski, J.R. 215
Taylor, J.L. 288
Taylor, P. 12, 115, 122, 123, 127, 225, 268, 303
Taylor, R. 177
Tennent, G. 175
Thapar, A. 165
Thomas, S. 82
Thomas, T. 274n3
Thomson, L.D.G. 172
Tidmarsh, D. 82, 309
Tiffin, P. 179n2
Tilt, R. 81
Toch, H. 196
Toffler, A. 192
Topp, D.O. 291
Towl, G. 56, 63
Treves-Brown, C. 174

Trethowan, W. 120, 160
Turner, T. 14n6
Tyrer, P. 161

Vandersall, T.A. 294
Vattakatuchery, J.J. 133
Vaughan, P. 66
Verkaik, R. 4
Vess, J. 258
Victor, T. 136
Vine, B. 108
Vizard, E. 258

Wachi, T. 288
Waddington, J.L. 243
Walker, N. 21, 23, 24, 75, 308
Walker, W.D. 197
Walmsley, R. 264
Walsh, E. 103, 115
Wambaugh, J. 163
Ward, M. 79
Ward, T. 24
Watson, W. 79
Watts, D. 196
Webster, C. 306
Weiner, J.M. 294
Weiss, E. 218
Wesseley, S.C. 115
West, D.J. 110, 220, 256, 257, 260, 267, 271, 274n3
Wheatley, M. 116
White, G.L. 118
White, T. 28, 111
Whiteley, J.S. 159
Whittaker, J. 134
Whitty, C.W.M. 133
Whyte, S. 126
Wiegersma, A. 198
Wilczynski, A. 218, 223
Wildgoose, J. 196
Wilkins, L. 306
Williams, M. 138
Wilson, D. 83, 222, 257, 274n4
Wilson, J. 313
Wilson, P. 225
Wilson, S. 134
Winick, B. 274n3
Winnicott, D.W. 175
Woddis, G.M. 128
Wooden, W.S. 294
Woodhams, J. 228, 282
Woodward, C.D. 289

Subject index

Munchausen's Syndrome 123, 134; by
    Proxy 123, 134
murder 3, 26, 69, 70, 213–33; defence to
    charge of 5, 28, 35, 46; definition of
    215–16; first degree 231; law on
    215–17; second degree 231; sexual
    268, 271–2; statistics of 214
Murder, Abolition of Death Penalty Act
    1965 6
Murdock, George 189
'mute of malice' 26
Muti killings 218
mysophilia 246

Napoleon 246
National Health Service 56–7, 82,
    201
National Health Service and
    Community Care Act 1990 79
National Probation Service 69, 325n6
necrophagy 270
necrophilia 37, 246, 250, 270–2;
    classification of 270; law on 271;
    symbolic 270
necrophilous character 270
negativism 113
negligence 20
neonaticide 218
neurobiology 164
neurology 158
neurophysiology 164
neuro-psychiatry 162
neuroses 107, 119, 127–34
neurosyphillis 135
Newton, Isaac 105
NGRI verdict 23, 24, 46, 53
Nilsen, Dennis 34–5, 36, 47n8, 217, 222,
    270
nurses 14n2, 55, 84–5, 197, 252
nutrition 164

obsessive-compulsive disorder/states
    107, 128
occult, the 272, 318
occupational therapists 14n2
offender profiling 13, 227–8
Old Testament 21, 213–14, 242, 261,
    274n3
oligophrenia 141
omission 20
Onoprienko, Anatoly 222
oral sex 14, 245, 264, 268

Othello 102, 118, 124
Othello Syndrome 118, 119, 123

paedophiles 192, 255–6, 274n4, 311;
    classification of 258–9; 'outing' of
    274n3; predatory 206n5, 257;
    stigmatisation of 257
paedophilia 244, 246, 247–8, 250, 252,
    255–61, 318; criteria for 256
paralysis 130
paranoid disorder/delusions 23, 33,
    115–122, 312
paraphilias 246–7; classification of 247
parental care 162
Parole Board 5, 86–7, 307, 315
Parole System 4, 85, 86
Paterson, Alexander 3
Payne, Sarah 274n3
'Peeping Tom' activities 246, 251
peine forte et dure 26
Peirce, Gareth 10
Perceval, Spencer 23
Pericles 170, 314
persecutory delusions 114–16
persistence 177
personality 159–61
personality disorders 35, 44, 47n8, 55,
    63, 103, 116–17, 119, 146, 157,
    159–61, 218, 295; definitions of
    160–1; severe 163, 166
petit mal 139
Phaeton 284
phallometric assessment 260
pharmacological treatments 12
phenylketonuria 142
phobias, hysterical 130
Phoenix, the 284
physiology 158
Piaget, Jean 226
Pinel, Philippe 157, 158
Pitchfork, Colin 163, 166
plea bargaining 315
Podola, Gunther 132
Poe, Edgar Allan 227
Police Act 1997 274n3
pollutants 164
polygraphy 260
Pompeii 251
Pope, Alexander 331
pornography 12, 124, 318; child 248, 250
'possession' 105, 123
post-traumatic stress disorder 107, 129